GUIDE
TO RESEARCH MATERIALS
IN THE NORTH CAROLINA
STATE ARCHIVES:

COUNTY RECORDS

Eleventh Revised Edition

Raleigh

Department of Cultural Resources

Division of Archives and History

Archives and Records Section

1997

This edition is dedicated to the memory of

Gene Jerome Williams

1948-1996

Archivist and Friend

INTRODUCTION

Since 1963, the North Carolina State Archives has been publishing guides to its holdings, including state agency records, county records, private manuscript collections and Civil War material. While each edition has been expanded and improved, this eleventh revised edition of the guide to county records represents a major advancement in accuracy and standardization. In conjunction with each annual inventory since January 1991 and continuing as a full-time responsibility of the supervisor of the Local Records Sub-unit of the Arrangement and Description Unit since April 1995, many descriptive titles have been improved and standardized, inclusive dates corrected, and new material added. This edition describes more than 9,000 bound volumes and 21,000 boxes of loose records, as well as over 24,000 reels of microfilm, all of which are available to researchers in the State Archives.

The North Carolina State Archives began systematically seeking and accepting non-current local records from the various counties in 1916 under authority of a 1907 statute permitting their transfer to the Archives. Thanks in large measure to the tactful determination of Colonel Fred A. Olds, director of the Hall of History, seven counties—Carteret, Chowan, Edgecombe, Halifax, Orange, Perquimans and Wilkes—took advantage of the act and transferred some of their oldest records to the Archives. Forty additional counties had followed suit by 1924, so that the handbook issued that year describing the county records in the Archives included approximately 500 volumes, 90 boxes of loose papers and 414 boxes of marriage bonds. By the time the Historical Records Survey of the Works Progress Administration inventoried the county records in the Archives in 1938, another 950 volumes, 100 boxes of papers and 160,000 documents had been transferred from the counties. In 1941 the Archives, with the assistance of the Genealogical Society of Utah, commenced a program for microfilming many of the records, such as will books and deed books, that were generally retained in the counties. This program was interrupted in 1943 because of the war and not fully resumed until ten years later.

In 1957, the General Assembly authorized the creation of an "inspector of county records" whose task it would be to visit all the courthouses in the state and, with his staff, inventory the records found in them, microfilm volumes of permanent value for purposes of security, determine which of the records were not worth permanent preservation, set up schedules for the orderly transfer of permanently valuable non-current records to the Archives, and arrange and describe them for public use once they were there. This officer and his staff provided a solid basis for an effective local records program. By 1970, the local records staff had completed records inventories and disposition schedules for all 100 counties, and many county officers had availed themselves of the opportunity to free up storage space in their offices.

In 1981, an internal reorganization of the Archives and Records Section divided the functions of the local records program between the Records Services Branch, which helps counties and municipalities manage their records through scheduling, microfilming, and records-keeping consultations, and the Archival Services Branch, which appraises, arranges, describes, and references the permanently valuable county records that have been sent to the State Archives in accordance with the disposition schedules. By the time of the reorganization, the local records staff had produced more than 46,000 reels of microfilm, many for security purposes only, supervised the restoration and rebinding of over 2,800 volumes in the Archives and in the counties, and encouraged the voluntary transfer of some 5,900 volumes and 6,000 cubic feet of loose records.

The Guide to County Records is a testament to the success of the local records program. Records listed herein are categorized as either original records or microfilm copies, and grouped within each category by series: bonds, census (county copies), corporations and partnerships, courts, elections, estates, land, marriage and vital statistics, military and pension, officials, roads and bridges, schools, tax and fiscal, and wills. Unfortunately, many very interesting and valuable records remain hidden under the heading of "Miscellaneous Records," but space considerations prevent a more elaborate listing. The brief descriptions included in this guide are not intended to replace the more detailed finding aids available to researchers in the Archives' Search Room.

The vast majority of the records listed in this guide have been transferred to the State Archives from the offices of clerks of superior court and registers of deeds. Others have originated in the offices of tax supervisors, boards of county commissioners, boards of education, health departments, and social services directors. The Archives maintains a very precise registration of the provenance of the county records in its custody, although there is some confusion as to the office of origin and date of transfer of certain records received in the early years of the program. Researchers needing such information are encouraged to contact the registrar of the Archives and Records Section.

The local records program owes a considerable debt to an inventory of county records conducted in the 1930s by the Historical Records Survey of the Works Progress Administration. Interested researchers are urged to consult the three-volume report of this survey, edited by Dr. C. Christopher Crittenden and Dan Lacy and published as The Historical Records of North Carolina: The County Records (Raleigh: North Carolina Historical Commission, 1938-1939). The introduction to the series, reprinted as a pamphlet entitled Introduction to the County Records of North Carolina (Raleigh: North Carolina Historical Commission, 1938), contains an excellent historical resume of the county court system in North Carolina and a detailed analysis of the various records produced by the courts. Both the Historical Records and the Introduction are out of print, but copies may be consulted in libraries throughout the state; there is a full set of the three-volume series in the Archives' Search Room.

Researchers whose interests range over a long period of time or concern a county that has been subdivided will find valuable information in The Formation of the North Carolina Counties, 1663-1943 (Raleigh: State Department of Archives and History, 1950, reprinted with corrections in 1975), by David Leroy Corbitt. This volume is the principal source for the dates and origins of county formations cited in this guide.

The first edition of the guide to county records was compiled in 1972 by Gregory B. Coudriet and other members of the Local Records staff from earlier drafts and finding aids. Subsequent editions reflecting additional holdings and changes to the finding aids were prepared under the direction of Frank D. Gatton, head of the Local Records Branch and later assistant state archivist and assistant records administrator. The fourth edition was particularly significant, as it was revised in its entirety. All entries were checked against the original records rather than the finding aids. Gaps in series were indicated and headnotes added to explain absences of records.

In the preparation of this the eleventh revised edition, the process utilized for the fourth edition was partially duplicated. After card catalogues had been carefully compared with titles, dates and call numbers of original records over the course of several annual inventories, all guide entries were then compared with the listings in the card catalogues (both original records and microfilm) and, when discrepancies were discovered, with the records. Gaps or overlaps in dates often suggested an error in the description, resulting in the discovery of many presumably "missing" volumes.

Whenever titles for like records varied from county to county, they have been standardized. Call numbers were also made uniform, although they are not indicated in the guide. The records of several older counties, such as Bertie, Hyde and Tyrrell, that were arranged and transferred before the creation of the "Local Records Procedures Manual" in 1966 have been brought into conformity with the standards of description established by the manual.

Throughout the guide, the attempt at uniformity will be most apparent in the court dockets and, to a lesser extent, in the series of estates records. Historically, clerks of county courts, inferior and superior, have maintained four principal dockets: the court minutes, a docket of civil causes, a docket of criminal cases, and an execution docket. During the colonial period and into the early years of statehood, the various components of the civil docket—trial, appearance, petition, reference and appeal—were usually kept together within a single volume. As cases proliferated in the early nineteenth century, most clerks found it expedient to maintain the several civil dockets in separate books. Over the years, archivists have described and numbered the early conjoined civil dockets in various ways. This edition of the guide brings these together within each county under a standardized title, in most cases as "Trial, Appearance and Reference Docket" or "Reference (Trial) and Appearance Docket." The call numbers have likewise been made uniform: 308 for the civil docket of the Court of Pleas and Quarter Sessions, and 322 for that of county superior court. Incidentally, in the process of sorting out the oldest civil dockets, we have discovered that the so-called reference dockets of the colonial county courts are in essence trial dockets, "reference" used in the sense of causes referred to the present term of court for trial. In later years, reference dockets served the more traditional purpose of tracking civil causes referred to a referee for determination.

Within the estates series, pre-1868 volumes that contain a multiplicity of records related to the administration of estates, including inventories, accounts of sale, annual accounts and final settlements, have been brought together under the heading "Record of

Estates," with a 501 call number. Records of appointments of executors have been retitled to indicate the inclusion of administrators, guardians, and masters of apprentices. Practically all records, both original and microfilm, relating to assignees, receivers, and trustees, except those truly concerned with estates matters, have been removed from the estates series to the miscellaneous records and assigned a 929 call number.

Other records affected by standardization include levy dockets, which have been removed from land or miscellaneous records and filed with court records (310); clerk's minute dockets, mistakenly classified with court minutes, which have been grouped with special proceedings and orders and decrees (922); civil actions concerning railroads, which have been retitled railroad records within the series of road records (925); and records concerning land sales for taxes, formerly classified as tax records, now filed under land (407). A variety of accounting records created by committees of finance, county treasurers, auditors and clerks of court have been collected under the heading "County Accounts and Claims" (910). One other title of microfilm records has been reclassified. The accounts of sales and resales of land by mortgagees and trustees have been removed from the estates series and assigned numbers in the land series.

Microfilm of county records has been produced either from originals that have been transferred to the State Archives or from volumes retained by the counties. Much of this film is stored in the Archives' vault for security purposes and may not be accessed for general reference. However, for the convenience of researchers, reading copies have been made of older records with considerable reference value. To avoid the confusion that might ensue for those wishing to order a copy from microfilm, the titles of reels were not as a rule corrected and standardized as were those of original records; only the most egregious errors, including the classification of the two titles mentioned above, were corrected. As a result, there will be many cases in which the title of an original record and that of its microfilm copy will not agree.

In previous editions of this guide, records were arranged strictly alphabetically within each series. This edition has adopted a more functional approach, grouping similar records within the series and arranging them by their (implied) call numbers. For example, all records relating to the naturalization of aliens are listed at the beginning of the miscellaneous records, reflecting their 902 call numbers.

One final word: Users of this edition should be aware that it, like its predecessors, is but a static indicator of a fluid process. The archival holdings of original and microfilmed records change constantly, as the Arrangement and Description Unit staff members continue to appraise and transfer records from the counties, and as reading copies of microfilm are added to the Search Room. This edition represents county records holdings as of May 1, 1997.

A number of staff members of the Archival Services Branch, interns, and volunteers have contributed to this revision of the guide to county records. Kenrick N. Simpson, supervisor of the Local Records Sub-unit of the Arrangement and Description Unit, compared descriptions in the previous edition with the county card catalogue; examined the original records in cases of discrepancies; made corrections to the guide, the cards, and labels on the records; selected standardized titles and call numbers in accordance with the "Local Records Procedures Manual" if applicable or, if the manual did not address a particular type of record, the law or code that dictated the creation of the record; reviewed the same process involving microfilm records; and provided general oversight to the project. J. Mark Valsame of the Local Records Sub-unit compared listings of microfilm records with the card catalogue descriptions. William H. Brown, microfilm reference archivist, and Daniel J. Salemson, temporary employee, made corrections to the microfilm cards and labels. Benjamin S. (Tres) Lovelace, a state government intern, entered all the corrections and additions to the guide, verified creation dates of counties, and selected photographs from the Iconographic Collection of the Archives. George Stevenson, private collections archivist, assisted in the identification of several obscure eighteenth-century court records. Druscilla R. Simpson, information management archivist, edited the final version for style and appearance. Temporary employee Andra M. Knecht copied the cards from the original and microfilm card catalogues to facilitate the comparison of descriptions and the guide. Volunteer Nora Jane Cain tabulated the volumes, boxes, and reels in this revision to provide the figures noted in this introduction.

The present edition marks a new high in our continuing effort to make the guide of maximum usefulness to those who consult it. With the new material that has been added and the corrections that have been made, this edition replaces in their entirety all earlier editions of the county records guide.

David J. Olson
State Archivist

LIST OF ILLUSTRATIONS

Interior view of Chowan County Courthouse, Edenton, 1976.
Photograph from the files of the State Archives

ALAMANCE COUNTY

Established in 1849 from Orange County.

ORIGINAL RECORDS

BONDS

Apprentice Bonds, 1878-1918; 1 volume.

Bastardy Bonds and Records, 1877-1917; 1 Fibredex box.

COURT RECORDS

County Court of Pleas and Quarter Sessions

Minutes, 1849-1860, 1866-1868; 3 volumes.

State Docket, 1849-1868; 1 volume.

Superior Court

Minutes, 1849-1920; 24 volumes.

Equity Minutes, 1849-1860; Clerk's Receipt Book (Land Sales), 1869-1872; 1 volume.

Civil Action Papers, 1870-1939; 2 Fibredex boxes.

Civil Action Papers Concerning Land, 1877-1915; 2 Fibredex boxes.

Criminal Action Papers, 1878-1917; 3 Fibredex boxes.

Inferior Court

Minutes, 1877-1879; 1 volume.

ELECTION RECORDS

Record of Elections, 1897-1968; 6 volumes.

ESTATES RECORDS

Record of Accounts, 1869-1929; 3 volumes.

Administrators' Bonds, 1882-1902; 3 volumes.

Appointment of Administrators, Executors and Guardians, 1869-1902; 1 volume.

Record of Dowers (Widows' Year's Support), 1878-1968; 3 volumes.

Estates Records, 1856-1949; 21 Fibredex boxes.

Guardians' Records, 1878-1949; 6 Fibredex boxes.

Guardians' Bonds, 1882-1909; 2 volumes.

Guardians' Returns, 1849-1868; 1 volume.

Inventories and Accounts of Sales, 1849-1932; 7 volumes.

Record of Settlements, 1870-1918; 3 volumes.

LAND RECORDS

Deeds, 1793-1905; 2 Fibredex boxes.

MARRIAGE, DIVORCE AND VITAL STATISTICS

Marriage Bonds, 1853-1867; 1 Fibredex box.

Record of Marriage Certificates, 1854-1868; 1 volume.

Divorce Records, 1889-1917; 1 Fibredex box.

Disinterment/Reinterment Permits, 1978; 1 manuscript box.

MILITARY AND PENSION RECORDS
     Record of Pensions, 1921-1945; 2 volumes.
MISCELLANEOUS RECORDS
     Alien Registration, 1931-1940; 1 volume.
     Miscellaneous Records, 1822-1939; 1 Fibredex box.
     Records of Assignees, Receivers and Trustees, 1884-1933; 1 Fibredex box.
     Record of Accounts of Trustees and Assignees, 1895-1933; 2 volumes.
ROADS AND BRIDGES
     Railroad Records, 1898-1919; 2 Fibredex boxes.
WILLS
     Wills, 1832-1900; 8 Fibredex boxes.

MICROFILM RECORDS

BONDS
     Apprentice Bonds, 1878-1918; 1 reel.
CORPORATIONS AND PARTNERSHIPS
     Record of Corporations, 1879-1946; 3 reels.
     Index to Corporations, 1883-1978; 1 reel.
     Index to Partnerships, various years; 1 reel.
COURT RECORDS
     County Court of Pleas and Quarter Sessions
          Minutes, 1849-1868; 1 reel.
     Superior Court
          Minutes, 1849-1944, 1961-1963; 12 reels.
          Equity Minutes, 1849-1860; Clerk's Receipt Book (Land Sales), 1869-
               1872; 1 reel.
          Index to Judgments, 1868-1939; 1 reel.
ELECTION RECORDS
     Record of Elections, 1897-1962; 1 reel.
ESTATES RECORDS
     Record of Estates, 1849-1858, 1916-1951; 4 reels.
     Record of Accounts, 1869-1951; 3 reels.
     Administrators' Bonds, 1882-1902; 1 reel.
     Record of Administrators, 1902-1963; 6 reels.
     Appointment of Executors, 1869-1902; 1 reel.
     Record of Dowers, 1878-1951; 2 reels.
     Record of Widows' Year's Support, 1928-1963; 1 reel.
     Guardians' Bonds, 1882-1909; 1 reel.
     Guardians' Returns, 1849-1868, 1879-1951; 3 reels.
     Record of Guardians, 1910-1963; 2 reels.
     Record of Trustees and Guardians, 1941-1962; 1 reel.
     Inheritance Tax Records, 1924-1963; 2 reels.
     Inventory Book, 1859-1863; 1 reel.
     Record of Sales and Inventories, 1916-1931; 1 reel.

Inventories of Estates, 1929-1951; 2 reels.

Record of Settlements, 1867-1951; 5 reels.

Index to Estates, 1900-1968; 2 reels.

LAND RECORDS

Record of Deeds, 1849-1945; 69 reels.

Index to Real Estate Conveyances, 1849-1941; 8 reels.

Plat Books, 1911-1976; 5 reels.

Index to Plats, 1911-1977; 1 reel.

Record of Sales and Resales of Land, 1926-1968; 4 reels.

MARRIAGE, DIVORCE AND VITAL STATISTICS

Marriage Bonds, 1849-1868; 3 reels.

Marriage Certificates, 1854-1946; 12 reels.

Marriage Registers, 1870-1961; 2 reels.

Index to Marriages, 1962; 1 reel.

Record of Maiden Names of Divorced Women, 1938-1963; 1 reel.

Index to Births, 1913-1961; 1 reel.

Index to Deaths, 1913-1962, 1 reel.

Index to Delayed Births, various years; 1 reel.

MILITARY AND PENSION RECORDS

Record of Armed Forces Discharges, 1917-1984; 11 reels.

Index to Armed Forces Discharges, 1917-1978; 1 reel.

Widows' and Soldiers' Pensions, 1938-1945; 1 reel.

MISCELLANEOUS RECORDS

Orders and Decrees, 1869-1951; 1 reel.

Special Proceedings, 1881-1946; 4 reels.

Index to Special Proceedings, 1877-1963; 3 reels.

Record of Accounts of Trustees and Assignees, 1895-1933; 1 reel.

Record of Receivership, 1925-1955; 1 reel.

OFFICIALS, COUNTY

Minutes, Board of County Commissioners, 1868-1956; 7 reels.

SCHOOL RECORDS

Minutes, County Board of Education, 1877-1948; 1 reel.

WILLS

Record of Wills, 1849-1963; 8 reels.

Cross Index to Wills, 1850-1963; 1 reel.

ALBEMARLE COUNTY

Established in 1663; abolished in 1738.

MICROFILM RECORDS

Miscellaneous Records, 1678-1737; 1 reel.

ALEXANDER COUNTY

Established in 1847 from Caldwell, Iredell and Wilkes counties.
Many court records burned by Federal troops in 1865.

ORIGINAL RECORDS

BONDS

Bastardy Bonds and Records, 1865-1900; 2 Fibredex boxes.

Officials' Bonds and Records, 1855-1908; 2 Fibredex boxes.

COURT RECORDS

County Court of Pleas and Quarter Sessions

Appearance Docket, 1865-1868; Apprentice Bonds, 1875-1878; 1 volume.

Execution Docket, 1861-1868; 1 volume.

State Docket, 1865-1868; 1 volume.

Superior Court

Minutes, 1866-1900; 3 volumes.

Equity Minutes, 1866-1868; Record of Probate of Deeds, 1866-1875; 1 volume.

Appearance Docket, 1866-1868; 1 volume.

Civil Action Papers, 1853-1927; 5 Fibredex boxes.

Civil Action Papers Concerning Land, 1860-1952; 5 Fibredex boxes.

Criminal Action Papers, 1861-1909; 9 Fibredex boxes.

ELECTION RECORDS

Record of Elections, 1869-1926; 5 volumes.

ESTATES RECORDS

Record of Estates, 1861-1868; 1 volume.

Record of Accounts, 1869-1894; 2 volumes.

Appointment of Administrators, Executors, Guardians and Masters, 1868-1914; 1 volume.

Estates Records, 1839, 1858-1939; 32 Fibredex boxes.

Guardians' Records, 1866-1909; 2 Fibredex boxes.

LAND RECORDS

Deeds of Sale, 1848-1953; 8 Fibredex boxes.

Mortgage Deeds, 1872-1956; 2 Fibredex boxes.

Miscellaneous Deeds, 1850-1963; 1 Fibredex box.

Cross Index to Deeds, 1847-1928; 3 volumes.

Division of Land, 1863-1942; 1 Fibredex box.

Land Entries, 1847-1911; 1 volume, 1 Fibredex box.

Miscellaneous Land Records, 1833-1958; 2 Fibredex boxes.

MARRIAGE, DIVORCE AND VITAL STATISTICS

Marriage Bonds, 1861; 1 Fibredex box.

Divorce Records, 1867-1905; 1 Fibredex box.

MISCELLANEOUS RECORDS
    Minutes and Accounts, Wardens of the Poor, 1847-1868; 1 volume.
    Miscellaneous Records, 1852-1957; 3 Fibredex boxes.
    Records of Assignees and Trustees, 1869-1910, 1941, 1945; 1 Fibredex box.
ROADS AND BRIDGES
    Road Records, 1863-1916; 1 Fibredex box.
    Railroad Records, 1869-1903; 1 Fibredex box.
WILLS
    Wills, 1847-1949; 4 Fibredex boxes.

MICROFILM RECORDS

BONDS
    Apprentice Bonds, 1875-1878; 1 reel.
CORPORATIONS AND PARTNERSHIPS
    Record of Incorporations, 1892-1968; 1 reel.
    Record of Partnerships, 1913-1970; 1 reel.
COURT RECORDS
    Superior Court
        Minutes, 1866-1956; 4 reels.
        Equity Minutes, 1866-1868; 1 reel.
        Cross Index to Civil Judgments, 1867-1963; 1 reel.
        Index to Judgments, 1871-1948; 2 reels.
ELECTION RECORDS
    Record of Elections, 1928-1968; 1 reel.
ESTATES RECORDS
    Record of Estates, 1861-1868; 1 reel.
    Record of Accounts, 1869-1968; 6 reels.
    Appointment of Administrators, Executors and Guardians, 1868-1933; 2 reels.
    Record of Administrators, 1930-1968; 2 reels.
    Record of Executors, 1930-1970; 1 reel.
    Record of Guardians, 1929-1970; 1 reel.
    Record of Accounts of Indigent Children, 1913-1946; 1 reel.
    Inheritance Tax Records, 1923-1968; 1 reel.
    Record of Settlements, 1869-1968; 2 reels.
    Index to Administrators and Executors, 1906-1945; 1 reel.
    Index to Guardians, 1907-1914; 1 reel.
    Index to Estates, Administrators, Executors, Guardians and Trustees, 1963-
        1968; 1 reel.
    Index to Estates and Wards, 1963-1968; 1 reel.
LAND RECORDS
    Record of Deeds, 1847-1955; 34 reels.
    Index to Deeds, Grantor, 1847-1954; 1 reel.
    Index to Deeds, Grantee, 1847-1968; 2 reels.
    Land Entries, 1847-1941; 1 reel.

Record of Resale of Land by Trustees and Mortgagees, 1921-1968; 1 reel.

MARRIAGE, DIVORCE AND VITAL STATISTICS

Marriage Bonds, 1865-1868; 1 reel.

Marriage Licenses, 1868-1961; 11 reels.

Marriage Registers, 1867-1937; 1 reel.

Maiden Names of Divorced Women, 1940-1968; 1 reel.

Index to Births, 1913-1966; 1 reel.

Index to Deaths, 1913-1960; 1 reel.

Index to Delayed Births, various years; 1 reel.

MILITARY AND PENSION RECORDS

Record of Armed Forces Discharges, 1919-1970; 3 reels.

Index to Armed Forces Discharges, 1969-1981; 1 reel.

MISCELLANEOUS RECORDS

Lunacy Dockets, 1907-1970; 1 reel.

Special Proceedings, 1870-1933; Minutes, Court of Pleas and Quarter
Sessions, 1865-1868; 1 reel.

Special Proceedings, 1898-1960; 5 reels.

Index to Special Proceedings, 1870-1981; 3 reels.

OFFICIALS, COUNTY

Minutes, Board of County Commissioners, 1868-1942; 3 reels.

SCHOOL RECORDS

Minutes, County Board of Education, 1921-1968; 1 reel.

TAX AND FISCAL RECORDS

Tax Lists, 1915, 1935, 1965; 1 reel.

WILLS

Record of Wills, 1865-1968; 2 reels.

Cross Index to Wills, 1865-1967; 1 reel.

ALLEGHANY COUNTY

Established in 1859 from Ashe County.
Courthouse fire in 1932 destroyed a few permanently valuable records.

ORIGINAL RECORDS

BONDS
> Apprentice Bonds, 1869-1909; 1 volume.
> Apprentice Bonds, 1863-1872; Bastardy Bonds, 1863-1910; Officials' Bonds
> > and Records, 1859-1927; 1 Fibredex box.
> Bastardy Bonds, 1872-1879; 1 volume.

COURT RECORDS
> County Court of Pleas and Quarter Sessions
> > Minutes, 1862-1868; 1 volume.
> > Execution Docket, 1863-1868; Execution Docket, Superior Court,
> > > 1869-1872; Minutes, Inferior Court, 1877-1883; 1 volume.
> Superior Court
> > Minutes, 1869-1907; 5 volumes.
> > Civil Action Papers, 1862-1928; 5 Fibredex boxes.
> > Civil Action Papers Concerning Land, 1867-1920; 4 Fibredex boxes.
> > Criminal Action Papers, 1862-1925; 5 Fibredex boxes.

ELECTION RECORDS
> Record of Elections, 1878-1944; 5 volumes.

ESTATES RECORDS
> Administrators' Bonds, 1911-1918; 1 volume.
> Estates Records, 1859-1928; 30 Fibredex boxes.
> Guardians' Records, 1864-1917; 3 Fibredex boxes.
> Guardians' Bonds, 1869-1940; 3 volumes.
> Record of Inventories, Marriages and Wills, 1862-1869; 1 volume.

LAND RECORDS
> Deeds and Grants, 1837-1908; 1 Fibredex box.
> Miscellaneous Land Records, 1874-1908; 1 Fibredex box.

MARRIAGE, DIVORCE AND VITAL STATISTICS
> Divorce Records, 1862-1932; 2 Fibredex boxes.

MISCELLANEOUS RECORDS
> Registry of Licenses to Trades, 1874-1906; Record of Strays, 1895, 1914;
> > 1 volume.
> Miscellaneous Records, 1848-1929; 2 Fibredex boxes.

ROADS AND BRIDGES
> Road Records, 1861-1910; 1 Fibredex box.

WILLS
> Wills, 1859-1912; 3 Fibredex boxes.

MICROFILM RECORDS

BONDS
> Apprentice Bonds, 1869-1909; 1 reel.
> Bastardy Bonds, 1872-1879; 1 reel.

CORPORATIONS AND PARTNERSHIPS
> Record of Corporations, 1903-1971; 1 reel.

COURT RECORDS
> County Court of Pleas and Quarter Sessions
> > Minutes, 1862-1868; 1 reel.
> Superior Court
> > Minutes, 1869-1955; 5 reels.
> > Tax Judgments, 1882-1889, 1950-1957; 21 reels.
> > Cross Index to Judgments, 1869-1970; 1 reel.

ELECTION RECORDS
> Record of Elections, 1878-1944; 1 reel.

ESTATES RECORDS
> Record of Inventories, Marriages and Wills, 1862-1869; 1 reel.
> Record of Accounts, 1870-1970; 4 reels.
> Administrators' Bonds, 1911-1918; 1 reel.
> Record of Administrators, Executors and Guardians, 1919-1951; 1 reel.
> Record of Administrators, 1939-1970; 1 reel.
> Record of Executors, 1948-1970; 1 reel.
> Guardians' Bonds, 1869-1940; 1 reel.
> Record of Guardians, 1951-1970; 1 reel.
> Inheritance Tax Records, 1920-1971; 1 reel.
> Record of Settlements, 1866-1970; 4 reels.
> Cross Index to Final Settlements, 1922-1970; 1 reel.
> Cross Index to Administrators, Executors and Guardians, 1911-1934, 1943-
> > 1970; 2 reels.
> Index to Estates, 1970-1971; 1 reel.

LAND RECORDS
> Record of Deeds, 1859-1961; 34 reels.
> Record of Deeds for Schools, 1884-1965; 1 reel.
> Index to Real Estate Conveyances, Grantor, 1859-1971; 3 reels.
> Index to Real Estate Conveyances, Grantee, 1859-1971; 3 reels.
> Record of Land Entries, 1870-1962; 1 reel.
> Federal Tax Lien Index, 1931-1970; 1 reel.
> Record of Taxes for Mortgagees, 1931-1935; 1 reel.
> Record of Surveys, 1905-1933; 1 reel.
> Record of Sales and Resales, 1937-1965; 1 reel.

MARRIAGE, DIVORCE AND VITAL STATISTICS
> Marriage Licenses, 1861-1961; 11 reels.
> Marriage Registers, 1867-1971; 2 reels.
> Maiden Names of Divorced Women, 1966-1970; 1 reel.

Index to Vital Statistics, various years; 1 reel.

MILITARY AND PENSION RECORDS

Record of Armed Forces Discharges, 1917-1989; 3 reels.

Organizational Minutes, Ex-Confederate Soldiers of Alleghany County, 1890-1920; 1 reel.

MISCELLANEOUS RECORDS

Record of Officials' Reports, 1876-1970; 1 reel.

Homestead Returns, 1870-1916; 1 reel.

Record of Lunacy, 1901-1970; 1 reel.

Orders and Decrees, 1870-1948; 1 reel.

Special Proceedings, 1884-1964; 5 reels.

Cross Index to Special Proceedings, 1939-1970; 1 reel.

OFFICIALS, COUNTY

Minutes, Board of County Commissioners, 1868-1971; 4 reels.

TAX AND FISCAL RECORDS

Tax Lists, 1915-1955; 2 reels.

Tax Scrolls, 1920-1980; 3 reels.

WILLS

Record of Wills, 1870-1970; 3 reels.

Cross Index to Wills, 1864-1933; 1 reel.

ANSON COUNTY

Established in 1750 from Bladen County.
Courthouse fire of 1868 destroyed many court records.

ORIGINAL RECORDS

BONDS
>Apprentice Bonds and Records, 1873-1891; 1 Fibredex box.
>Bastardy Bonds and Records, 1870-1903; 1 Fibredex box.
>Officials' Bonds, 1889-1895; 1 volume.

COURT RECORDS
>County Court of Pleas and Quarter Sessions
>>Minutes, 1771-1777, 1848-1858, 1868; 4 volumes.
>>Appearance Dockets, 1837-1845, 1856-1868; 2 volumes.
>>Execution Docket, 1861-1868; 1 volume.
>>Recognizance Docket, 1843-1845; Sheriffs' Settlements, 1846-1861;
>>>1 volume.
>>Trial Docket, 1852-1868; 1 volume.
>Superior Court
>>Minutes, 1868-1909; Trial Docket, 1847-1850; 11 volumes.
>>Equity Minutes, 1847-1868; Equity Trial Docket, 1861-1868;
>>>2 volumes.
>>Civil Action Papers, 1864-1908; 12 Fibredex boxes.
>>Civil Action Papers Concerning Land, 1870-1910; 2 Fibredex boxes.
>>Criminal Action Papers, 1868-1904; 25 Fibredex boxes.

ELECTION RECORDS
>Record of Elections, 1878-1910; 3 volumes.

ESTATES RECORDS
>Record of Estates, 1849-1855, 1868; 2 volumes.
>Record of Accounts, 1868-1915; 4 volumes.
>Administrators' Bonds, 1873-1903; 3 volumes.
>Estates Records, 1805-1953; 54 Fibredex boxes.
>Guardians' Records, 1848-1924; 7 Fibredex boxes.
>Guardians' Bonds, 1873-1902; 1 volume.
>Record of Settlements, 1875-1910; 2 volumes.
>Probate Court Minutes, 1869-1872; 1 volume.

LAND RECORDS
>Record of Deeds, 1749-1838; 30 volumes.
>Deeds, 1786-1909; 1 Fibredex box.
>Deeds of Trust, 1863-1910; 4 Fibredex boxes.
>Index to Deeds, 1749-1916; 5 volumes.
>Miscellaneous Land Records, 1755-1909; 1 Fibredex box.

MARRIAGE, DIVORCE AND VITAL STATISTICS
>Marriage Bonds, 1741-1868; 1 manuscript box.

Divorce Records, 1872-1925; 2 Fibredex boxes.

Index to Vital Statistics, 1922-1932; 1 volume.

Disinterment/Reinterment Permits, 1967-1976; 1 manuscript box.

MILITARY AND PENSION RECORDS

Record of Pensions, 1885-1960; 5 volumes.

MISCELLANEOUS RECORDS

Declaration of Intent (to Become a Citizen), 1911-1920; 1 volume.

Naturalization Record, 1913-1924; 1 volume.

Orders and Decrees, 1868-1932; 1 volume.

Special Proceedings, 1874-1911; 6 volumes.

Miscellaneous Records, 1759-1960; 3 Fibredex boxes.

ROADS AND BRIDGES

Road Records, 1855, 1871-1903; 1 Fibredex box.

TAX AND FISCAL RECORDS

Tax Records, 1887; 1 Fibredex box.

WILLS

Record of Wills, 1751-1848; 3 volumes.

Wills, 1754-1946; 16 Fibredex boxes.

Cross Index to Wills, 1751-1929; 1 volume.

MICROFILM RECORDS

CORPORATIONS AND PARTNERSHIPS

Record of Incorporations, 1888-1960; 1 reel.

Record of Partnerships, 1913-1973; 1 reel.

COURT RECORDS

County Court of Pleas and Quarter Sessions

Minutes, 1771-1777, 1848-1858, 1868; 1 reel.

Superior Court

Minutes, 1868-1927; 9 reels.

Equity Minutes, 1847-1868; 1 reel.

Cross Index to Judgments, 1868-1956; 1 reel.

ELECTION RECORDS

Record of Elections, 1880-1962; 1 reel.

ESTATES RECORDS

Accounts of Sales, 1868; 1 reel.

Record of Accounts, 1868-1944; 5 reels.

Administrators' Bonds, 1873-1954; 2 reels.

Record of Administrators, Executors and Guardians, 1868-1948; 3 reels.

Record of Executors, 1948-1960; 1 reel.

Guardians' Bonds, 1873-1953; 1 reel.

Record of Guardians, 1945-1962; 1 reel.

Record of Accounts of Indigent Orphans, 1908-1948; 1 reel.

Inheritance Tax Records, 1920-1962; 1 reel.

Inventories and Accounts, 1849-1855; 1 reel.

Record of Settlements, 1875-1945; 3 reels.

LAND RECORDS

Record of Deeds, 1749-1950; 53 reels.

Index to Deeds, Grantor, 1749-1973; 11 reels.

Index to Deeds, Grantee, 1749-1973; 9 reels.

Land Entries, 1851-1927; 1 reel.

Map Books, 1913-1967; 2 reels.

Index to Map Books, 1913-1961; 1 reel.

Record of Resale of Land by Trustees, 1920-1962; 1 reel.

MARRIAGE, DIVORCE AND VITAL STATISTICS

Marriage Bonds, 1749-1868; 2 reels.

Marriage Licenses, 1869-1962; 7 reels.

Marriage Registers, 1870-1962; 1 reel.

Index to Births, 1913-1982; 2 reels.

Index to Deaths, 1913-1973; 1 reel.

Index to Delayed Births, various years; 1 reel.

MILITARY AND PENSION RECORDS

Record of Pensions, 1885-1960; 1 reel.

Record of Armed Forces Discharges, 1917-1982; 5 reels.

Index to Armed Forces Discharges, 1917-1962; 1 reel.

MISCELLANEOUS RECORDS

Declaration of Intent, 1911-1920; 1 reel.

Naturalization Record, 1913-1924; 1 reel.

Record of Lunacy, 1899-1968; 1 reel.

Orders and Decrees, 1868-1968; 1 reel.

Special Proceedings, 1874-1946, 1961-1962; 10 reels.

Index to Special Proceedings, 1886-1920; 1 reel.

Appointment of Receivers, 1911-1938; 1 reel.

OFFICIALS, COUNTY

Minutes, Board of County Commissioners, 1868-1931; 4 reels.

SCHOOL RECORDS

Minutes, County Board of Education, 1873-1919; 1 reel.

WILLS

Record of Wills, 1751-1955; 4 reels.

Cross Index to Wills, 1751-1968; 1 reel.

ASHE COUNTY

Established in 1799 from Wilkes County.
Courthouse fire of 1865 destroyed many court records.

ORIGINAL RECORDS

BONDS
    Apprentice Bonds, 1876-1923; 1 volume.
    Bastardy Bonds, 1828-1910; 1 volume, 1 Fibredex box.
    Officials' Bonds and Records, 1821-1907; 2 Fibredex boxes.
CENSUS RECORDS (County Copy)
    Census, 1880; 1 manuscript box.
COURT RECORDS
    County Court of Pleas and Quarter Sessions
        Minutes, 1806-1866; 6 volumes.
        Trial and Appearance Dockets, 1829-1868; 2 volumes.
    Superior Court
        Minutes, 1807-1912; 12 volumes.
        Equity Minutes and Equity Trial Dockets, 1824-1868; 2 volumes.
        Execution Dockets, 1826-1841; 2 volumes.
        State Docket, 1829-1853; 1 volume.
        Trial and Appearance Dockets, 1807-1849; 2 volumes.
        Civil Action Papers, 1807-1934; 19 Fibredex boxes.
        Civil Action Papers Concerning Land, 1827-1911; 13 Fibredex boxes.
        Criminal Action Papers, 1805-1930; 11 Fibredex boxes.
    Inferior Court
        Minutes, 1877-1885; 1 volume.
ELECTION RECORDS
    Record of Elections, 1878-1930; 4 volumes.
ESTATES RECORDS
    Record of Estates, 1828-1842, 1853-1873; 2 volumes.
    Record of Accounts, 1869-1911; 2 volumes.
    Administrators' Bonds, 1876-1920, 1925; 4 volumes.
    Appointment of Administrators, Executors and Guardians, 1868-1920;
        1 volume.
    Estates Records, 1819-1935; 34 Fibredex boxes.
    Guardians' Records, 1829-1918; 5 Fibredex boxes.
    Guardians' Bonds, 1876-1925; 3 volumes.
    Record of Settlements, 1869-1920; 2 volumes.
LAND RECORDS
    Deeds and Grants, 1778-1849; 13 volumes.
    Deeds, 1802-1954; 8 Fibredex boxes.
    Mortgage Deeds, Deeds of Trust and Miscellaneous Land Records, 1828-
        1949; 1 Fibredex box.

Ejectments, 1827-1911; 1 Fibredex box.

Land Entries, 1803-1906; 6 volumes.

Miscellaneous Land Records, 1826-1911; 1 Fibredex box.

Processioners' Record, 1879-1883; 1 volume.

MARRIAGE, DIVORCE AND VITAL STATISTICS

Marriage Bonds, 1828-1868; 4 Fibredex boxes.

Record of Marriage Certificates, 1851-1881; 1 volume.

Divorce Records, 1822-1912; 5 Fibredex boxes.

MILITARY AND PENSION RECORDS

Pension Records, 1885-1919; 1 Fibredex box.

MISCELLANEOUS RECORDS

Homestead and Personal Property Exemptions, 1857-1938; 1 Fibredex box.

Settlement of County Accounts, Committee of Finance, 1839-1847; 1 volume.

Clerk's Minute Docket (Special Proceedings), 1895-1922; 1 volume.

Minutes and Accounts, Wardens of the Poor, 1832-1855; 1 volume.

Miscellaneous Records, 1801-1954; 2 Fibredex boxes.

Records of Assignees, Receivers and Trustees, 1811-1933; 1 Fibredex box.

Record of Receivers, 1883, 1889, 1907; 1 volume.

ROADS AND BRIDGES

Road Records, 1846-1909; 1 Fibredex box.

Railroad Records, 1885-1911; 1 Fibredex box.

SCHOOL RECORDS

School Census, 1883-1903; 3 Fibredex boxes.

School Teachers' Vouchers, 1881-1903; 3 Fibredex boxes.

WILLS

Wills, 1801-1912; 5 Fibredex boxes.

MICROFILM RECORDS

BONDS

Apprentice Bonds, 1876-1923; 1 reel.

Bastardy Bonds, 1876-1880, 1883; 1 reel.

CORPORATIONS AND PARTNERSHIPS

Record of Incorporations, 1910-1966; 1 reel.

Record of Partnerships, 1933-1966; 1 reel.

COURT RECORDS

County Court of Pleas and Quarter Sessions

Minutes, 1806-1866; 2 reels.

Superior Court

Minutes, 1807-1818, 1834-1959; 10 reels.

Equity Minutes, 1824-1868; Land Entries, 1870-1872; Tax Judgments, 1872-1874; 1 reel.

Witness Fee Docket, 1826-1841; 1 reel.

Cross Index to Judgments, 1869-1947; 2 reels.

ELECTION RECORDS
 Record of Elections, 1878-1956; 1 reel.
ESTATES RECORDS
 Record of Estates, 1853-1873; 1 reel.
 Record of Accounts, 1869-1966; 6 reels.
 Administrators' Bonds, 1876-1925; 1 reel.
 Record of Administrators, Executors and Guardians, 1920-1927; 1 reel.
 Record of Administrators, 1924-1966; 2 reels.
 Record of Executors, 1869-1919, 1943-1970; 2 reels.
 Guardians' Bonds, 1876-1941; 1 reel.
 Record of Guardians, 1927-1966; 2 reels.
 Record of Accounts of Indigent Orphans, 1939-1966; 1 reel.
 Record of Settlements, 1869-1966; 5 reels.
 Cross Index to Administrators, Executors and Guardians, 1906-1966; 1 reel.
LAND RECORDS
 Record of Deeds, 1800-1955; 57 reels.
 Cross Index to Deeds, 1799-1935; 4 reels.
 Index to Real Estate Conveyances, Grantor, 1935-1966; 4 reels.
 Index to Real Estate Conveyances, Grantee, 1935-1966; 4 reels.
 Land Entries, 1803-1906; 1 reel.
 Record of Surveys, 1905-1918; 1 reel.
 Plats, various years, 1966-1979; 2 reels.
 Index to Plats, no date; 1 reel.
 Record of Sale and Resale of Land by Trustees and Mortgagees, 1924-1966;
  2 reels.
MARRIAGE, DIVORCE AND VITAL STATISTICS
 Marriage Bonds, 1799-1868; 5 reels.
 Marriage Certificates, 1853-1881; 1 reel.
 Marriage Registers, 1853-1966; 1 reel.
 Maiden Names of Divorced Women, 1944-1966; 1 reel.
 Index to Births, 1913-1979; 1 reel.
 Index to Deaths, 1913-1979; 1 reel.
 Index to Delayed Births, various years; 1 reel.
MILITARY AND PENSION RECORDS
 Record of Armed Forces Discharges, 1918-1979; 5 reels.
MISCELLANEOUS RECORDS
 Minutes, Committee of Finance, 1839-1847; 1 reel.
 Inquisition of Lunacy, 1900-1961; 1 reel.
 Clerk's Minute Docket, 1895-1922; 1 reel.
 Orders and Decrees, 1868-1956; 9 reels.
 Special Proceedings, 1896-1970; 2 reels.
 Index to Special Proceedings, 1892-1966, 1970-1979; 2 reels.
 Wardens of the Poor, 1832-1855; 1 reel.
OFFICIALS, COUNTY
 Minutes, Board of County Commissioners, 1870-1955; 3 reels.

SCHOOL RECORDS

Minutes, County Board of Education, 1885-1966; 1 reel.

TAX AND FISCAL RECORDS

Tax Lists, 1925, 1935; 1 reel.

Tax Scrolls, 1955; 1 reel.

Tax Ledgers, 1915-1945; 1 reel.

County Tax Book, 1915-1916; 1 reel.

WILLS

Record of Wills, 1816-1966; 3 reels.

Cross Index to Wills, 1816-1966; 1 reel.

AVERY COUNTY

Established in 1911 from Caldwell, Mitchell and Watauga counties.

ORIGINAL RECORDS

ELECTION RECORDS
Record of Elections, 1912-1938; 3 volumes.
MARRIAGE, DIVORCE AND VITAL STATISTICS
Disinterment/Reinterment Permits, 1976-1986; 1 manuscript box.
MILITARY AND PENSION RECORDS
Record of Pensions, 1914-1940; 1 volume.
MISCELLANEOUS RECORDS
Alien Registration, 1940; 1 volume.
Alien Registration Records, 1940-1943; Abstract of Elections, 1932-1938;
1 manuscript box.

MICROFILM RECORDS

CORPORATIONS AND PARTNERSHIPS
Record of Corporations, 1911-1969; 1 reel.
Record of Partnerships, 1946-1964; 1 reel.
COURT RECORDS
Superior Court
Minutes, 1911-1957; 5 reels.
Judgment Dockets, Land Tax Sales, 1930-1958; 2 reels.
Tax Judgment Docket, 1947-1950; 1 reel.
Cross Index to Judgments, 1911-1963; 1 reel.
ELECTION RECORDS
Record of Elections, 1912-1970; 1 reel.
ESTATES RECORDS
Record of Accounts, 1912-1968; 3 reels.
Record of Administrators, Executors and Guardians, 1911-1955; 1 reel.
Record of Administrators, 1939-1968; 1 reel.
Record of Executors, 1955-1968; 1 reel.
Record of Dowers, 1913-1925; 1 reel.
Record of Guardians, 1937-1968; 1 reel.
Record of Accounts of Indigent Orphans, 1924-1931; 1 reel.
Inheritance Tax Records, 1923-1969; 1 reel.
Record of Settlements, 1912-1968; 1 reel.
Cross Index to Administrators and Executors, 1911-1968; 1 reel.
Cross Index to Guardians, 1911-1964; 1 reel.
LAND RECORDS
Record of Deeds, 1911-1966; 28 reels.
Index to Real Estate Conveyances, Grantor and Grantee, 1911-1944; 1 reel.

Index to Real Estate Conveyances, Grantor, 1944-1970; 2 reels.
Index to Real Estate Conveyances, Grantee, 1944-1970; 2 reels.
Land Entries, 1912-1957; 1 reel.
Land Title Guaranty Proceedings, 1914-1915; 1 reel.
Record of Taxes for Mortgages, 1931-1932; 1 reel.
Right of Way and Easements, 1962-1969; 1 reel.
Federal Tax Lien Index, 1928-1968; 1 reel.
Registration of Titles (Torrens Act), 1925; 1 reel.
Plat Books, 1914-1977; 4 reels.

MARRIAGE, DIVORCE AND VITAL STATISTICS

Marriage Licenses, 1913-1977; 15 reels.
Marriage Registers, 1911-1970; 1 reel.
Maiden Names of Divorced Women, 1939-1961; 1 reel.
Index to Births and Deaths, 1914-1970; 1 reel.
Index to Delayed Births, various years; 1 reel.

MILITARY AND PENSION RECORDS

Record of Armed Forces Discharges, 1919-1970; 2 reels.
Record of Pensions, 1914-1940; 1 reel.

MISCELLANEOUS RECORDS

Minutes, County Finance Committee, 1917-1918; 1 reel.
Lunacy Docket, 1911-1968; 1 reel.
Clerk's Minute Dockets, 1923-1968; 1 reel.
Orders and Decrees, 1911-1968; 1 reel.
Special Proceedings, 1911-1968; 3 reels.
Cross Index to Special Proceedings, 1911-1968; 1 reel.
Appointment of Receivers, 1924-1931; 1 reel.

OFFICIALS, COUNTY

Minutes, Board of County Commissioners, 1911-1970; 2 reels.

SCHOOL RECORDS

Minutes, County Board of Education, 1911-1970; 1 reel.

WILLS

Record of Wills, 1911-1968; 1 reel.
Cross Index to Wills, 1911-1968; 1 reel.

BATH COUNTY

Established in 1696 from Albemarle County. Divided into Archdale, Pamptecough and Wickham precincts in 1705. Abolished in 1738.

No records exist except a few which may be found in those of Beaufort County.

BEAUFORT COUNTY

Established in 1705 as Pamptecough Precinct of Bath County.
Name changed to Beaufort in 1712.

ORIGINAL RECORDS

BONDS
> Bastardy Books, 1846-1860, 1866-1875; 1 manuscript box.
> Officials' Bonds and Records, 1758, 1777, 1801-1871; 1 Fibredex box.
> Record of Officials' Bonds, 1868-1931; 2 volumes.

COURT RECORDS
> County Court of Pleas and Quarter Sessions
>> Minutes, 1756-1868; 10 volumes.
>> Appearance Dockets, 1828-1868; 3 volumes.
>> Execution Dockets, 1808-1868; 7 volumes.
>> State Dockets, 1846-1868; 2 volumes.
>> Trial and Appearance Dockets, 1744-1745, 1794-1828; 4 volumes.
>> Trial Dockets, 1838-1868; 10 volumes.
>
> Superior Court
>> Minutes, 1817-1902; 9 volumes.
>> Equity Minutes, 1807-1868; 3 volumes.
>> Equity Execution Docket, 1835-1868; 1 volume.
>> Equity Trial Docket, 1834-1868; 1 volume.
>> Appearance Docket, 1811-1817; 1 volume.
>> State Docket, 1855-1868; 1 volume.
>> Trial Dockets, 1835-1845, 1855-1868; 4 volumes.
>> Civil Issues Dockets, 1870, 1871, 1873-1885; 2 manuscript boxes.
>> Criminal Issues Dockets, 1870, 1873-1885; 2 manuscript boxes.
>> Civil Action Papers, 1785-1915; 8 Fibredex boxes.
>> Civil Action Papers Concerning Land, 1855-1938; 8 Fibredex boxes.
>
> Inferior Court
>> Minutes, 1878-1886; 1 volume.

ELECTION RECORDS
> Record of Elections, 1878-1922; 4 volumes.
> Voter Registration Books, 1868, 1872-1898; 9 manuscript boxes.

ESTATES RECORDS
> Record of Estates (Orphan Books), 1808-1868; 13 volumes.
> Record of Accounts, 1868-1904; 3 volumes.
> Record of Administrators, 1897-1911; 1 volume.
> Estates Records, 1760-1949; 28 Fibredex boxes.
> Guardians' Records, 1794-1918, 1948; 2 Fibredex boxes.
> Record of Guardians, 1842-1870; 1 volume.

Guardians' Bonds, 1867-1925; 2 volumes.

Record of Settlements, 1869-1914; 2 volumes.

Partitions and Divisions, 1794-1909; 1 volume.

Reports on Devised Estates, 1908-1913; 2 volumes.

Clerk's Account Book (Estates), 1849-1873; 1 volume.

LAND RECORDS

Record of Deeds, 1695-1881; 43 volumes.

Record of Corrections to Transcribed Records of Deeds, 1835-1836;
1 volume.

Index to Deeds, Grantee, 1701-1877; 3 volumes.

Index to Deeds, Grantor, 1701-1877; 3 volumes.

Cross Index to Deeds, 1854-1888; 3 volumes.

Land Entries, 1867-1926; 1 volume.

Attachments, Executions, Liens and Levies on Land, 1791-1904;
2 Fibredex boxes.

Miscellaneous Land Records, 1750-1947; 2 Fibredex boxes.

Patent Record, 1798-1816; 1 volume.

MARRIAGE, DIVORCE AND VITAL STATISTICS

Record of Marriages, 1851-1866; Record of Cohabitation, 1866-1867;
1 volume.

Marriage Registers, 1867-1930; 7 volumes.

Divorce Records, 1868-1902, 1923; 2 Fibredex boxes.

Disinterment/Reinterment Permits, 1979; 1 manuscript box.

MILITARY AND PENSION RECORDS

Record of Pensions, 1912-1931; 1 volume.

MISCELLANEOUS RECORDS

Record of Stock Marks, 1878-1921; 1 manuscript box.

Record of Official Reports, 1880-1944; 3 volumes.

Account Book, Deputy Register of Deeds, 1850-1860; 1 volume.

Homestead and Personal Property Exemptions, 1869-1906; 2 Fibredex boxes.

Minutes, Board of Magistrates, 1878-1895; 1 volume.

Nurses' Certificates of Registration, 1909-1960; 1 manuscript box.

Optometrists' Certificates of Registration, 1909-1957; 1 manuscript box.

Physicians' Certificates of Registration, 1889-1950; 1 manuscript box.

Minutes, Wardens of the Poor, 1847-1868; 1 volume.

Miscellaneous Records, 1755-1942; 1 Fibredex box.

Assignees, Receivers and Trustees Record, 1859; 1 volume.

Records of Assignees, Receivers and Trustees, 1869-1913; 2 Fibredex boxes.

ROADS AND BRIDGES

Record of Appointment of Road Overseers, 1843-1869; 1 volume.

Railroad Records, 1878-1903; 2 Fibredex boxes.

TAX AND FISCAL RECORDS

Lists of Taxables, 1841-1860, 1866; 6 volumes.

Tax Records, 1832-1852, 1878-1905; 1 manuscript box.

Assessment of Land for Taxation, 1860; 1 volume.

Beaufort County Courthouse, Washington, completed circa 1786.
Early twentieth-century photograph from the files of the State Archives.

Tax Abstract, 1879-1896; Record of Allowances to Outside Poor, 1868-1874;
1 volume.

WILLS

Wills, 1720-1903; 6 volumes, 1 Fibredex box.

MICROFILM RECORDS

CORPORATIONS AND PARTNERSHIPS

Record of Corporations, 1886-1960; 2 reels.

Partnership Record, 1918-1960; 1 reel.

Index to Corporations, 1886-1982; 1 reel.

COURT RECORDS

County Court of Pleas and Quarter Sessions

Minutes, 1785-1868; 3 reels.

Minutes, Appearance, Prosecution and Trial Dockets, 1756-1761;
1 reel.

Clerk's Account Book, 1849-1878; 1 reel.

Superior Court

Minutes, 1817-1960; 18 reels.

Equity Minutes, 1807-1868; 2 reels.

Index to Judgments, Plaintiff, 1868-1949; 2 reels.

Index to Judgments, Defendant, 1868-1949; 2 reels.

Inferior Court

Minutes, 1878-1886; 1 reel.

ELECTION RECORDS

Record of Elections, 1878-1960; 1 reel.

ESTATES RECORDS

Record of Estates (Orphan Books), 1808-1868; 5 reels.

Index to Record of Estates (Orphan Books), 1808-1868; 1 reel.

Record of Accounts, 1868-1960; 7 reels.

Administrators' Bonds, 1867-1898; 1 reel.

Record of Administrators, 1897-1960; 8 reels.

Appointment of Executors, 1868-1937; 1 reel.

Guardians' Bonds, 1867-1899; 1 reel.

Record of Guardians, 1845-1968; 3 reels.

Clerk's Receiver Accounts, 1908-1932; 1 reel.

Inheritance Tax Records, 1920-1960; 1 reel.

Record of Settlements, 1862-1960; 5 reels.

Index to Administrators, Executors and Guardians, 1868-1968; 1 reel.

Index to Administrators, 1897-1940; 1 reel.

Index to Executors, 1869-1940; 1 reel.

Index to Guardians, 1899-1940; 1 reel.

LAND RECORDS

Record of Deeds, 1701-1946; 181 reels.

Record of Real Estate Conveyances, 1946-1960; 75 reels.

Index to Real Estate Conveyances, Grantor, 1701-1959; 11 reels.
Index to Real Estate Conveyances, Grantee, 1701-1959; 11 reels.
Deeds, Mortgages and Bills of Sale, 1784, 1803-1807; 1 reel.
Land Entries, 1778-1795; 1 reel.
Land Entries and Claims Journal, 1882-1926; 1 reel.
Partitions and Divisions, 1736-1878; 1 reel.
Patent Book (Grants), 1798-1816; 2 reels.
Registration of Titles, 1915-1959; 4 reels.
Record of Land Sold for Taxes, 1876-1905; 1 reel.
Deeds Proved in Court, 1802-1805; 1 reel.
Plat Books, 1913-1982; 8 reels.
Index to Plats, 1913-1982; 1 reel.
Record of Sale and Resale under Mortgages and Deeds of Trust, 1915-1960; 5 reels.

MARRIAGE, DIVORCE AND VITAL STATISTICS

Record of Marriages, 1851-1868; Record of Cohabitation, 1866; 1 reel.
Marriage Registers, 1847-1963; 9 reels.
Index to Marriage Registers, no date; 1 reel.
Maiden Names of Divorced Women, 1926-1960; 1 reel.
Record of Delayed Births, various years; 5 reels.
Index to Delayed Births, various years; 1 reel.
Index to Births, 1913-1980; 7 reels.
Index to Deaths, 1913-1963; 2 reels.

MILITARY AND PENSION RECORDS

Record of Armed Forces Discharges, 1917-1982; 8 reels.
Index to Armed Forces Discharges, 1917-1982; 1 reel.
Record of Pensions, 1912-1930; 1 reel.

MISCELLANEOUS RECORDS

Alien Registration, various years; 1 reel.
Inquisition of Lunacy, 1900-1968; 2 reels.
Clerk's Minute Docket, 1908; 1 reel.
Orders and Decrees, 1869-1963; 15 reels.
Special Proceedings, 1874-1960; 4 reels.
Index to Special Proceedings, Plaintiff, 1874-1968; 2 reels.
Index to Special Proceedings, Defendant, 1874-1960; 2 reels.
Minutes, Wardens of the Poor, 1839-1868; 1 reel.

OFFICIALS, COUNTY

Minutes, Board of County Commissioners, 1868-1971; 12 reels.
Index to Minutes, Board of County Commissioners, 1919-1972; 1 reel.
Minutes, County Board of Health, 1960-1975; 1 reel.
Minutes of Magistrates, 1875-1895; 1 reel.

ROADS AND BRIDGES

Record of Overseers, 1845-1868; 1 reel.

SCHOOL RECORDS

Minutes, County Board of Education, 1909-1960; 2 reels.

Annual Reports, Public Schools of Washington, 1898-1913; 1 reel.
TAX AND FISCAL RECORDS
Tax Lists and Scrolls, 1779-1927; 24 reels.
WILLS
Wills, 1720-1867; 4 reels.
Record of Wills, 1868-1968; 6 reels.
Cross Index to Wills, 1720-1949; 1 reel.
Index to Wills, Devisor, 1950-1968; 1 reel.

BERTIE COUNTY

Established in 1722 from Chowan Precinct as a precinct of Albemarle County.

ORIGINAL RECORDS

BONDS

    Apprentice Bonds and Records, 1750-1889; 5 volumes, 4 Fibredex boxes, 1 manuscript box.

    Bastardy Bonds and Records, 1739-1880; 1 volume, 2 Fibredex boxes.

    Constables' Bonds, 1812-1869; 3 volumes.

    Officials' Bonds, 1755-1889; 2 Fibredex boxes.

COURT RECORDS

    County Court of Pleas and Quarter Sessions

        Minutes, 1724-1868; 21 volumes, 1 pamphlet.

        Appearance Dockets, 1838-1861, 1866-1868; 2 volumes.

        Costs Docket, 1760-1763; 1 pamphlet.

        Execution Dockets, 1748-1868; 16 volumes.

        Crown Dockets, 1748-1775; 2 volumes.

        State Dockets, 1778-1868; 5 volumes.

        Trial, Appearance and Reference Dockets, 1725-1797; 11 volumes.

        Trial and Appearance Dockets, 1798-1868; 8 volumes.

        Trial Dockets (Rough), 1761-1862; 1 Fibredex box.

        Clerk's Account Book, 1755-1761; 1 volume.

        Clerk's Receipt Book, 1824-1828; 1 volume.

    Superior Court

        Minutes, 1807-1915; 11 volumes, 1 manuscript box.

        Equity Execution Docket, 1824-1835; 1 volume.

        Equity Trial Dockets, 1808, 1818, 1820-1833; 2 volumes.

        Execution Dockets, 1808-1868; 3 volumes, 1 manuscript box.

        State Dockets, 1817-1868; 2 volumes.

        Criminal Issues Dockets, 1871-1900; 1 Fibredex box.

        Trial and Appearance Dockets, 1807-1871; 5 volumes.

        Civil Issues Dockets, 1870-1900; 1 Fibredex box.

        Miscellaneous Dockets, 1814-1875; 1 manuscript box.

        Civil Action Papers, 1737-1905; 28 Fibredex boxes.

        Criminal Action Papers, 1734-1868; 6 Fibredex boxes.

    Inferior Court

        Minutes, 1877-1887; 1 volume.

ELECTION RECORDS

    Record of Elections, 1878-1926; 2 volumes.

    Election Returns, 1769, 1790-1914; 4 Fibredex boxes.

ESTATES RECORDS

    Record of Estates, 1728-1868; 27 volumes.

    Record of Accounts, 1868-1915; 7 volumes.

Administrators' Bonds, 1762-1769, 1848-1909; 6 volumes.

Estates Records, 1730-1920; 114 Fibredex boxes.

Guardians' Records, 1730-1920; 16 Fibredex boxes.

Guardians' Accounts, 1817-1868; 5 volumes.

Guardians' Bonds, 1848-1894; 2 volumes.

Record of Settlements, 1869-1916; 2 volumes.

LAND RECORDS

Record of Deeds, 1765-1772; 1 volume.

Deeds, 1723-1890; 12 Fibredex boxes.

Mortgage Deeds and Deeds of Trust, 1723-1890; 2 Fibredex boxes.

Land Records, 1736-1861; 2 Fibredex boxes.

Miscellaneous Land Records, 1720-1861; 1 Fibredex box.

MARRIAGE, DIVORCE AND VITAL STATISTICS

Marriage Bonds, 1762-1868; 5 Fibredex boxes.

Marriage Licenses, 1870-1903; 5 Fibredex boxes.

Miscellaneous Marriage Records, 1749-1914; 1 Fibredex box.

Disinterment/ Reinterment Permits, 1980-1986; 1 manuscript box.

MILITARY AND PENSION RECORDS

Court Martial Minutes, 1842; 1 manuscript box.

Pension Board Minutes, 1903-1965; 1 volume.

MISCELLANEOUS RECORDS

Alien Registration, 1940, 1954; 1 volume.

Cotton Reports, 1889-1890; 2 manuscript boxes.

County Accounts, 1741-1903; 2 Fibredex boxes.

Personal Accounts, 1718-1860; 2 Fibredex boxes.

Stock Marks, 1722-1741; 1 pamphlet.

Merchants' Accounts, 1800-1900; 1 Fibredex box.

Merchants' Purchase Returns, 1880-1887, 1897; 2 manuscript boxes.

Minutes, Wardens of the Poor, 1838-1851; 1 volume.

Miscellaneous Records, 1723-1914; 5 Fibredex boxes.

Promissory Notes, 1746-1800; 1 Fibredex box.

Slave Records, 1744-1865; 3 Fibredex boxes.

ROADS AND BRIDGES

Road, Bridge and Ferry Records, 1734-1903; 2 Fibredex boxes.

SCHOOL RECORDS

Minutes and Accounts, Board of Superintendents of Common Schools, and County Board of Education, 1847-1878; 1 volume.

School Records, 1850-1878, 1895; 3 manuscript boxes.

TAX AND FISCAL RECORDS

Lists of Taxables, 1755-1860; 13 Fibredex boxes.

Miscellaneous Tax Records, 1843-1903; 1 manuscript box.

WILLS

Wills, 1749-1897; 18 Fibredex boxes.

MICROFILM RECORDS

BONDS
>Apprentice Bonds, 1811-1889; 2 reels.
>Bastardy Bonds, 1875-1877; 1 reel.

CORPORATIONS AND PARTNERSHIPS
>Record of Corporations, 1907-1957; 1 reel.

COURT RECORDS
>County Court of Pleas and Quarter Sessions
>>Minutes, 1724-1743, 1758-1868; 7 reels.
>
>Superior Court
>>Minutes, 1807-1955; 11 reels.
>>Cross Index to Judgments, 1868-1940; 4 reels.
>>Index to Civil Judgments, Plaintiff, 1941-1968; 1 reel.
>>Index to Civil Judgments, Defendant, 1941-1968; 1 reel.
>
>Inferior Court
>>Minutes, 1877-1887; 1 reel.

ELECTION RECORDS
>Record of Elections, 1878-1968; 2 reels.

ESTATES RECORDS
>Record of Estates, 1728-1871; 11 reels.
>Record of Accounts, 1868-1954; 7 reels.
>Cross Index to Accounts, 1868-1942; 1 reel.
>Administrators' Bonds, 1762-1769, 1848-1903; 5 reels.
>Appointment of Administrators, Executors and Guardians, 1909-1948; 6 reels.
>Appointment of Executors, 1868-1917; 1 reel.
>Record of Executors, 1940-1968; 1 reel.
>Guardians' Accounts, 1817-1868; 1 reel.
>Guardians' Bonds, 1848-1931; 2 reels.
>Record of Guardians, 1935-1968; 1 reel.
>Clerk's Receiver Accounts, 1906-1921; 1 reel.
>Amounts Paid to Indigent Children, 1929-1942; 1 reel.
>Inheritance Tax Records, 1923-1959; 1 reel.
>Record of Settlements, 1866-1968; 4 reels.
>Cross Index to Guardians and Administrators, 1858-1907; 1 reel.
>Index to Executors and Administrators, 1905-1968; 1 reel.
>Cross Index to Guardians, 1905-1960; 1 reel.

LAND RECORDS
>Record of Real Estate Conveyances, 1721-1948; 147 reels.
>Index to Real Estate Conveyances, Grantor, 1722-1959; 4 reels.
>Index to Real Estate Conveyances, Grantee, 1722-1959; 4 reels.
>Land Entries, 1778-1794; 1 reel.
>Record of Processions, 1851-1869; 1 reel.
>Map Books, 1915-1957, 1973-1985; 3 reels.
>Index to Map Books, 1771-1976; 1 reel.

Record of Resale of Land, 1925-1968; 4 reels.

MARRIAGE, DIVORCE AND VITAL STATISTICS

Marriage Bonds, 1741-1868; 4 reels.

Marriage Certificates, 1851-1868; 1 reel.

Marriage Registers, 1851-1945; 2 reels.

Cross Index to Marriage Registers, 1872-1900; 1 reel.

Maiden Names of Divorced Women, 1938-1968; 1 reel.

Record of Cohabitation, 1866; 1 reel.

Index to Births and Deaths, 1914-1921; 1 reel.

Index to Births, 1916-1975; 2 reels.

Index to Deaths, 1917-1975; 1 reel.

Index to Delayed Births, various years; 1 reel.

MILITARY AND PENSION RECORDS

Court Martial Minutes, 1842; 1 reel.

Confederate Veterans Association Roster, 1919-1935; 1 reel.

Pension Board Minutes, 1903-1960; 1 reel.

Record of Armed Forces Discharges, 1917-1978; 7 reels.

Index to Armed Forces Discharges, no date; 1 reel.

MISCELLANEOUS RECORDS

Alien Registration, 1940, 1954; 1 reel.

Record of Lunacy, 1899-1968; 1 reel.

Orders and Decrees, 1868-1959; 17 reels.

Special Proceedings, 1868-1955; 2 reels.

Index to Special Proceedings and Civil Actions, 1923-1968; 2 reels.

Minutes, Wardens of the Poor, 1838-1847; 1 reel.

OFFICIALS, COUNTY

Minutes, Board of County Commissioners, 1868-1947; 5 reels.

SCHOOL RECORDS

Minutes, Board of Superintendents of Common Schools, 1847-1878; 1 reel.

TAX AND FISCAL RECORDS

Tax Lists, 1755-1860, 1877, 1906, 1908-1909; 7 reels.

WILLS

Record of Wills, 1761-1968; 7 reels.

Index to Wills, 1761-1970; 1 reel.

BLADEN COUNTY

Established in 1734 from New Hanover Precinct as a precinct of Bath County. Courthouse fires of 1800 and 1893 destroyed most of the court records and several land records.

ORIGINAL RECORDS

COURT RECORDS
County Court of Pleas and Quarter Sessions
Minutes, 1866-1867; 1 volume.
Superior Court
Minutes, 1869-1890, 1893-1901; 4 volumes.
ELECTION RECORDS
Record of Elections, 1896-1934; 4 volumes.
ESTATES RECORDS
Record of Accounts, 1868-1885, 1893-1917; 2 volumes.
Administrators' Bonds, 1909-1912; 1 volume.
Guardians' Bonds, 1893-1912; 2 volumes.
Record of Settlements, 1885-1923; 2 volumes.
LAND RECORDS
Deeds and Grants, 1738-1804; 2 volumes.
Land Entry Books, 1893-1920; 2 volumes.
MARRIAGE, DIVORCE AND VITAL STATISTICS
Marriage Register, 1892-1904; 1 volume.
MISCELLANEOUS RECORDS
Alien Registration, 1940; 1 volume.
Special Proceedings Docket, 1869-1892; 1 volume.
Miscellaneous Records, 1761-1912; 1 manuscript box.

MICROFILM RECORDS

CORPORATIONS AND PARTNERSHIPS
Record of Corporations, 1899-1973; 2 reels.
Partnership Record, 1913-1929; 1 reel.
Index to Partners, Assumed Names and Corporations, 1899-1984; 1 reel.
COURT RECORDS
County Court of Pleas and Quarter Sessions
Minutes, 1866-1867; 1 reel.
Superior Court
Minutes, 1869-1968; 8 reels.
Index to Minutes, Plaintiff, 1869-1968; 2 reels.
Index to Minutes, Defendant, 1869-1968; 2 reels.
Index to Judgments, Plaintiff, 1869-1968; 1 reel.
Index to Judgments, Defendant, 1869-1968; 1 reel.

ELECTION RECORDS

Record of Elections, 1896-1960; 1 reel.

ESTATES RECORDS

Record of Accounts, 1868-1917; 1 reel.

Record of Administrators, Executors, Guardians and Trustees, 1911-1926; 1 reel.

Record of Accounts of Administrators, Executors and Guardians, 1918-1968; 3 reels.

Administrators' Bonds, 1909-1912; 1 reel.

Record of Administrators, 1917-1968; 3 reels.

Record of Executors, 1946-1968; 1 reel.

Guardians' Bonds, 1893-1912; 1 reel.

Record of Guardians, 1922-1968; 2 reels.

Inheritance Tax Records, 1924-1970; 2 reels.

Record of Division of Estates, 1899-1936; 1 reel.

Record of Settlements, 1885-1919; 1 reel.

Index to Final Accounts: Executors, Administrators and Guardians, 1869-1968; 1 reel.

Index to Final Accounts: Wards, 1872-1968; 1 reel.

LAND RECORDS

Record of Deeds, 1774-1961; 79 reels.

Deeds and Grants, 1738-1804; 1 reel.

Index to Real Estate Conveyances, Grantor, 1784-1961; 14 reels.

Index to Real Estate Conveyances, Grantee, 1784-1961; 12 reels.

Record of Entry Takers, 1893-1917, 1923-1940; 1 reel.

Map Books, 1877-1973; 5 reels.

Index to Maps, 1877-1973; 1 reel.

Record of Resale of Land by Mortgagees and Trustees, 1923-1966; 2 reels.

MARRIAGE, DIVORCE AND VITAL STATISTICS

Marriage Licenses, 1909-1961; 3 reels.

Marriage Registers, 1892-1971; 2 reels.

Index to Births, 1913-1972; 1 reel.

Index to Deaths, 1914-1972; 1 reel.

Index to Delayed Births, various years, 1873-1966; 2 reels.

MILITARY AND PENSION RECORDS

Record of Armed Forces Discharges, 1917-1984; 4 reels.

Index to Armed Forces Discharges, 1917-1973; 1 reel.

Roll Book, Bladen Guards (Co. K, 8th Regt. N. C. V., Artillery), 1861-1862; 1 reel.

MISCELLANEOUS RECORDS

Alien Registration, 1940; 1 reel.

Record of Inquisition of Lunacy, 1899-1959; 1 reel.

Clerk's Minute Dockets, 1933-1968; 2 reels.

Orders and Decrees, 1868-1968; 9 reels.

Special Proceedings, 1868-1924; 1 reel.

Index to Special Proceedings, Plaintiff, 1868-1968; 1 reel.

Index to Special Proceedings, Defendant, 1868-1968; 1 reel.

OFFICIALS, COUNTY

Minutes, Board of County Commissioners, 1893-1905; 1 reel.

SCHOOL RECORDS

Minutes, County Board of Education, 1881-1933; 1 reel.

TAX AND FISCAL RECORDS

Tax Lists, 1883, 1895, 1898-1900, 1905, 1915, 1925-1926; 3 reels.

WILLS

Record of Wills, 1766-1968; 3 reels.

Index to Wills, Devisor, 1766-1968; 1 reel.

Index to Wills, Devisee, 1766-1968; 1 reel.

BRUNSWICK COUNTY

Established in 1764 from Bladen and New Hanover counties.
Many court records were destroyed by Federal troops in 1865.

ORIGINAL RECORDS

BONDS
> Apprentice Bonds and Records, 1810-1907; 1 Fibredex box.
> Bastardy Bonds and Records, 1810-1930; 1 Fibredex box.
> Officials' Bonds and Records, 1794-1904; 3 volumes, 1 Fibredex box.
> Sheriffs' Bonds and Records, 1818-1901; 1 Fibredex box.

COURT RECORDS
> County Court of Pleas and Quarter Sessions
>> Minutes, 1782-1868; 11 volumes.
>> Trial Dockets, 1792, 1820-1868; 2 volumes, 1 manuscript box.
> Superior Court
>> Minutes, 1845-1912; 5 volumes.
>> Civil Action Papers, 1790-1926; 11 Fibredex boxes.
>> Civil Action Papers Concerning Land, 1807-1911; 3 Fibredex boxes.
>> Criminal Action Papers, 1800-1920; 3 Fibredex boxes.

ELECTION RECORDS
> Record of Elections, 1898-1920; 3 volumes.
> Election Records, 1809-1916; 1 Fibredex box.

ESTATES RECORDS
> Record of Accounts, 1868-1915; 1 volume.
> Appointment of Administrators, Executors, Guardians and Masters, 1868-1914; 1 volume.
> Estates Records, 1783-1920; 14 Fibredex boxes.
> Guardians' Records, 1819-1909; 2 Fibredex boxes.

LAND RECORDS
> Record of Deeds, 1790-1796, 1809-1814; 2 volumes.
> Deeds of Sale, 1821-1926; 2 Fibredex boxes.
> Mortgage Deeds and Warranty Deeds, 1798-1929; 1 Fibredex box.
> Index to Deeds, 1764-1900; 1 volume.
> Entry Books, 1853-1958; 2 volumes.
> Miscellaneous Land Records, 1808-1924; 1 Fibredex box.
> Record of Surveys, 1905-1920; 1 volume.

MARRIAGE, DIVORCE AND VITAL STATISTICS
> Marriage Bonds, 1804-1868; 2 Fibredex boxes.
> Marriage Registers, 1870-1877, 1893-1904; 2 volumes.
> Divorce and Marriage Records, 1844, 1866, 1869-1905; 1 Fibredex box.
> Disinterment/Reinterment Permits, 1963-1981; 1 manuscript box.

MILITARY AND PENSION RECORDS
> Record of Pensions, 1927-1954; 1 volume.

MISCELLANEOUS RECORDS
>Alien Registration, 1940; 1 volume.
>Stock Marks, 1869-1941, 1947; 2 volumes.
>Miscellaneous Records, 1786-1925; 2 Fibredex boxes.
>Records of Assignees, Receivers and Trustees, 1893-1907; 1 Fibredex box.

ROAD AND BRIDGES
>Railroad Records, 1868-1908; 1 Fibredex box.

SCHOOL RECORDS
>Minutes, Board of Superintendents of Common Schools, 1841-1854; 1 pamphlet.

WILLS
>Record of Wills, 1781-1847; 3 volumes.
>Wills, 1765-1912; 6 Fibredex boxes.

MICROFILM RECORDS

BONDS
>Officials' Bonds, 1794-1829, 1868-1904; 1 reel.

CORPORATIONS AND PARTNERSHIPS
>Record of Corporations, 1889-1963; 1 reel.
>Record of Partnerships, 1917-1959; 1 reel.

COURT RECORDS
>County Court of Pleas and Quarter Sessions
>>Minutes, 1782-1786, 1789-1801, 1805-1868; 2 reels.
>Superior Court
>>Minutes, 1845-1954; 6 reels.
>>Index to Judgments, 1868-1963; 2 reels.

ELECTION RECORDS
>Record of Elections, 1898-1972; 1 reel.

ESTATES RECORDS
>Record of Accounts, 1868-1963; 2 reels.
>Appointment of Administrators, Executors and Guardians, 1868-1929; 1 reel.
>Record of Administrators, 1929-1955; 2 reels.
>Record of Executors, 1929-1963; 1 reel.
>Record of Guardians, 1930-1968; 1 reel.
>Division of Land and Dowers, 1894-1917; 1 reel.
>Inheritance Tax Records, 1923-1963; 1 reel.
>Record of Settlements, 1868-1963; 1 reel.
>Index to Administrators, Executors and Guardians, 1929-1963; 1 reel.

LAND RECORDS
>Record of Real Estate Conveyances, 1764-1946; 50 reels.
>Record of Deeds and Land Grants, 1788-1815; 1 reel.
>Index to Real Estate Conveyances, Grantor, 1764-1963; 6 reels.
>Index to Real Estate Conveyances, Grantee, 1764-1963; 6 reels.
>Land Entries, 1853-1953; 1 reel.

Record of Surveys, 1905-1920; 1 reel.

Certificate Record of Land Sold for Taxes, 1931; 1 reel.

Index to Federal Tax Liens, 1933-1972; 1 reel.

Registration of Land Titles, 1914-1940; 1 reel.

Plat Books, 1915-1973; 4 reels.

Index to Maps, 1914-1974; 1 reel.

Record of Resale of Land by Mortgagees and Trustees, 1920-1963; 2 reels.

MARRIAGE, DIVORCE AND VITAL STATISTICS

Marriage Bonds, 1804-1868; 3 reels.

Marriage Registers, 1850-1974; 2 reels.

Record of Marriages, 1962-1969; 1 reel.

Record of Births, 1913-1985; 17 reels.

Index to Births, 1914-1974; 1 reel.

Record of Deaths, 1913-1991; 13 reels.

Index to Deaths, 1914-1974; 1 reel.

Record of Delayed Births, various years; 3 reels.

Index to Delayed Births, various years; 1 reel.

MILITARY AND PENSION RECORDS

Record of Pensions, 1927-1953; 1 reel.

Record of Armed Forces Discharges, 1927-1974; 2 reels.

MISCELLANEOUS RECORDS

Alien Registration, 1940; 1 reel.

Record of Lunacy, 1914-1961; 1 reel.

Special Proceedings Dockets, 1890-1963; 5 reels.

Cross Index to Special Proceedings, 1938-1963; 1 reel.

OFFICIALS, COUNTY

Minutes, Board of County Commissioners, 1868-1963; 5 reels.

SCHOOL RECORDS

Minutes, Board of Superintendents of Common Schools, 1841-1854; 1 reel.

Minutes, County Board of Education, 1872-1963; 2 reels.

TAX AND FISCAL RECORDS

Tax Scrolls, 1873-1945; 4 reels.

WILLS

Record of Wills, 1764-1954; 1 reel.

Cross Index to Wills, 1764-1963; 1 reel.

BUNCOMBE COUNTY

Established in 1791 from Burke and Rutherford counties.
Courthouse fires of 1830 and 1865 destroyed many court records.

ORIGINAL RECORDS

BONDS
>Apprentice Bonds, 1794-1919; 4 volumes.
>Bastardy Bonds and Records, 1824-1928; 1 volume, 2 Fibredex boxes.

CORPORATIONS AND PARTNERSHIPS
>Record of Incorporations, 1885-1909; 1 Fibredex box.

COURT RECORDS
>County Court of Pleas and Quarter Sessions
>>Minutes, 1792-1868; 7 volumes.
>>Appearance Docket, 1852-1868; 1 volume.
>>Execution Dockets, 1807-1868; 10 volumes.
>>State Dockets, 1826-1868; 3 volumes.
>>Trial and Appearance Dockets, 1796-1851; 4 volumes.
>>Trial Dockets, 1851-1868; 2 volumes.

>Superior Court
>>Minutes, 1812-1815, 1857-1909; 25 volumes.
>>Appearance Docket, 1866-1869; 1 volume.
>>Equity Trial and Appearance Docket, 1808-1845; 1 volume.
>>Execution Dockets, 1850-1868; 4 volumes.
>>State Docket, 1833-1869; 1 volume.
>>Trial Docket, 1851-1867; 1 volume.
>>Miscellaneous Dockets (Abstracts), 1808-1862; 1 volume.
>>Civil Action Papers, 1812-1918; 31 Fibredex boxes.
>>Civil Action Papers Concerning Land, 1808-1925; 46 Fibredex boxes.
>>Criminal Action Papers, 1832-1944; 20 Fibredex boxes.

>Inferior Court
>>Minutes, 1883-1889; 1 volume.
>>Execution Docket, 1883-1888; 1 volume.

>Circuit Criminal Court/Western District Criminal Court
>>Minutes, 1893-1900; 3 volumes.

ELECTION RECORDS
>Election Records, 1871-1900; 1 Fibredex box.

ESTATES RECORDS
>Record of Estates, 1845-1868; 2 volumes.
>Record of Accounts, 1868-1912; 7 volumes.
>Administrators' Bonds, 1870-1897; 5 volumes.
>Appointment of Administrators, Executors, Guardians and Masters, 1868-1890; 1 volume.
>Appointment of Administrators, 1896-1907; 2 volumes.

Appointment of Guardians, 1899-1907; 1 volume.

Estates Records, 1801, 1815-1924; 122 Fibredex boxes.

Guardians' Records, 1829-1915, 1933; 15 Fibredex boxes.

Guardians' Bonds, 1870-1900; 4 volumes.

Record of Inventories, 1899-1917; 1 volume.

Record of Settlements, 1864-1909; 3 volumes.

LAND RECORDS

Deeds, 1807-1919; 1 Fibredex box.

Miscellaneous Deeds, 1841-1924; 2 Fibredex boxes.

Index to Deeds, 1794-1924; 5 volumes.

Attachments, Executions, Levies and Liens on Land, 1814-1915;
    4 Fibredex boxes.

Ejectments, 1818-1905; 1 Fibredex box.

Land Entries, 1794-1919; 16 volumes, 1 manuscript box.

Miscellaneous Land Records, 1798-1920; 3 Fibredex boxes.

Probate of Deeds, 1798-1804, 1820-1825; 2 volumes.

MARRIAGE, DIVORCE AND VITAL STATISTICS

Marriage Bonds, 1842-1867; 1 Fibredex box.

Divorce Records, 1830-1918; 26 Fibredex boxes.

Disinterment/Reinterment Permits, 1972-1986; 1 manuscript box.

MILITARY AND PENSION RECORDS

Record of Pensions, 1893, 1903-1959; 6 volumes.

MISCELLANEOUS RECORDS

Alien Registration, 1927-1941; 1 Fibredex box.

Naturalization Records, 1906, 1909-1910; 2 volumes.

Coroners' Inquests, 1875-1929; 2 Fibredex boxes.

Homestead and Personal Property Exemptions, 1866-1906; 2 Fibredex boxes.

Clerk's Minute Dockets (Special Proceedings), 1873-1884; 2 volumes.

Orders and Decrees, 1868-1899; 1 volume.

Special Proceedings Docket, 1869-1878; 1 volume.

Cross Index to Special Proceedings, no date; 1 volume.

Cross Index to Special Proceedings Minutes, [1869-1911]; 1 volume.

Miscellaneous Records, 1786-1946; 7 Fibredex boxes.

Records of Assignees, Receivers and Trustees, 1837-1911; 13 Fibredex boxes.

OFFICIALS, COUNTY

Minutes, Board of County Commissioners, 1868-1912; 12 volumes.

ROADS AND BRIDGES

Road Docket, 1812-1816; 1 volume.

Road Records, 1838-1916; 2 Fibredex boxes.

Railroad Records, 1857-1912; 9 Fibredex boxes.

WILLS

Record of Wills, 1831-1868; 1 volume.

Wills, 1826-1909; 10 Fibredex boxes.

MICROFILM RECORDS

BONDS
        Apprentice Indentures, 1794-1874; 1 reel.
        Bastardy Bonds, 1875-1879; 1 reel.

CORPORATIONS AND PARTNERSHIPS
        Record of Corporations, 1884-1947; 8 reels.
        Record of Partnerships, 1913-1974; 2 reels.
        Index to Corporations, 1884-1964; 1 reel.

COURT RECORDS
        County Court of Pleas and Quarter Sessions
                Minutes, 1792-1812, 1819-1825, 1832-1868; 3 reels.
                Appearance Docket, 1852-1868; 1 reel.
                Execution Dockets, 1807-1814, 1823-1843, 1858-1868; 2 reels.
        Superior Court
                Minutes, 1812-1815, 1857-1909 (includes Special Proceedings, 1868-1885); 9 reels.
                Civil Minutes, 1909-1948; 12 reels.
                Criminal Minutes, 1883-1953; 6 reels.
                Equity Minutes, 1854-1857; Special Proceedings, 1870-1877; 1 reel.
                Bills and Answers in Equity, 1809-1832; 1 reel.
                Execution Dockets, 1869-1870, 1883-1884; 1 reel.
                Motion Docket, 1868-1869; 1 reel.
                Summons Docket, 1868-1893; 1 reel.
                Trial Docket, 1867-1870; 1 reel.
                Cross Index to Civil Issues Docket, no date; 1 reel.
                Judgment Docket, Justice of the Peace Transcripts, 1930-1960; 1 reel.
                Cross Index to Civil Actions, 1858-1879, 1896-1955; 5 reels.
                Cross Index to Judgments, Plaintiff, 1868-1943; 2 reels.
                Cross Index to Judgments, Defendant, 1915-1942; 2 reels.
        Inferior Court
                Criminal Docket, 1883-1889; 1 reel.
                Judgment Docket, 1887-1897; 1 reel.
        Circuit Criminal Court/Western District Criminal Court
                Minutes, 1889-1900; 2 reels.
        General County Court
                Minutes, 1929-1941; 4 reels.
                Cross Index to Civil Actions, 1929-1941; 1 reel.

ESTATES RECORDS
        Record of Accounts, 1868-1964; 13 reels.
        Administrators' Bonds, 1870-1897; 2 reels.
        Appointment of Administrators, Executors and Guardians, 1868-1890; 1 reel.
        Record of Administrators, 1896-1963; 12 reels.
        Cross Index to Administrators, 1896-1960; 1 reel.
        Guardians' Bonds, 1870-1900; 1 reel.

Appointment and Record of Guardians, 1855-1867; 1 reel.

Record of Guardians, 1899-1962; 6 reels.

Index to Guardians, 1899-1918; 1 reel.

Inheritance Tax Records, 1919-1953; 2 reels.

Commitment of Indigent Children to County Home, 1890-1911; 1 reel.

Record of Amounts Paid for Indigent Children, 1916-1920; 1 reel.

Record of Trusts for Minors and Incompetents, 1935-1953; 1 reel.

Record of Qualification of Trustees for Guardians and Administrators, 1936-1967; 1 reel.

Record of Inventories, 1845-1868, 1899-1961; 4 reels.

Record of Settlements, 1864-1964; 13 reels.

Cross Index to Settlements, 1869-1970; 1 reel.

LAND RECORDS

Record of Deeds, 1789-1964; 294 reels.

Index to Deeds, Grantor, 1791-1962; 31 reels.

Index to Deeds, Grantee, 1798-1962; 30 reels.

Land Entries, 1794, 1795, 1832-1837; 1 reel.

Land Grants, 1794-1832; 1 reel.

Record of Mountain Retreat Leases, 1898-1914; 1 reel.

Plat Books, 1912-1969; 15 reels.

Index to Plats, 1919-1965; 2 reels.

MARRIAGE, DIVORCE AND VITAL STATISTICS

Marriage Bonds, 1791-1868; 1 reel.

Marriage Registers, Male, 1851-1969; 3 reels.

Marriage Registers, Female, 1851-1961; 2 reels.

Births and Deaths, City of Asheville, 1887-1915; 1 reel.

Deaths, City of Asheville, 1898-1914; 1 reel.

Index to Births, 1913-1974; 5 reels.

Index to Deaths, 1913-1968; 3 reels.

MILITARY AND PENSION RECORDS

Record of Pensions, 1893, 1903-1959; 2 reels.

War of 1812 Claims of Service, 1855; 1 reel.

Record of Armed Forces Discharges, 1919-1973; 18 reels.

Index to Armed Forces Discharges, 1919-1970; 1 reel.

MISCELLANEOUS RECORDS

Alien Registration, 1927-1941; 1 reel.

Record of Naturalization, 1906, 1909-1910; 1 reel.

Record of Lunacy, 1899-1949; 3 reels.

Orders and Decrees, 1868-1899; 1 reel.

Minute Docket, Orders and Decrees, Liquidation Book, 1933-1936; 1 reel.

Special Proceedings, 1869-1953; 20 reels.

Cross Index to Special Proceedings, 1869-1954; 2 reels.

Cross Index to Special Proceedings, Unrecorded, 1874-1957; 1 reel.

OFFICIALS, COUNTY

Minutes, Board of County Commissioners, 1872-1962; 12 reels.

Minutes, Board of Trustees, Magistrates' and Commissioners' Bonds, 1878-1917; 1 reel.
ROADS AND BRIDGES
Road Docket, 1812-1816; 1 reel.
TAX AND FISCAL RECORDS
Tax List, 1915; 1 reel.
WILLS
Record of Wills, 1831-1964; 18 reels.
Cross Index to Wills, 1831-1970; 1 reel.

BURKE COUNTY

Established in 1777 from Rowan County.
Many court records and most land records burned by Federal troops in 1865.

ORIGINAL RECORDS

BONDS
>   Apprentice Bonds and Records, 1784-1908; 1 volume, 1 Fibredex box.
>   Bastardy Bonds and Records, 1777-1899; 1 volume, 3 Fibredex boxes.
>   Constables' Bonds and Records, 1782-1875, 1892; 2 Fibredex boxes.
>   Officials' Bonds and Records, 1778-1949; 1 Fibredex box.

COURT RECORDS
>   County Court of Pleas and Quarter Sessions
>>   Minutes, 1791-1868; 13 volumes.
>>   Execution Dockets, 1837-1840, 1843-1855; 3 volumes.
>>   Trial and Appearance Dockets, 1792-1857; 5 volumes.
>   Superior Court
>>   Minutes, 1830-1857, 1866-1907; 15 volumes.
>>   Execution Dockets, 1824-1856; 8 volumes.
>>   Judgment Dockets, 1878-1895, 1917-1926; 4 volumes.
>>   Presentment Dockets, 1879-1912; 3 volumes.
>>   State Dockets, 1830-1851, 1866-1879; 3 volumes.
>>   Trial, Appearance and Reference Dockets, 1830-1859; 4 volumes.
>>   Civil Action Papers, 1755-1905; 14 Fibredex boxes.
>>   Civil Action Papers Concerning Land, 1779-1927; 5 Fibredex boxes.
>>   Criminal Action Papers, 1779-1921; 21 Fibredex boxes.
>>   Supplementary Proceedings, 1871-1876; 1 volume.
>   Western District Criminal Court
>>   Minutes, 1899-1900; 1 volume.
>>   Criminal Issues Docket, 1899-1900; 1 volume.
>>   Judgment Docket, 1899-1900; 1 volume.
>>   Half Fee Docket, 1899-1900; 1 volume.

ELECTION RECORDS
>   Record of Elections, 1896-1908; 1 volume.
>   Election Records, 1806-1931; 3 Fibredex boxes.

ESTATES RECORDS
>   Record of Estates, 1832-1845, 1865-1868; 3 volumes.
>   Record of Accounts, 1868-1900; 2 volumes.
>   Administrators' Bonds, 1868-1896; 3 volumes.
>   Appointment of Administrators, Executors, Guardians and Masters, 1868-
>   1898; 1 volume.
>   Estates Records, 1776-1934; 62 Fibredex boxes.
>   Guardians' Records, 1785-1933; 6 Fibredex boxes.
>   Guardians' Bonds, 1870-1896; 2 volumes.

Inventories and Accounts of Sale, 1880-1899; 1 volume.

Record of Settlements, 1869-1899; 1 volume.

Clerk's Receipt Docket (Estates), 1896-1916; 1 volume.

Index to Estates, 1868-1887; 1 volume.

LAND RECORDS

Deeds of Sale, 1805-1928; 1 Fibredex box.

Miscellaneous Deeds, 1772-1919; 1 Fibredex box.

Ejectments, 1784-1868; 1 Fibredex box.

Land Entries, 1770-1909; 1 volume, 1 Fibredex box.

Levies on Land for Taxes, 1875-1888; 1 volume.

Petitions for Partition, 1870-1910; 1 Fibredex box.

MARRIAGE, DIVORCE AND VITAL STATISTICS

Marriage Bonds, 1780-1868; 4 Fibredex boxes.

Marriage Certificates, 1865-1867. SEE Court Records, County Court of Pleas and Quarter Sessions, Minutes, 1865.

Divorce Records, 1828-1911; 3 Fibredex boxes.

MILITARY AND PENSION RECORDS

Confederate Oaths, 1865; 1 volume.

Record of Confederate Pensions, 1885-1901; 2 volumes.

MISCELLANEOUS RECORDS

Alien Registration, 1927-1940; 1 volume.

Declarations of Citizenship, 1911-1928; 1 volume.

Petitions for Naturalization, 1919-1930; 2 volumes.

Lunacy Records, 1899-1917; 1 volume.

Orders and Decrees, 1868-1923; 2 volumes.

Special Proceedings, 1870-1901; 7 volumes.

Miscellaneous Records, 1776-1949; 4 Fibredex boxes.

Records of Assignees and Trustees, 1783-1905; 1 Fibredex box.

OFFICIALS, COUNTY

Record of Justices of the Peace, Magistrates and Notaries Public, 1923-1953; 3 volumes.

ROADS AND BRIDGES

Road Records, 1787-1897; 5 Fibredex boxes.

TAX AND FISCAL RECORDS

Tax Records, 1782-1894; 3 Fibredex boxes.

WILLS

Wills, 1790-1905; 1 Fibredex box.

MICROFILM RECORDS

BONDS

Apprentice Bonds, 1868-1907; 1 reel.

Bastardy Bonds, 1868-1879; 1 reel.

CORPORATIONS AND PARTNERSHIPS

Record of Corporations, 1886-1963; 2 reels.

Record of Partnerships, 1944-1963; 1 reel.

COURT RECORDS

County Court of Pleas and Quarter Sessions

Minutes, 1791-1834, 1841-1849, 1865-1868; 4 reels.

Execution Dockets, 1837-1855; 1 reel.

Superior Court

Minutes, 1830-1857, 1866-1966; 18 reels.

Minutes, Criminal, 1938-1943; Papers of Frances Silver Trial, 1832; 1 reel.

Judgment Dockets, 1885-1895; 1 reel.

Cross Index to Judgments, 1897-1962; 2 reels.

State Dockets, 1830-1851; 1 reel.

Western District Criminal Court

Minutes, 1899-1900; 1 reel.

Judgment Dockets, 1899-1900; 2 reels.

ELECTION RECORDS

Record of Elections, 1880-1970; 1 reel.

ESTATES RECORDS

Record of Accounts, 1896-1916; 1 reel.

Record of Annual Accounts, 1868-1963; 6 reels.

Administrators' Bonds, 1868-1896; 1 reel.

Appointment of Administrators, Executors and Guardians, 1868-1898; 1 reel.

Record of Administrators, 1897-1963; 6 reels.

Record of Executors and Guardians, 1897-1916; 1 reel.

Record of Executors, 1915-1959; 1 reel.

Record of Guardians, 1913-1963; 3 reels.

Record of Money Paid by Administrators, Executors and Guardians, 1916-1962; 1 reel.

Inheritance Tax Records, 1924-1963; 1 reel.

Record of Inventories and Sales of Estates, 1832-1963; 5 reels.

Record of Settlements, 1869-1963; 6 reels.

LAND RECORDS

Record of Deeds, 1865-1960; 141 reels.

Index to Real Estate Conveyances, Grantor, 1865-1965; 9 reels.

Index to Real Estate Conveyances, Grantee, 1865-1965; 8 reels.

Land Entries, 1778-1795, 1833-1900, 1913-1945; 3 reels.

Record of Surveys, 1905-1935; 1 reel.

Levies on Land for Taxes, 1867-1888, 1931-1941; 2 reels.

Plat Books, 1922-1980; 4 reels.

Record of Resale by Trustees and Mortgagees, 1932-1952; 1 reel.

MARRIAGE, DIVORCE AND VITAL STATISTICS

Marriage Bonds, 1777-1868; 3 reels.

Marriage Registers, 1867-1980; 2 reels.

Index to Births, 1913-1978; 4 reels.

Index to Deaths, 1913-1978; 2 reels.

MILITARY AND PENSION RECORDS

Record of Armed Forces Discharges, 1918-1980; 10 reels.

Index to Armed Forces Discharges, 1918-1980; 1 reel.

MISCELLANEOUS RECORDS

Record of Inquisition of Lunacy, 1899-1959; 2 reels.

Orders and Decrees, 1868-1923, 1935; 1 reel.

Special Proceedings, 1868-1885; Trial and Appearance Docket, Superior Court, 1866-1868; 1 reel.

Special Proceedings, 1884-1954; 11 reels.

Index to Special Proceedings, 1866-1980; 4 reels.

OFFICIALS, COUNTY

Minutes, Board of County Commissioners, 1871-1882, 1892-1959; 5 reels.

Minutes, County Board of Health, 1937-1949; 1 reel.

SCHOOL RECORDS

Minutes, County Board of Education, 1885-1948; 1 reel.

WILLS

Record of Wills, 1793-1963; 5 reels.

Index to Wills, 1863-1954; 1 reel.

BUTE COUNTY

Established in 1764 from Granville County.
Divided into Franklin and Warren counties in 1779; additional
records of Bute County may be found in the records of those counties.

ORIGINAL RECORDS

COURT RECORDS
        County Court of Pleas and Quarter Sessions
                Minutes, 1767-1779; 2 volumes.
                Execution Docket, 1765-1768; 1 volume.
                Recording Docket (Clerk of the Pleas), 1764-1787; 1 volume.
                Trial and Appearance Docket, 1766-1767; 1 volume.
                Trial, Appearance and Petitions Docket, 1772-1778; 1 volume.
ESTATES RECORDS
        Estates Records, 1764-1779; 1 Fibredex box.
        Guardians' Accounts, 1770-1778; 1 volume.
LAND RECORDS
        Land Entries, 1778-1785; 1 volume.
MARRIAGE, DIVORCE AND VITAL STATISTICS
        Marriage Bonds, 1764-1779; 1 Fibredex box.
MISCELLANEOUS RECORDS
        Miscellaneous Records, 1764-1779; 1 Fibredex box.
TAX AND FISCAL RECORDS
        Miscellaneous Tax Records, 1765-1778; 1 manuscript box.
WILLS
        Wills and Inventories, 1760-1800; 3 volumes.

MICROFILM RECORDS

COURT RECORDS
        County Court of Pleas and Quarter Sessions
                Minutes, 1767-1779; Reference, Trial and New Action Docket, 1766-
                        1767; Execution Docket, 1765-1768; 1 reel.
                Recording Docket, 1764-1787; Reference Docket, 1772-1778; 1 reel.
MARRIAGE, DIVORCE AND VITAL STATISTICS
        Marriage Bonds, 1764-1779; 1 reel.
MISCELLANEOUS RECORDS
        Miscellaneous Unbound Records, 1764-1779; 1 reel.
TAX AND FISCAL RECORDS
        List of Taxables, 1771; 1 reel.
WILLS
        Wills and Inventories, 1760-1800; Guardians' Accounts, 1770-1778; 1 reel.
        Record Book I (wills, deeds, and inventories), 1764-1767; 1 reel.

CABARRUS COUNTY

Established in 1792 from Mecklenburg County.
Courthouse fire of 1876 resulted in the loss of a few court records.

ORIGINAL RECORDS

BONDS
>   Apprentice Bonds, 1875-1901; 2 volumes.
>   Bastardy Bonds and Records, 1869-1918; 1 Fibredex box.

COURT RECORDS
>   County Court of Pleas and Quarter Sessions
>   >   Minutes, 1793-1817, 1821-1867; 9 volumes.
>   >   Appearance Dockets, 1821-1829, 1843-1868; 2 volumes.
>   >   Execution Dockets, 1821-1826, 1843-1868; 6 volumes.
>   >   State Docket, 1797-1819; 1 volume.
>   >   Trial and Appearance Docket, 1793-1808; 1 volume.
>   >   Trial Dockets, 1821-1829, 1843-1868; 3 volumes.
>   Superior Court
>   >   Minutes, 1819-1913; 11 volumes.
>   >   Equity Minutes, 1846-1868; 1 volume.
>   >   Civil Issues Dockets, 1869-1904; 3 volumes.
>   >   Civil Action Papers, 1824-1935; 12 Fibredex boxes.
>   >   Civil Action Papers Concerning Land, 1856-1944; 4 Fibredex boxes.
>   >   Criminal Action Papers, 1873-1923; 8 Fibredex boxes.

ELECTION RECORDS
>   Record of Elections, 1878-1920; 4 volumes.

ESTATES RECORDS
>   Record of Accounts, 1875-1908; 3 volumes.
>   Administrators' Bonds, 1875-1881; 1 volume.
>   Appointment of Administrators, Executors, Guardians and Masters, 1868-1911; 1 volume.
>   Estates Records, 1793-1953; 48 Fibredex boxes.
>   Guardians' Records, 1847-1932, 1940, 1945; 6 Fibredex boxes.
>   Guardians' Bonds, 1853-1882; 2 volumes.
>   Record of Inventories, Accounts and Settlements, 1846-1868; 3 volumes.
>   Record of Inventories and Accounts, 1869-1905; 3 volumes.
>   Record of Settlements, 1869-1898; 3 volumes.
>   Clerk's Receipt Book (Land Sales), 1861-1919; 1 volume.

LAND RECORDS
>   Deeds, 1821, 1869-1945; 4 Fibredex boxes.
>   Attachments, Executions, Liens and Levies on Land, 1844-1925; 1 Fibredex box.
>   Miscellaneous Land Records, 1818-1945; 1 Fibredex box.
>   Record of Probate, 1878-1885; 1 volume.

MARRIAGE, DIVORCE AND VITAL STATISTICS
>   Marriage Bonds, 1792-1868; 10 Fibredex boxes.
>   Marriage Register, 1867-1905; 1 volume.
>   Divorce Records, 1866, 1868, 1873-1930; 4 Fibredex boxes.
>   Disinterment/Reinterment Permits, 1977-1979; 1 manuscript box.

MILITARY AND PENSION RECORDS
>   Record of Pensions, 1919-1940; 1 volume.
>   Minutes and Roster, Confederate Veterans Association of Cabarras County, 1895, 1897; 1 volume.
>   Record of Soldiers in World War I, 1917-1919; 1 volume.

MISCELLANEOUS RECORDS
>   Alien Registration, 1927, 1940-1941; 1 volume.
>   Declaration of Intent (to Become a Citizen), 1909-1921; 1 volume.
>   Petitions for Naturalization, 1909-1921; 1 volume.
>   Special Proceedings Docket, 1875-1914; 1 volume.
>   Miscellaneous Records, 1794-1945; 2 Fibredex boxes.
>   Records of Assignees, Trustees and Receivers, 1854-1928; 3 Fibredex boxes.

ROADS AND BRIDGES
>   Record of Appointment of Road Overseers, 1837; 1 volume.
>   Railroad Records, 1869-1924; 3 Fibredex boxes.

TAX AND FISCAL RECORDS
>   Miscellaneous Tax Records, 1860-1921; 1 Fibredex box.

WILLS
>   Wills, 1794-1921; 12 Fibredex boxes.

MICROFILM RECORDS

BONDS
>   Apprentice Bonds, 1875-1901; 1 reel.

CORPORATIONS AND PARTNERSHIPS
>   Record of Corporations, 1885-1965; 2 reels.
>   Record of Partnerships, 1917-1965; 1 reel.
>   Index to Partnerships, Corporations and Assumed Names, 1899-1982; 1 reel.

COURT RECORDS
>   County Court of Pleas and Quarter Sessions
>> Minutes, 1793-1817, 1828-1867; 6 reels.
>   Superior Court
>> Minutes, 1819-1954; 16 reels.
>> Equity Minutes, 1846-1868; 1 reel.
>> Index to Minutes, Civil, Plaintiff, 1819-1970; 2 reels.
>> Index to Minutes, Civil and Criminal, Defendant, 1819-1970; 3 reels.
>> Index to Judgments, Plaintiff, 1898-1970; 2 reels.
>> Index to Judgments, Defendant, 1898-1970; 2 reels.

ELECTION RECORDS

    Record of Elections, 1878-1972; 1 reel.

    Voter Registration Lists (by Township), 1902-1908; 1 reel.

ESTATES RECORDS

    Record of Estates, 1846-1869; 1 reel.

    Record of Accounts, 1875-1965; 8 reels.

    Accounts of Sale of Estates, 1869-1894; 1 reel.

    Administrators' Bonds, 1875-1881; 1 reel.

    Record of Administrators, 1891-1966; 8 reels.

    Administrator and Guardian Proceedings, 1881-1899; 1 reel.

    Appointment of Executors, 1868-1911; 1 reel.

    Record of Executors, 1926-1966; 2 reels.

    Guardians' Bonds, 1853-1867, 1875-1882, 1899-1924; 1 reel.

    Record of Guardians, 1924-1970; Appointment of Trustees Under Wills, 1941-1970; 3 reels.

    Record of Receivership of Minors' Accounts, 1918-1922, 1931-1966; 1 reel.

    Record of Widows' Year's Support, 1946-1962; 1 reel.

    Inheritance Tax Records, 1923-1966; 2 reels.

    Record of Estates Not Exceeding $300, 1929-1966; 1 reel.

    Record of Inventories and Accounts of Sale, 1869-1965; 3 reels.

    Record of Settlements, 1846-1965; 12 reels.

    Index to Final Accounts: Administrators, Executors and Guardians, 1846-1970; 2 reels.

    Index to Final Accounts: Wards, 1846-1970; 3 reels.

LAND RECORDS

    Record of Deeds, 1784-1962; 120 reels.

    Index to Deeds, Grantor and Grantee, 1792-1891; 1 reel.

    Index to Deeds, Grantor, 1892-1967; 12 reels.

    Index to Deeds, Grantee, 1892-1967; 12 reels.

    Registration of Titles, 1914-1923; 1 reel.

    Plats, 1914-1923, 1933-1964; 3 reels.

    Index to Plats, 1894-1964; 1 reel.

    Record of Resale of Land Under Mortgagees and Trustees, 1921-1966; 3 reels.

MARRIAGE, DIVORCE AND VITAL STATISTICS

    Marriage Bonds, 1792-1868; 7 reels.

    Marriage Licenses, 1864-1965; 13 reels.

    Marriage Registers, 1867-1982; 3 reels.

    Maiden Names of Divorced Women, 1938-1966; 1 reel.

    Index to Births, 1914-1981; 3 reels.

    Index to Deaths, 1913-1981; 3 reels.

    Index to Delayed Births, various years; 1 reel.

MILITARY AND PENSION RECORDS

    Record of Pensions, 1889-1940; 1 reel.

    Record of Armed Forces Discharges, 1917-1982; 16 reels.

Index to Armed Forces Discharges, 1917-1982; 1 reel.

Minutes, Eleventh Company, N. C. Reserve Militia, 1909-1915; 1 reel.

MISCELLANEOUS RECORDS

Alien Registration, 1921, 1940-1941; 1 reel.

Record of Naturalization, 1918-1921; 1 reel.

Record of Lunacy, 1899-1946; 1 reel.

Orders and Decrees, 1868-1957; 14 reels.

Index to Special Proceedings, Plaintiff, 1868-1970; 2 reels.

Index to Special Proceedings, Defendant, 1868-1970; 2 reels.

Appointment of Receivers, 1915-1917; 1 reel.

OFFICIALS, COUNTY

Minutes, Board of County Commissioners, 1868-1961; 7 reels.

SCHOOL RECORDS

Minutes, Board of Superintendents of Common Schools, 1841-1885; 1 reel.

Minutes, County Board of Education, 1885-1966; 2 reels.

Common School Register, 1857-1903; 1 reel.

Records of Association of Teachers, 1901-1915; 1 reel.

TAX AND FISCAL RECORDS

Tax Lists, 1881-1884; 1 reel.

Tax Scrolls, 1872-1900, 1905, 1915; 7 reels.

Board of Assessors, Record of Assessment List, 1860, 1863-1868; 1 reel.

WILLS

Record of Wills, 1798-1958; 4 reels.

Index to Wills, Devisor, 1794-1970; 1 reel.

Index to Wills, Devisee, 1794-1970; 1 reel.

CALDWELL COUNTY

Established in 1841 from Burke and Wilkes counties.

ORIGINAL RECORDS

BONDS

Apprentice Bonds and Records, 1841-1906; 1 Fibredex box.

Bastardy Bonds and Records, 1843-1925; 3 Fibredex boxes.

Officials' Bonds and Records, 1841-1917; 3 Fibredex boxes.

Sheriffs' Bonds and Records, 1841-1903; 1 Fibredex box.

COURT RECORDS

County Court of Pleas and Quarter Sessions

Minutes, 1841-1868; 3 volumes.

Execution Docket, 1841-1848, 1863; 1 volume.

State Docket, 1848-1868; 1 volume.

Superior Court

Minutes, 1843-1911; 10 volumes.

Equity Minutes, 1844-1868; Civil and Criminal Issues Dockets, 1883-1887; 1 volume.

Civil Action Papers, 1838-1934; 23 Fibredex boxes.

Civil Action Papers Concerning Land, 1840-1930; 13 Fibredex boxes.

Criminal Action Papers, 1840-1932; 26 Fibredex boxes.

ELECTION RECORDS

Record of Elections, 1898-1932; 4 volumes.

ESTATES RECORDS

Record of Estates, 1847-1867; 1 volume.

Record of Accounts, 1868-1914; 2 volumes.

Appointment of Administrators, Executors, Guardians and Masters, 1868-1911; 1 volume.

Estates Records, 1841-1934; 47 Fibredex boxes.

Guardians' Records, 1842-1934; 3 Fibredex boxes.

Record of Settlements, 1868-1913; 1 volume.

LAND RECORDS

Deeds of Sale, 1849-1920; 1 Fibredex box.

Miscellaneous Deeds, 1841-1931; 1 Fibredex box.

Ejectments, 1841-1904; 1 Fibredex box.

Miscellaneous Land Records, 1841-1934; 2 Fibredex boxes.

MARRIAGE, DIVORCE AND VITAL STATISTICS

Miscellaneous Marriage Records, 1867-1933; 1 Fibredex box.

Divorce Records, 1850-1925; 3 Fibredex boxes.

Disinterment/Reinterment Permits, 1974-1978; 1 manuscript box.

MISCELLANEOUS RECORDS

Alien Registration, 1940; 1 volume.

Grand Jury Records, 1843-1924; 1 Fibredex box.

Magistrates' Records, 1849-1915; 1 Fibredex box.

Registry of Licenses to Trades, 1901-1916; 1 volume.

Orders and Decrees, 1869-1906; 3 volumes.

Miscellaneous Records, 1837-1934; 5 Fibredex boxes.

Slave Records, 1842-1866; 1 Fibredex box.

Records of Assignees, Receivers and Trustees, 1841-1930; 2 Fibredex boxes.

OFFICIALS, COUNTY

Minutes, Board of County Commissioners, 1868-1870; Common School
Register, 1858; 1 volume.

ROADS AND BRIDGES

Road Records, 1838-1913; 2 Fibredex boxes.

Railroad Records, 1876-1911; 3 Fibredex boxes.

TAX AND FISCAL RECORDS

Lists of Taxables, 1841-1853, 1868; 2 volumes.

WILLS

Wills, 1830-1925; 3 Fibredex boxes.

MICROFILM RECORDS

CORPORATIONS AND PARTNERSHIPS

Record of Corporations, 1885-1945; 1 reel.

COURT RECORDS

County Court of Pleas and Quarter Sessions
Minutes, 1841-1868; 2 reels.
Superior Court
Minutes, 1843-1954; 12 reels.
Equity Minutes, 1844-1868; 1 reel.
Index to Judgments, Plaintiff, 1940-1963; 5 reels.
Index to Judgments, Defendant, 1940-1963; 5 reels.

ELECTION RECORDS

Record of Elections, 1898-1968; 1 reel.

ESTATES RECORDS

Record of Accounts, 1868-1966; 7 reels.

Appointment of Administrators, Executors and Guardians, 1868-1948; 2 reels.

Record of Administrators, 1897-1966; 4 reels.

Appointment of Executors, 1948-1966; 1 reel.

Appointment of Guardians, 1941-1966; 1 reel.

Record of Minors' Accounts, 1944-1956; 1 reel.

Inheritance Tax Records, 1920-1967; 1 reel.

Inventories of Estates, 1847-1867, 1885-1966; 5 reels.

Record of Settlements, 1868-1966; 6 reels.

LAND RECORDS

Record of Deeds, 1841-1956; 78 reels.

Index to Real Estate Conveyances, Grantor, 1841-1971; 13 reels.

Index to Real Estate Conveyances, Grantee, 1841-1971; 10 reels.

Land Entries, 1841-1954; 1 reel.
Record of Surveys, 1905-1937; 1 reel.
Plat Books, 1913-1946; 1 reel.
Index to Plats, 1915-1980; 1 reel.
Record of Sales by Trustees, Mortgagees and Executors, 1917-1959; 2 reels.

MARRIAGE, DIVORCE AND VITAL STATISTICS
Marriage Licenses, 1841-1961; 15 reels.
Marriage Registers, 1851-1969; 3 reels.
Cohabitation and Marriage Records, 1866-1872; 1 reel.
Index to Births, 1914-1971; 2 reels.
Index to Deaths, 1914-1980; 2 reels.
Index to Delayed Births, various years; 1 reel.

MILITARY AND PENSION RECORDS
Record of Armed Forces Discharges, 1917-1954; 5 reels.
Index to Armed Forces Discharges, 1917-1980; 1 reel.

MISCELLANEOUS RECORDS
Record of Lunacy, 1908-1959; 1 reel.
Orders and Decrees, 1869-1938; 3 reels.
Special Proceedings, 1903-1952; 7 reels.

OFFICIALS, COUNTY
Minutes, Board of County Commissioners, 1870-1964; 7 reels.

SCHOOL RECORDS
Minutes, County Board of Education, 1885-1952; 1 reel.
Minutes, Board of Education, City of Lenoir, 1903-1957; 1 reel.

TAX AND FISCAL RECORDS
Tax Lists, 1841-1853; 1 reel.

WILLS
Record of Wills, 1827-1966; 5 reels.
Index to Wills, 1841-1966; 1 reel.

CAMDEN COUNTY

Established in 1777 from Pasquotank County.
Some records were said to have been destroyed in a
storage rom fire; many records missing.

ORIGINAL RECORDS

BONDS
>Apprentice Bonds, 1871-1886; 1 volume.
>Bastardy Bonds, 1871-1879; 1 volume.

COURT RECORDS
>County Court of Pleas and Quarter Sessions
>>Minutes, 1855-1868; 1 volume.
>>Execution Docket, 1858-1862, 1866-1868; 1 volume.
>>Trial, Appearance and Petition Dockets, 1857-1862, 1865-1868;
>>>2 volumes.

>Superior Court
>>Minutes, 1853-1861, 1866-1911; 4 volumes.
>>Equity Minutes, 1807-1861, 1866-1868; 2 volumes.
>>Equity Trial Dockets, 1807-1861; 2 volumes.
>>Execution Docket, 1854-1860, 1866-1869; 1 volume.
>>State Docket, 1854-1861, 1866-1869; 1 volume.
>>Trial and Appearance Dockets, 1842-1861, 1866-1869; 2 volumes.
>>Civil Action Papers, 1802-1929; 2 Fibredex boxes.
>>Criminal Action Papers, 1808-1928; 1 Fibredex box.

ELECTION RECORDS
>Record of Elections, 1878-1916; 3 volumes.

ESTATES RECORDS
>Record of Estates, 1853-1869; 1 volume.
>Record of Accounts, 1866-1906; 3 volumes.
>Administrators' Bonds, 1853-1872, 1895-1916; 4 volumes.
>Widows' Dowers, 1894-1918; 1 volume.
>Estates Records, 1790-1929; 22 Fibredex boxes.
>Guardians' Records, 1809-1925; 5 Fibredex boxes.
>Guardians' Accounts, 1805-1809, 1858-1869; 2 volumes.
>Guardians' Bonds, 1856-1918; 3 volumes.
>Record of Inventories, 1853-1868; 1 volume.
>Record of Settlements, 1869-1914; 1 volume.

LAND RECORDS
>Deeds, 1739-1912; 1 Fibredex box.
>Processioners' Reports, 1874-1904; 1 volume.
>Miscellaneous Land Records, 1807-1925; 1 Fibredex box.

MISCELLANEOUS RECORDS
>Orders and Decrees, 1869-1904; 3 volumes.

Miscellaneous Records, 1786-1928; 3 Fibredex boxes.

Records of Assignees, Receivers and Trustees, 1859-1928; 1 Fibredex box.

ROADS AND BRIDGES

Minutes, Board of Supervisors of Public Roads, 1879-1903; 1 volume.

Minutes, Board of County Highway Commissioners, 1917-1931; 1 volume.

TAX AND FISCAL RECORDS

Miscellaneous Tax Records, 1848-1890; 1 Fibredex box.

WILLS

Wills, 1766-1922; 5 Fibredex boxes.

MICROFILM RECORDS

BONDS

Apprentice Bonds, 1871-1886; 1 reel.

Bastardy Bonds, 1871-1879; 1 reel.

CORPORATIONS AND PARTNERSHIPS

Record of Corporations, 1908-1972; 1 reel.

COURT RECORDS

County Court of Pleas and Quarter Sessions

Minutes, 1855-1868; 1 reel.

Superior Court

Minutes, 1853-1959; 4 reels.

Equity Minutes, 1807-1868; 1 reel.

Index to Judgments, 1929-1966; 1 reel.

Index to Civil Actions, Plaintiff, 1966-1983; 1 reel.

Index to Civil Actions, Defendant, 1966-1983; 1 reel.

Index to Criminal Actions, 1966-1983; 1 reel.

ELECTION RECORDS

Record of Elections, 1878-1968; 1 reel.

ESTATES RECORDS

Record of Accounts, 1866-1966; 4 reels.

Accounts and Sales of Estates, 1853-1869; 1 reel.

Administrators' Bonds, 1853-1916; 2 reels.

Record of Administrators, Executors and Guardians, 1915-1966; 1 reel.

Record of Administrators, 1929-1966; 1 reel.

Guardians' Accounts, 1800-1809; 1 reel.

Record of Widows' Dowers, 1894-1914; 1 reel.

Inheritance Tax Records, 1923-1966; 1 reel.

Inventories of Estates, 1853-1868; 1 reel.

Record of Settlements, 1862-1967; 2 reels.

LAND RECORDS

Record of Deeds, 1777-1949; 36 reels.

General Index to Deeds, Grantor and Grantee, 1777-1927; 1 reel.

Index to Real Estate Conveyances, Grantor, 1927-1946; 1 reel.

Index to Real Estate Conveyances, Grantee, 1927-1946; 1 reel.

Land Entries, 1866-1903; 1 reel.

Processioners' Record, 1875-1904; 1 reel.

Record of Sales by Trustees and Mortgagees, 1919-1967; 1 reel.

MARRIAGE, DIVORCE AND VITAL STATISTICS

Marriage Licenses, 1868-1945; 32 reels.

Marriage Registers, 1840-1967; 3 reels.

Maiden Names of Divorced Women, 1945-1965; 1 reel.

Index to Births, 1913-1982; 1 reel.

Index to Deaths, 1913-1982; 1 reel.

Index to Delayed Births, various years; 1 reel.

MILITARY AND PENSION RECORDS

Record of Armed Forces Discharges, 1944-1982; 1 reel.

MISCELLANEOUS RECORDS

Minutes, Committee of Finance, 1861-1877; 1 reel.

Record of Lunacy, 1907-1967; 1 reel.

Orders and Decrees, 1869-1966; 5 reels.

OFFICIALS, COUNTY

Minutes, Board of County Commissioners, 1868-1959; 2 reels.

SCHOOL RECORDS

Minutes, Board of Superintendents of Common Schools, 1857-1867; 1 reel.

Minutes, County Board of Education, 1872-1960; 1 reel.

TAX AND FISCAL RECORDS

Tax Scrolls, 1872-1893, 1915, 1925, 1935, 1945; 3 reels.

WILLS

Record of Wills, 1815-1966; 3 reels.

Index to Wills, 1822-1966; 1 reel.

Road construction crew, Carteret County, circa 1920s.
Photograph from the files of the State Archives.

CARTERET COUNTY

Established in 1722 from Craven Precinct as a precinct of Bath County.

ORIGINAL RECORDS

BONDS
>Bastardy Bonds and Records, 1771-1906; 2 Fibredex boxes.
>Officials' Bonds and Records, 1755-1909; 2 Fibredex boxes.

COURT RECORDS
>County Court of Pleas and Quarter Sessions
>>Minutes, 1723-1868; 19 volumes.
>>Appearance Dockets, 1793-1868; 4 volumes, 1 manuscript box.
>>Execution Dockets, 1785-1839, 1847-1856, 1867-1868; 8 volumes, 1 manuscript box.
>>State Dockets, 1775-1849; 1 volume, 1 manuscript box.
>>Trial and Appearance Dockets, 1731-1792; 4 volumes, 1 manuscript box.
>>Trial Dockets, 1793-1868; 3 volumes, 1 manuscript box.
>>Clerk's Fee Book, 1849-1862; 1 pamphlet.

>Superior Court
>>Minutes, 1809-1907; 5 volumes, 1 manuscript box.
>>Equity Minutes, 1816-1847, 1859-1867; 2 volumes.
>>Equity Execution Docket, 1818-1859; 1 volume.
>>Equity Trial and Appearance Dockets, 1810-1868; 3 volumes.
>>Appearance Dockets, 1816-1869; 1 volume, 1 manuscript box.
>>Execution Docket, 1849-1868; 1 volume.
>>State Docket, 1866-1881; 1 volume.
>>Trial Dockets, 1816-1868; 1 manuscript box.
>>Prosecution Bonds, 1836-1845; 1 volume.
>>Civil Action Papers, 1741-1913; 18 Fibredex boxes.
>>Civil Action Papers Concerning County and Municipal Officials, 1869-1894; 1 Fibredex box.
>>Civil Action Papers Concerning Land, 1779-1938; 6 Fibredex boxes.
>>Criminal Action Papers, 1771-1913; 6 Fibredex boxes.

ELECTION RECORDS
>Record of Elections, 1896-1944; 2 volumes.

ESTATES RECORDS
>Record of Estates, 1829-1862; 6 volumes.
>Record of Accounts, 1868-1915; 1 volume.
>Administrators' Bonds, 1884-1902; 1 volume.
>Estates Records, 1744-1957; 40 Fibredex boxes.
>Guardians' Records, 1789-1962; 16 Fibredex boxes.
>Guardians' Bonds, 1884-1903; 1 volume.
>Guardians' Dockets, 1818-1846; 1 manuscript box.

LAND RECORDS

Record of Deeds, 1721-1839, 1845-1852; 47 volumes.

Deeds, 1803-1952; 3 Fibredex boxes.

Grants and Miscellaneous Papers, 1717-1844; 1 volume.

Miscellaneous Land Records, 1743-1948; 1 Fibredex box.

MARRIAGE, DIVORCE AND VITAL STATISTICS

Marriage Bonds, 1746-1868; 8 Fibredex boxes.

Record of Marriages, 1864-1872; 1 volume.

Divorce Records, 1877-1939; 1 Fibredex box.

Disinterment/Reinterment Permits, 1976-1980; 1 manuscript box.

MISCELLANEOUS RECORDS

Declaration of Intent (to Become a Citizen), 1910-1911, 1940; 1 volume.

Vestry Books (St. John's Parish, Beaufort), 1742-1843; 3 volumes.

Minutes, Wardens of the Poor, 1844-1866; 1 volume.

Miscellaneous Records, 1741-1919; 3 Fibredex boxes.

Oyster Bed Records, 1879-1906; 1 volume, 1 Fibredex box.

Slave Records, 1793-1867; 1 Fibredex box.

Records of Assignees, Receivers and Trustees, 1795-1918; 2 Fibredex boxes.

ROADS AND BRIDGES

Road Records, 1811-1911; 2 Fibredex boxes.

Railroad Records, 1858-1913; 2 Fibredex boxes.

SCHOOL RECORDS

Minutes, Board of Superintendents of Common Schools, 1841-1860;
1 volume.

Minutes, Beaufort Peabody Educational Association, 1871-1872; 1 volume.

TAX AND FISCAL RECORDS

Lists of Taxables, 1802-1860; 10 volumes.

Tax Records, 1745-1899; 1 Fibredex box.

WILLS

Wills, 1744-1921; 10 Fibredex boxes.

MICROFILM RECORDS

CORPORATION AND PARTNERSHIPS

Record of Corporations, 1878-1957; 1 reel.

Record of Partnerships, 1917-1982; 1 reel.

Record of Dissolutions and Agreements, 1924-1946; 1 reel.

Index to Corporations, 1878-1982; 1 reel.

COURT RECORDS

County Court of Pleas and Quarter Sessions
Minutes, 1732-1868; 11 reels.

Superior Court
Minutes, 1809-1949; 8 reels.
Equity Minutes, 1816-1868; 1 reel.
Prosecution Bonds, 1836-1845; 1 reel.

Index to Judgments, Plaintiff, 1869-1968; 2 reels.

Index to Judgments, Defendant, 1869-1968; 2 reels.

ELECTION RECORDS

Record of Elections, 1897-1958; 1 reel.

ESTATES RECORDS

Record of Estates, 1829-1862; 2 reels.

Record of Accounts, 1868-1961; 3 reels.

Administrators' Bonds, 1884-1936; 3 reels.

Record of Administrators, Executors and Guardians, 1758-1959; 14 reels.

Record of Administrators, 1922-1959; 1 reel.

Appointment of Executors, 1868-1902; 1 reel.

Record of Executors and Guardians, 1928-1959; 1 reel.

Record of Guardians, 1852-1962; 9 reels.

Guardians' Bonds, 1884-1903; 1 reel.

Inheritance Tax Records, 1923-1955; 1 reel.

Record of Settlements, 1880-1955; 2 reels.

LAND RECORDS

Record of Real Estate Conveyances, 1722-1947; 79 reels.

Sheriffs' Deeds, 1800; 1 reel.

Index to Real Estate Conveyances, Grantor, 1722-1972; 9 reels.

Index to Real Estate Conveyances, Grantee, 1722-1972; 10 reels.

Land Entries, 1866-1895, 1905-1958; 1 reel.

Plat Books, 1926-1953; 1 reel.

Index to Plats, 1904-1982; 1 reel.

Record of Sales and Resales by Mortgagees and Trustees, 1922-1955; 2 reels.

MARRIAGE, DIVORCE AND VITAL STATISTICS

Marriage Bonds, 1741-1868; 6 reels.

Record of Marriages, 1864-1872; 1 reel.

Marriage Registers, 1850-1981; 3 reels.

Index to Marriages, Female, 1850-1981; 1 reel.

Maiden Names of Divorced Women, 1938-1968; 1 reel.

Index to Births, 1913-1961; 2 reels.

Index to Deaths, 1913-1957; 1 reel.

MILITARY AND PENSION RECORDS

Record of Armed Forces Discharges, 1918-1968; 4 reels.

Index to Armed Forces Discharges, 1918-1981; 1 reel.

MISCELLANEOUS RECORDS

Declaration of Intent, 1910-1911, 1914; 1 reel.

Record of Lunacy, 1899-1945; 1 reel.

Orders and Decrees, 1868-1968; 7 reels.

Special Proceedings, 1882-1968; 2 reels.

Index to Special Proceedings, Plaintiff, 1869-1968; 1 reel.

Index to Special Proceedings, Defendant, 1869-1968; 1 reel.

OFFICIALS, COUNTY

Minutes, Board of County Commissioners, 1879-1959; 5 reels.

Index to Minutes, Board of County Commissioners, 1868-1939; 2 reels.

SCHOOL RECORDS

Minutes, Board of Superintendents of Common Schools, 1844-1858; 1 reel.

Minutes, County Board of Education, 1872-1956; 1 reel.

Minutes, Beaufort Peabody Educational Association, 1871-1872; 1 reel.

TAX AND FISCAL RECORDS

Lists of Taxables, 1802-1841; 1 reel.

WILLS

Record of Wills, 1745-1968; 5 reels.

Index to Wills, Devisor, 1745-1968; 1 reel.

Index to Wills, Devisee, 1745-1968; 1 reel.

CASWELL COUNTY

Established in 1777 from Orange County.
Some records were said to have been destroyed during occupation
by militia troops during Reconstruction.

ORIGINAL RECORDS

BONDS

    Apprentice Bonds and Records, 1777-1921; 2 volumes, 2 Fibredex boxes.

    Bastardy Bonds and Records, 1780-1905; 1 volume, 2 Fibredex boxes.

    Officials' Bonds and Records, 1777-1907; 1 volume, 3 Fibredex boxes.

    Tavern Bonds, 1777-1868; 1 Fibredex box.

COURT RECORDS

    County Court of Pleas and Quarter Sessions

        Minutes, 1777-1868; 17 volumes.

        Appearance Docket, 1843-1849; 1 volume.

        Execution Dockets, 1778-1868; 9 volumes.

        State Dockets, 1777-1789, 1804-1868; 5 volumes.

        Trial, Appearance and Reference Dockets, 1777-1843; 10 volumes.

        Trial Dockets, 1843-1868; 2 volumes.

        Clerk's Fee Book, 1801-1822; 1 volume.

        Costs Docket (State Prosecutions), 1822-1845; 1 volume.

        Prosecution Bond Docket, 1788-1805; 1 volume.

    Superior Court

        Minutes, 1807-1837, 1853-1924; 13 volumes.

        Equity Minutes, 1807-1868; 3 volumes.

        Equity Receipt Books, 1840-1872; 3 volumes.

        Equity Trial and Appearance Docket, 1856-1868; 1 volume.

        Execution Dockets, 1823-1868; 4 volumes.

        State Dockets, 1823-1868; 3 volumes.

        Criminal Issues Docket, 1869-1892; 1 volume.

        Trial and Appearance Docket, 1834-1848; 1 volume.

        Trial Dockets, 1854-1873; 2 volumes.

        Civil Action Papers, 1767-1944; 61 Fibredex boxes.

        Civil Action Papers Concerning Land, 1778-1927; 5 Fibredex boxes.

        Criminal Action Papers, 1777-1911; 42 Fibredex boxes.

ELECTION RECORDS

    Election Records, 1803-1920; 1 Fibredex box.

    Record of Elections, 1872-1912; 2 volumes.

ESTATES RECORDS

    Record of Accounts, 1868-1930; 8 volumes.

    Administrators' Bonds, 1876-1918; 4 volumes.

    Appointment of Administrators, Executors and Guardians, 1868-1907;
        2 volumes.

Union (Yellow) Tavern, Milton, Caswell County, built circa 1818.
The noted free black cabinetmaker, Thomas Day, had his workshop and residence in this building.
Photograph from the files of the State Archives.

Estates Records, 1772-1941; 106 Fibredex boxes.
Guardians' Records, 1777-1930; 23 Fibredex boxes.
Guardians' Accounts, 1794-1868; 5 volumes.
Guardians' Bonds, 1875-1936; 4 volumes.
Record of Receivers of Estates, 1887-1934; 2 volumes.
Record of Settlements, 1868-1926; 3 volumes.
Cross Index to Estates, 1859-1887; 1 volume.

LAND RECORDS
Deeds, 1780-1884; 5 Fibredex boxes.
Deeds of Gift, 1787-1864; Deeds of Trust, 1803-1884; 1 Fibredex box.
Ejectments, 1799-1878; 1 Fibredex box.
Land Entries, 1778-1795, 1841-1863; 1 volume.
Attachments, Executions, Liens and Levies, 1799-1900; 1 Fibredex box.
Miscellaneous Land Records, 1778-1918; 1 Fibredex box.

MARRIAGE, DIVORCE AND VITAL STATISTICS
Marriage Bonds, 1778-1868; 17 Fibredex boxes.
Divorce Records, 1818-1928; 2 Fibredex boxes.

MILITARY AND PENSION RECORDS
Pension Records, 1909-1937; 1 volume.

MISCELLANEOUS RECORDS
County Accounts, 1771-1867; 5 Fibredex boxes.
County Claims Allowed, 1808-1832; 1 volume.
Insolvents Records, 1786-1858; 1 Fibredex box.
Jury Lists and Tickets, 1786-1869; 3 Fibredex boxes.
Orders and Decrees, 1868-1924; 5 volumes.
Special Proceedings Docket, 1869-1883; 1 volume.
Miscellaneous Records, 1775-1900; 4 Fibredex boxes.
Powers of Attorney, 1785-1876; 1 Fibredex box.
Records of Assignees, Trustees and Receivers, 1815-1934; 1 Fibredex box.

ROADS AND BRIDGES
Bridge Records, 1787-1872; 1 Fibredex box.
Minutes, Highway Commission of Caswell County, 1919-1923;
    1 manuscript box.
Road Dockets, 1801-1867; 8 volumes.
Road Records, 1785-1922; 1 Fibredex box.

SCHOOL RECORDS
Common School Register, 1859; 1 volume.
School Records, 1816-1877; 3 Fibredex boxes.

TAX AND FISCAL RECORDS
Lists of Taxables, 1777-1867; 9 volumes, 3 Fibredex boxes.

WILLS
Wills, 1771-1927; 7 Fibredex boxes.
Extracts from County Court Minutes, 1780-1782; 1 volume.

MICROFILM RECORDS

BONDS

    Apprentice Bonds, 1880-1921; 1 reel.

    Bastardy Bonds, 1780-1799, 1830-1905; 2 reels.

    Officials' Bonds, 1868-1907; 1 reel.

CORPORATIONS AND PARTNERSHIPS

    Certificates of Incorporation, 1899-1963; 1 reel.

COURT RECORDS

    County Court of Pleas and Quarter Sessions

        Minutes, 1777-1862, 1866-1868; 5 reels.

        Orders of Allowance, 1808-1832; 1 reel.

    Superior Court

        Minutes, 1807-1826, 1853-1970; 7 reels.

        Equity Minutes, 1807-1868; 1 reel.

        Index to Judgments, 1948-1970; 1 reel.

        Index to Civil Actions, 1970-1986; 1 reel.

        Index to Criminal Actions, 1948-1970; 1 reel.

ELECTION RECORDS

    Record of Elections, 1884-1933, 1940-1970; 2 reels.

ESTATES RECORDS

    Record of Accounts, 1867-1970; 10 reels.

    Administrators' Bonds, 1876-1918; 1 reel.

    Appointment of Administrators, Executors and Guardians, 1892-1907; 1 reel.

    Record of Administrators, 1868-1889, 1919-1951; 2 reels.

    Record of Executors and Guardians, 1868-1892, 1923-1936, 1949-1970; 3 reels.

    Application for Guardianship, 1937-1962, 1967-1970; 1 reel.

    Guardians' Accounts, 1794-1868; 3 reels.

    Guardians' Bonds, 1875-1929; 2 reels.

    Accounts for Indigent Children, 1905-1936; 1 reel.

    Clerk's Receiver Accounts, 1920-1940; 1 reel.

    Inheritance Tax Records, 1923-1970; 1 reel.

    Record of Final Accounts, 1890-1958; 4 reels.

    Record of Trustees Under Wills, 1963; 1 reel.

    Index to Administrators and Guardians, 1864-1887, 1924-1948; 1 reel.

    Index to Estates, 1948-1963; 1 reel.

LAND RECORDS

    Record of Deeds, 1777-1963; 52 reels.

    Index to Real Estate Conveyances, Grantor, 1777-1985; 6 reels.

    Index to Real Estate Conveyances, Grantee, 1777-1985; 5 reels.

    Land Entries, 1778-1795, 1841-1863; 1 reel.

    Index to Federal Tax Liens, 1935-1969; 1 reel.

    Plat Books, 1914-1953; 2 reels.

    Record of Sales and Resales by Mortgagees and Trustees, 1920-1970; 1 reel.

MARRIAGE, DIVORCE AND VITAL STATISTICS
        Marriage Bonds, 1780-1868; 6 reels.
        Marriage Licenses, 1867-1965; 23 reels.
        Marriage Registers, 1853-1963; 2 reels.
        Maiden Names of Divorced Women, 1936-1961; 1 reel.
        Index to Births, 1913-1956; 1 reel.
        Index to Deaths, 1913-1985; 1 reel.
        Delayed Birth Certificates, 1941-1946; Index to Delayed Births, various years;
            3 reels.

MILITARY AND PENSION RECORDS
        Record of Armed Forces Discharges, 1944-1985; 3 reels.

MISCELLANEOUS RECORDS
        Record of Lunacy, 1899-1963; 1 reel.
        Orders and Decrees, 1868-1970; 9 reels.
        Special Proceedings, 1884-1970; 2 reels.
        Index to Special Proceedings, 1884-1970; 2 reels.

OFFICIALS, COUNTY
        Minutes, Board of County Commissioners, 1868-1961; 4 reels.

ROADS AND BRIDGES
        Road Docket, 1801-1867; 1 reel.
        Minutes, County Highway Commission, 1919-1923; 1 reel.

SCHOOL RECORDS
        Minutes, County Board of Education, 1882-1963; 2 reels.
        School Register, Common School, 1859; 1 reel.
        School Registers, 1901-1923; 7 reels.
        School Census, 1905-1909, 1919; 1 reel.

TAX AND FISCAL RECORDS
        Lists of Taxables, 1777-1806, 1823-1824, 1838-1839, 1863-1864; 3 reels.
        Tax Scrolls, 1866-1867, 1876-1902, 1907, 1911, 1917; 7 reels.

WILLS
        Record of Wills, 1777-1970; 12 reels.
        Original Wills, 1785-1864; 1 reel.
        Index to Wills, 1777-1970; 3 reels.

CATAWBA COUNTY

Established in 1842 from Lincoln County.
Many court records missing; reason unknown.

ORIGINAL RECORDS

BONDS
>   Bastardy Bonds and Records, 1868-1911; 2 Fibredex boxes.

COURT RECORDS
>   County Court of Pleas and Quarter Sessions
>>   Minutes, 1843-1868; 2 volumes.
>>   Appearance Docket, 1843-1868; List of Commissioners of Affidavits, 1883; 1 volume.
>>   Execution Docket, 1843-1868; 1 volume.
>>   Levy Docket, 1843-1868; Minutes, Board of County Commissioners, 1868-1880; 1 volume.
>>   State Docket, 1843-1868; 1 volume.
>   Superior Court
>>   Minutes, 1843-1886; 3 volumes.
>>   Equity Minutes, 1843-1868; Record of Widows' Year's Support, 1871-1893; 1 volume.
>>   Equity Trial Docket, 1844-1868; 1 volume.
>>   Appearance Docket, 1844-1868; 1 volume.
>>   State Docket, 1845-1868; 1 volume.
>>   Civil Action Papers, 1858-1926; 22 Fibredex boxes.
>>   Civil Action Papers Concerning Land, 1867-1925; 6 Fibredex boxes.
>>   Criminal Action Papers, 1866-1923; 14 Fibredex boxes.

ELECTION RECORDS
>   Record of Elections, 1878-1924; 3 volumes.

ESTATES RECORDS
>   Record of Estates, 1843-1868; 2 volumes.
>   Record of Dowers and Land Divisions, 1875-1907; 2 volumes.
>   Record of Widows' Year's Support, 1894-1907; 1 volume.
>   Estates Records, 1851-1922; 32 Fibredex boxes.
>   Guardians' Records, 1856-1912; 9 Fibredex boxes.
>   Record of Settlements, 1868-1908; 3 volumes.
>   Cross Index to Executors and Administrators, 1843-1927; 1 volume.
>   Cross Index to Guardians and Wards, 1843-1937; 1 volume.

LAND RECORDS
>   Miscellaneous Land Records, 1864-1906; 1 Fibredex box.

MARRIAGE, DIVORCE AND VITAL STATISTICS
>   Marriage Bonds, 1843-1868; 1 Fibredex box.
>   Divorce Records, 1869-1927; 4 Fibredex boxes.
>   Disinterment/Reinterment Permits, 1968-1984; 1 manuscript box.

MISCELLANEOUS RECORDS
    Special Proceedings Dockets, 1880-1915; 2 volumes.
    Miscellaneous Records, 1851-1922; 3 Fibredex boxes.
    Records of Assignees, Trustees and Receivers, 1853-1911; 2 Fibredex boxes.
ROADS AND BRIDGES
    Road and Bridge Records, 1869-1911; 1 Fibredex box.
SCHOOL RECORDS
    Minutes, County Board of Education, 1881-1884; 1 volume.
    School Fund Account Book, 1899-1908; 1 volume.
TAX AND FISCAL RECORDS
    Lists of Taxables, 1857-1868; 1 volume.
    Tax Records, 1894-1912; 2 Fibredex boxes.
WILLS
    Wills, 1843-1966; 48 Fibredex boxes.
    Cross Index to Wills, 1843-1926; 1 volume.

MICROFILM RECORDS

CORPORATIONS AND PARTNERSHIPS
    Record of Corporations, 1883-1949; 3 reels.
    Record of Partnerships, 1913-1968; 1 reel.
    Index to Corporations, 1883-1968; 1 reel.
COURT RECORDS
    County Court of Pleas and Quarter Sessions
        Minutes, 1843-1868; 1 reel.
    Superior Court
        Minutes, 1843-1960; 15 reels.
        Equity Minutes, 1843-1868; Widows' Year's Support, 1871-1893;
            1 reel.
        Index to Judgments, Defendant, 1912-1967; 3 reels.
        Index to Civil Actions, Plaintiff, 1966-1980; 2 reels.
        Index to Civil Actions, Defendant, 1966-1974; 3 reels.
ELECTION RECORDS
    Record of Elections, 1906-1966; 1 reel.
ESTATES RECORDS
    Record of Estates, 1843-1868; 2 reels.
    Record of Accounts and Inventories, 1869-1966; 14 reels.
    Record of Administrators, Executors and Guardians, 1868-1925; 6 reels.
    Record of Administrators, 1916-1966; 9 reels.
    Record of Executors, 1925-1966; 4 reels.
    Record of Guardians, 1925-1966; 3 reels.
    Record of Guardians of World War I Veterans, 1930-1938; 1 reel.
    Record of Dowers, 1871-1948; 1 reel.
    Record of Widows' Year's Support, 1894-1907; 1 reel.
    Inheritance Tax Records, 1923-1968; 2 reels.

Record of Estates Not Exceeding $300, 1930-1942; 1 reel.

Record of Settlements, 1868-1966; 10 reels.

Index to Administrators, Executors and Guardians, 1843-1966; 2 reels.

LAND RECORDS

Record of Deeds, 1843-1955; 103 reels.

Index to Real Estate Conveyances, Grantor, 1837-1954; 7 reels.

Index to Real Estate Conveyances, Grantee, 1837-1954; 7 reels.

Entry Takers' Book, 1904-1918; 1 reel.

Tax Levies on Land, 1843-1868; 1 reel.

Index to Federal Tax Liens, 1906-1969; 1 reel.

Maps, 1911-1954; 2 reels.

Index to Plats, 1842-1980; 1 reel.

Record of Sale and Resale, 1925-1967; 3 reels.

MARRIAGE, DIVORCE AND VITAL STATISTICS

Marriage Bonds, 1842-1868; 1 reel.

Marriage Bond Abstracts, 1842-1868; 1 reel.

Marriage Licenses, 1864-1946; 8 reels.

Marriage Registers, 1851-1968; 2 reels.

Freedmen's Marriage Records, 1866; 1 reel.

Index to Births, 1913-1967; 3 reels.

Index to Deaths, 1909-1979; 1 reel.

Index to Delayed Births, various years; 1 reel.

MILITARY AND PENSION RECORDS

Record of Armed Forces Discharges, 1917-1972; 11 reels.

Index to Armed Forces Discharges, 1917-1980; 1 reel.

MISCELLANEOUS RECORDS

Record of Lunacy, 1899-1967; 3 reels.

Clerk's Minute Dockets, 1880-1915, 1927-1966; 4 reels.

Orders and Decrees, 1868-1966; 19 reels.

Index to Orders and Decrees, Plaintiff, 1868-1966; 1 reel.

Index to Orders and Decrees, Defendant, 1868-1966; 1 reel.

Index to Special Proceedings, 1912-1922, 1966-1980; 2 reels.

OFFICIALS, COUNTY

Minutes, Board of County Commissioners, 1880-1960; 4 reels.

SCHOOL RECORDS

Minutes, County Board of Education, 1881-1968; 2 reels.

TAX AND FISCAL RECORDS

List of Taxables, 1857-1868; 1 reel.

Tax Scrolls, 1869-1896, 1905, 1915, 1925, 1935, 1945, 1955, 1965; 7 reels.

WILLS

Record of Wills, 1843-1966; 5 reels.

Index to Wills, Devisor, 1843-1966; 1 reel.

Index to Wills, Devisee, 1843-1966; 1 reel.

CHATHAM COUNTY

Established in 1771 from Orange County.
Many court records missing; reason unknown.

ORIGINAL RECORDS

BONDS

    Apprentice Bonds and Records, 1784-1919; 3 volumes, 2 Fibredex boxes.

    Bastardy Bonds and Records, 1869-1931; 2 Fibredex boxes.

    Constables' Bonds, 1771-1928; 3 Fibredex boxes.

    Officials' Bonds, 1782-1912; 1 Fibredex box.

COURT RECORDS

    County Court of Pleas and Quarter Sessions

        Minutes, 1774-1864; 16 volumes.

        Appearance Dockets, 1839-1867; 3 volumes.

        Execution Dockets, 1807-1868; 7 volumes.

        State and Recognizance Dockets, 1824-1866; 2 volumes.

        Trial, Appearance and Reference Dockets, 1774-1821; 6 volumes.

        Trial Dockets, 1839-1866; 3 volumes.

    Superior Court

        Minutes, 1807-1931; 15 volumes, 1 manuscript box.

        Equity Minutes, 1821-1842, 1859-1868; 2 volumes.

        Equity Execution Docket, 1860-1868; 1 volume.

        Equity Trial Dockets, 1854-1868; 2 volumes.

        Execution Dockets, 1816-1874; 5 volumes.

        State Dockets, 1849-1892; 3 volumes.

        Trial and Appearance Dockets, 1821-1868; 3 volumes.

        Civil Issues Dockets, 1868-1898; 2 volumes.

        Civil Action Papers, 1772-1937; 15 Fibredex boxes.

        Civil Action Papers Concerning Land, 1868-1940; 17 Fibredex boxes.

        Civil Action Papers Concerning Mines, 1863-1930; 1 Fibredex box.

        Criminal Action Papers, 1846-1934; 15 Fibredex boxes.

    Inferior Court

        Criminal Issues Docket, 1878-1885; 1 volume.

        Execution Docket, 1878-1885; 1 volume.

ELECTION RECORDS

    Record of Elections, 1878-1942; 4 volumes.

    Democratic Canvass Book, 1888-1890; Registration Book, 1890, 1892, 1896;
        1 manuscript box.

ESTATES RECORDS

    Record of Estates, 1799-1868; 16 volumes.

    Record of Accounts, 1868-1934; 9 volumes.

    Administrators' Bonds, 1867-1896; 4 volumes.

Appointment of Executors, Administrators, Guardians and Masters, 1868-1903; 1 volume.

Estates Records, 1771-1948, 1955; 164 Fibredex boxes.

Guardians' Records, 1775, 1784-1939; 17 Fibredex boxes.

Guardians' Bonds, 1874-1911; 3 volumes.

Guardians' Accounts, 1800-1868; 3 volumes.

Record of Settlements, 1869-1934; 4 volumes.

Probate Court Docket, 1868-1902; 1 volume.

LAND RECORDS

Deeds, 1775-1952; 5 Fibredex boxes.

Deeds of Trust, 1821-1867, 1913-1939; 1 Fibredex box.

Index to Deeds, 1771-1873; 2 manuscript boxes.

Attachments, Executions, Liens and Levies on Land, 1800-1937; 5 Fibredex boxes.

Ex Parte Proceedings Concerning Land, 1872-1930; 1 Fibredex box.

Land Entry Book, 1843-1913; 1 manuscript box.

Land Grants, 1779-1870; 1 oversized manuscript box.

Levies on Land, 1853-1944; 4 Fibredex boxes.

Miscellaneous Land Records, 1778-1938; 2 Fibredex boxes.

MARRIAGE, DIVORCE AND VITAL STATISTICS

Marriage Bonds, 1778-1867; 5 Fibredex boxes.

Divorce Records, 1829-1934; 7 Fibredex boxes.

MISCELLANEOUS RECORDS

Accounts of Outside Poor and Lunatics, 1879-1916; 3 volumes.

County Accounts and Claims, 1868-1910; 2 volumes.

Homestead and Personal Property Exemptions, 1869-1939; 2 Fibredex boxes.

Homestead Returns, 1888-1945; 1 volume.

Orders and Decrees, 1870-1902; 2 volumes.

Coroners' Inquests, 1796-1971; 3 Fibredex boxes.

Records of Slaves and Free Persons of Color, 1782-1870; 1 Fibredex box.

Miscellaneous Records, 1772-1956; 4 Fibredex boxes.

Records of Assignees, Trustees and Receivers, 1872-1935; 5 Fibredex boxes.

OFFICIALS, COUNTY

Minutes, Board of County Commissioners, 1868-1874; 1 volume.

Records Relating to County Commissioners, 1871-1930; 1 Fibredex box.

Minutes, Board of Magistrates, 1877-1894; 1 volume.

ROADS AND BRIDGES

Road and Bridge Records, 1781-1921; 1 Fibredex box.

Railroad Records, 1874-1933; 4 Fibredex boxes.

SCHOOL RECORDS

Record of Expenditures, County Superintendent of Public Instruction, 1883-1887; 1 volume.

Miscellaneous School Records, 1843-1934; 1 Fibredex box.

TAX AND FISCAL RECORDS

Poll Tax Register, 1902-1908; 1 volume.

WILLS

      Deeds, Bills of Sale, Inventories and Wills, 1782-1794; 1 volume.

      Record of Wills, 1794-1857; 5 volumes.

      Wills, 1771-1964; 27 Fibredex boxes.

MICROFILM RECORDS

BONDS

      Apprentice Bonds, 1875-1920; 1 reel.

      Officials' Bonds, 1868-1892; 1 reel.

CORPORATIONS AND PARTNERSHIPS

      Record of Corporations, 1889-1977; 3 reels.

      Record of Partnerships, 1913-1952; 1 reel.

COURT RECORDS

      County Court of Pleas and Quarter Sessions

            Minutes, 1774-1864; 5 reels.

      Superior Court

            Minutes, 1827-1839, 1867-1960; 10 reels.

            Equity Minutes, 1821-1842, 1858-1868; 2 reels.

            Judgment Dockets, 1868-1956; 1 reel.

            Index to Civil Actions, 1968-1977; 1 reel.

            Index to Criminal Actions, 1968-1977; 1 reel.

            Index to Judgments, Plaintiff, 1956-1968; 1 reel.

            Index to Judgments, Defendant, 1956-1968; 1 reel.

      General County Court

            Minutes, 1929-1959; 2 reels.

ELECTION RECORDS

      Record of Elections, 1878-1968; 3 reels.

ESTATES RECORDS

      Record of Estates, 1782-1857, 1862-1868; 5 reels.

      Record of Accounts, 1868-1968; 8 reels.

      Administrators' Bonds, 1867-1894; 1 reel.

      Record of Administrators, 1896-1954; 4 reels.

      Appointment of Executors, 1868-1903, 1915-1968; 2 reels.

      Record of Dowers and Widows' Year's Support, 1888-1968; 1 reel.

      Guardians' Bonds, 1874-1907; 1 reel.

      Record of Guardians, 1800-1868, 1906-1958; 2 reels.

      Accounts for Indigent Children, 1922-1926; 1 reel.

      Inheritance Tax Records, 1923-1971; 1 reel.

      Record of Settlements, 1868-1968; 5 reels.

      Index to Administrators, Executors and Guardians, 1867-1966; 1 reel.

LAND RECORDS

      Record of Deeds, 1771-1950; 60 reels.

      Index to Real Estate Conveyances, Grantor, 1771-1974; 7 reels.

      Index to Real Estate Conveyances, Grantee, 1771-1974; 7 reels.

Land Entry Book, 1843-1913; 1 reel.

Land Grants, 1837-1858; 1 reel.

Federal Farm Loan Mortgages, 1923-1930; 1 reel.

Index to Tax Liens, 1932-1959; 1 reel.

Maps, 1911-1949; 1 reel.

Index to Plats, 1814-1986; 1 reel.

Record of Sales by Trustees and Mortgagees, 1921-1969; 3 reels.

MARRIAGE, DIVORCE AND VITAL STATISTICS

Marriage Bonds, 1772-1868; 3 reels.

Marriage Licenses, 1877-1960; 8 reels.

Marriage Registers, 1851-1977; 3 reels.

Index to Marriages, 1903-1971; 2 reels.

Maiden Names of Divorced Women, 1945-1959; 1 reel.

Index to Births, 1913-1985; 2 reels.

Index to Deaths, 1913-1976; 1 reel.

Index to Delayed Births, various years; 1 reel.

MILITARY AND PENSION RECORDS

Record of Armed Forces Discharges, 1944-1979; 4 reels.

MISCELLANEOUS RECORDS

Homestead Returns, 1888-1916; 1 reel.

Record of Lunacy, 1899-1968; 2 reels.

Orders and Decrees, 1870-1968; 9 reels.

Special Proceedings, 1905-1968; 2 reels.

Index to Special Proceedings, 1935-1968; 1 reel.

Poor House Book, 1871-1885; 1 reel.

Accounts of Outside Poor and Lunatics, 1879-1932; 1 reel.

Index to Notaries Public, 1969-1971; 1 reel.

Revolutionary History of Chatham, 1876; 1 reel.

OFFICIALS, COUNTY

Minutes, Board of County Commissioners, 1869-1962; 5 reels.

Index to Minutes, Board of County Commissioners, 1875-1978; 1 reel.

Commissioners' Ledgers, 1878-1909; 1 reel.

Record of Magistrates, 1877-1894; 1 reel.

ROADS AND BRIDGES

Record of Road Overseers, 1869; 1 reel.

SCHOOL RECORDS

Minutes, County Board of Education, 1841-1954; 2 reels.

TAX AND FISCAL RECORDS

Tax Lists, 1874-1896, 1905; 5 reels.

Tax Scrolls, 1865, 1875-1945; 12 reels.

WILLS

Record of Wills, 1780-1968; 7 reels.

Index to Wills, 1916-1971; 1 reel.

Index to Wills, Devisee, 1970-1977; 1 reel.

CHEROKEE COUNTY

Established in 1839 from Macon County.
Courthouse fires of 1865 (Federal troops), 1895 and 1926
destroyed many court records.

ORIGINAL RECORDS

BONDS
> Apprentice Bonds, 1896, 1906; Bastardy Bonds, 1866-1912; Officials' Bonds, 1866-1948; 1 Fibredex box.

COURT RECORDS
> County Court of Pleas and Quarter Sessions
>> Minutes, 1865-1868; Minutes, Board of County Commissioners, 1870-1882; Merchants' Taxes, 1873-1882; 1 volume.
>
> Superior Court
>> Minutes, 1869-1913; 8 volumes.
>> Equity Enrolling Docket, 1866-1868; Minutes, Superior Court, 1868-1869; 1 volume.
>> Civil Action Papers, 1846-1919; 10 Fibredex boxes.
>> Civil Action Papers Concerning Land, 1862-1926; 23 Fibredex boxes.
>> Criminal Action Papers, 1863-1913; 12 Fibredex boxes.

ELECTION RECORDS
> Record of Elections, 1878-1934; 6 volumes.

ESTATES RECORDS
> Record of Accounts, 1868-1928; 1 volume.
> Administrators' Bonds, 1914-1936; 1 volume.
> Estates Records, 1843-1940; 24 Fibredex boxes.
> Guardians' Records, 1869-1936; 2 Fibredex boxes.

LAND RECORDS
> Record of Deeds, 1839-1856, 1859-1889, 1897-1898; 20 volumes.
> Deeds, 1889-1950; 2 Fibredex boxes.
> Deeds of Trust and Mortgage Deeds, 1893-1954; 1 Fibredex box.
> Cross Index to Deeds, various dates; 2 volumes.
> Land Entries, 1883-1931; 3 Fibredex boxes.
> Record of Probate, 1869-1880; Equity Minutes, 1866-1868; 1 volume.
> Miscellaneous Land Records, 1869-1946; 1 Fibredex box.
> Pre-emption Bond Book, 1838-1857; 1 volume.
> Record of Solvent and Insolvent Principals, 1844-1845; 1 volume.

MARRIAGE, DIVORCE AND VITAL STATISTICS
> Record of Marriage Licenses Issued, 1865-1870; Registry of Licenses to Trades, 1869-1870, 1883-1890; 1 volume.
> Marriage Registers, 1868-1906; 2 volumes.
> Divorce Records, 1869-1914, 1942; 3 Fibredex boxes.

MISCELLANEOUS RECORDS
>   Alien Registration, 1927, 1940, 1957; 1 volume.
>   Record of Ear Marks and Brands, 1888-1918; 1 volume.
>   Homestead and Personal Property Exemptions, 1869-1926; 1 Fibredex box.
>   Orders and Decrees, 1869-1914; 2 volumes.
>   Wardens of the Poor Account Book, 1843-1868; 1 volume.
>   Miscellaneous Records, 1866-1948; 3 Fibredex boxes.
>   Records of Assignees, Receivers and Trustees, 1872-1919; 6 Fibredex boxes.

ROADS AND BRIDGES
>   Road Records, 1874-1927; 1 Fibredex box.
>   Railroad Records, 1880-1914; 4 Fibredex boxes.

TAX AND FISCAL RECORDS
>   Tax Book, 1867-1869; 1 volume.
>   Tax Records, 1870-1946; 1 Fibredex box.
>   Tax Scrolls, 1933, 1936, 1937; 3 volumes.

WILLS
>   Wills, 1857-1941; 3 Fibredex boxes.

MICROFILM RECORDS

CORPORATIONS AND PARTNERSHIPS
>   Record of Corporations, 1898-1963; 2 reels.
>   Record of Partnerships, 1913-1957; 1 reel.

COURT RECORDS
>   County Court of Pleas and Quarter Sessions
>   >   Minutes, 1865-1868; 1 reel.
>   Superior Court
>   >   Minutes, 1868-1945; 12 reels.
>   >   Equity Minutes, 1866-1868; 1 reel.
>   >   Index to Civil Actions, 1890-1979; 3 reels.
>   >   Index to Criminal Actions, 1966-1979; 1 reel.
>   >   Index to Judgments, 1898-1966; 4 reels.

ELECTION RECORDS
>   Record of Elections, 1878-1966; 2 reels.

ESTATES RECORDS
>   Record of Accounts, 1868-1966; 3 reels.
>   Administrators' Bonds, 1914-1936; 1 reel.
>   Record of Administrators, Executors and Guardians, 1925-1956; 2 reels.
>   Record of Administrators, 1948-1966; 1 reel.
>   Appointment of Executors, 1868-1925; 1 reel.
>   Record of Executors and Guardians, 1956-1966; 1 reel.
>   Record of Guardians, 1947-1966; 1 reel.
>   Inheritance Tax Records, 1919-1967; 1 reel.
>   Record of Settlements, 1871-1966; 2 reels.

LAND RECORDS
Record of Deeds, 1839-1955; 61 reels.
Index to Deeds, Grantor, 1839-1967; 8 reels.
Index to Deeds, Grantee, 1839-1967; 8 reels.
Land Entries, 1853-1936; 2 reels.
Record of Surveys, 1905-1915; 1 reel.
Plat Book, various years; 1 reel.
Index to Plats, various years; 1 reel.
Record of Solvent and Insolvent Purchasers, 1844-1845; 1 reel.
Pre-emption Bonds, 1838-1857; 2 reels.
Record of Sales and Resales by Mortgagees and Trustees, 1920-1966; 1 reel.

MARRIAGE, DIVORCE AND VITAL STATISTICS
Marriage Licenses, 1868-1961; 7 reels.
Marriage Registers, 1837-1978; 4 reels.
Index to Births, 1913-1945; 1 reel.
Index to Deaths, 1913-1945; 1 reel.

MILITARY AND PENSION RECORDS
Record of Armed Forces Discharges, 1918-1979; 5 reels.

MISCELLANEOUS RECORDS
Alien Registration, 1927, 1940, 1957; 1 reel.
Record of Ear Marks and Brands, 1888-1918; 1 reel.
Record of Lunacy, 1919-1966; 1 reel.
Orders and Decrees, 1869-1966; 6 reels.
Special Proceedings, 1921-1951; 1 reel.
Index to Special Proceedings, 1869-1967; 3 reels.
Record of Wardens of the Poor, 1843-1868; 1 reel.
Record of Memorials, 1927-1965; 1 reel.

OFFICIALS, COUNTY
Minutes, Board of County Commissioners, 1870-1965; 5 reels.

SCHOOL RECORDS
Minutes, County Board of Education, 1926-1979; 1 reel.

TAX AND FISCAL RECORDS
Tax List, 1867-1869; 1 reel.
Tax Scrolls, 1933, 1936-1937; 1 reel.

WILLS
Record of Wills, 1869-1966; 2 reels.
Cross Index to Wills, 1869-1966; 1 reel.

Chowan County Courthouse, Edenton, circa 1932. Built in 1767, it is considered one of the finest examples of Georgian architecture in the state. Photograph from the files of the State Archives.

CHOWAN COUNTY

Established by 1670 as a precinct of Albemarle County.
Many court records said to have been destroyed
by acting clerk of court in 1848.

ORIGINAL RECORDS

BONDS

      Apprentice Bonds and Records, 1737-1909; 1 volume, 4 Fibredex boxes.

      Bastardy Bonds and Records, 1736-1933; 1 volume, 4 Fibredex boxes.

      Officials' Bonds and Records, 1737-1921; 5 Fibredex boxes.

      Ordinary Bonds and Records, 1739-1867; 2 Fibredex boxes.

COURT RECORDS

      County Court of Pleas and Quarter Sessions

            Minutes, 1714-1868; 21 volumes.

            Execution Dockets, 1757-1859; 11 volumes, 1 manuscript box.

            Levy Docket, 1849-1850; 1 volume.

            State (Crown) Dockets, 1774-1862; 4 volumes, 1 manuscript box.

            Trial, Appearance and Reference Dockets, 1757-1868; 18 volumes,
                2 manuscript boxes.

            Clerk's Account Book, 1804-1811; 1 volume.

            Clerk's Account and Receipt Book, 1840-1850; 1 volume.

            Costs Dockets, 1806-1813, 1841-1850; 2 volumes.

      Superior Court

            Minutes, 1809-1910; 11 volumes, 1 manuscript box.

            Equity Minutes, 1816-1861, 1866-1868; 2 volumes.

            Equity Trial Docket, 1849-1868; 1 volume.

            Execution Dockets, 1814-1868; 2 volumes.

            State Docket, 1826-1868; 1 volume.

            Trial, Appearance and Reference Dockets, 1807-1868; 5 volumes,
                1 manuscript box.

            Rough Minutes and Dockets, 1725-1867; 1 Fibredex box.

            Civil Action Papers, 1730-1922; 103 Fibredex boxes.

            Civil Action Papers Concerning Land, 1761-1911; 12 Fibredex boxes.

            Civil Action Papers Concerning Timber, 1795-1908; 1 Fibredex box.

            Criminal Action Papers, 1720-1933; 38 Fibredex boxes.

ELECTION RECORDS

      Record of Elections, 1878-1912; 2 volumes.

      Election Returns and Lists of Voters, 1772-1914; 2 Fibredex boxes.

ESTATES RECORDS

      Record of Estates, 1811-1868; 2 volumes.

      Accounts of Sale, 1779-1796, 1812-1868; 7 volumes.

      Administrators' Bonds, 1867-1911; 4 volumes.

      Appointment of Administrators, 1777-1784; 1 pamphlet.

Appointment of Administrators, Executors, Guardians and Masters, 1868-1911; 1 volume.

Dowers and Widows' Year's Support, 1815-1858; 2 volumes.

Estates Records, 1728-1951; 118 Fibredex boxes.

Guardians' Records, 1741-1913; 7 Fibredex boxes.

Guardians' Accounts, 1812-1868; 3 volumes.

Guardians' Bonds, 1850-1911; 2 volumes.

Orphans' Court Docket, 1767-1775; 1 volume.

Inventories of Estates, 1811-1866; 1 volume.

Record of Inheritance Tax, 1919; 1 volume.

Record of Hiring of Slaves Belonging to Estates, 1808-1817; 1 volume.

LAND RECORDS

Record of Deeds, 1715-1758; 8 volumes.

Deeds, 1714-1900; 2 Fibredex boxes.

Miscellaneous Deeds, 1678-1893; 1 Fibredex box.

Ejectments, 1767-1879; 1 Fibredex box.

Entry Book, 1794-1801; 1 volume.

Record of Deeds Proved, 1811-1852; 1 volume.

Miscellaneous Land Records, 1708-1923; 2 Fibredex boxes.

MARRIAGE, DIVORCE AND VITAL STATISTICS

Marriage Bonds, 1747-1868; 8 Fibredex boxes.

Record of Marriage Certificates, 1851-1867; 1 volume.

Miscellaneous Marriage Records, 1754-1909; 1 Fibredex box.

Divorce Records, 1823-1909; 2 Fibredex boxes.

MISCELLANEOUS RECORDS

County Accounts, 1742-1929; 2 Fibredex boxes.

Accounts, Letters and Receipts of Edmund Hoskins, 1801-1835; 4 Fibredex boxes.

Accounts, Letters and Receipts of Elisha Norfleet, Clerk of Court of Pleas and Quarter Sessions, 1796-1811; 1 Fibredex box.

Jury Lists, 1722-1877; 1 Fibredex box.

Record of Jury Tickets, 1873-1906; 1 volume.

Ferriage Docket, 1781-1783; 1 volume.

Insolvent Debtors, 1769-1869; 4 Fibredex boxes.

Loyalty Oath Stubs, 1865; 1 volume.

Special Proceedings, 1870-1895; 2 volumes.

Miscellaneous Accounts, 1752-1879; 1 Fibredex box.

Miscellaneous Records, 1685-1916; 20 volumes, 5 Fibredex boxes.

Personal Accounts, 1700-1895; 2 Fibredex boxes.

Promissory Notes and Receipts, 1721-1909; 1 Fibredex box.

Shipping Records, 1731-1894; 5 Fibredex boxes.

Slave Records, 1730-1869; 7 Fibredex boxes.

Record (Entry) of Strays, 1906-1919; 1 volume.

Records of Assignees, Receivers and Trustees, 1763-1918; 2 Fibredex boxes.

OFFICIALS, COUNTY
    Justices of the Peace Records, 1753-1920; 1 Fibredex box.
ROADS AND BRIDGES
    Minutes, County Road Commissioners, 1921-1929; 1 volume.
    Road Records, 1717-1912; 6 Fibredex boxes.
SCHOOL RECORDS
    Common School Records, 1839-1897; 1 Fibredex box.
TAX AND FISCAL RECORDS
    Taxables, 1717-1909; 2 volumes, 9 Fibredex boxes.
WILLS
    Wills, 1694-1938; 24 Fibredex boxes.

MICROFILM RECORDS

BONDS
    Apprentice Bonds, 1871-1909; 1 reel.
    Bastardy Bonds, 1755-1878; 2 reels.
    Officials' Bonds, 1690-1959; 3 reels.
    Tavern Bonds, 1785-1837; 1 reel.
CORPORATIONS AND PARTNERSHIPS
    Record of Corporations, 1888-1950; 1 reel.
    Record of Partnerships, 1922-1976; 1 reel.
COURT RECORDS
    County Court of Pleas and Quarter Sessions
        Minutes, 1714-1719, 1730-1868; 11 reels.
        Trial Dockets, 1788-1804; 1 reel.
        Levy Docket, 1849-1850; 1 reel.
        Court Letterbook, 1816-1858; 1 reel.
        Orders of the Court, 1780-1830; 1 reel.
    Superior Court
        Minutes, 1807-1956; 6 reels.
        Equity Minutes, 1807-1810, 1816-1868; 2 reels.
        Index to Civil Actions, 1966-1984; 3 reels.
        Index to Criminal Actions, 1966-1984; 1 reel.
        Index to Judgments, 1966-1985; 1 reel.
ELECTION RECORDS
    Record of Elections, 1880-1914, 1924-1958; 1 reel.
ESTATES RECORDS
    Record of Accounts, 1785-1794, 1811-1958; 6 reels.
    Accounts of Sale of Estates, 1779-1796, 1811-1868; 5 reels.
    Administrators' Bonds, 1867-1911; 2 reels.
    Record of Administrators, Executors and Guardians, 1911-1943; 1 reel.
    Record of Administrators, 1919-1966; 3 reels.
    Appointment of Executors, 1868-1911; 1 reel.
    Record of Executors and Guardians, 1936-1966; 2 reels.

Guardians' Accounts, 1811-1868; 1 reel.

Record of Guardians, 1877-1883; 1 reel.

Guardians' Bonds, 1787, 1811-1911; 3 reels.

Orphans' Court Docket, 1767-1775; 1 reel.

Record of Widows' Year's Support, 1869-1966; 2 reels.

Inheritance Tax Records, 1914-1967; 2 reels.

Inventories of Estates, 1811-1866; 1 reel.

Record of Settlements, 1859-1969; 3 reels.

Index to Administrators, Executors and Guardians, 1811-1966; 1 reel.

Index to Estates, 1811-1966; 1 reel.

LAND RECORDS

Record of Deeds, 1715-1946; 36 reels.

Index to Deeds, Grantor, 1695-1975; 3 reels.

Index to Deeds, Grantee, 1695-1975; 3 reels.

Land Entries, 1787-1941; 1 reel.

Processioners' Record, 1756, 1795-1808; 1 reel.

Record of Deeds Proved, 1811-1852; 1 reel.

Sales and Resales of Land Under Mortgagees and Trustees, 1926-1966;
    2 reels.

MARRIAGE, DIVORCE AND VITAL STATISTICS

Marriage Bonds, 1741-1868; 2 reels.

Marriage Registers, 1851-1947; 1 reel.

Record of Divorce, 1868-1960; 1 reel.

Index to Births, 1913-1993; 1 reel.

Index to Deaths, 1913-1993; 1 reel.

Index to Delayed Births, various years; 1 reel.

MILITARY AND PENSION RECORDS

Record of Armed Forces Discharges, 1942-1994; 3 reels.

MISCELLANEOUS RECORDS

Ferriage Docket, 1781-1783; 1 reel.

Registry of Licenses to Trades, 1873-1902; 1 reel.

Record of Lunacy, 1899-1966; 1 reel.

Clerk's Minute Docket, 1921-1966; 1 reel.

Orders and Decrees, 1868-1968; 2 reels.

Special Proceedings, 1868-1895, 1911-1967; Widows' Dowers and Year's
    Provisions, 1859-1868; 2 reels.

Record of Petitions, 1770-1887; 3 reels.

OFFICIALS, COUNTY

Minutes, Board of County Commissioners, 1868-1899, 1942-1953; 2 reels.

Minutes of Commissioners and Magistrates, 1876-1896; 1 reel.

ROADS AND BRIDGES

Minutes, County Road Commissioners, 1921-1929; 1 reel.

SCHOOL RECORDS

Minutes, Board of Superintendents of Common Schools, 1841-1861; 1 reel.

Minutes, County Board of Education, 1885-1982; 2 reels.

TAX AND FISCAL RECORDS
      Lists of Taxables, 1801-1810, 1814-1826; 1 reel.
      Tax Ledger, 1865-1867; 1 reel.
      Tax Scrolls, 1888-1892; 1 reel.
WILLS
      Record of Wills, 1760-1966; 7 reels.
      List of Wills, 1777-1784; 1 reel.
      Index to Wills, Devisor, 1760-1966; 1 reel.
      Index to Wills, Devisee, 1760-1966; 1 reel.

CLAY COUNTY

Established in 1861 from Cherokee County.
Fire (not courthouse) destroyed all records of the county in 1870.

ORIGINAL RECORDS

BONDS
>Apprentice Bonds, 1871-1910; 1 volume.
>Bastardy Bonds, 1879; 1 volume.
>Officials' Bonds and Records, 1879-1939; 1 Fibredex box.

COURT RECORDS
>Superior Court
>>Minutes, 1870-1902; 2 volumes.
>>Civil Action Papers, 1868-1911; 2 Fibredex boxes.
>>Civil Action Papers Concerning Land, 1870-1942; 4 Fibredex boxes.
>>Criminal Action Papers, 1870-1909; 6 Fibredex boxes.

ELECTION RECORDS
>Record of Elections, 1878-1932; 4 volumes.

ESTATES RECORDS
>Administrators' Bonds, 1870-1915; 2 volumes.
>Record of Dowers, 1871-1901; 1 volume.
>Estates Records, 1862-1943; 16 Fibredex boxes.
>Guardians' Records, 1869-1921; 2 Fibredex boxes.
>Guardians' Bonds, 1870-1921; 2 volumes.

LAND RECORDS
>Deeds, 1845-1937; 1 Fibredex box.
>Cross Index to Deeds, 1870-1906; 1 volume.
>Entry Books, 1871-1929; 4 volumes.
>Land Entries, 1877-1928; 1 Fibredex box.
>Probate of Deeds, 1870-1908; 2 volumes.
>Record of Processioners of Land, 1881-1891; 1 volume.

MILITARY AND PENSION RECORDS
>Minutes, Board of Pensions, 1908-1939; 1 volume.

MISCELLANEOUS RECORDS
>Registry of Licenses to Trades, 1876-1904; 1 volume.
>Miscellaneous Records, 1869-1939; 1 Fibredex box.

ROADS AND BRIDGES
>Road Records, 1871-1903; 1 Fibredex box.

WILLS
>Wills, 1870-1928; 1 Fibredex box.

MICROFILM RECORDS

BONDS
> Apprentice Bonds, 1871-1910; 1 reel.
> Bastardy Bonds, 1879; 1 reel.

CORPORATIONS AND PARTNERSHIPS
> Record of Corporations, 1919-1970; 1 reel.
> Record of Partnerships, 1919-1960; 1 reel.

COURT RECORDS
> Superior Court
> > Minutes, 1870-1966; 4 reels.
> > Judgment Docket, 1870-1889; 1 reel.
> > Cross Index to Judgments, 1870-1966; 1 reel.

ELECTION RECORDS
> Record of Elections, 1878-1966; 1 reel.

ESTATES RECORDS
> Record of Accounts, 1870-1966; 2 reels.
> Administrators' Bonds, 1870-1910; 1 reel.
> Administrators' and Executors' Bonds, 1877-1915; 1 reel.
> Record of Administrators, Executors and Guardians, 1915-1966; 1 reel.
> Record of Administrators, 1939-1966; 1 reel.
> Guardians' Bonds, 1870-1921; 1 reel.
> Record of Guardians, 1952-1966; 1 reel.
> Record of Dowers, 1871-1931; 1 reel.
> Inheritance Tax Records, 1920-1966; 1 reel.
> Record of Settlements, 1873-1946; 1 reel.

LAND RECORDS
> Record of Deeds, 1870-1958; 23 reels.
> Cross Index to Deeds, 1870-1944; 1 reel.
> Index to Real Estate Conveyances, Grantor, 1945-1977; 1 reel.
> Index to Real Estate Conveyances, Grantee, 1945-1977; 1 reel.
> Land Entry Books, 1871-1929; 1 reel.
> Record of Processioners of Land, 1881-1891; 1 reel.
> Registration of Land Titles, 1945-1968; 1 reel.
> Federal Farm Loan Mortgages, 1922-1969; 1 reel.
> Record of Taxes for Mortgages, 1927-1932; 1 reel.
> Record of Sales and Resales by Mortgagees and Trustees, 1933-1966; 1 reel.

MARRIAGE, DIVORCE AND VITAL STATISTICS
> Marriage Licenses, 1889-1964; 2 reels.
> Marriage Registers, 1870-1970; 1 reel.
> Index to Births, 1913-1970; 1 reel.
> Index to Deaths, 1913-1970; 1 reel.

MILITARY AND PENSION RECORDS
> Record of Armed Forces Discharges, 1918-1993; 2 reels.
> Minutes, Board of Pensions, 1908-1939; 1 reel.

MISCELLANEOUS RECORDS
      Registry of Licenses to Trades, 1876-1904; 1 reel.
      Clerk's Minute Docket, 1909-1966; 1 reel.
      Orders and Decrees, 1870-1966; 3 reels.
      Cross Index to Special Proceedings and Orders and Decrees, 1870-1966;
            1 reel.
OFFICIALS, COUNTY
      Minutes, Board of County Commissioners, 1874-1972; 3 reels.
SCHOOL RECORDS
      Minutes, County Board of Education, 1921-1979; 1 reel.
WILLS
      Record of Wills, 1870-1966; 1 reel.
      Cross Index to Wills, 1870-1966; 1 reel.

CLEVELAND COUNTY

Established in 1841 from Lincoln and Rutherford counties.

ORIGINAL RECORDS

BONDS
>
> Apprentice Bonds and Records, 1841-1888; 1 volume, 1 Fibredex box.
>
> Bastardy Bonds and Records, 1841-1919; 3 Fibredex boxes.
>
> Officials' Bonds and Records, 1841-1909; 1 Fibredex box.

COURT RECORDS
>
> County Court of Pleas and Quarter Sessions
>> Minutes, 1841-1867; 4 volumes.
>>
>> Appearance Docket, 1844-1868; 1 volume.
>>
>> Execution Dockets, 1841-1868; 3 volumes.
>>
>> Levy Docket, 1841-1868, 1876; 1 volume.
>>
>> State Docket, 1841-1859; 1 volume.
>>
>> Trial Dockets, 1841-1868; 2 volumes.
>
> Superior Court
>> Minutes, 1841-1910; 12 volumes.
>>
>> Equity Enrolling Docket, 1856-1867; 1 volume.
>>
>> Equity Execution Docket, 1843-1868; 1 volume.
>>
>> Equity Trial Docket, 1842-1857; 1 volume.
>>
>> Execution Docket, 1854-1867; 1 volume.
>>
>> Trial and Appearance Docket, 1841-1854; 1 volume.
>>
>> Civil Action Papers, 1838-1921; 30 Fibredex boxes.
>>
>> Civil Action Papers Concerning Land, 1842-1911; 11 Fibredex boxes.
>>
>> Criminal Action Papers, 1841-1879; 19 Fibredex boxes.

ELECTION RECORDS
>
> Record of Elections, 1878-1908; 1 volume.
>
> Election Records, 1841-1922; 2 Fibredex boxes.

ESTATES RECORDS
>
> Record of Estates, 1841-1868; 4 volumes.
>
> Record of Accounts, 1868-1909; 4 volumes.
>
> Estates Records, 1795-1915; 56 Fibredex boxes.
>
> Guardians' Records, 1845-1910; 4 Fibredex boxes.
>
> Guardians' Accounts, 1841-1867; 2 volumes.
>
> Record of Settlements, 1869-1919; 4 volumes.

LAND RECORDS
>
> Deeds and Grants, 1775-1898; 1 Fibredex box.
>
> Ejectments, 1841-1895; 3 Fibredex boxes.
>
> Processioners' Returns, 1841-1860; 1 volume.
>
> Attachments, Executions, Levies and Liens on Land, 1841-1899;
>> 2 Fibredex boxes.
>
> Miscellaneous Land Records, 1790-1905; 1 Fibredex box.

MARRIAGE, DIVORCE AND VITAL STATISTICS
        Marriage Bonds, 1865-1866; 1 Fibredex box.
        Marriage Register, 1905-1917; 1 volume.
        Divorce Records, 1842-1907; 4 Fibredex boxes.
MISCELLANEOUS RECORDS
        County Accounts, Claims and Court Orders, 1841-1889; 2 Fibredex boxes.
        Insolvent Debtors and Homestead and Personal Property Exemptions, 1841-1891; 1 Fibredex box.
        Lunacy Records, 1845-1907; 1 Fibredex box.
        Mill Records, 1850-1896; 1 Fibredex box.
        Orders and Decrees, 1869-1904; 5 volumes.
        Minutes, Wardens of the Poor, 1847-1868; 1 volume.
        Records of Slaves and Free Persons of Color, 1841-1869; 2 Fibredex boxes.
        Miscellaneous Records, 1833, 1841-1938; 3 Fibredex boxes.
        Records of Assignees, Receivers and Trustees, 1860-1909; 1 Fibredex box.
ROADS AND BRIDGES
        Overseers of Roads and Hands, 1829-1867; 3 Fibredex boxes.
        Road Petitions, 1841-1899; 2 Fibredex boxes.
        Railroad Records, 1857-1908; 4 Fibredex boxes.
SCHOOL RECORDS
        School Records, 1841-1905; 1 Fibredex box.
TAX AND FISCAL RECORDS
        Tax List, 1918; 1 volume.
        Tax Records, 1823-1896; 1 Fibredex box.
WILLS
        Wills, 1841-1919; 12 Fibredex boxes.

MICROFILM RECORDS

BONDS
        Apprentice Bonds, 1869-1888; 1 reel.
CORPORATIONS AND PARTNERSHIPS
        Record of Corporations, 1888-1960; 2 reels.
        Record of Partnerships, 1913-1961; 1 reel.
        Index to Corporations, 1883-1977; 1 reel.
COURT RECORDS
        County Court of Pleas and Quarter Sessions
            Minutes, 1841-1867; 3 reels.
        Superior Court
            Minutes, 1841-1950; 11 reels.
            Criminal Minutes, 1866-1906; 2 reels.
            Index to Civil Actions, 1939-1978; 3 reels.
            Index to Criminal Actions, 1968-1978; 1 reel.
            Index to Judgments and Liens, Plaintiff, 1921-1968; 3 reels.
            Index to Judgments and Liens, Defendant, 1921-1968; 4 reels.

ELECTION RECORDS

Record of Elections, 1878-1908, 1924-1936; 2 reels.

ESTATES RECORDS

Record of Estates, 1841-1855; 1 reel.

Record of Accounts, 1868-1959; 7 reels.

Record of Administrators, 1896-1956; 5 reels.

Appointment of Executors, 1868-1958; 2 reels.

Cross Index to Executors and Administrators, 1869-1964; 1 reel.

Record of Guardians, 1897-1959; 2 reels.

Cross Index to Guardians, 1870-1960; 1 reel.

Inheritance Tax Records, 1923-1960; 1 reel.

Record of Settlements, 1869-1960; 6 reels.

LAND RECORDS

Record of Deeds, 1841-1956; 77 reels.

Index to Deeds, Grantor, 1841-1959; 5 reels.

Index to Deeds, Grantee, 1841-1959; 5 reels.

Entry Book, 1888-1925; 1 reel.

Processioners' Returns, 1841-1859; 1 reel.

Federal Tax Lien Index, 1935-1941, 1951-1964; 1 reel.

Plats, 1912-1957; 1 reel.

Index to Plats, various years; 1 reel.

Record of Land Sales, 1924-1960; 2 reels.

MARRIAGE, DIVORCE AND VITAL STATISTICS

Marriage Licenses, 1882-1906; 5 reels.

Marriage Records, 1851-1965; 1 reel.

Marriage Registers, 1870-1945; 1 reel.

Maiden Names of Divorced Women, 1945-1970; 1 reel.

Index to Births and Deaths, 1913-1962; 3 reels.

Index to Delayed Births, 1908-1935, various years; 3 reels.

MILITARY AND PENSION RECORDS

Record of Armed Forces Discharges, 1918-1919, 1943-1988; 12 reels.

Index to Armed Forces Discharges, 1918-1977; 2 reels.

MISCELLANEOUS RECORDS

Record of Lunacy, 1899-1963; 2 reels.

Orders and Decrees, 1868-1968; 17 reels.

Special Proceedings, 1874-1968; 2 reels.

Cross Index to Special Proceedings, 1874-1910, 1968-1978; 2 reels.

Minutes, Wardens of the Poor, 1847-1868; 1 reel.

OFFICIALS, COUNTY

Minutes, Board of County Commissioners, 1868-1955; 5 reels.

SCHOOL RECORDS

Minutes, County Board of Education, 1913-1977; 1 reel.

TAX AND FISCAL RECORDS

Tax List, 1918; 1 reel.

Record of Taxes, 1840-1857; 1 reel.

WILLS
Record of Wills, 1841-1965; 5 reels.
Cross Index to Wills, 1841-1960; 1 reel.

COLUMBUS COUNTY

Established in 1808 from Bladen and Brunswick counties.

ORIGINAL RECORDS

BONDS
>Apprentice Bonds, 1874-1891; 1 volume.
>Officials' Bonds, 1868-1881, 1891-1914; 2 volumes.

CENSUS RECORDS (County Copy)
>Census (partial), 1810; 1 volume of photostats.

COURT RECORDS
>County Court of Pleas and Quarter Sessions
>>Minutes, 1819-1868; 6 volumes.
>>Appeal Docket, 1856-1868; 1 volume.
>>Appearance Docket, 1856-1868; 1 volume.
>>Execution Dockets, 1842-1868; 2 volumes.
>>State Docket, 1856-1868; 1 volume.
>>Trial Docket, 1856-1868; 1 volume.

>Superior Court
>>Minutes, 1817-1912; 10 volumes.
>>Equity Minutes, 1843-1868; 1 volume.
>>Equity Decrees, 1858-1860; 1 volume.
>>Equity Execution Docket, 1858-1868; 1 volume.
>>Equity Trial Docket, 1859-1861, 1866-1868; 1 volume.
>>Appearance Docket, 1858-1869; 1 volume.
>>State Docket, 1847-1868; 1 volume.

ELECTION RECORDS
>Record of Elections, 1878-1900, 1906-1936; 4 volumes.

ESTATES RECORDS
>Record of Accounts, 1869-1913; 3 volumes.
>Administrators' Bonds, 1873-1912; 4 volumes.
>Appointment of Administrators, Executors and Guardians, 1868-1915;
>>1 volume.
>Estates Records, 1812-1923; 13 Fibredex boxes.
>Guardians' Records, 1844-1919; 1 Fibredex box.
>Guardians' Accounts, 1857-1868; 1 volume.
>Record of Settlements, 1869-1899; 1 volume.

LAND RECORDS
>Entry Books, 1809-1900; 4 volumes.

MARRIAGE, DIVORCE AND VITAL STATISTICS
>Disinterment/Reinterment Permits, 1967-1987; 1 manuscript box.

MISCELLANEOUS RECORDS
>Alien Registration, 1927, 1940, 1946, 1958; 1 volume.
>Settlement of County Accounts, Committee of Finance, 1824-1857; 1 volume.

Registry of Licenses to Trades, 1876-1893; 1 volume.
Orders and Decrees, 1875-1907; 1 volume.
Miscellaneous Records, 1816, 1884; 1 manuscript box.
WILLS
Wills, 1808-1917; 3 Fibredex boxes.

MICROFILM RECORDS

CORPORATIONS AND PARTNERSHIPS
Record of Incorporations, 1887-1938; 1 reel.
CENSUS RECORDS (County Copy)
Census, 1860; 1 reel.
COURT RECORDS
County Court of Pleas and Quarter Sessions
Minutes, 1819-1868; 3 reels.
Superior Court
Minutes, 1851-1960; 17 reels.
Equity Minutes, 1817-1868; 1 reel.
ESTATES RECORDS
Record of Accounts, 1869-1967; 7 reels.
Record of Administrators and Executors, 1912-1957; 2 reels.
Record of Administrators, 1920-1967; 4 reels.
Appointment of Executors, 1868-1915; 1 reel.
Record of Guardians, 1902-1967; 2 reels.
Record of Amounts Paid to Indigent Children, 1912-1967; 1 reel.
Inheritance Tax Records, 1923-1967; 1 reel.
Division of Estates, 1887-1967; 3 reels.
Record of Settlements, 1869-1967; 3 reels.
Index to Administrators, Executors and Guardians, 1869-1967; 1 reel.
LAND RECORDS
Record of Deeds, 1805-1960; 113 reels.
Index to Real Estate Conveyances, Grantor, 1808-1966; 9 reels.
Index to Real Estate Conveyances, Grantee, 1808-1966; 8 reels.
Land Entries, 1809-1953; 1 reel.
Plats, 1919-1967; 1 reel.
Record of Resale of Land by Trustees and Mortgagees, 1922-1954; 3 reels.
MARRIAGE, DIVORCE AND VITAL STATISTICS
Record of Marriages, 1851-1868; 1 reel.
Marriage Registers, 1868-1974; 2 reels.
Cohabitation Records, 1866-1868; 1 reel.
Maiden Names of Divorced Women, 1939-1969; 1 reel.
Index to Births, 1913-1974; 3 reels.
Index to Delayed Births, various years; 1 reel.
MILITARY AND PENSION RECORDS
Record of Armed Forces Discharges, 1918-1974; 7 reels.

Index to Armed Forces Discharges, 1917-1967; 1 reel.
MISCELLANEOUS RECORDS
Orders and Decrees, 1869-1953; 9 reels.
Special Proceedings Dockets, 1885-1945, 1954-1967; 2 reels.
Cross Index to Special Proceedings, 1885-1967; 2 reels.
OFFICIALS, COUNTY
Minutes, Board of County Commissioners, 1868-1954; 7 reels.
SCHOOL RECORDS
Minutes, County Board of Education, 1885-1936; 2 reels.
TAX AND FISCAL RECORDS
Tax Lists and Tax Scrolls, 1869, 1925; 1 reel.
WILLS
Record of Wills, 1808-1967; 4 reels.
Cross Index to Wills, 1808-1967; 1 reel.

CRAVEN COUNTY

Established in 1705 as Archdale Precinct of Bath County.
Name changed to Craven in 1712.

ORIGINAL RECORDS

BONDS

    Apprentice Bonds and Records, 1748-1910; 2 volumes, 7 Fibredex boxes.

    Bastardy Bonds and Records, 1803-1880; 1 volume, 3 Fibredex boxes.

    Constables' Bonds, 1850-1859; 1 volume.

    Officials' Bonds, 1753-1867; 1 Fibredex box.

COURT RECORDS

    County Court of Pleas and Quarter Sessions

        Minutes, 1712-1715, 1730-1868; 43 volumes.

        Appearance Dockets, 1791-1868; 9 volumes.

        Execution Dockets, 1754-1867; 28 volumes.

        Levy Docket, 1842-1857; 1 volume.

        State Dockets, 1786-1859; 4 volumes.

        Reference (Trial) and Appearance Dockets, 1778-1791; 2 volumes.

        Trial and Reference Dockets, 1789-1807; 3 volumes.

        Trial and Petition Dockets, 1807-1868; 14 volumes.

        Writs Docket, 1850-1854; 1 volume.

    Superior Court

        Minutes, 1807-1820, 1829-1914; 26 volumes.

        Equity Minutes, 1850-1868; 3 volumes.

        Equity Execution Docket, 1858-1868; Clerk's Receipt Book (Land Sales), 1869-1872; 1 volume.

        Equity Trial and Appearance Docket, 1850-1859; 1 volume.

        Clerk and Master in Equity Sale and Hiring Book, 1858-1875; 1 volume.

        Appearance Docket, 1843-1867; 1 volume.

        Execution Dockets, 1806-1830, 1840-1869; 5 volumes.

        State Dockets, 1815-1861, 1866-1867, 1869; 4 volumes.

        Trial, Appearance, Argument and Reference Docket, 1807-1813; 1 volume.

        Trial and Argument Docket, 1814-1832; 1 volume.

        Trial Dockets, 1845-1868; 2 volumes.

        Civil Issues Docket, 1868-1870; 1 volume.

        Civil Action Papers, 1756-1908; 71 Fibredex boxes.

        Civil Action Papers Concerning Land, 1809-1920; 7 Fibredex boxes.

        Criminal Action Papers, 1778-1906; 20 Fibredex boxes.

    Circuit Criminal Court/Eastern District Criminal Court

        Minutes, 1895-1901; 1 volume.

ELECTION RECORDS

    Record of Elections, 1874-1914; 3 volumes.

    Election Returns, 1835-1895; 4 Fibredex boxes.

    Election Returns for Sheriffs, 1830-1860; 2 Fibredex boxes.

ESTATES RECORDS

    Record of Accounts, 1829-1902; 11 volumes.

    Administrators' Bonds, 1868-1917; 5 volumes.

    Estates Records, 1745-1945; 167 Fibredex boxes.

    Guardians' Records, 1766-1945; 16 Fibredex boxes.

    Guardians' Bonds, 1869-1910; 5 volumes.

    Record of Guardians, 1808-1869; 2 volumes.

    Inventories, Accounts of Sale and Deeds, 1763-1767; 1 volume.

    Inventories and Accounts of Sale, 1781-1789, 1807, 1830-1867; 11 volumes.

    Record of Probate (Estates), 1877-1885; 1 volume.

    Fiduciary Account Book (Estate of Major Willis), 1844-1845; 1 volume.

LAND RECORDS

    Deeds, Inventories, Wills and Miscellaneous Records, 1729-1855;
        21 volumes.

    Deeds, Patents, Grants, Deeds of Trust and Mortgage Deeds, 1724-1904;
        2 Fibredex boxes.

    Acknowledgment of Deeds and Powers of Attorney, 1786-1799; 1 volume.

    Index to Deeds, 1744-1846; 3 volumes.

    Ejectments, 1787-1872, 1896; 3 Fibredex boxes.

    Land Entries, 1789-1861, 1893; Division and Sale of Land, 1803-1910;
        1 Fibredex box.

    Land Entries, 1834-1903; 1 volume.

    Grants and Surveys, 1716-1802 (includes Land Entry Book, 1809-1813);
        2 volumes.

    Plats, Surveys and Miscellaneous Land Records, 1754-1901; 1 Fibredex box.

MARRIAGE, DIVORCE AND VITAL STATISTICS

    Marriage Bonds, 1773-1868; 17 Fibredex boxes.

    Divorce Records, 1828-1897, 1955; 4 Fibredex boxes.

MILITARY AND PENSION RECORDS

    Blind Pensioners, 1902-1927; 1 volume.

    State Pension Book, 1903-1938; 1 volume.

MISCELLANEOUS RECORDS

    Buildings, Claims, County Lines and Trustee Settlements, 1780-1918;
        1 Fibredex box.

    Sheriff's Settlements, 1811-1854, and State of County Finance, 1834-1856;
        1 Fibredex box.

    Certificates of Claims, 1829-1846; 2 volumes.

    County Trustees' Settlements, 1817-1868; 3 volumes.

    Sheriffs' Receipt Book, 1836-1845; 1 volume.

    Treasurer's Account Book, 1881-1887; 1 volume.

    Treasurer of Public Buildings Accounts, 1817-1857; 1 Fibredex box.

Insolvent Debtors, 1757-1866; 4 Fibredex boxes.
List of Active Dentists in County, 1887; 1 volume.
Orders and Decrees, 1869-1879; 1 volume.
Personal Accounts, 1750-1894; 1 Fibredex box.
Minutes, Wardens of the Poor, 1837-1871; 1 volume.
Records of Wardens of the Poor, 1803-1861; 1 Fibredex box.
Miscellaneous Records, 1757-1929; 5 Fibredex boxes.
Letters to Clerk, 1814-1871; 1 Fibredex box.
List of Commissioners of Affidavits, 1851-1884; 1 volume.
Coroners' Inquests, 1782-1905; 2 Fibredex boxes.
Records of Ships and Merchants, 1770-1858; 3 Fibredex boxes.
Civil Action Papers Concerning Slaves and Free Persons of Color, 1788, 1806-1860, 1885; 1 Fibredex box.
Criminal Action Papers Concerning Slaves and Free Persons of Color, 1781-1868; 2 Fibredex boxes.
Slaves and Free Negroes, 1775-1861; 1 Fibredex box.

OFFICIALS, COUNTY
Oath Book, 1811-1872; 1 volume.

ROADS AND BRIDGES
Appointment of Constables and Overseers, 1784-1857; 2 volumes.
Road Records, 1767-1868; 3 Fibredex boxes.
Railroad Records, 1855-1908; 2 Fibredex boxes.

SCHOOL RECORDS
Minutes, Board of Superintendents of Common Schools, 1841-1859; 1 volume.
Lists of School Children and Teacher Applications, 1841-1861; 1 Fibredex box.
School Committees, 1841-1861; 2 Fibredex boxes.
Miscellaneous School Records, 1823-1874; 1 Fibredex box.

TAX AND FISCAL RECORDS
Tax Book, 1829-1856; 1 volume.
Tax Records, 1764-1904; 1 Fibredex box.

WILLS
Wills (includes inventories and deeds), 1737-1868; 12 volumes.
Wills, 1748-1941; 16 Fibredex boxes.
Cross Index to Wills, 1750-1914; 1 volume.

MICROFILM RECORDS

BONDS
Apprentice Bonds, 1868-1910; 1 reel.
Bastardy Bonds, 1870-1880; 1 reel.
COURT RECORDS
County Court of Pleas and Quarter Sessions
Minutes, 1712-1868; 15 reels.

Superior Court
        Minutes, 1801-1820, 1829-1933; 15 reels.
        Equity Minutes, 1850-1860; 1 reel.

ESTATES RECORDS
        Record of Estates, 1829-1960; 6 reels.
        Record of Accounts, 1868-1951; 7 reels.
        Administrators' Bonds, 1868-1947; 2 reels.
        Record of Administrators, 1935-1946; 1 reel.
        Guardians' Bonds, 1868-1927; 2 reels.
        Record of Guardians, 1919-1960; 2 reels.
        Citations to Guardians, Administrators and Executors, 1869-1885; 1 reel.
        Inventories and Accounts of Sale, 1763-1767, 1781-1789, 1807, 1830-1867;
            7 reels.
        Inventory of the Estate of Major Willis, 1844; 1 reel.
        Land Divisions and Plats, 1803-1868; 1 reel.
        Record of Settlements, 1869-1955; 5 reels.
        Miscellaneous Estates Records, 1740-1870; 6 reels.
        Cross Index to Executors and Administrators, 1869-1910; 1 reel.
        Cross Index to Guardians, 1868-1910; 1 reel.
        Cross Index to Fiduciaries, 1909-1968; 1 reel.

LAND RECORDS
        Record of Deeds, 1739-1914; 94 reels.
        Index to Deeds and Mortgages, Grantor, 1739-1980; 13 reels.
        Index to Deeds and Mortgages, Grantee, 1739-1980; 12 reels.
        Land Entries, 1778-1959; 1 reel.
        Land Grants, 1783-1809; 1 reel.
        Index to Land Grants, no date; 1 reel.
        Record of Patents, 1770-1859; 2 reels.
        Record of Land Sales by Mortgagees and Trustees, 1921-1946; 3 reels.

MARRIAGE, DIVORCE AND VITAL STATISTICS
        Marriage Bond Abstracts, 1740-1868; 1 reel.
        Marriage Licenses, 1892-1946; 8 reels.
        Marriage Registers, 1851-1960; Record of Cohabitation, 1865-1867; 3 reels.
        Marriage Registers, Women, 1851-1946; 3 reels.

MILITARY AND PENSION RECORDS
        Record of Armed Forces Discharges, 1927-1981; 7 reels.
        Index to Armed Forces Discharges, various years; 1 reel.

MISCELLANEOUS RECORDS
        Orders and Decrees, 1868-1925; 2 reels.
        Special Proceedings, 1869-1949; 9 reels.
        Cross Index to Special Proceedings, 1869-1960; 1 reel.
        Minutes, Wardens of the Poor, 1837-1871; 1 reel.

OFFICIALS, COUNTY
        Minutes, Board of County Commissioners, 1868-1902; 3 reels.

TAX AND FISCAL RECORDS
     Lists of Taxables, 1829-1856; 1 reel.
     Tax Lists, 1881-1893, 1896, 1900, 1916-1917, 1925, 1935; 7 reels.
WILLS
     Record of Wills, 1708-1716, 1784-1968; 14 reels.
     Original Wills, 1746-1890; 3 reels.
     Wills and Estates Papers, 1736-1857; 4 reels.
     Cross Index to Wills, 1784-1970; 2 reels.

CUMBERLAND COUNTY

Established in 1754 from Bladen County.

ORIGINAL RECORDS

BONDS
>
> Apprentice Bonds and Records, 1812-1909; 1 volume, 2 Fibredex boxes.
>
> Bastardy Bonds and Records, 1760-1910; 1 volume, 1 Fibredex box.
>
> Constables' Bonds, 1779-1883, 1920; 1 Fibredex box.
>
> Officials' Bonds, 1777-1954; 2 Fibredex boxes.

CENSUS RECORDS (County Copy)
>
> Census, 1840; 1 volume.

COURT RECORDS
>
> County Court of Pleas and Quarter Sessions
>> Minutes, 1755-1868; 44 volumes.
>>
>> Appeal Dockets, 1791-1834, 1857-1868; 5 volumes.
>>
>> Appearance Dockets, 1789-1868; 7 volumes.
>>
>> Execution Dockets, 1785-1868; 14 volumes.
>>
>> Judgment Docket, 1823-1825; 1 volume.
>>
>> Levy Dockets, 1821-1835; 2 volumes.
>>
>> Recognizance Docket, 1789-1806; 1 volume.
>>
>> State Dockets, 1784-1860; 4 volumes.
>>
>> Trial, Appearance and Reference Dockets, 1774-1787; 2 volumes.
>>
>> Trial Dockets, 1788-1868; 11 volumes.
>
> Superior Court
>> Minutes, 1806-1818, 1831-1913; 24 volumes.
>>
>> Equity Minutes, 1830-1868; 3 volumes.
>>
>> Equity Enrolling Docket, 1845-1867; 1 volume.
>>
>> Equity Execution Docket, 1862-1868; 1 volume.
>>
>> Equity Trial Dockets, 1840-1868; 2 volumes.
>>
>> Equity Costs Docket, 1827-1855; 1 volume.
>>
>> Appearance Docket, 1853-1869; 1 volume.
>>
>> Argument Docket, 1807-1816; 1 volume.
>>
>> Execution Dockets, 1818-1868; 6 volumes.
>>
>> State Dockets, 1816-1847; 3 volumes.
>>
>> Trial Docket, 1830-1846; 1 volume.
>>
>> Civil Action Papers, 1759-1914; 4 Fibredex boxes.
>>
>> Civil Action Papers Concerning Land, 1857-1945; 2 Fibredex boxes.
>>
>> Criminal Action Papers, 1772-1927; 3 Fibredex boxes.
>
> Circuit Criminal Court/Eastern District Criminal Court
>> Minutes, 1897-1901; 1 volume.

ELECTION RECORDS
>
> Record of Elections, 1900-1921; 2 volumes.
>
> Election Records, 1793-1925; 4 Fibredex boxes.

ESTATES RECORDS

Record of Estates, 1825-1868; 6 volumes.

Record of Accounts, 1868-1900; 3 volumes.

Administrators' Bonds, 1869-1906; 4 volumes.

Appointment of Administrators, Executors, Guardians and Masters, 1868-1906; 1 volume.

Division of Estates, 1818-1860; 1 volume.

Estates Records, 1758-1930; 79 Fibredex boxes.

Guardians' Records, 1795-1916; 10 Fibredex boxes.

Guardians' Accounts, 1830-1868; 3 volumes.

Guardians' Bonds, 1869-1906; 3 volumes.

Record of Settlements, 1869-1916; 2 volumes.

Clerk's Account Book, 1898-1908; 1 volume.

LAND RECORDS

Deeds, 1787-1956; 20 Fibredex boxes.

Deeds of Trust, 1837, 1852, 1903-1956; 1 Fibredex box.

Mortgage Deeds, 1894-1947; 1 Fibredex box.

Index to Deeds, 1752-1856; 2 volumes.

Miscellaneous Land Records, 1784-1955; 1 Fibredex box.

Chattel Mortgages, 1899-1901; 1 volume.

MARRIAGE, DIVORCE AND VITAL STATISTICS

Marriage Bonds, 1800-1868; 15 Fibredex boxes.

Marriage Licenses, 1868-1906; 1 Fibredex box.

Marriage Registers, 1851-1941; 8 volumes.

Disinterment/Reinterment Permits, 1953-1981; 1 Fibredex box.

MILITARY AND PENSION RECORDS

Record of Pensions, 1915-1926; 1 volume.

MISCELLANEOUS RECORDS

Alien Registration, 1927-1942; 1 volume.

Applications for Naturalization, 1894-1904; 1 volume.

Coroners' Inquests, 1791-1909; 1 Fibredex box.

County Trustee Accounts, 1845-1855; 1 volume.

Record of Claims Allowed, 1797-1836; 1 volume.

Orders and Decrees, 1869-1913; 9 volumes.

Account Book, Cumberland Agricultural Society, 1823-1825; 1 volume.

Miscellaneous Records, 1758-1965; 7 Fibredex boxes.

Records of Assignees, Receivers and Trustees, 1839-1926; 3 Fibredex boxes.

Record of Assignments, 1894-1912; 1 volume.

ROADS AND BRIDGES

Road Dockets, 1825-1855; 2 volumes.

TAX AND FISCAL RECORDS

Lists of Taxables, 1777-1884; 7 volumes.

Poll Tax Register, 1902-1904; 1 volume.

WILLS

Wills, 1757-1955; 37 Fibredex boxes.

Cross Index to Wills, 1796-1933; 1 volume.

MICROFILM RECORDS

BONDS
>Apprentice Bonds, 1873-1894; 1 reel.
>
>Bastardy Bonds, 1867-1883; 1 reel.

CENSUS RECORDS (County Copy)
>Census, 1840, 1850; 1 reel.

CORPORATIONS AND PARTNERSHIPS
>Record of Incorporations, 1898-1923; 1 reel.

COURT RECORDS
>County Court of Pleas and Quarter Sessions
>>Minutes, 1755-1868; 9 reels.
>
>Superior Court
>>Minutes, 1867-1947, 1952-1955; 15 reels.
>>
>>Equity Minutes, 1830-1868; 1 reel.

ELECTION RECORDS
>Record of Elections, 1906-1960; 1 reel.

ESTATES RECORDS
>Record of Estates, 1825-1868; 3 reels.
>
>Record of Division of Estates, 1808-1860; 1 reel.
>
>Accounts and Inventories, 1868-1962; 10 reels.
>
>Appointment of Administrators, Executors, Guardians and Trustees, 1956-1962; 3 reels.
>
>Index to Appointment of Administrators, Executors, Guardians and Trustees, 1849-1962; 1 reel.
>
>Record of Administrators, 1906-1956; 7 reels.
>
>Guardians' Accounts, 1820-1862; 2 reels.
>
>Record of Guardians, 1906-1956; 2 reels.
>
>Inheritance Tax Records, 1921-1962; 1 reel.
>
>Record of Estates not Exceeding $300, 1930-1956; 1 reel.
>
>Record of Settlements, 1869-1962; 5 reels.
>
>Index to Estates, 1949-1962; 1 reel.

LAND RECORDS
>Record of Deeds, 1754-1947; 176 reels.
>
>Index to Deeds, Grantor, 1754-1942; 7 reels.
>
>Index to Deeds, Grantee, 1754-1942; 7 reels.
>
>Record of Grants, 1897-1926; 1 reel.
>
>Index to Record of Grants, 1774-1927; 1 reel.
>
>Record of Surveys and Plats, 1904-1910; 1 reel.
>
>Plat Books, 1911-1950, 1957-1962; 2 reels.
>
>Index to Plats, 1905-1973; 1 reel.
>
>Land Sales by Trustees and Mortgagees, 1921-1962; 5 reels.
>
>Index to Land Sales by Trustees and Mortgagees, 1956-1962; 1 reel.

MARRIAGE, DIVORCE AND VITAL STATISTICS
       Marriage Bonds, 1803-1868; 5 reels.
       Marriage Bond Abstracts, 1808-1868; 1 reel.
       Marriage Licenses, 1868-1961; 19 reels.
       Marriage Registers, 1851-1962; 9 reels.
       Index to Births, 1913-1962; 4 reels.
       Index to Deaths, 1913-1962; 3 reels.

MILITARY AND PENSION RECORDS
       Record of Armed Forces Discharges, 1919-1973; 10 reels.
       Index to Armed Forces Discharges, 1919-1973; 1 reel.

MISCELLANEOUS RECORDS
       Orders and Decrees, 1869-1959; 10 reels.
       Index to Special Proceedings and Orders and Decrees, Plaintiff, 1869-1962;
           2 reels.
       Index to Special Proceedings and Orders and Decrees, Defendant, 1869-1962;
           2 reels.

OFFICIALS, COUNTY
       Minutes, Board of County Commissioners, 1868-1924; 2 reels.
       Index to Minutes, Board of County Commissioners, 1871-1940; 1 reel.

SCHOOL RECORDS
       Minutes, County Board of Education, 1885-1962; 1 reel.

TAX AND FISCAL RECORDS
       Lists of Taxables, 1771-1783, 1816-1823, 1837-1849, 1857-1884; 5 reels.
       Tax Levies on Land, 1833-1835; 1 reel.

WILLS
       Record of Wills, 1761-1962; 7 reels.
       Index to Wills, 1796-1962; 1 reel.

CURRITUCK COUNTY

Established by 1670 as a precinct of Albemarle County.
Many records of the county are missing; reason unknown.

ORIGINAL RECORDS

BONDS

    Apprentice Bonds, 1868-1884, 1888; 2 volumes.

    Bastardy Bonds, 1830-1879; 2 volumes.

COURT RECORDS

    County Court of Pleas and Quarter Sessions

        Minutes, 1799-1832, 1838-1868; 12 volumes.

        Execution Dockets, 1821-1868; 5 volumes.

        State Dockets, 1807-1868; 2 volumes.

        Trial, Appearance and Reference Dockets, 1806-1861; 5 volumes.

    Superior Court

        Minutes, 1851-1862, 1866-1907; 4 volumes.

        Equity Minutes, 1808-1868; 2 volumes.

        Equity Execution and Costs Docket, and Receipts in Equity, 1841-1857; 1 volume.

        Execution Docket, 1847-1862, 1866-1875; 1 volume.

        State Docket, 1856-1861, 1866-1869; 1 volume.

        Trial and Appearance Docket, 1856-1861, 1866-1868; 1 volume.

        Civil Action Papers, 1781, 1840-1923; 1 Fibredex box.

        Civil Action Papers Concerning Land, 1858-1915; 1 Fibredex box.

        Criminal Action Papers, 1858-1902; 1 Fibredex box.

ELECTION RECORDS

    Record of Elections, 1878-1916; 2 volumes.

ESTATES RECORDS

    Accounts of Sale, 1830-1918; 5 volumes.

    Record of Accounts, 1869-1905; 2 volumes.

    Administrators' Bonds, 1827-1927; 7 volumes.

    Appointment of Administrators, Executors, Guardians and Masters, 1868-1919; 1 volume.

    Record of Dowers and Widows' Year's Support, 1869-1918; 1 volume.

    Estates Records, 1812-1926; 14 Fibredex boxes.

    Guardians' Records, 1841-1928; 4 Fibredex boxes.

    Guardians' Accounts, 1830-1870; 5 volumes.

    Guardians' Bonds, 1827-1927; 7 volumes.

    Inventories of Estates, 1830-1906; 2 volumes.

    Record of Settlements, 1830-1899; 3 volumes.

    Miscellaneous Estates Records, 1772-1827; 1 volume.

LAND RECORDS

    Land Divisions, 1877-1911; 1 Fibredex box.

Miscellaneous Land Records, 1808-1899; 1 Fibredex box.

MARRIAGE, DIVORCE AND VITAL STATISTICS

Marriage Bonds, 1858-1867; 1 Fibredex box.

MISCELLANEOUS RECORDS

Alien Registration, 1940; 1 volume.

County Accounts, 1840-1874; 1 volume.

Account Book, Wardens of the Poor, 1803-1868; 1 volume.

Miscellaneous Records, 1787-1914; 1 Fibredex box.

TAX AND FISCAL RECORDS

Oyster Tax Receipts, 1895-1899; 1 volume.

WILLS

Wills, 1841-1924; 4 Fibredex boxes.

MICROFILM RECORDS

BONDS

Apprentice Bonds, 1844, 1868-1883; 1 reel.

Bastardy Bonds, 1830-1833, 1872-1879; 1 reel.

CORPORATIONS AND PARTNERSHIPS

Record of Incorporations and Partnerships, 1868-1966; 1 reel.

COURT RECORDS

County Court of Pleas and Quarter Sessions

Minutes, 1799-1832, 1838-1868; 4 reels.

Superior Court

Minutes, 1872-1966; 6 reels.

Equity Minutes, 1808-1847, 1850-1868; 1 reel.

Index to Judgments, 1867-1966; 3 reels.

ELECTION RECORDS

Minutes, Board of Elections, 1896-1916; 1 reel.

Record of Elections, 1880-1968; 1 reel.

ESTATES RECORDS

Accounts of Sale, 1830-1918; 3 reels.

Record of Accounts, 1861-1966; 3 reels.

Administrators' Bonds, 1827-1847, 1856-1927; 2 reels.

Record of Administrators, 1795-1820, 1830-1841, 1930-1945; 2 reels.

Appointment of Executors, 1868-1919; 1 reel.

Appointment of Administrators, Executors and Guardians, 1907-1953; 1 reel.

Record of Executors and Guardians, 1953-1966; 1 reel.

Guardians' Accounts, 1830-1870; 2 reels.

Guardians' Bonds, 1827-1834, 1840-1927; 3 reels.

Inheritance Tax Records, 1923-1967; 1 reel.

Record of Inventories, 1830-1967; 2 reels.

Record of Settlements, 1841-1966; 3 reels.

Cross Index to Administrators and Executors, 1907-1938; 1 reel.

LAND RECORDS
    Record of Deeds, 1739-1965; 61 reels.
    Index to Deeds, 1761-1929; 2 reels.
    Index to Real Estate Conveyances, Grantor, 1928-1977; 2 reels.
    Index to Real Estate Conveyances, Grantee, 1928-1977; 2 reels.
    Land Entries, 1872-1955; 2 reels.
MARRIAGE, DIVORCE AND VITAL STATISTICS
    Marriage Registers, 1868-1983; 4 reels.
    Cross Index to Marriage Registers, 1852-1972; 1 reel.
    Cohabitation Certificates, 1866; 1 reel.
    Index to Vital Statistics, 1914-1983; 1 reel.
MILITARY AND PENSION RECORDS
    Record of Armed Forces Discharges, 1942-1983; 1 reel.
MISCELLANEOUS RECORDS
    Alien Registration, 1940; 1 reel.
    Accounts of the Clerk, Treasurer and Sheriff, 1840-1974; 1 reel.
    Clerk's Minute Docket, 1868-1899; 1 reel.
    Orders and Decrees, 1868-1966; 3 reels.
    Special Proceedings, 1879-1918; 1 reel.
    Record of Wardens of the Poor, 1803-1862; 1 reel.
OFFICIALS, COUNTY
    Minutes, Board of County Commissioners, 1868-1951; 2 reels.
SCHOOL RECORDS
    Minutes, County Board of Education, 1885-1895, 1915-1960; 1 reel.
TAX AND FISCAL RECORDS
    Tax Scrolls, 1915-1950; 3 reels.
WILLS
    Record of Wills, 1761-1960; 3 reels.
    Index to Wills, 1761-1966; 2 reels.

DARE COUNTY

Established in 1870 from Currituck, Hyde and Tyrrell counties.

ORIGINAL RECORDS

BONDS

> Bastardy Bonds and Records, 1869-1957; 1 volume, 1 Fibredex box.
> Officials' Bonds and Records, 1871-1917; 1 Fibredex box.

COURT RECORDS

> Superior Court
>> Minutes, 1870-1924; 3 volumes.
>> Civil Action Papers, 1869-1966; 14 Fibredex boxes.
>> Civil Action Papers Concerning Land, 1874-1968; 16 Fibredex boxes.
>> Criminal Action Papers, 1870-1965; 13 Fibredex boxes.

ELECTION RECORDS

> Record of Elections, 1878-1926; 2 volumes.
> Election Records, 1878-1955; 3 Fibredex boxes.

ESTATES RECORDS

> Record of Accounts, 1870-1927; 2 volumes.
> Administrators' Bonds, 1904-1936; 1 volume.
> Record of Dowers, Widows' Year's Support and Land Partitions, 1869-1915;
>> 1 volume.
> Estates Records, 1832-1964; 8 Fibredex boxes.
> Guardians' Records, 1866-1959; 1 Fibredex box.
> Record of Settlements, 1867-1926; 1 volume.

LAND RECORDS

> Attachments, Executions, Levies and Liens on Land, 1874-1965;
>> 1 Fibredex box.
> Tax Levies on Land, 1872-1949; 1 Fibredex box.
> Miscellaneous Land Records, 1804-1962; 1 Fibredex box.

MARRIAGE, DIVORCE AND VITAL STATISTICS

> Marriage Registers, 1870-1903; 2 volumes.
> Divorce Records, 1882-1969; 9 Fibredex boxes.

MISCELLANEOUS RECORDS

> Fishing and Shipping Records, 1868-1915; 1 Fibredex box.
> Grand Jury Reports, 1870-1966; 1 Fibredex box.
> Miscellaneous Records, 1821-1966; 4 Fibredex boxes.
> Records of Assignees, Receivers and Trustees, 1875-1961; 2 Fibredex boxes.

TAX AND FISCAL RECORDS

> Miscellaneous Tax Records, 1873-1942; 2 Fibredex boxes.

WILLS

> Wills, 1872-1959; 2 Fibredex boxes.

MICROFILM RECORDS

CORPORATIONS AND PARTNERSHIPS

Record of Incorporations, 1906-1967; 3 reels.

COURT RECORDS

Superior Court

Minutes, 1870-1956; 3 reels.

Index to Minutes, Plaintiff, 1870-1967; 1 reel.

Index to Minutes, Defendant, 1870-1967; 1 reel.

ELECTION RECORDS

Record of Elections, 1878-1948; 1 reel.

ESTATES RECORDS

Record of Accounts, 1870-1967; 4 reels.

Administrators' Bonds, 1936-1967; 1 reel.

Appointment of Administrators, Executors and Guardians, 1906-1967; 3 reels.

Cross Index to Administrators, Executors and Guardians, 1870-1966; 2 reels.

Guardians' Bonds, 1904-1932, 1937-1967; 1 reel.

Cross Index to Guardians, 1870-1940; 1 reel.

Inheritance Tax Records, 1923-1967; 1 reel.

LAND RECORDS

Record of Deeds, 1871-1958; 54 reels.

Index to Real Estate Conveyances, Grantor, 1870-1965; 3 reels.

Index to Real Estate Conveyances, Grantee, 1870-1966; 3 reels.

Entry Takers' Books, 1870-1959; 2 reels.

Record of Surveys, 1905-1923; 1 reel.

Registration of Land Titles, 1924-1964; 1 reel.

MARRIAGE, DIVORCE AND VITAL STATISTICS

Marriage Registers, 1870-1967; 1 reel.

Maiden Names of Divorced Women, 1943-1967; 1 reel.

MILITARY AND PENSION RECORDS

Record of Armed Forces Discharges, 1918-1986; 2 reels.

MISCELLANEOUS RECORDS

Orders and Decrees, 1871-1966; 2 reels.

Special Proceedings, 1906-1960; 2 reels.

OFFICIALS, COUNTY

Minutes, Board of County Commissioners, 1870-1954; 4 reels.

SCHOOL RECORDS

Minutes, County Board of Education, 1896-1963; 1 reel.

TAX AND FISCAL RECORDS

Tax Lists, 1915, 1925, 1935, 1945; 2 reels.

Tax Scrolls, 1881-1905; 1 reel.

WILLS

Record of Wills, 1870-1966; 3 reels.

Index to Wills, 1870-1968; 2 reels.

DAVIDSON COUNTY

Established in 1822 from Rowan County.
Courthouse fire in 1866 may have destroyed some records.

ORIGINAL RECORDS

BONDS
> Apprentice Bonds and Records, 1824-1919; 2 volumes, 1 Fibredex box.
> Bastardy Bonds and Records, 1823-1935; 9 Fibredex boxes.
> Officials' Bonds and Records, 1827-1930; 3 Fibredex boxes.

CENSUS RECORDS (County Copy)
> Census, 1880; 1 pamphlet.

COURT RECORDS
> County Court of Pleas and Quarter Sessions
>> Minutes, 1823-1868; 7 volumes.
>> Appearance Dockets, 1823-1868; 2 volumes.
>> Execution Dockets, 1823-1868; 8 volumes.
>> Recognizance Dockets, 1827-1861; 2 volumes.
>> State Dockets, 1823-1868; 3 volumes.
>> Trial Dockets, 1823-1868; 4 volumes.
>
> Superior Court
>> Minutes, 1824-1910; 15 volumes.
>> Equity Minutes, 1824-1856; 2 volumes.
>> Equity Execution Docket, 1824-1868; 1 volume.
>> Equity Trial and Appearance Dockets, 1824-1868; 2 volumes.
>> Appearance Docket, 1824-1868; 1 volume.
>> Execution Dockets, 1824-1861; 2 volumes.
>> Recognizance Dockets, 1824-1867; 2 volumes.
>> State Dockets, 1824-1868; 2 volumes.
>> Trial Dockets, 1824-1868; 2 volumes.
>> Civil Action Papers, 1821-1946; 65 Fibredex boxes.
>> Civil Action Papers Concerning Land, 1820-1946; 42 Fibredex boxes.
>> Criminal Action Papers, 1822-1940; 33 Fibredex boxes.
>
> Thomasville Recorders Court
>> Minutes, 1941-1969; 2 volumes.
>> Judgment Dockets, 1941-1970; 3 volumes.

ELECTION RECORDS
> Record of Elections, 1878-1926; 2 volumes.
> Election Returns, 1823-1888; 3 Fibredex boxes.
> Miscellaneous Election Records, 1833-1928; 2 Fibredex boxes.
> Division of Lexington, Thomasville and Conrad Hill Townships into Voting
>> Precincts, 1896; 1 volume.

ESTATES RECORDS

     Record of Estates, 1830-1868; 9 volumes.

     Record of Accounts, 1868-1910; 7 volumes.

     Administrators' Bonds, 1868-1916; 7 volumes.

     Appointment of Administrators, Executors, Guardians and Masters, 1868-1910; 1 volume.

     Record of Widows' Year's Support, 1900-1970; 4 volumes.

     Record of Dowers, 1915-1952; 1 volume.

     Estates Records, 1817-1948; 249 Fibredex boxes.

     Guardians' Records, 1823-1941; 34 Fibredex boxes.

     Guardians' Accounts, 1830-1868; 3 volumes.

     Guardians' Bonds, 1870-1909; 5 volumes.

     Record of Notice to Guardians to Renew Bonds, 1877-1895; 1 volume.

     Record of Settlements, 1869-1897; 3 volumes.

     Record of Executors of Persons Who Died Prior to 1916, 1915-1916; 1 pamphlet.

LAND RECORDS

     Deeds, 1808-1922; 2 Fibredex boxes.

     Cross Index to Deeds, 1826-1902; 5 volumes.

     Ejectments, 1822-1935; 4 Fibredex boxes.

     Land Entries, 1874-1916; 2 volumes.

     Levies on Land, 1831-1938; 6 Fibredex boxes.

     Processions and Surveys, 1827-1941; 2 Fibredex boxes.

     Miscellaneous Land Records, 1817-1937; 1 Fibredex box.

MARRIAGE, DIVORCE AND VITAL STATISTICS

     Marriage Bonds, 1823-1868; 8 Fibredex boxes.

     Marriage Licenses, 1869-1893; 1 manuscript box.

     Marriage Registers, 1851-1921; 9 volumes.

     Divorce Records, 1831-1944; 30 Fibredex boxes.

MISCELLANEOUS RECORDS

     Alien Registration, 1927, 1940; 1 volume.

     County Accounts, 1868, 1876-1882; 2 volumes.

     County Claims, 1823-1867; 2 volumes.

     Treasurers' Accounts, 1876-1882; 1 volume.

     Treasurer's Reports, 1879-1914; 1 volume.

     Homestead and Personal Property Exemptions, 1869-1944; 2 volumes.

     Insolvent Debtors, 1831-1933; 3 Fibredex boxes.

     List of Jurors, 1875-1906; 1 volume.

     Registry of Licenses to Trades, 1871-1878; 1 volume.

     Certificates of Registration, 1887-1970; 1 manuscript box.

     Certificates of Registration for Optometrists, 1909-1916; 1 volume.

     Orders and Decrees, 1869-1908; 4 volumes.

     Special Proceedings, 1871-1916; 1 volume.

     Mining Records, 1835-1931; 8 Fibredex boxes.

     Records of Slaves and Free Persons of Color, 1826-1896; 1 Fibredex box.

Miscellaneous Records, 1824-1946; 11 Fibredex boxes.
Records of Assignees, Receivers and Trustees, 1846-1943; 13 Fibredex boxes.

ROADS AND BRIDGES
Bridges and Ferries, 1824-1929; 1 Fibredex box.
Road Orders, 1833-1865; 1 volume.
Road Records, 1823-1939; 5 Fibredex boxes.
Railroad Records, 1847-1941; 10 Fibredex boxes.

SCHOOL RECORDS
School Records, 1855-1934; 2 Fibredex boxes.

TAX AND FISCAL RECORDS
Tax Lists, 1827-1863; 5 volumes, 1 manuscript box.

WILLS
Wills, 1823-1940; 13 Fibredex boxes.
Cross Index to Wills, 1919-1947; 1 volume.

MICROFILM RECORDS

BONDS
Apprentice Bonds, 1870-1919; 1 reel.

CORPORATIONS AND PARTNERSHIPS
Record of Incorporations, 1884-1957; 5 reels.
Index to Incorporations, 1884-1966; 1 reel.
Record of Partnerships, 1913-1958; 1 reel.

COURT RECORDS
County Court of Pleas and Quarter Sessions
    Minutes, 1823-1868; 4 reels.
Superior Court
    Minutes, 1824-1955; 14 reels.

ELECTION RECORDS
Record of Elections, 1878-1966; 1 reel.

ESTATES RECORDS
Record of Accounts, 1868-1961; 12 reels.
Administrators' Bonds, 1868-1916; 1 reel.
Appointment of Administrators, Executors and Guardians, 1868-1912; 2 reels.
Record of Administrators, 1910-1955; 7 reels.
Record of Executors, 1918-1966; 2 reels.
Guardians' Bonds, 1870-1909; 1 reel.
Record of Guardians, 1918-1967; 3 reels.
Record of Dowry, 1915-1952; 1 reel.
Record of Widows' Year's Support, 1900-1967; 2 reels.
Inheritance Tax Records, 1923-1956; 1 reel.
Inventories and Accounts of Sale, 1830-1897; 5 reels.
Record of Settlements, 1904-1960; 12 reels.
Cross Index to Administrators and Executors, 1868-1966; 1 reel.
Cross Index to Guardians, 1900-1970; 1 reel.

LAND RECORDS

Record of Deeds, 1822-1953; 124 reels.

Index to Real Estate Conveyances, Grantor, 1823-1953; 16 reels.

Index to Real Estate Conveyances, Grantee, 1823-1953; 18 reels.

Division of Land, 1835-1966; 3 reels.

Registration of Land Titles, 1914-1943; 1 reel.

MARRIAGE, DIVORCE AND VITAL STATISTICS

Marriage Registers, 1822-1954; 3 reels.

Maiden Names of Divorced Women, 1937-1966; 1 reel.

Index to Vital Statistics, 1914-1980; 4 reels.

Index to Delayed Births, various years; 1 reel.

MILITARY AND PENSION RECORDS

Record of Armed Forces Discharges, 1919-1969; 11 reels.

Index to Armed Forces Discharges, 1919-1967; 1 reel.

MISCELLANEOUS RECORDS

Homestead Returns, 1878-1944; 1 reel.

Orders and Decrees, 1869-1959; 16 reels.

Special Proceedings, 1871-1928; 2 reels.

Cross Index to Special Proceedings, 1886-1936; 1 reel.

OFFICIALS, COUNTY

Minutes, Board of County Commissioners, 1868-1951; 6 reels.

SCHOOL RECORDS

Minutes, Board of Superintendents of Common Schools, 1843-1864; 1 reel.

Minutes, County Board of Education, 1885-1906, 1931-1963; 1 reel.

TAX AND FISCAL RECORDS

Tax Lists, 1827-1863; 2 reels.

WILLS

Record of Wills, 1823-1967; 12 reels.

Cross Index to Wills, 1823-1955; 1 reel.

Index to Wills, Devisor, 1956-1966; 1 reel.

Index to Wills, Devisee, 1956-1966; 1 reel.

Ferry crossing the Yadkin River, between Lexington and Mocksville, circa 1900. Photograph from the files of the State Archives.

DAVIE COUNTY

Established in 1836 from Rowan County.

ORIGINAL RECORDS

BONDS
Apprentice Bonds and Records, 1829-1925; 1 volume, 2 Fibredex boxes.
Bastardy Bonds and Records, 1837-1897; 2 Fibredex boxes.
Officials' Bonds and Records, 1830-1908; 3 Fibredex boxes.

COURT RECORDS
County Court of Pleas and Quarter Sessions
Appearance Dockets, 1837-1868; 2 volumes.
Execution Dockets, 1837-1859; 2 volumes.
Levy Docket, 1843-1868; 1 volume.
State Docket, 1847-1868; 1 volume.
Trial Dockets, 1837-1853; 2 volumes.

Superior Court
Minutes, 1837-1905; 8 volumes, 1 manuscript box.
Equity Minutes, 1837-1868; 1 volume.
Equity Enrolling Docket, 1837-1839, 1858; 1 volume.
Equity Trial and Appearance Docket, 1837-1867; 1 volume.
Civil Action Papers, 1829-1913; 23 Fibredex boxes.
Civil Action Papers Concerning Land, 1869-1913; 9 Fibredex boxes.
Criminal Action Papers, 1837-1905; 12 Fibredex boxes.

Inferior Court
Minutes, 1877-1883; 1 volume.

ELECTION RECORDS
Record of Elections, 1878-1928; 5 volumes.
Election Records, 1838-1898; 4 Fibredex boxes.

ESTATES RECORDS
Record of Estates, 1855-1868; 1 volume.
Record of Accounts, 1868-1895; 2 volumes.
Appointment of Administrators, Executors, Guardians and Masters, 1868-1917; 1 volume.
Estates Records, 1809-1936; 77 Fibredex boxes.
Guardians' Records, 1834-1918; 9 Fibredex boxes.
Guardians' Accounts, 1846-1868; 1 volume.
Record of Settlements, 1840-1904, 1923; 3 volumes.

LAND RECORDS
Record of Probate, 1891-1894; 1 volume.
Processioners' Records, 1840-1884; 1 volume.
Miscellaneous Land Records, 1792-1914; 2 Fibredex boxes.

MARRIAGE, DIVORCE AND VITAL STATISTICS

Divorce Records, 1849-1908; 3 Fibredex boxes.

MISCELLANEOUS RECORDS

Homestead and Personal Property Exemptions, 1869-1899; 3 Fibredex boxes.

Insolvent Debtors, 1837-1890; 1 Fibredex box.

Orders and Decrees, 1868-1883; 1 volume.

Special Proceedings, 1883-1906; 2 volumes.

Miscellaneous Records, 1813-1927; 8 Fibredex boxes.

Records of Assignees, Receivers and Trustees, 1872-1897; 1 Fibredex box.

ROADS AND BRIDGES

Bridge, Ferry and Road Records, 1837-1909; 3 Fibredex boxes.

Railroad Records, 1878-1910; 1 Fibredex box.

SCHOOL RECORDS

Minutes, Board of Superintendents of Common Schools, 1841-1864; 1 volume.

School Records, 1839-1908; 3 Fibredex boxes.

TAX AND FISCAL RECORDS

Tax Records, 1838-1905; 3 Fibredex boxes.

WILLS

Wills, 1808-1902; 2 Fibredex boxes.

MICROFILM RECORDS

BONDS

Apprentice Bonds, 1889-1925; 1 reel.

CORPORATIONS AND PARTNERSHIPS

Record of Incorporations, 1891-1962; 1 reel.

Record of Partnerships, 1913-1967; 1 reel.

COURT RECORDS

County Court of Pleas and Quarter Sessions
Minutes, 1837-1868; 2 reels.

Superior Court
Minutes, 1837-1948; 5 reels.

Equity Minutes, 1837-1868; 1 reel.

ELECTION RECORDS

Record of Elections, 1880-1967; 1 reel.

ESTATES RECORDS

Accounts of Sale, 1846-1854; 1 reel.

Record of Accounts, 1868-1967; 5 reels.

Record of Administrators, Executors and Guardians, 1912-1931; 1 reel.

Record of Administrators, 1920-1967; 2 reels.

Record of Executors, 1868-1916, 1925-1964; 1 reel.

Record of Guardians, 1925-1967; 1 reel.

Guardians' Settlements, 1846-1868; 1 reel.

Accounts of Indigent Orphans, 1917-1967; 1 reel.

Record of Widows' Year's Support, 1955-1966; 1 reel.

Inheritance Tax Records, 1923-1957; 1 reel.

Record of Settlements, 1846-1967; 5 reels.

Index to Administrators and Estates, 1837-1967; 1 reel.

General Index to Administrators, 1837-1967; 1 reel.

Cross Index to Administrators and Executors, 1869-1937; 1 reel.

Index to Guardians and Wards, 1868-1935; 1 reel.

LAND RECORDS

Record of Deeds, 1837-1953; 27 reels.

Index to Real Estate Conveyances, Grantor, 1837-1967; 4 reels.

Index to Real Estate Conveyances, Grantee, 1837-1967; 4 reels.

Land Entries, 1837-1910; 1 reel.

Record of Resale, 1920-1967; 1 reel.

MARRIAGE, DIVORCE AND VITAL STATISTICS

Marriage Bonds, 1836-1868; 2 reels.

Marriage Registers, 1867-1959; 3 reels.

Cohabitation Record, 1866-1867; 1 reel.

Maiden Names of Divorced Women, 1940-1966; 1 reel.

Index to Births, 1912-1961; 1 reel.

Index to Deaths, 1913-1966; 1 reel.

Index to Delayed Births, various years; 1 reel.

MILITARY AND PENSION RECORDS

Record of Armed Forces Discharges, 1912-1981; 4 reels.

Index to Armed Forces Discharges, 1913-1980; 1 reel.

MISCELLANEOUS RECORDS

Special Proceedings, 1883-1946; 4 reels.

Index to Special Proceedings, Plaintiff, 1883-1967; 1 reel.

Index to Special Proceedings, Defendant, 1883-1967; 1 reel.

Minutes, Wardens of the Poor, 1839-1854; 1 reel.

OFFICIALS, COUNTY

Minutes, Board of County Commissioners, 1868-1967; 2 reels.

SCHOOL RECORDS

Minutes, Board of Superintendents of Common Schools, 1841-1864; 1 reel.

Minutes, County Board of Education, 1885-1967; 1 reel.

TAX AND FISCAL RECORDS

Tax Lists, 1843-1860, 1866-1872; 4 reels.

Tax Scrolls, 1869-1900, 1905, 1915; 8 reels.

Schedule B Taxes, 1883-1903; 1 reel.

WILLS

Record of Wills, 1837-1967; 2 reels.

Index to Wills, 1837-1967; 2 reels.

DOBBS COUNTY

Established in 1758 (effective 1759) from Johnston County.
Divided into Glasgow and Lenoir counties in 1791.
Land records destroyed by fire at Lenoir County courthouse in 1880.

ORIGINAL RECORDS

LAND RECORDS
Index to Deeds, no date; 4 volumes.
MISCELLANEOUS RECORDS
Miscellaneous Records, 1762-1792; 1 manuscript box.

MICROFILM RECORDS

LAND RECORDS
(includes records of Johnston County, 1746-1759, and Lenoir County, 1792-1880)
Index to Deeds, Grantor, 1746-1880; 1 reel.
Index to Deeds, Grantee, 1746-1880; 1 reel.

DUPLIN COUNTY

Established in 1750 from New Hanover County.
Many court records are missing; reason unknown.

ORIGINAL RECORDS

BONDS

Apprentice Bonds, 1871-1916; 1 volume.

Apprentice Bonds and Records, 1801-1908; Bastardy Bonds and Records, 1868-1921; 1 Fibredex box.

Officials' Bonds and Records, 1779-1936; 2 Fibredex boxes.

COURT RECORDS

County Court of Pleas and Quarter Sessions

Minutes, 1784-1868; 20 volumes.

Appearance Dockets, 1847-1868; 2 volumes.

Execution Dockets, 1847-1868; 5 volumes.

State Docket, 1847-1868; 1 volume.

Trial Dockets, 1847-1868; 3 volumes.

Prosecution Bonds, 1866-1868; 1 volume.

Superior Court

Minutes, 1815-1908; 10 volumes.

Equity Minutes, 1824-1868; 2 volumes.

Equity Trial Docket, 1824-1868; 1 volume.

Trial Docket, 1851-1867; 1 volume.

Civil Action Papers, 1799-1935; 7 Fibredex boxes.

Civil Action Papers Concerning Land, 1868-1946; 25 Fibredex boxes.

Criminal Action Papers, 1871-1927; 6 Fibredex boxes.

Inferior Court

Minutes, 1881-1885; 1 volume.

ELECTION RECORDS

Record of Elections, 1878-1932; 4 volumes.

ESTATES RECORDS

Record of Estates, 1830-1876; 6 volumes.

Administrators' Bonds, 1846-1871, 1885-1923; 7 volumes.

Estates Records, 1752-1930; 100 Fibredex boxes.

Guardians' Records, 1787-1943; 12 Fibredex boxes.

Guardians' Accounts, 1854-1882; 2 volumes.

Guardians' Bonds, 1846-1856, 1871-1919; 3 volumes.

Record of Probate (Estates), 1868-1878; 1 volume.

LAND RECORDS

Attachments, Executions, Levies and Liens on Land, 1804-1950; 3 Fibredex boxes.

Land Divisions, Partitions and Sales, 1796-1936; 2 Fibredex boxes.

Land Sales for Taxes, 1933; 1 volume.

Meridian Record, 1902-1932; 1 volume.

Miscellaneous Land Records, 1776-1935; 2 Fibredex boxes.

Processioners' Record, 1859-1877; 1 volume.

MARRIAGE, DIVORCE AND VITAL STATISTICS

Marriage Bonds, 1755-1869; 5 Fibredex boxes.

Marriage Registers, 1867-1928; 4 volumes.

Divorce Records, 1869-1952; 4 Fibredex boxes.

MISCELLANEOUS RECORDS

Alien Registration, 1940; 1 volume.

Record of Officials' Reports, 1868-1893; 1 volume.

Homestead and Personal Property Exemptions, 1869-1942; 2 Fibredex boxes.

St. Gabriel's Parish Wardens' Records, 1799-1817; 1 volume.

Timber Records, 1903-1918; 2 Fibredex boxes.

Miscellaneous Records, 1754-1947; 4 Fibredex boxes.

Records of Assignees, Receivers and Trustees, 1822-1930; 2 Fibredex boxes.

OFFICIALS, COUNTY

Minutes, Board of County Commissioners, 1878-1906; 4 volumes.

ROADS AND BRIDGES

Railroad Records, 1877-1922; 6 Fibredex boxes.

SCHOOL RECORDS

School Records, 1861-1921; 1 Fibredex box.

TAX AND FISCAL RECORDS

Lists of Taxables, 1783-1838; 2 volumes, 1 manuscript box.

Tax Returns, 1895-1925; 2 volumes.

WILLS

Wills, 1759-1913; 12 Fibredex boxes.

MICROFILM RECORDS

BONDS

Apprentice Bonds, 1871-1916; 1 reel.

COURT RECORDS

County Court of Pleas and Quarter Sessions

Minutes, 1784-1868; 5 reels.

Superior Court

Minutes, 1815-1930; 8 reels.

Equity Minutes, 1824-1868; 1 reel.

ELECTION RECORDS

Record of Elections, 1880-1952; 1 reel.

ESTATES RECORDS

Record of Estates, 1830-1874; 2 reels.

Record of Accounts, 1869-1962; 6 reels.

Administrators' Bonds, 1846-1923; 1 reel.

Record of Administrators, 1918-1962; 4 reels.

Guardians' Bonds, 1846-1918; 1 reel.

Guardians' Accounts, 1854-1882; 1 reel.

Record of Guardians, 1918-1962; 1 reel.

Record and Index of Commissioners to Divide Real Estate, 1800-1960; 3 reels.

Inheritance Tax Records, 1919-1962; 1 reel.

Inventories and Accounts of Estates, 1754-1800; 3 reels.

Record of Settlements, 1869-1961; 3 reels.

LAND RECORDS

Record of Deeds, 1784-1935; 91 reels.

Index to Real Estate Conveyances, Grantor, 1784-1940; 3 reels.

Index to Real Estate Conveyances, Grantee, 1784-1940; 3 reels.

Land Entries, 1896-1941; 1 reel.

Divisions of Land, 1800-1860; 1 reel.

Processioners' Records, 1859-1877; 1 reel.

Plat Books, 1784-1962; 1 reel.

Index to Plat Books, 1784-1962; 1 reel.

Registration of Land Titles, 1929-1967; 1 reel.

Record of Mortgage Resales, 1922-1933; 1 reel.

MARRIAGE, DIVORCE AND VITAL STATISTICS

Marriage Licenses, 1893-1961; 9 reels.

Record of Marriages, 1866-1868; 1 reel.

Marriage Registers, 1867-1938; 1 reel.

Record of Cohabitation, 1866; 1 reel.

Maiden Names of Divorced Women, 1944-1969; 1 reel.

Index to Births, 1913-1981; 3 reels.

Index to Deaths, 1913-1981; 2 reels.

Index to Delayed Births, 1913-1981; 1 reel.

MILITARY AND PENSION RECORDS

Record of Armed Forces Discharges, 1918-1976; 3 reels.

Index to Armed Forces Discharges, 1918-1981; 1 reel.

MISCELLANEOUS RECORDS

Orders and Decrees, 1872-1948, 1952-1968; 13 reels.

Special Proceedings, 1872-1962; 3 reels.

Cross Index to Special Proceedings, 1872-1926; 1 reel.

Record of Home Demonstration Club, Calypso, 1952-1962; 1 reel.

Miscellaneous Historical Essays: County and People, no date; 1 reel.

OFFICIALS, COUNTY

Minutes, Board of County Commissioners, 1878-1932; 4 reels.

Minutes, County Board of Social Services, 1946-1962; 1 reel.

SCHOOL RECORDS

Minutes, County Board of Education, 1872-1935; 1 reel.

TAX AND FISCAL RECORDS

Tax Lists, 1786-1838, 1895-1925; 2 reels.

WILLS

Record of Wills, 1760-1968; 7 reels.

Cross Index to Wills, 1760-1970; 2 reels.

DURHAM COUNTY

Established in 1881 from Orange and Wake counties.

ORIGINAL RECORDS

BONDS

Apprentice Bonds, 1882-1913; 1 volume.

COURT RECORDS

Superior Court

Minutes, 1887-1924; 17 volumes.

Civil Action Papers, 1879-1926; 2 Fibredex boxes.

Criminal Action Papers, 1882-1936; 4 Fibredex boxes.

ELECTION RECORDS

Record of Elections, 1881-1904; 1 volume.

Election Returns and Vote Abstracts, 1896-1936; 3 Fibredex boxes.

ESTATES RECORDS

Record of Accounts, 1881-1946; 10 volumes.

Administrators' Bonds, 1891-1896; 1 volume.

Appointment of Administrators, Executors and Guardians, 1881-1892;
1 volume.

Record of Widows' Dowers and Year's Support, 1881-1944; 1 volume.

Estates Records, 1875-1926; 1 Fibredex box.

Guardians' Accounts, 1881-1909, 1921-1950; 7 volumes.

Guardians' Bonds, 1881-1898; 2 volumes.

Record of Guardians, 1898-1912; 1 volume.

Record of Amounts Paid for Indigent Children, 1915-1916; 1 pamphlet.

Record of Settlements, 1882-1939; 9 volumes.

Index to Administrators and Executors, 1881-1890; 1 volume.

MISCELLANEOUS RECORDS

Alien Registration, 1927-1928, 1940-1941; 1 volume.

Alien, Naturalization and Citizenship Records, 1882-1904; 2 Fibredex boxes.

Petitions for Naturalization, 1909-1922, 1943-1944; 2 volumes.

Record of Officials' Reports, 1885-1917; 1 volume.

Record of Special Licenses Issued, 1908-1918; 4 volumes.

Registry of Licenses to Trades, 1881-1913; 1 volume.

Miscellaneous Records, 1825-1934; 1 Fibredex box.

OFFICIALS, COUNTY

Justices of the Peace Oaths, 1889-1900; 1 volume.

Minutes of the Board of Justices, 1881-1894; 1 volume.

WILLS

Cross Index to Wills, 1881-1915; 1 volume.

MICROFILM RECORDS

BONDS

Apprentice Bonds, 1882-1913; 1 reel.

CORPORATIONS AND PARTNERSHIPS

Record of Incorporations, 1905-1945; 2 reels.

Index to Incorporations, 1890-1957; 1 reel.

COURT RECORDS

Superior Court

Minutes, 1884-1959; 26 reels.

Index to Judgments, Plaintiff, 1929-1966; 2 reels.

Index to Judgments, Defendant, 1929-1966; 3 reels.

ELECTION RECORDS

Record of Elections, 1881-1904; 1 reel.

ESTATES RECORDS

Record of Accounts, 1881-1965; 16 reels.

Administrators' Bonds, 1891-1896; 1 reel.

Appointment of Administrators, Executors and Guardians, 1881-1892; 1 reel.

Record of Administrators, 1896-1966; 14 reels.

Guardians' Bonds, 1881-1898; 1 reel.

Guardians' Accounts, 1881-1966; 10 reels.

Record of Guardians, 1898-1964; 6 reels.

Record of Next Friend of Minors and Incompetents, 1935-1967; 1 reel.

Record of Widows' Dowers and Year's Support, 1881-1969; 2 reels.

Inheritance Tax Records, 1922-1966; 3 reels.

Record of Trustees Under Wills, 1941-1966; 1 reel.

Record of Trust Funds of Estates and Special Proceedings, 1920-1966; 4 reels.

Record of Settlements, 1882-1966; 14 reels.

General Index to Estates, 1881-1968; 3 reels.

Index to Administrators and Executors, 1881-1890; 1 reel.

Index to Beneficiaries, 1966-1968; 1 reel.

LAND RECORDS

Record of Deeds, 1881, 1883-1961; 168 reels.

Index to Deeds, Grantor, 1881-1961; 6 reels.

Index to Deeds, Grantee, 1881-1961; 6 reels.

Record of Sales of Trustees and Mortgagees, 1923-1967; 10 reels.

MARRIAGE, DIVORCE AND VITAL STATISTICS

Marriage Registers, 1881-1969; 3 reels.

Marriage Licenses, Colored, 1898-1968; 14 reels.

Marriage Licenses, White, 1898-1968; 22 reels.

Maiden Names of Divorced Women, 1937-1969; 1 reel.

MILITARY AND PENSION RECORDS

Record of Armed Forces Discharges, 1918-1987; 11 reels.

MISCELLANEOUS RECORDS

Record of Homesteads, 1882-1939; 1 reel.

Special Proceedings, 1892-1961; 18 reels.

Special Proceedings Dockets, 1881-1952; 3 reels.

Cross Index to Special Proceedings, 1883-1966; 1 reel.

OFFICIALS, COUNTY

Minutes, Board of County Commissioners, 1881-1950; 7 reels.

TAX AND FISCAL RECORDS

Tax Scrolls, 1882-1902, 1905, 1910, 1915, 1925, 1935, 1945; 14 reels.

WILLS

Record of Wills, 1881-1966; 8 reels.

Index to Wills, 1881-1968; 1 reel.

EDGECOMBE COUNTY

Established in 1741 from Bertie County.
Land records prior to 1759 are among those of Halifax County.

ORIGINAL RECORDS

BONDS

      Apprentice Bonds, 1875-1924; 2 volumes.

      Bastardy Bonds and Records, 1771-1909; 3 volumes, 1 Fibredex box.

COURT RECORDS

      County Court of Pleas and Quarter Sessions

            Minutes, 1744-1746, 1757-1868; 27 volumes.

            Execution Dockets, 1769-1856; 4 volumes, 1 manuscript box.

            State (and Crown) Dockets, 1755-1762, 1778-1868; 3 volumes,
                1 manuscript box.

            Reference (Trial) and Appearance Dockets, 1758-1790; 1 volume,
                2 manuscript boxes.

            Trial and Appearance Dockets, 1794-1868; 15 volumes, 1 pamphlet.

            Canal Docket, 1867-1868; 1 volume.

            Clerk's Docket, 1745-1746; 1 manuscript box.

            Clerk's Fee Books, 1753-1765; 2 volumes.

      Superior Court

            Minutes, 1807-1834, 1862-1910; 14 volumes.

            Equity Minutes, 1808-1868; 3 volumes.

            Equity Enrolling Docket, 1807-1814; 1 manuscript box.

            Equity Trial Dockets, 1847-1868; 2 volumes, 1 manuscript box.

            Receipts in Equity, 1866-1874; 1 volume.

            Execution Docket, 1807-1817; 1 manuscript box.

            State Dockets, 1807-1841; 1 volume, 1 manuscript box.

            Trial and Appearance Docket, 1807-1817; 1 volume.

            Civil Action Papers, 1756-1910; 116 Fibredex boxes.

            Civil Action Papers Concerning Land, 1791-1918; 13 Fibredex boxes.

            Criminal Action Papers, 1756-1910; 14 Fibredex boxes.

      Inferior Court

            Minutes, 1877-1895; 2 volumes.

      Circuit Criminal Court/Eastern District Criminal Court

            Minutes, 1895-1901; 1 volume.

ELECTION RECORDS

      Record of Elections, 1878-1942; 5 volumes.

ESTATES RECORDS

      Record of Estates, 1730-1896; 30 volumes.

      Administrators' Bonds, 1866-1907; 6 volumes.

      Appointment of Administrators, Executors, Guardians and Masters, 1868-
            1915; 2 volumes.

Estates Records, 1748-1917; 139 Fibredex boxes.

Guardians' Records, 1787-1917; 20 Fibredex boxes.

Guardians' Accounts, 1764-1778, 1820-1914; 11 volumes.

Guardians' Bonds, 1867-1916; 6 volumes.

Record of Settlements, 1869-1916; 4 volumes.

LAND RECORDS

Record of Deeds, 1732-1741; 4 volumes.

Land Entries, 1795-1853; 1 volume.

Miscellaneous Land Records, 1742-1913; 1 Fibredex box.

MARRIAGE, DIVORCE AND VITAL STATISTICS

Marriage Bonds, 1760-1868; 9 Fibredex boxes.

Cohabitation Certificates, 1866; 2 Fibredex boxes.

Divorce Records, 1835-1901; 3 Fibredex boxes.

MILITARY AND PENSION RECORDS

Pension Records, 1878-1927; 2 volumes.

MISCELLANEOUS RECORDS

Alien Registration, 1940; 1 volume.

Petitions for Naturalization, 1903-1920; 1 volume.

Record of Declaration of Intent (to Become a Citizen), 1907-1920; 1 volume.

County Claims, 1839-1855; 1 volume.

Minutes, Committee of Finance, 1852-1866; 1 volume.

Insolvents, 1788-1857; 1 Fibredex box.

Orders and Decrees, 1868-1922; 1 volume.

Minutes, Wardens of the Poor, 1859-1869; 1 volume.

Miscellaneous Records, 1769-1929; 4 Fibredex boxes.

Promissory Notes, 1753-1876; 1 Fibredex box.

Slave Records, 1780-1857, 1871; 1 Fibredex box.

Stock Marks, 1732-1809, 1835; 1 volume.

Records of Assignees, Receivers and Trustees, 1891-1922; 2 Fibredex boxes.

ROADS AND BRIDGES

Bridge and Mill Records, 1760-1891; 1 Fibredex box.

Canal and Drainage Records, 1821-1912; 1 Fibredex box.

Road Records, 1761-1897; 2 Fibredex boxes.

Railroad Records, 1837-1905; 3 Fibredex boxes.

SCHOOL RECORDS

Minutes, Board of Superintendents of Common Schools, 1846-1860;
1 volume.

Minutes, County Board of Education, 1883-1886; 1 volume.

TAX AND FISCAL RECORDS

Poll Tax Records, 1908, no date; 2 volumes.

Record of Federal Direct Taxes Collected, 1866; 1 volume.

WILLS

Wills, 1750-1945; 34 Fibredex boxes.

MICROFILM RECORDS

COURT RECORDS
County Court of Pleas and Quarter Sessions
Minutes, 1744-1746, 1757-1868; 10 reels.
Superior Court
Minutes, 1862-1924; 8 reels.

ELECTION RECORDS
Record of Elections, 1878-1960; 1 reel.

ESTATES RECORDS
Appointment of Administrators, Executors and Guardians, 1868-1949; 4 reels.
Record of Administrators, 1897-1961; 8 reels.
Record of Executors, 1936-1961; 1 reel.
Guardians' Bonds, 1908-1915; 1 reel.
Record of Payments to Indigent Children, 1900-1961; 1 reel.
Record of Widows' Year's Allowance, 1928-1961; 1 reel.
Inventories and Accounts of Sale, 1733-1753, 1764-1772, 1783-1790, 1830-
1896; 4 reels.
Inventories and Accounts of Trustees, 1894-1951; 4 reels.
Estates Not Exceeding $300, 1929-1953; 1 reel.
Estates Not Exceeding $500, 1948-1961; 1 reel.
Inheritance Tax Records, 1920-1970; 2 reels.
Record of Settlements, 1869-1961; 7 reels.
Index to Estates, Wills, Guardians and Trustees, 1930-1968; 1 reel.
Cross Index to Guardians, 1887-1937; 1 reel.

LAND RECORDS
Record of Real Estate Conveyances, 1759-1928; 93 reels.
General Index to Deeds and Mortgages, 1759-1920; 4 reels.
Maps, 1891-1972; 2 reels.
Index to Maps, 1759-1974; 1 reel.

MARRIAGE, DIVORCE AND VITAL STATISTICS
Marriage Bonds, 1760-1868; 3 reels.
Marriage Licenses, 1866-1961; 17 reels.
Marriage Registers, 1851-1937, 1950-1961; 4 reels.
Maiden Names of Divorced Women, 1948-1960; 1 reel.
Index to Births, 1914-1961; 2 reels.
Index to Deaths, 1914-1972; 2 reels.
Index to Delayed Births, 1909-1981; 1 reel.

MILITARY AND PENSION RECORDS
Record of Armed Forces Discharges, 1918-1987; Index to Armed Forces
Discharges, 1918-1961; 6 reels.
Record of Pensions, 1878-1893, 1903-1927; 1 reel.

MISCELLANEOUS RECORDS
Alien Registration Record, 1940; 1 reel.
Record of Declaration of Intent, 1907-1920; 1 reel.

Petitions for Naturalization, 1903-1920; 1 reel.

Inquisitions of Lunacy, 1899-1952; 2 reels.

Orders and Decrees, 1868-1928; 1 reel.

Special Proceedings, 1874-1931; 8 reels.

Cross Index to Special Proceedings, 1887-1961; 1 reel.

OFFICIALS, COUNTY

Minutes, Board of County Commissioners, 1868-1971; 11 reels.

SCHOOL RECORDS

Minutes, County Board of Education, 1883-1907; 2 reels.

WILLS

Record of Wills, 1749-1968; 10 reels.

Index to Wills, 1760-1936; 1 reel.

FORSYTH COUNTY

Established in 1849 from Stokes County.

ORIGINAL RECORDS

BONDS

    Apprentice Bonds, 1875-1891; 1 volume.

    Apprentice Bonds, 1850-1916; Bastardy Bonds, 1849-1917; Officials' Bonds,
        1877; 1 Fibredex box.

COURT RECORDS

    County Court of Pleas and Quarter Sessions

        Minutes, 1849-1868; 3 volumes.

    Superior Court

        Minutes, 1848-1900; 13 volumes.

        Equity Minutes, 1849-1868; 1 volume.

        State Docket, 1849-1872; 1 volume.

        Civil Action Papers, 1851-1930; 16 Fibredex boxes.

        Civil Action Papers Concerning Land, 1849-1930; 5 Fibredex boxes.

    Inferior Court

        Minutes, 1878-1885; 1 volume.

        Judgment Docket, 1878-1885; 1 volume.

    Western District Criminal Court

        Minutes, 1899-1901; 1 volume.

ELECTION RECORDS

    Record of Elections, 1898-1900, 1908-1924; 3 volumes.

ESTATES RECORDS

    Record of Accounts, 1868-1926; 16 volumes.

    Estates Records, 1845-1956; 419 Fibredex boxes.

    Inventories of Estates, 1849-1868; 4 volumes.

    Index to Administrators, Executors and Guardians, 1849-1940; 4 volumes.

    Cross Index to Administrators and Executors, no date; 1 volume.

LAND RECORDS

    Cross Index to Deeds, 1849-1907; 5 volumes.

    Land Records, 1876-1947; 15 Fibredex boxes.

    Processioners' Record, 1884-1886; 1 volume.

MARRIAGE, DIVORCE AND VITAL STATISTICS

    Marriage Bonds, 1850-1859; 1 Fibredex box.

    Divorce Records, 1871-1929; 2 Fibredex boxes.

MILITARY AND PENSION RECORDS

    Salem Militia Record Book, 1831-1861; 1 volume.

MISCELLANEOUS RECORDS

    Alien Registration, 1927-1940; 1 volume.

    Record of Declaration of Intent, 1908-1919; 1 volume.

    Petitions for Naturalization, 1891-1921; 1 volume.

    County Claims, 1849-1878; 1 volume.

Homestead and Personal Property Exemptions, 1877-1943; 4 Fibredex boxes.

Lunacy Records, 1852-1949; 4 Fibredex boxes.

Special Proceedings, 1903-1942; 1 Fibredex box.

Miscellaneous Records, 1849-1954; 6 Fibredex boxes.

Petitions to Change Name, 1891-1949; 2 Fibredex boxes.

Stokes County Records (includes civil actions, estates), 1808-1848;
1 Fibredex box.

Records of Assignees, Receivers and Trustees, 1858-1930; 6 Fibredex boxes.

ROADS AND BRIDGES

Road Docket, 1850-1879; 1 volume.

Minutes, Board of Road Supervisors, 1907-1912; 1 volume.

Railroad Records, 1870-1930; 2 Fibredex boxes.

SCHOOL RECORDS

Minutes, Board of Superintendents of Common Schools, 1851-1854;
1 volume.

WILLS

Wills, 1840-1900; 7 Fibredex boxes.

Cross Index to Wills, 1857-1929; 2 volumes.

MICROFILM RECORDS

BONDS

Apprentice Bonds, 1875-1920; 2 reels.

Bastardy Bonds, 1874-1879; 1 reel.

CORPORATIONS AND PARTNERSHIPS

Record of Corporations, 1884-1957; 7 reels.

Index to Corporations, 1884-1969; 1 reel.

COURT RECORDS

County Court of Pleas and Quarter Sessions

Minutes, 1849-1868; 2 reels.

Superior Court

Minutes, 1849-1932; 26 reels.

Equity Minutes, 1849-1868; 1 reel.

Index to Civil Actions, Plaintiff, 1849-1949; 1 reel.

Index to Civil Actions, Defendant, 1849-1949; 2 reels.

Forsyth County Court

Minutes, 1915-1931; 5 reels.

ELECTION RECORDS

Record of Elections, 1878-1952; 1 reel.

ESTATES RECORDS

Record of Accounts, 1868-1932; 12 reels.

Administrators' Bonds, 1882-1893; 1 reel.

Bonds of Administrators, Surviving Partners and Collectors, 1936-1950;
9 reels.

Appointment of Administrators, Executors and Guardians, 1899-1936; 4 reels.

Record of Administrators, 1893-1952; 7 reels.

Reports of Administrators, Executors and Guardians, 1902-1914, 1932-1935; 7 reels.

Inventories and Accounts of Fiduciaries, 1935-1949; 20 reels.

Appointment of Executors, 1868-1928; 2 reels.

Guardians' Bonds, 1875-1903, 1910-1946; 9 reels.

Appointment of Guardians and Guardians' Oath Book, 1903-1910; 1 reel.

Record of Guardians, 1946-1953; 2 reels.

Record of Widows' Year's Allowances, 1934-1939; 1 reel.

Inheritance Tax Records, 1923-1949; 2 reels.

Inventories of Estates, 1849-1868; 2 reels.

Record of Final Settlements, 1868-1934; 8 reels.

Record of Receivers for Estates, 1912-1930; 1 reel.

Record of Trustees Under Wills, 1933-1949; 1 reel.

Index to Administrators, Executors, Guardians and Trustees, 1849-1968; 5 reels.

Index to Accounts in Trust, 1924-1969; 1 reel.

LAND RECORDS

Record of Deeds, 1849-1957; 316 reels.

Index to Real Estate Conveyances, Grantor, 1849-1956; 18 reels.

Index to Real Estate Conveyances, Grantee, 1849-1956; 18 reels.

Land Title Guaranty Proceeding Docket, 1914-1927; 1 reel.

Record of Processioners, 1884-1886; 1 reel.

Federal Tax Lien Index, 1932-1966; 1 reel.

Record of Foreclosure Sales, 1932-1935; 1 reel.

Record of Sales by Mortgagees, Trustees and Executors, 1917-1949; 6 reels.

Index to Sales by Trustee, Commissioner and Owner, 1917-1968; 1 reel.

Index to Sales by Trustee and Commissioner, 1917-1968; 1 reel.

MARRIAGE, DIVORCE AND VITAL STATISTICS

Marriage Bonds and Licenses, 1849-1869; 3 reels.

Marriage Licenses, 1870-1967; 78 reels.

Marriage License Index, 1849-1965; 6 reels.

Cohabitation Certificates, 1866; 1 reel.

Maiden Names of Divorced Women, 1937-1969; 1 reel.

MILITARY AND PENSION RECORDS

Record of Armed Forces Discharges, 1917-1972; 33 reels.

Index to Armed Forces Discharges, 1917-1969; 1 reel.

Militia Records, 1831-1861; 1 reel.

MISCELLANEOUS RECORDS

Record of Lunacy, 1899-1960; 4 reels.

Index to Persons Adjudged Mentally Disordered, 1899-1968; 1 reel.

Clerk's Minute Dockets, 1931-1940; 1 reel.

Orders and Decrees, 1869-1952; 24 reels.

Special Proceedings, 1879-1935; 4 reels.

Index to Special Proceedings, Plaintiff, 1849-1953; 1 reel.

Index to Special Proceedings, Defendant, 1849-1953; 1 reel.
Cross Index to Special Proceedings, 1849-1953; 1 reel.
Record of Assignments, 1894-1948; 2 reels.
Appointment of Receivers, 1910-1940; 1 reel.
Inventories and Accounts of Receivers, 1930-1949; 1 reel.
Index to Receiverships and Assignments, 1956-1960; 1 reel.
Miscellaneous Index, 1849-1968; 2 reels.

SCHOOL RECORDS
Minutes, Board of Graded Schools, Town of Winston, 1883-1890; 1 reel.

TAX AND FISCAL RECORDS
Tax Scrolls, 1945-1955; 10 reels.

WILLS
Record of Wills, 1842-1953; 15 reels.
Index to Wills, Devisor, 1849-1969; 1 reel.
Index to Wills, Devisee, 1849-1969; 2 reels.

FRANKLIN COUNTY

Established in 1779 from Bute County.

ORIGINAL RECORDS

BONDS

Bastardy Bonds and Records, 1784-1906; 2 Fibredex boxes.

Officials' Bonds, 1820-1898; 3 volumes, 2 Fibredex boxes.

CORPORATIONS AND PARTNERSHIPS

Record of Incorporations, 1905-1924; 1 volume.

COURT RECORDS

County Court of Pleas and Quarter Sessions

Minutes, 1785-1868; 23 volumes.

Execution Dockets, 1785-1828, 1846-1858; 5 volumes.

State Dockets, 1786-1794, 1803-1868; 5 volumes.

Trial and Appearance Dockets, 1798-1868; 15 volumes.

Superior Court

Minutes, 1807-1836, 1846-1883; 6 volumes.

Equity Minutes, 1818-1863; 3 volumes.

Equity Receipts, 1839-1856; 1 volume.

Equity Trial Dockets, 1827-1868; 3 volumes.

Execution Docket, 1850-1869, 1903-1915; 1 volume.

State Dockets, 1818-1868; 2 volumes.

Trial and Appearance Dockets, 1807-1868; 5 volumes.

Civil Action Papers, 1774-1932; 34 Fibredex boxes.

Civil Action Papers Concerning Land, 1792-1934; 4 Fibredex boxes.

Criminal Action Papers, 1779, 1784-1914; 9 Fibredex boxes.

ELECTION RECORDS

Record of Elections, 1897-1932; 3 volumes.

Election Records, 1810-1926; 4 Fibredex boxes.

ESTATES RECORDS

Record of Accounts, 1868-1901; 4 volumes.

Administrators' Bonds, 1866-1869, 1900-1913; 3 volumes.

Appointment of Administrators, Executors, Guardians and Masters, 1868-1902; 2 volumes.

Record of Administrators, Executors and Guardians, 1890-1893; 1 volume.

Estates Records, 1781-1934; 88 Fibredex boxes.

Guardians' Records, 1793-1916; 4 Fibredex boxes.

Guardians' Bonds, 1866-1869, 1913-1914; 2 volumes.

Record of Settlements, 1869-1901; 1 volume.

LAND RECORDS

Record of Deeds, 1797-1800; 2 volumes.

Deeds, 1784-1925; 2 Fibredex boxes.

Deeds of Trust, 1820-1927; 1 Fibredex box.

Mortgage Deeds, 1870-1924; 1 Fibredex box.

Ejectments, 1804-1899; 1 Fibredex box.

Miscellaneous Land Records, 1793-1931; 1 Fibredex box.

MARRIAGE, DIVORCE AND VITAL STATISTICS

Marriage Bonds, 1789-1868; 10 Fibredex boxes.

Record of Marriage Licenses and Certificates, 1851-1867; 1 volume.

Marriage Registers, 1872-1919; 3 volumes.

Cohabitation Certificates, 1866; 1 volume.

Divorce Records, 1820-1928; 3 Fibredex boxes.

MILITARY AND PENSION RECORDS

Court Martial Minutes, 1820-1852; 1 volume.

MISCELLANEOUS RECORDS

Minutes and Accounts, Committee of Finance, 1853-1868; 1 volume.

Audit of County Claims, 1868-1879; 1 volume.

Insolvents, Homestead and Personal Property Exemptions, 1820-1900;
1 Fibredex box.

Louisburg Dispensary Records, 1897-1908; 3 Fibredex boxes.

Special Proceedings Dockets, 1868-1909; 2 volumes.

Miscellaneous Records, 1784-1933; 4 Fibredex boxes.

Personal and Merchants' Accounts, 1788-1900; 1 Fibredex box.

Records of Assignees, Receivers and Trustees, 1844-1931; 1 Fibredex box.

SCHOOL RECORDS

Minutes, Board of Superintendents of Common Schools, 1841-1864;
1 volume.

Minutes, County Board of Education, 1872-1882; 1 volume.

TAX AND FISCAL RECORDS

Assessment of Land and Slaves for Taxation, 1859-1868; 1 volume.

Poll Tax Register, 1902-1904; 1 volume.

Tax Lists, 1804-1836, 1855-1871; 5 volumes.

Tax Records, 1785-1898; 1 Fibredex box.

WILLS

Wills, 1787-1929; 8 Fibredex boxes.

Cross Index to Wills, 1789-1945; 1 volume.

MICROFILM RECORDS

COURT RECORDS

County Court of Pleas and Quarter Sessions
Minutes, 1785-1868; 7 reels.

Superior Court
Minutes, 1884-1945; 5 reels.

ELECTION RECORDS

Record of Elections, 1924-1932; 1 reel.

ESTATES RECORDS

Record of Accounts, 1901-1964; 3 reels.

Appointment of Administrators, Executors and Guardians, 1902-1922; 1 reel.

Appointment of Administrators, 1920-1964; 4 reels.

Appointment of Executors, 1913-1964; 1 reel.

Appointment of Guardians, 1914-1964; 1 reel.

Record of Dowers and Widows' Year's Support, 1925-1964; 1 reel.

Inheritance Tax Records, 1920-1964; 1 reel.

Record of Settlements, 1898-1964; 3 reels.

Index to Administrators, Executors and Guardians, 1872-1964; 1 reel.

LAND RECORDS

Record of Deeds, 1779-1951; 101 reels.

Index to Real Estate Conveyances, Grantor, 1776-1949; 10 reels.

Index to Real Estate Conveyances, Grantee, 1776-1949; 11 reels.

Land Entries, 1778-1898; 2 reels.

Land Sold for Taxes, 1926-1933; 1 reel.

Record of Sales by Trustees and Mortgagees, 1922-1964; 2 reels.

Record of Taxes for Mortgagees, 1931-1932; 1 reel.

MARRIAGE, DIVORCE AND VITAL STATISTICS

Marriage Bonds, 1779-1868; 5 reels.

Marriage Registers, 1869-1964; 2 reels.

Cohabitation Certificates, 1866; 1 reel.

Index to Vital Statistics, 1913-1963; 2 reels.

Index to Delayed Births, various years; 1 reel.

MILITARY AND PENSION RECORDS

Record and Index of Armed Forces Discharges, 1918-1964; 4 reels.

Minutes of Militia Court Martial, 1820-1852; 1 reel.

MISCELLANEOUS RECORDS

Inquisition of Lunacy, 1900-1964; 1 reel.

Orders and Decrees and Index, 1868-1964; 9 reels.

Special Proceedings, 1910-1964; 1 reel.

Owelty Docket, Special Proceedings, 1900-1963; 1 reel.

OFFICIALS, COUNTY

Minutes, Board of County Commissioners, 1868-1940; 4 reels.

SCHOOL RECORDS

Minutes, Board of Superintendents of Common Schools, 1841-1864; 1 reel.

Minutes, County Board of Education, 1885-1941; 1 reel.

TAX AND FISCAL RECORDS

Assessment of Real Property for Taxation, 1859-1868; 1 reel.

Lists of Taxables, 1804-1871; 3 reels.

Tax Lists, 1915, 1925; 1 reel.

WILLS

Record of Wills, 1785-1964; 12 reels.

Original Wills, 1787-1838; 1 reel.

Index to Wills, Devisor, 1785-1978; 1 reel.

Index to Wills, Devisee, 1785-1978; 1 reel.

GASTON COUNTY

Established in 1846 from Lincoln County.
Courthouse fire of 1874 destroyed many court records.

ORIGINAL RECORDS

BONDS
>
> Bastardy Bonds and Records, 1849-1905; 1 volume, 2 Fibredex boxes.
>
> Record of Officials' Bonds, 1868-1889; 1 volume.

COURT RECORDS
>
> County Court of Pleas and Quarter Sessions
>
>> Minutes, 1847-1860; 1 volume.
>>
>> Appearance Docket, 1847-1868; 1 volume.
>>
>> State Docket, 1847-1868; 1 volume.
>
> Superior Court
>
>> Minutes, 1847-1885, 1897-1911; 7 volumes.
>>
>> Equity Minutes, 1847-1868; 1 volume.
>>
>> Civil Action Papers, 1850-1912; 16 Fibredex boxes.
>>
>> Civil Action Papers Concerning Land, 1868-1912; 6 Fibredex boxes.
>>
>> Criminal Action Papers, 1860-1910; 32 Fibredex boxes.
>>
>> Miscellaneous Court Records, 1870-1902; 1 Fibredex box.

ELECTION RECORDS
>
> Record of Elections, 1880-1932; 3 volumes.
>
> Election Records, 1856-1888; 1 Fibredex box.

ESTATES RECORDS
>
> Record of Accounts, 1869-1912; 6 volumes.
>
> Appointment of Administrators, Executors, Guardians and Masters, 1869-1901; 1 volume.
>
> Appointment of Administrators, Executors and Guardians, 1901-1924; 3 volumes.
>
> Estates Records, 1839-1928; 60 Fibredex boxes.
>
> Guardians' Records, 1849-1833; 4 Fibredex boxes.
>
> Record of Settlements, 1869-1915; 3 volumes.

LAND RECORDS
>
> Deeds of Sale and Miscellaneous Deeds, 1860-1944; 1 Fibredex box.
>
> Cross Index to Deeds, 1847-1898; 5 volumes.
>
> Record of Probate, 1883-1885; 1 volume.

MARRIAGE, DIVORCE AND VITAL STATISTICS
>
> Record of Marriages, 1865-1870; 1 manuscript box.
>
> Marriage Registers, 1871-1905; 2 volumes.
>
> Divorce Records, 1859-1910; 3 Fibredex boxes.

MISCELLANEOUS RECORDS
>
> Orders and Decrees, 1869-1912; 4 volumes.
>
> Special Proceedings, 1848-1911; 33 Fibredex boxes.
>
> Miscellaneous Records, 1847-1910; 4 Fibredex boxes.

Records of Assignees, Receivers and Trustees, 1869-1911; 2 Fibredex boxes.
ROADS AND BRIDGES
Road and Bridge Records, 1859-1909; 1 Fibredex box.

Railroad Records, 1872-1912; 3 Fibredex boxes.
SCHOOL RECORDS
School Records, 1855-1884; 2 Fibredex boxes.
TAX AND FISCAL RECORDS
Tax Lists, 1847-1868; 3 volumes.

Tax Records, 1851-1902; 1 Fibredex box.
WILLS
Wills, 1849-1924; 9 Fibredex boxes.

MICROFILM RECORDS

BONDS
Apprentice Bonds, 1869-1919; 1 reel.

Bastardy Bonds, 1869-1882; 1 reel.
CORPORATIONS AND PARTNERSHIPS
Record of Incorporations, 1883-1945; 3 reels.
COURT RECORDS
County Court of Pleas and Quarter Sessions
Minutes, 1847-1860; 1 reel.

Superior Court
Minutes, 1847-1948; 14 reels.

Equity Minutes, 1847-1868; 1 reel.
ELECTION RECORDS
Record of Elections, 1890-1932; 1 reel.
ESTATES RECORDS
Record of Estates, 1847-1863; Index to Estates, 1963; 1 reel.

Record of Accounts, 1869-1963; 11 reels.

Administrators' Bonds, 1868-1904; 1 reel.

Appointment of Administrators, Executors and Guardians, 1901-1918; Index
to Administrators, Executors and Guardians, 1963; 2 reels.

Record of Administrators, 1913-1963; Index to Administrators, 1925-1936;
8 reels.

Record of Executors, 1869-1901, 1936-1961; Index to Executors, 1921-1936;
2 reels.

Record of Executors and Guardians, 1913-1936; 1 reel.

Record of Guardians, 1925-1963; Index to Guardians, 1917-1933; 2 reels.

Guardians' Bonds, 1868-1908; 1 reel.

Inheritance Tax Records, 1923-1959; 1 reel.

Sales and Inventories of Estates, 1863-1869; 1 reel.

Record of Settlements, 1869-1963; 7 reels.
LAND RECORDS
Record of Deeds, 1847-1953; 121 reels.

Index to Deeds and Mortgages, Grantor, 1846-1961; 13 reels.
Index to Deeds and Mortgages, Grantee, 1846-1961; 16 reels.
Record of State Grants, 1845-1891; 1 reel.
Record of Processions, 1847-1886; 1 reel.
Plat Books, 1913-1964; 4 reels.
Record of Resale of Land, 1919-1963; 5 reels.

MARRIAGE, DIVORCE AND VITAL STATISTICS

Marriage Licenses, 1848-1963; 16 reels.
Marriage Registers, 1848-1963; 2 reels.
Maiden Names of Divorced Women, 1939-1963; 1 reel.
Index to Births, 1913-1977; 5 reels.
Index to Deaths, 1913-1962; 2 reels.
Index to Delayed Births, various years; 1 reel.

MILITARY AND PENSION RECORDS

Record of Armed Forces Discharges, 1922-1977; 17 reels.
Index to Armed Forces Discharges, 1922-1962; 1 reel.

MISCELLANEOUS RECORDS

Orders and Decrees, 1869-1954; 10 reels.
Special Proceedings Dockets, 1883-1953; 2 reels.

OFFICIALS, COUNTY

Minutes, Board of County Commissioners, 1868-1955; 6 reels.

SCHOOL RECORDS

Minutes, County Board of Education, 1885-1964; 1 reel.

WILLS

Record of Wills, 1847-1963; 5 reels.
Cross Index to Wills, 1847-1963; 1 reel.

GATES COUNTY

Established in 1779 from Chowan, Hertford and Perquimans counties.

ORIGINAL RECORDS

BONDS

Apprentice Bonds and Records, 1779-1911; 2 volumes, 2 Fibredex boxes.

Bastardy Bonds and Records, 1779-1910; 3 Fibredex boxes.

Constables' Bonds, 1834-1838, 1846-1861; 2 volumes.

Officials' Bonds and Records, 1779-1897; 7 Fibredex boxes.

COURT RECORDS

County Court of Pleas and Quarter Sessions

Minutes, 1779-1868; 15 volumes.

Execution Dockets, 1786-1860; 4 volumes, 2 manuscript boxes.

State Dockets, 1779-1854; 5 volumes.

Trial and Appearance Dockets, 1779-1867; 9 volumes,
1 manuscript box.

Clerk's Fee Books, 1791-1807; 2 volumes.

Superior Court

Minutes, 1807-1857; 3 volumes.

Equity Minutes, 1808-1830, 1855-1868; 2 volumes.

Equity Execution Docket and Receipts in Equity, 1847-1878;
1 volume.

Equity Trial Docket, 1831-1867; 1 volume.

Execution Dockets, 1814-1869; 4 volumes.

State Dockets, 1807-1860; 2 volumes.

Trial and Appearance Dockets, 1807-1859; 3 volumes.

Civil Action Papers, 1768-1911; 36 Fibredex boxes.

Civil Action Papers Concerning Land, 1780-1912; 6 Fibredex boxes.

Civil Action Papers Concerning Timber, 1849-1911; 2 Fibredex boxes.

Criminal Action Papers, 1775-1912; 23 Fibredex boxes.

ELECTION RECORDS

Record of Elections, 1906-1922; 1 volume.

Election Records, 1783-1882; 1 Fibredex box.

ESTATES RECORDS

Record of Estates, 1807-1868; 7 volumes.

Administrators' Bonds, 1812-1847, 1892-1914; 6 volumes.

Estates Records, 1765-1920; 134 Fibredex boxes.

Guardians' Records, 1785-1915; 21 Fibredex boxes.

Guardians' Accounts, 1808-1868; 7 volumes.

Guardians' Bonds, 1810-1904; 13 volumes.

Record of Settlements, 1807-1841; 2 volumes.

Index to Administrators and Executors, no date; 4 volumes.

Index to Guardians, no date; 1 volume.

LAND RECORDS

Deeds of Sale, 1788-1903; 2 Fibredex boxes.

Miscellaneous Deeds, 1776-1908; 1 Fibredex box.

Ejectments, 1795-1911; 2 Fibredex boxes.

Land Divisions, 1810-1911; 1 Fibredex box.

Land Entries, 1811-1817, 1831-1833; 1 volume.

Record of Probate, 1868-1882; 3 volumes.

MARRIAGE, DIVORCE AND VITAL STATISTICS

Marriage Bonds, 1779-1868; 11 Fibredex boxes.

Record of Marriage Certificates, 1851-1867; 1 volume.

Miscellaneous Marriage Records, 1784, 1821-1908; 1 Fibredex box.

Divorce Records, 1817-1911; 1 Fibredex box.

MISCELLANEOUS RECORDS

Record of Claims Allowed by County Court, 1845-1868; 1 volume.

Register of Slaves to Work in Great Dismal Swamp, 1847-1861; 1 volume.

Slave Records, 1783-1867; 3 Fibredex boxes.

Miscellaneous Records, 1780-1912; 5 Fibredex boxes.

Records of Assignees, Receivers and Trustees, 1796-1915; 4 Fibredex boxes.

ROADS AND BRIDGES

Bridge Records, 1786-1910; 1 Fibredex box.

Road Records, 1779-1912; 2 Fibredex boxes.

Railroad Records, 1849-1912; 2 Fibredex boxes.

SCHOOL RECORDS

Minutes, Board of Superintendents of Common Schools, 1841-1861;
1 volume.

TAX AND FISCAL RECORDS

Lists of Taxables, 1784-1868; 6 volumes.

Tax Lists, 1924, 1926, 1935; 3 volumes.

WILLS

Wills, 1762-1904; 12 Fibredex boxes.

MICROFILM RECORDS

BONDS

Apprentice Bonds, 1878-1917; 1 reel.

CORPORATIONS AND PARTNERSHIPS

Record of Incorporations, 1866-1964; 1 reel.

COURT RECORDS

County Court of Pleas and Quarter Sessions
Minutes, 1779-1868; 4 reels.

Superior Court
Minutes, 1859-1964; 5 reels.

Equity Minutes, 1808-1830, 1855-1868; Equity Minutes and Trial
Docket, 1831-1867; 2 reels.

ELECTION RECORDS

Record of Elections, 1880-1964; 1 reel.

ESTATES RECORDS

Record of Estates, 1806-1851; 3 reels.

Record of Accounts, 1869-1964; 5 reels.

Administrators' Bonds, 1870-1914; 1 reel.

Appointment of Administrators, Executors and Guardians, 1868-1964; Cross Index to Administrators and Executors, 1868-1934; 3 reels.

Guardians' Returns, 1828-1837; Guardians' Accounts and Minutes of Probate Court, 1857-1888; 1 reel.

Guardians' Accounts, 1840-1868; 1 reel.

Guardians' Bonds, 1854-1904; 1 reel.

Cross Index to Guardians, 1868-1944; 1 reel.

Inheritance Tax Records, 1923-1964; 1 reel.

Inventories of Estates, 1819-1842; 1 reel.

Record of Settlements, 1804-1841, 1867-1964; 4 reels.

LAND RECORDS

Record of Deeds, 1776-1964; 51 reels.

Cross Index to Deeds, 1776-1910; 1 reel.

Index to Deeds, Grantor, 1910-1964; 1 reel.

Index to Deeds, Grantee, 1910-1964; 1 reel.

Registration of Land Titles, 1923-1964; 1 reel.

Surveyors' Book, 1894-1922; 1 reel.

Federal Tax Lien Index, 1950-1964; 1 reel.

Plats, 1928-1964; 1 reel.

MARRIAGE, DIVORCE AND VITAL STATISTICS

Marriage Bonds, 1778-1868; 4 reels.

Marriage Licenses, 1886-1963; 5 reels.

Marriage Registers, 1867-1964; 1 reel.

Index to Vital Statistics, 1913-1964; 1 reel.

MILITARY AND PENSION RECORDS

Record of Armed Forces Discharges, 1943-1987; 1 reel.

MISCELLANEOUS RECORDS

Orders and Decrees, 1868-1964; 3 reels.

Special Proceedings, 1910-1957; Cross Index to Special Proceedings, 1869-1964; 1 reel.

Registration of Slaves to Work in Great Dismal Swamp, 1847-1861; 1 reel.

OFFICIALS, COUNTY

Minutes, Board of County Commissioners, 1887-1922; 1 reel.

SCHOOL RECORDS

Minutes, County Board of Education, 1885-1927; 1 reel.

TAX AND FISCAL RECORDS

Tax Lists, 1784-1868, 1874, 1890, 1897, 1900, 1924-1926, 1935; 6 reels.

WILLS

Record of Wills, 1779-1964; 4 reels.
Cross Index to Wills, 1779-1964; 1 reel.

GRAHAM COUNTY

Established in 1872 from Cherokee County.

ORIGINAL RECORDS

BONDS
Officials' Bonds, 1871-1914; 1 Fibredex box.
COURT RECORDS
Superior Court
Minutes, 1873-1908; 4 volumes.
Civil Action Papers, 1864-1931; 2 Fibredex boxes.
Civil Action Papers Concerning Land, 1872-1928; 3 Fibredex boxes.
Criminal Action Papers, 1874-1920; 1 Fibredex box.
ELECTION RECORDS
Record of Elections, 1878-1938; 3 volumes.
ESTATES RECORDS
Administrators' Bonds, 1879-1887; 1 volume.
Estates Records, 1847-1930; 3 Fibredex boxes.
Guardians' Bonds, 1877-1898; 1 volume.
LAND RECORDS
Record of Deeds, 1867-1924; 11 volumes.
Deeds, 1789-1921; 1 Fibredex box.
Cross Index to Deeds, 1873-1933; 4 volumes.
Land Entry Books, 1872-1919; 2 volumes.
MARRIAGE, DIVORCE AND VITAL STATISTICS
Marriage Register, 1873-1926; 1 volume.
MISCELLANEOUS RECORDS
Miscellaneous Records (including wills), 1836-1940; 3 Fibredex boxes.
TAX AND FISCAL RECORDS
Miscellaneous Tax Records, 1874-1921; 1 Fibredex box.

MICROFILM RECORDS

CORPORATIONS AND PARTNERSHIPS
Record of Corporations, 1907-1970; 1 reel.
Record of Partnerships, 1927-1928; 1 reel.
COURT RECORDS
Superior Court
Minutes, 1873-1960; 5 reels.
ELECTION RECORDS
Record of Elections, 1878-1966; 1 reel.
ESTATES RECORDS
Record of Accounts, 1873-1966; 2 reels.
Administrators' Bonds, 1879-1966; 1 reel.
Guardians' Bonds, 1877-1898, 1910-1966; 1 reel.

Inheritance Tax Records, 1928-1966; 1 reel.

Record of Settlements, 1886-1903, 1928-1961; 1 reel.

LAND RECORDS

Record of Deeds, 1873-1960; 30 reels.

Index to Deeds, Grantor, 1873-1967; 3 reels.

Index to Deeds, Grantee, 1873-1967; 3 reels.

Land Entry Books, 1872-1961; 1 reel.

Land Sales for Taxes, 1929-1966; 3 reels.

Record of Sales and Foreclosures, 1934-1944; 1 reel.

Record of Sales by Mortgagees, 1934-1966; 1 reel.

MARRIAGE, DIVORCE AND VITAL STATISTICS

Marriage Registers, 1873-1979; 2 reels.

Index to Births, 1913-1979; 1 reel.

Index to Deaths, 1913-1979; 1 reel.

MILITARY AND PENSION RECORDS

Record of Armed Forces Discharges, 1918-1979; 2 reels.

MISCELLANEOUS RECORDS

Orders and Decrees, 1878-1951; 1 reel.

Special Proceedings, 1915-1953; 1 reel.

OFFICIALS, COUNTY

Minutes, Board of County Commissioners, 1873-1961; 4 reels.

WILLS

Record of Wills, 1873-1966; 1 reel.

GRANVILLE COUNTY

Established in 1746 from Edgecombe County.

ORIGINAL RECORDS
BONDS
Apprentice Bonds and Records, 1749-1913; 1 volume, 6 Fibredex boxes.

Bastardy Bonds and Records, 1746-1910; 1 volume, 5 Fibredex boxes.

Constables' Bonds, 1781-1886; 3 Fibredex boxes.

Sheriffs' Bonds, 1748-1887; 1 Fibredex box.

Officials' Bonds, 1754-1898; 3 Fibredex boxes.

Ordinary Bonds, 1748-1838; 1 Fibredex box.

COURT RECORDS
County Court of Pleas and Quarter Sessions

Minutes, 1754-1868; 24 volumes.

Minutes (Rough), 1867-1868; Minutes (Rough), Superior Court, 1868-1869; Record of Probate, 1868-1869; 1 volume.

Appeal Docket, 1792-1807; 1 manuscript box.

Execution Dockets, 1765-1867; 14 volumes.

Levy Docket, 1795-1801, 1837-1838; 1 volume.

State Dockets, 1774-1867; 9 volumes.

Trial, Appearance and Reference Dockets, 1753-1853; 26 volumes.

Trial and Appearance Dockets, 1853-1868; 3 volumes.

Clerk's Fee Books, 1764-1769, 1830-1857; 3 volumes.

Clerk's Receipt Book, 1795-1796; 1 volume.

Costs Docket, State Cases, 1859-1868; 1 volume.

Witness Ticket Books, 1814-1848; 2 volumes.

Superior Court

Minutes, 1807-1867; 7 volumes.

Equity Minutes, 1807-1867; 4 volumes.

Equity Trial and Appearance Dockets, 1807-1868; 5 volumes.

Execution Dockets, 1807-1813, 1854-1866; 2 volumes.

State Dockets, 1812-1868; 4 volumes.

Trial, Appearance and Reference Dockets, 1807-1847; 3 volumes.

Civil Action Papers, 1742-1916; 153 Fibredex boxes.

Civil Action Papers Concerning Land, 1778-1913; 7 Fibredex boxes.

Criminal Action Papers, 1746-1921; 63 Fibredex boxes.

Clerk's Receipt Book, 1832-1857, 1866-1867; Half Fee Docket, 1879-1886; 1 volume.

Receipt Books, Clerk and Master in Equity, 1844-1868; 3 volumes.

Inferior Court

Minutes, 1877-1885; 1 volume.

Costs Docket, 1878-1885; 1 volume.

ELECTION RECORDS
Election Records, 1790-1878; 3 Fibredex boxes.

Miscellaneous Election Records, 1817-1917; 1 Fibredex box.

ESTATES RECORDS

Administrators' Bonds, 1868-1891; 3 volumes.

Record of Appointment of Administrators, Executors and Guardians, 1898-1901; 1 volume.

Estates Records, 1746-1919; 200 Fibredex boxes.

Guardians' Records, 1758-1913, 1927; 25 Fibredex boxes.

Guardians' Accounts, 1810-1868; 8 volumes.

Guardians' Bonds, 1888-1897; 1 volume.

Record of Appointment of Guardians, 1791-1850, 1860-1868; 2 volumes.

LAND RECORDS

Deeds, 1742-1874; 4 Fibredex boxes.

Bills of Sale, Mortgage Deeds and Deeds of Trust, 1757-1912; 1 Fibredex box.

Ejectments, 1788-1886; 5 Fibredex boxes.

Land Entries, 1778-1877; 3 volumes.

Attachments, Executions, Levies and Liens on Land, 1785-1918; 9 Fibredex boxes.

Miscellaneous Land Records, 1748-1914; 2 Fibredex boxes.

MARRIAGE, DIVORCE AND VITAL STATISTICS

Marriage Bonds, 1758-1868; 17 Fibredex boxes.

Record of Cohabitation, 1866-1867; 2 volumes.

Divorce Records, 1819-1895, 1914; 2 Fibredex boxes.

MILITARY AND PENSION RECORDS

Record of Pensions, 1907-1931; 1 volume.

MISCELLANEOUS RECORDS

Alien Registration, 1940; 1 volume.

Declaration of Intent (to Become a Citizen), 1909-1929; 1 volume.

Naturalization Certificates, 1915-1927; 1 volume.

Petitions for Naturalization, 1913-1927; 1 volume.

County Accounts and Claims, 1829-1866; 2 volumes.

County Accounts, Court Orders and Memoranda, 1746-1908; 5 Fibredex boxes.

Insolvent Debtors, 1746-1871; 12 Fibredex boxes.

Homestead and Personal Property Exemptions, 1844-1908; 1 Fibredex box.

Record of Jurors, 1849-1868; 2 volumes.

Jury and Witness Tickets, 1757-1865; 2 Fibredex boxes.

Jury Lists, 1746-1881; 1 Fibredex box.

Grand Jury Presentments and Reports, 1749-1901; 1 Fibredex box.

Lunacy Records, 1798-1913; 1 Fibredex box.

Oaths of Allegiance, 1865; 1 volume.

Wardens of the Poor, 1787-1868; 1 Fibredex box.

Wardens of the Poor, County Home and Outside Paupers List, 1851-1921; 3 volumes.

Miscellaneous Records, 1722, 1747-1920; 5 Fibredex boxes.

Bankruptcy Proceedings, 1804-1884; 1 Fibredex box.

Coroners' Inquests, 1755-1905, 1920; 2 Fibredex boxes.

Correspondence, 1759-1914; 1 Fibredex box.

Mill Records, 1747-1865; 2 Fibredex boxes.

Personal and Merchants' Accounts, 1742-1906; 2 Fibredex boxes.

Powers of Attorney, 1749-1877; 2 Fibredex boxes.

Attachments and Levies on Slaves, 1794-1863; 2 Fibredex boxes.

Civil Action Papers Concerning Slaves and Free Persons of Color, 1754-1875; 4 Fibredex boxes.

Criminal Action Papers Concerning Slaves and Free Persons of Color, 1764-1876; 6 Fibredex boxes.

Miscellaneous Records of Slaves and Free Persons of Color, 1755-1871; 1 Fibredex box.

OFFICIALS, COUNTY

Justices of the Peace Records, 1749-1886; 1 Fibredex box.

Minutes, Board of Justices of the Peace, 1899-1902; 1 volume.

ROADS AND BRIDGES

Bridge Records, 1748-1868; 1 Fibredex box.

Road Records, 1747-1905; 7 Fibredex boxes.

Railroad Records, 1837-1891; 1 Fibredex box.

SCHOOL RECORDS

Common School Register, 1860-1861; 1 volume.

Public School Register, Oxford Graded School, 1893-1904; 1 volume.

Lists of School Children, 1825-1878; 3 Fibredex boxes.

Miscellaneous School Records, 1804-1895; 2 Fibredex boxes.

TAX AND FISCAL RECORDS

Lists of Taxables, 1796-1864; 19 volumes.

Taxables, 1747-1887; 9 Fibredex boxes.

Miscellaneous Tax Records, 1754-1886; 3 Fibredex boxes.

WILLS

Wills, 1749-1879; 2 Fibredex boxes.

MICROFILM RECORDS

BONDS

Apprentice Bonds, 1802-1913; 1 reel.

Bastardy Bonds, 1869-1879; 1 reel.

CENSUS RECORDS

State Census, Granville County, 1786; 1 reel.

CORPORATIONS AND PARTNERSHIPS

Record of Corporations, 1895-1961; 1 reel.

Partnership Record Index, 1916-1958; 1 reel.

COURT RECORDS

County Court of Pleas and Quarter Sessions
Minutes, 1746-1868; 12 reels.

Superior Court
>> Minutes, 1807-1947; 12 reels.
>> Equity Minutes, 1807-1867; 2 reels.
>> Index to Civil Actions, 1968-1990; 1 reel.
>> Index to Criminal Actions, 1968-1990; 1 reel.
>> Index to Judgments, 1868-1968; 2 reels.

ESTATES RECORDS

>> Record of Accounts, 1868-1961; 10 reels.
>> Administrators' Bonds, 1868-1891; 1 reel.
>> Appointment of Administrators, Executors, Collectors and Masters, 1888-1901; 1 reel.
>> Appointment of Administrators, 1896-1961; 5 reels.
>> Appointment of Executors, 1868-1869, 1896-1933; 1 reel.
>> Guardians' Bonds, 1790-1917; 1 reel.
>> Guardians' Accounts, 1810-1868; 4 reels.
>> Record of Guardians, 1899-1940; 2 reels.
>> Inheritance Tax Records, 1923-1950; 1 reel.
>> Record of Settlements, 1868-1961; 9 reels.
>> Index to Administrators, Executors and Guardians, 1896-1961; 1 reel.

LAND RECORDS

>> Record of Deeds, 1746-1946; 76 reels.
>> Index to Deeds, Grantor, 1746-1947; 3 reels.
>> Index to Deeds, Grantee, 1746-1947; 3 reels.
>> Land Entries, 1778-1904; 2 reels.
>> Record of Sale and Resale of Land by Mortgagees and Trustees, 1920-1948; 2 reels.

MARRIAGE, DIVORCE AND VITAL STATISTICS

>> Marriage Bonds, 1753-1868; 5 reels.
>> Index to Marriage Bonds, 1753-1868; 1 reel.
>> Marriage Certificates, 1851-1868; 1 reel.
>> Marriage Registers, 1867-1961; 2 reels.
>> Marriages of Freed People, 1866-1867; 1 reel.
>> Index to Births, 1914-1961; 1 reel.
>> Index to Deaths, 1913-1961; 1 reel.
>> Index to Delayed Births, various years; 1 reel.

MILITARY AND PENSION RECORDS

>> Record of Armed Forces Discharges, 1921-1974; 4 reels.
>> Index to Armed Forces Discharges, 1918-1961; 1 reel.

MISCELLANEOUS RECORDS

>> Special Proceedings, 1868-1925; 6 reels.
>> Special Proceedings and Orders and Decrees, 1960-1961; 1 reel.
>> Cross Index to Special Proceedings, 1868-1961; 1 reel.

OFFICIALS, COUNTY

>> Minutes, Board of County Commissioners, 1868-1925; 6 reels.

SCHOOL RECORDS
    Minutes, Board of Superintendents of Common Schools, 1842-1865; 1 reel.
    Minutes, County Board of Education, 1885-1975; 2 reels.
    Minutes, Oxford Graded School Board of Trustees, 1903-1959; 1 reel.
TAX AND FISCAL RECORDS
    Tax Lists, 1755-1902, 1915, 1925, 1935, 1945, 1955; 16 reels.
WILLS
    Unrecorded Wills, 1749-1771; 1 reel.
    Record of Wills, 1772-1954; 16 reels.
    Cross Index to Wills, 1762-1971; 2 reels.

GREENE COUNTY

Established in 1791 as Glasgow County from Dobbs County.
Name changed to Greene in 1799.
Courthouse fire of 1876 destroyed many court records and all land records.

ORIGINAL RECORDS

BONDS
>Apprentice Bonds, 1869-1888, 1911-1912; 2 volumes.
>Officials' Bonds and Records, 1874-1933; 2 Fibredex boxes.

COURT RECORDS
>County Court of Pleas and Quarter Sessions
>>Execution Docket, 1861-1862, 1866-1868; 1 volume.
>>Trial Docket, 1867-1868; 1 volume.
>Superior Court
>>Minutes, 1869-1911; 6 volumes.
>>Civil Action Papers, 1868-1959; 16 Fibredex boxes.
>>Civil Action Papers Concerning Land, 1871-1967; 22 Fibredex boxes.
>>Clerk's Receipt Book, 1868-1871; 1 volume.
>Inferior Court
>>Minutes, 1877-1884; 1 volume.
>>Criminal Issues Docket, 1877-1883; 1 volume.

ELECTION RECORDS
>Record of Elections, 1878-1928; 4 volumes.

ESTATES RECORDS
>Record of Estates, 1839-1845; 1 volume.
>Record of Accounts, 1869-1905; 2 volumes.
>Appointment of Administrators, Executors, Guardians and Masters, 1869-1871, 1891-1918; 1 volume.
>Estates Records, 1809-1962; 68 Fibredex boxes.
>Guardians' Records, 1860-1947; 9 Fibredex boxes.
>Guardians' Bonds, 1857-1918; 4 volumes.
>Record of Settlements, 1869-1908; 1 volume.

LAND RECORDS
>Deeds, 1857-1926; 2 Fibredex boxes.
>Mortgage Deeds, 1875-1927; 1 Fibredex box.
>Land Entries, 1906-1913; 1 volume.
>Tax Liens on Land, 1892-1943; 2 Fibredex boxes.
>Attachments, Executions, Levies and Liens on Land, 1876-1969; 3 Fibredex boxes.
>Miscellaneous Land Records, 1880-1958; 1 Fibredex box.

MARRIAGE, DIVORCE AND VITAL STATISTICS
>Marriage Registers, 1875-1958; 6 volumes.
>Divorce Records, 1875-1959; 23 Fibredex boxes.

MISCELLANEOUS RECORDS
Alien Registration, 1927, 1940; 1 volume.
Homestead and Personal Property Exemptions, 1881-1966; 1 Fibredex box.
Registry of Licenses to Trades, 1875-1899; 1 volume.
Special Proceedings Docket, 1871-1918; 1 volume.
Bankruptcy Proceedings, 1879-1943; 1 Fibredex box.
Miscellaneous Records, 1802-1956; 5 Fibredex boxes.
Records of Assignees, Receivers and Trustees, 1872-1947; 6 Fibredex boxes.

ROADS AND BRIDGES
Road Records, 1874-1940; 1 Fibredex box.
Railroad Records, 1874-1942; 3 Fibredex boxes.

TAX AND FISCAL RECORDS
Tax Records, 1875-1894; 1 Fibredex box.

WILLS
Wills, 1846-1944; 4 Fibredex boxes.
Cross Index to Wills, 1869-1935; 1 volume.

MICROFILM RECORDS

BONDS
Apprentice Bonds, 1869-1888; 1 reel.
Record of Officials' Bonds, 1860-1937; 1 reel.

CORPORATIONS AND PARTNERSHIPS
Record of Incorporations, 1915-1966; Record of Partnerships, 1917-1936;
1 reel.

COURT RECORDS
Superior Court
Minutes, 1869-1963; 6 reels.
Index to Minutes, Plaintiff, 1875-1966; 1 reel.
Index to Minutes, Defendant, 1875-1966; 2 reels.

ELECTION RECORDS
Record of Elections, 1878-1966; 1 reel.

ESTATES RECORDS
Record of Estates, 1839-1845; 1 reel.
Record of Accounts, 1868-1925; 1 reel.
Record of Accounts and Inventories, 1891-1956; 6 reels.
Record of Administrators, Executors and Guardians, 1918-1926; 1 reel.
Record of Administrators, 1921-1964; 2 reels.
Appointment of Executors, 1869-1918; Record of Executors, 1942-1967;
1 reel.
Guardians' Bonds, 1869-1918; 1 reel.
Record of Guardians, 1926-1966; 1 reel.
Qualifications, Inventories and Accounts, and Wards, 1869-1966; 1 reel.
Record of Amounts Paid for Indigent Children, 1912-1913; 1 reel.
Inheritance Tax Records, 1923-1967; 1 reel.

Appointment and Accounts of Receivers of Estates, 1905-1934; 1 reel.

Record of Settlements, 1869-1952; 3 reels.

Cross Index to Administrators and Executors, 1869-1920; 1 reel.

Cross Index to Guardians, 1872-1917; 1 reel.

LAND RECORDS

Record of Deeds, 1861-1960; 55 reels.

Index to Real Estate Conveyances, Grantor, 1875-1966; 3 reels.

Index to Real Estate Conveyances, Grantee, 1875-1966; 3 reels.

Record of Sale and Resale, 1921-1966; 1 reel.

MARRIAGE, DIVORCE AND VITAL STATISTICS

Index to Marriages, 1876-1966; 1 reel.

Index to Births, 1913-1966; 1 reel.

Index to Deaths, 1913-1966; Index to Delayed Births, 1880-1966; 1 reel.

Index to Vital Statistics, various years; 1 reel.

MILITARY AND PENSION RECORDS

Record of Armed Forces Discharges, 1917-1982; 5 reels.

Index to Armed Forces Discharges, 1926-1982; 1 reel.

MISCELLANEOUS RECORDS

Orders and Decrees, 1869-1948; 8 reels.

Special Proceedings, 1871-1894; 1 reel.

Cross Index to Special Proceedings, 1868-1967; 1 reel.

Index to Special Proceedings, Plaintiff, 1875-1967; 1 reel.

Index to Special Proceedings, Defendant, 1875-1967; 1 reel.

OFFICIALS, COUNTY

Minutes, Board of County Commissioners, 1875-1931; 5 reels.

SCHOOL RECORDS

Minutes, County Board of Education, 1911-1967; 1 reel.

TAX AND FISCAL RECORDS

Tax Lists, 1881-1908, 1917-1924, 1935-1955; 2 reels.

WILLS

Record of Wills, 1868-1966; 3 reels.

Index to Wills, 1868-1966; 1 reel.

GUILFORD COUNTY

Established in 1771 from Orange and Rowan counties.
Courthouse fire of 1872 resulted in slight loss of records.

ORIGINAL RECORDS

BONDS

Apprentice Bonds and Records, 1817-1922; 3 volumes, 4 Fibredex boxes.
Bastardy Bonds and Records, 1779, 1816-1877, 1923; 3 Fibredex boxes.
Officials' Bonds, 1774-1892; 4 Fibredex boxes.

CORPORATIONS AND PARTNERSHIPS

Record of Incorporations, 1885-1896; 1 volume.

COURT RECORDS

County Court of Pleas and Quarter Sessions

Minutes, 1781-1868; 18 volumes, 2 manuscript boxes.
Execution Dockets, 1813-1868; 12 volumes.
State Dockets, 1811-1868; 7 volumes.
Trial Dockets, 1779-1817; 4 volumes.
Trial and Appearance Dockets, 1817-1868; 9 volumes.

Superior Court

Minutes, 1850-1924; 21 volumes.
Equity Minutes, 1826-1867; 2 volumes.
Equity Execution Docket, 1858-1868; 1 volume.
Equity Trial and Appearance Docket, 1822-1824; 1 volume.
Equity Trial Dockets, 1833-1868; 2 volumes.
Execution Dockets, 1858-1887; 2 volumes.
State Docket, 1855-1868; 1 volume.
Trial and Appearance Dockets, 1852-1869; 3 volumes.
Supplementary Proceedings, 1894-1899; 1 volume.
Clerk's Fee Dockets, 1853-1860; 2 volumes.
Clerk's Receipt Docket, 1886-1890; 1 volume.
Civil Action Papers, 1774-1930; 9 Fibredex boxes.
Civil Action Papers Concerning Land, 1817-1935; 8 Fibredex boxes.
Civil Action Papers Concerning Mines, 1845-1892; 1 Fibredex box.

ELECTION RECORDS

Record of Elections, 1880-1922; 3 volumes.
Election Returns, 1841-1918; 5 Fibredex boxes.

ESTATES RECORDS

Record of Estates, 1816-1868; 17 volumes.
Record of Accounts, 1869-1903; 7 volumes.
Administrators' Bonds, 1871-1899; 6 volumes.
Appointment of Administrators, Executors, Guardians and Masters, 1868-
1890; 1 volume.
Appointment of Administrators, Executors and Guardians, 1890-1897;
1 volume.

Record of Dowers, 1887-1897; 1 volume.

Record of Widows' Year's Support, 1886-1921; 1 volume.

Estates Records, 1778-1942; 275 Fibredex boxes.

Guardians' Records, 1775-1933; 31 Fibredex boxes.

Guardians' Accounts, 1821-1868, 1879-1897; 8 volumes.

Guardians' Bonds, 1871-1899; 4 volumes.

Record of Settlements, 1816-1862, 1869-1898; 9 volumes.

Probate Fee Docket, 1868-1869, 1880-1890; 1 volume.

Clerk's Receipt Book (Estates), 1890-1930; 1 volume.

LAND RECORDS

Deeds, 1785-1930; 16 Fibredex boxes.

Deeds of Trust and Mortgage Deeds, 1816-1926; 6 Fibredex boxes.

Record of Deeds Proved, 1853-1872; 1 volume.

Ejectments, 1808-1908; 5 Fibredex boxes.

Land Condemnations, 1909-1937; 3 Fibredex boxes.

Land Divisions, Partitions and Surveys, 1825-1939; 9 Fibredex boxes.

Land Foreclosures and Mortgage Sales, 1873-1931; 15 Fibredex boxes.

Miscellaneous Land Records, 1784-1959; 2 Fibredex boxes.

MARRIAGE, DIVORCE AND VITAL STATISTICS

Marriage Bonds, 1770-1868; 21 Fibredex boxes.

Marriage Registers (White), 1853-1937; 8 volumes.

Marriage Registers (Colored), 1867-1937; 3 volumes.

Divorce Records, 1820-1929; 7 Fibredex boxes.

Maiden Names of Divorced Women, 1937-1969; 1 volume.

MILITARY AND PENSION RECORDS

Court Martial Minutes, 1806-1852; 1 volume.

Confederate Pension Records, 1890-1972; 4 Fibredex boxes.

MISCELLANEOUS RECORDS

Alien Registration, 1927, 1935, 1940-1941; 2 volumes.

Insolvent Debtors, 1846-1868; 3 Fibredex boxes.

Homestead and Personal Property Exemptions, 1869-1931; 1 Fibredex box.

Lunacy Records, 1826-1930; 2 Fibredex boxes.

Orders and Decrees, 1869-1901; 3 volumes.

Special Proceedings Dockets, 1871-1900; 2 volumes.

Minutes, Wardens of the Poor, 1838-1868; 1 volume.

Miscellaneous Records, 1771-1934; 5 Fibredex boxes.

Powers of Attorney, 1805-1929; 1 Fibredex box.

Records of Slaves and Free Persons of Color, 1781-1864; 1 Fibredex box.

Records of Assignees, Trustees and Receivers, 1867-1935; 2 Fibredex boxes.

ROADS AND BRIDGES

Road and Bridge Records, 1799-1890; 3 Fibredex boxes.

Road Dockets, 1824-1827, 1832-1869; 4 volumes.

SCHOOL RECORDS

Minutes, County Board of Education, 1872-1899; 1 volume.

School Records, 1853-1929; 2 Fibredex boxes.

WILLS

Wills, 1771-1968; 228 Fibredex boxes.

Cross Index to Wills, 1771-1934; 3 volumes.

MICROFILM RECORDS

BONDS

Apprentice Bonds, 1871-1922; 1 reel.

CORPORATIONS AND PARTNERSHIPS

Record of Incorporations, 1886-1962; 37 reels.

Index to Incorporations, 1885-1970; 1 reel.

COURT RECORDS

County Court of Pleas and Quarter Sessions

Minutes, 1781-1868; 8 reels.

Superior Court

Minutes, 1850-1932; 15 reels.

Minutes, Civil, 1932-1952, 1959-1964; 7 reels.

Minutes, Criminal, 1932-1963; 5 reels.

Equity Minutes, 1826-1867; 1 reel.

Index to Civil Actions, Plaintiff, 1900-1968; 4 reels.

Index to Civil Actions, Defendant, 1900-1962; 3 reels.

Index to Judgments, Plaintiff, 1925-1954; 3 reels.

Index to Judgments, Defendant, 1925-1954; 3 reels.

ELECTION RECORDS

Minutes, Board of Elections, 1948-1969; 1 reel.

Record of Elections, 1880-1968; 1 reel.

ESTATES RECORDS

Record of Estates, 1820-1879, 1886-1932; 13 reels.

Record of Accounts and Settlements, 1857-1863, 1889-1893, 1939-1942;
2 reels.

Record of Accounts, 1879-1962; 27 reels.

Annual Accounts of Administrators, Executors and Trustees, 1887-1903;
1 reel.

Record of Accounts and Final Settlements (Wachovia and Security National
Banks), 1940-1962; 26 reels.

Administrators' Bonds, 1871-1899; 1 reel.

Index to Administrators' Bonds, 1871-1899; 1 reel.

Record of Administrators' and Guardians' Bonds, 1935-1969; 5 reels.

Record of Administrators, Executors and Guardians, 1868-1908; 3 reels.

Appointment of Administrators, 1899-1968; 23 reels.

Record of Executors, 1844-1848, 1868-1887, 1915-1957; 4 reels.

Appointment of Executors, 1957-1968; 2 reels.

Guardians' Bonds, 1871-1899; 1 reel.

Record of Guardians, 1821-1849, 1864-1866, 1914-1926; 4 reels.

Appointment of Guardians, 1899-1968; 7 reels.

Guardians' Docket, 1821-1868; 1 reel.

Appointment of Administrators, Executors and Guardians, 1966-1968; 1 reel.

Record of Dowers, 1887-1891; 1 reel.

Record of Widows' Year's Support, 1886-1962; 2 reels.

Inheritance Tax Records, 1912-1968; 7 reels.

General Index to Inheritance Tax Records, 1912-1970; 1 reel.

Record of Settlements, 1820-1825, 1836-1862, 1869-1888, 1898-1962; 17 reels.

Qualifications of Trustees Under Wills, 1934-1968; 1 reel.

Index to Estates, 1818-1970; 5 reels.

Index to Renunciations and Disclaimers, 1961-1968; 1 reel.

LAND RECORDS

Record of Deeds, 1771-1957; 386 reels.

Index to Real Estate Conveyances, Grantor, 1771-1951; 13 reels.

Index to Real Estate Conveyances, Grantee, 1771-1951; 12 reels.

Land Divisions, 1873-1893, 1921-1930; 1 reel.

Land Entries, 1779-1795; 1 reel.

Maps, Hamilton Lakes, 1926; 1 reel.

Plat Books, 1895-1954; 5 reels.

Index to Plats, 1853-1984; 1 reel.

MARRIAGE, DIVORCE AND VITAL STATISTICS

Marriage Bonds, 1770-1868; 6 reels.

Marriage Bond Abstracts, 1770-1868; 1 reel.

Marriage Licenses (White), 1871-1961; 56 reels.

Marriage Licenses (Black), 1871-1961; 15 reels.

Record of Marriages, 1853-1867; 1 reel.

Marriage Registers (White), 1867-1952; 4 reels.

Marriage Registers (Black), 1867-1970; 2 reels.

Maiden Names of Divorced Women, 1937-1969; 1 reel.

Non-Jury Divorce Judgments, 1966-1967; 1 reel.

Index to Births, 1913-1981; 10 reels.

Index to Deaths, 1913-1980; 5 reels.

Index to Delayed Births, various years; 1 reel.

MILITARY AND PENSION RECORDS

Record of Armed Forces Discharges, various years, 1967-1980; 26 reels.

Index to Armed Forces Discharges, 1912-1981; 1 reel.

Record of Court Martial Proceedings, 1806-1852; 1 reel.

MISCELLANEOUS RECORDS

Record of Lunacy, 1899-1946; 3 reels.

Inquisition of Inebriety, 1938-1958; 1 reel.

Index to Lunacy and Inebriety, 1908-1968; 1 reel.

Orders and Decrees, 1869-1953; 26 reels.

Special Proceedings Dockets, 1884-1968; 6 reels.

Index to Special Proceedings and Orders and Decrees, 1869-1968; 5 reels.

Minutes, Wardens of the Poor, 1838-1868; 1 reel.

Appointment of Receivers of Judgment Debtors, 1894-1899; 1 reel.

Accounts of Receivers, 1911-1931; 1 reel.

Final Reports of Receivers, 1933-1949; 1 reel.

Inventories, Reports and Accounts of Receivership, 1950-1962; 1 reel.

Index to Liquidations (N. C. Bank and Trust Company and United Bank and Trust Company), 1930-1946; 1 reel.

OFFICIALS, COUNTY

Minutes, Board of County Commissioners, 1868-1970; 15 reels.

Index to Minutes, Board of County Commissioners, 1899-1966; 1 reel.

ROADS AND BRIDGES

Road Dockets, 1824-1869; 2 reels.

SCHOOL RECORDS

Minutes, County Board of Education, 1872-1965; 3 reels.

WILLS

Record of Wills, 1779-1963; 24 reels.

Index to Wills, 1771-1969; 4 reels.

HALIFAX COUNTY

Established in 1758 (effective 1759) from Edgecombe County.
Many court records are missing; reason unknown.
Land records of Edgecombe County and Bertie Precinct are included
in the Record of Deeds series.

ORIGINAL RECORDS

BONDS

Bastardy Bonds and Records, 1858-1899; 1 Fibredex box.

Officials' Bonds and Records, 1820-1913; 1 Fibredex box.

CORPORATIONS AND PARTNERSHIPS

Incorporation Records, 1889-1894; 1 Fibredex box.

COURT RECORDS

County Court of Pleas and Quarter Sessions

Minutes, 1784-1787, 1796-1802, 1822-1868; 9 volumes.

Crown Docket, 1759-1770; 1 volume.

Execution Dockets, 1836-1840, 1848-1868; 4 volumes.

Trial and Appearance Dockets, 1766-1770, 1837-1868; 6 volumes.

Superior Court

Minutes, 1868-1902; 17 volumes.

Equity Minutes, 1822-1851; 1 volume.

Execution Docket, 1846-1869; Land Entries, 1844-1859; 1 volume.

State Docket, 1848-1868; 1 volume.

Trial and Appearance Docket, 1846-1866; 1 volume.

Civil Action Papers, 1765-1829, 1860-1922; 41 Fibredex boxes.

Civil Action Papers Concerning Land, 1868-1922; 25 Fibredex boxes.

Criminal Action Papers, 1844-1898; 1 Fibredex box.

Circuit Criminal Court

Minutes, 1899-1901; 1 volume.

ELECTION RECORDS

Record of Elections, 1878-1922; 2 volumes.

ESTATES RECORDS

Record of Estates, 1773-1779, 1828-1862; 6 volumes.

Record of Accounts, 1868-1898; 7 volumes.

Estates Records, 1762-1924; 108 Fibredex boxes.

Guardians' Records, 1808-1922; 12 Fibredex boxes.

Record of Settlements, 1870-1900; 3 volumes.

LAND RECORDS

Record of Deeds, 1758-1856; 10 volumes, 1 manuscript box.

Deeds and Bills of Sale, 1722-1855; 4 manuscript boxes.

Cross Index to Deeds, 1732-1893; 9 volumes.

Attachments, Executions, Levies and Liens on Land, 1867-1917;
1 Fibredex box.

Miscellaneous Land Records, 1716-1917; 1 Fibredex box.

Halifax County Jail, Halifax, date unknown. Photograph from the files of the State Archives.

Petitions to Divide and Sell Land, 1872-1922; 4 Fibredex boxes.

Record of Probate, 1869-1873; 1 volume.

MARRIAGE, DIVORCE AND VITAL STATISTICS

Marriage Bonds, 1770-1868; 10 Fibredex boxes.

Marriage Register, 1872-1895; 1 volume.

Divorce Records, 1870-1922; 16 Fibredex boxes.

MISCELLANEOUS RECORDS

Naturalization Record, 1916-1925; 1 volume.

County Accounts, 1826-1851; 1 volume.

Homestead and Personal Property Exemptions, 1869-1911; 1 Fibredex box.

Miscellaneous Records, 1761-1927; 6 Fibredex boxes.

Roanoke Navigation and Water Power Company Records, 1818-1913;
2 Fibredex boxes.

Records of Assignees, Receivers and Trustees, 1868-1920; 6 Fibredex boxes.

ROADS AND BRIDGES

Railroad Records, 1868-1921; 7 Fibredex boxes.

TAX AND FISCAL RECORDS

Lists of Taxables, 1784-1834, 1863; 2 volumes, 1 manuscript box.

WILLS

Record of Wills, 1759-1779; 2 volumes.

Wills, 1772-1916; 12 Fibredex boxes.

Cross Index to Wills, 1759-1963; 3 volumes.

MICROFILM RECORDS

CORPORATIONS AND PARTNERSHIPS

Record of Corporations, 1887-1947; 1 reel.

COURT RECORDS

County Court of Pleas and Quarter Sessions
Minutes, 1784-1787, 1796-1802, 1822-1824, 1832-1868; 4 reels.

Superior Court
Minutes, 1868-1940; 17 reels.
Equity Minutes, 1822-1851; 1 reel.
Trial and Appearance Docket, 1846-1866; 1 reel.

Circuit Criminal Court
Minutes, 1899-1901; 1 reel.

ELECTION RECORDS

Record of Elections, 1878-1968; 3 reels.

ESTATES RECORDS

Record of Accounts, 1817-1954; 9 reels.

Record of Estates, 1828-1862; 3 reels.

Administrators' and Guardians' Accounts and Inventories, 1826-1849; 3 reels.

Appointment of Administrators, Executors and Guardians, 1868-1909; 1 reel.

Record of Administrators, 1903-1946; 3 reels.

Record of Executors, 1903-1963; 1 reel.

Record of Guardians, 1904-1950; 1 reel.

Qualification of Trustees Under Wills, 1962; 1 reel.

Index to Administrators, Executors and Guardians, 1934-1968; 1 reel.

Inheritance Tax Records, 1920-1963; 1 reel.

Record of Inventories, 1773-1779, 1931-1950; 2 reels.

Record of Settlements, 1867-1950; 5 reels.

LAND RECORDS

Record of Deeds, 1732-1934; 123 reels.

Index to Deeds and Mortgages, Grantor, 1732-1934; 7 reels.

Index to Deeds and Mortgages, Grantee, 1732-1934; 7 reels.

Record of Resale of Land by Trustees, 1913-1940; 2 reels.

MARRIAGE, DIVORCE AND VITAL STATISTICS

Marriage Bonds, 1758-1868; 2 reels.

Record of Marriages, 1851-1903; 1 reel.

Marriage Registers, 1867-1974; 6 reels.

Index to Marriage Registers, 1867-1962; 2 reels.

Maiden Names of Divorced Women, 1938-1963; 1 reel.

Index to Births, 1913-1981; 4 reels.

Index to Deaths, 1913-1981; 3 reels.

Index to Delayed Births, various years; 1 reel.

MILITARY AND PENSION RECORDS

Record of Armed Forces Discharges, 1923-1963; 4 reels.

Index to Armed Forces Discharges, 1923-1963; 1 reel.

MISCELLANEOUS RECORDS

Orders and Decrees, 1932-1938; 1 reel.

Special Proceedings, 1868-1947; 7 reels.

Cross Index to Special Proceedings, 1868-1963, 1968-1981; 2 reels.

Index to Miscellaneous Records, 1968-1981; 1 reel.

OFFICIALS, COUNTY

Minutes, Board of County Commissioners, 1873-1921; 4 reels.

SCHOOL RECORDS

Minutes, County Board of Education, 1909-1951; 1 reel.

TAX AND FISCAL RECORDS

Lists of Taxables, 1784-1834; 1 reel.

Tax Scrolls, 1915, 1925, 1935; 2 reels.

WILLS

Record of Wills, 1758-1968; 7 reels.

Index to Wills, 1759-1968; 4 reels.

HARNETT COUNTY

Established in 1855 from Cumberland County.
Courthouse fires of 1892 and 1894 destroyed
court records and many of the land records.

ORIGINAL RECORDS

BONDS
> Officials' Bonds, 1893-1918; 1 volume.

ELECTION RECORDS
> Record of Elections, 1896-1932; 4 volumes.
> Record of Released Polls, 1887-1927; 1 volume.

ESTATES RECORDS
> Appointment of Administrators, Executors and Guardians, 1892-1908;
> > 1 volume.
> Appointment of Guardians, 1910-1927; 1 volume.
> Amounts Paid for Indigent Children, 1929-1948; 1 volume.

MISCELLANEOUS RECORDS
> County Accounts, 1875-1906; 2 volumes.
> Miscellaneous Records, 1855; 1 manuscript box.

TAX AND FISCAL RECORDS
> Tax List, 1915; 1 volume.

MICROFILM RECORDS

CORPORATIONS AND PARTNERSHIPS
> Record of Corporations, 1901-1939; 1 reel.

COURT RECORDS
> Superior Court
> > Minutes, 1892-1956; 8 reels.

ELECTION RECORDS
> Record of Elections, 1936-1966; 1 reel.

ESTATES RECORDS
> Record of Accounts, 1884-1956; 5 reels.
> Record of Administrators, 1910-1959; 4 reels.
> Record of Guardians, 1927-1967; 1 reel.
> Trust Funds for Minors and Incompetents, 1943-1966; 2 reels.
> Record of Dowers, 1893-1938; 1 reel.
> Record of Widow's Year's Support, 1938-1967; 1 reel.
> Estates Not Exceeding $300, 1930-1966; Estates Not Exceeding $1,000,
> > 1966-1967; 1 reel.
> Inheritance Tax Records, 1947-1967; 1 reel.
> Record of Monies Paid to Courts, Administrators and Executors, 1922-1951;
> > 1 reel.
> Record of Inventories, 1908-1962; 2 reels.

Record of Settlements, 1889-1957; 4 reels.

Cross Index to Administrators, Executors and Guardians, 1919-1954; 1 reel.

Index to Estates, 1950-1967; 1 reel.

LAND RECORDS

Record of Deeds, 1877-1952; 109 reels.

Index to Real Estate Conveyances, Grantor, 1855-1955; 5 reels.

Index to Real Estate Conveyances, Grantee, 1855-1955; 6 reels.

Record of Division and Partition of Land, 1898-1921; 1 reel.

Record of Resale of Land by Trustees and Mortgagees, 1919-1957; 6 reels.

MARRIAGE, DIVORCE AND VITAL STATISTICS

Marriage Registers, 1892-1967; 1 reel.

Maiden Names of Divorced Women, 1936-1967; 1 reel.

Index to Births, 1914-1974; 4 reels.

Index to Deaths, 1924-1966; 1 reel.

Index to Delayed Births, 1914-1973; 2 reels.

MILITARY AND PENSION RECORDS

Record of Armed Forces Discharges, various years, 1946-1971; 4 reels.

Index to Armed Forces Discharges, 1916-1967; 1 reel.

MISCELLANEOUS RECORDS

Orders and Decrees, 1892-1956; 11 reels.

Special Proceedings Dockets, 1894-1952; 2 reels.

Cross Index to Special Proceedings, 1892-1967; 1 reel.

Reports of Receivers, 1922-1942; 1 reel.

OFFICIALS, COUNTY

Minutes, Board of County Commissioners, 1876-1943; 4 reels.

SCHOOL RECORDS

Minutes, County Board of Education, 1885-1931; 1 reel.

Old Teachers' Register, 1857-1860; 1 reel.

WILLS

Record of Wills, 1885-1967; 6 reels.

Index to Wills, 1883-1967; 1 reel.

HAYWOOD COUNTY

Established in 1808 from Buncombe County.

ORIGINAL RECORDS

BONDS

Apprentice Bonds and Records, 1812-1861, 1870, 1905, 1908;
1 Fibredex box.

Bastardy Bonds and Records, 1814-1936; 4 Fibredex boxes.

Officials' Bonds and Records, 1812-1942; 2 Fibredex boxes.

COURT RECORDS

County Court of Pleas and Quarter Sessions

Minutes, 1809-1815, 1820-1868; 9 volumes.

Execution Dockets, 1816-1868; 3 volumes, 1 manuscript box.

State Dockets, 1811-1868; 2 volumes, 1 manuscript box.

Trial and Appearance Dockets, 1809-1834; 1 manuscript box.

Trial Dockets, 1835-1866; 3 volumes.

Miscellaneous Dockets, 1843-1868; 1 manuscript box.

Superior Court

Minutes, 1815-1913; 16 volumes, 2 manuscript boxes.

Equity Minutes, 1846-1868; 1 volume.

Equity Trial Docket, 1843-1868; 1 volume.

Appearance and Motion Docket, 1847-1882; 1 volume.

Execution Dockets, 1838-1867; 2 volumes.

State Dockets, 1840-1869; 2 volumes.

Trial Docket, 1840-1867; 1 volume.

Miscellaneous Dockets, 1810-1845; 1 manuscript box.

Civil Action Papers, 1802, 1810-1939; 87 Fibredex boxes.

Civil Action Papers Concerning Land, 1815-1948; 29 Fibredex boxes.

Criminal Action Papers, 1814-1944; 35 Fibredex boxes.

Circuit Criminal Court/Western District Criminal Court

Minutes, 1895-1900; 1 volume.

ELECTION RECORDS

Record of Elections, 1878-1902, 1924-1930; 2 volumes.

Certificates of Permanent Registration and Oaths, 1902-1908;
3 Fibredex boxes.

Miscellaneous Election Records, 1832-1936; 2 Fibredex boxes.

ESTATES RECORDS

Record of Accounts, 1866-1909; 4 volumes.

Appointment of Administrators, Executors, Guardians and Masters, 1868-1909; 1 volume.

Estates Records, 1809-1942; 82 Fibredex boxes.

Guardians' Records, 1815-1941; 9 Fibredex boxes.

Record of Settlements, 1869-1921; 2 volumes.

LAND RECORDS

Record of Deeds, 1809-1865; 13 volumes.

Deeds, 1801-1948; 9 Fibredex boxes.

Deeds of Trust, Mortgage Deeds and Land Grants, 1786-1948;
1 Fibredex box.

Cross Index to Deeds, 1809-1877; 1 volume.

Ejectments, 1812-1935; 3 Fibredex boxes.

Land Entries, 1809-1904; 3 volumes.

Tax Levies on Land, 1927-1936; 9 Fibredex boxes.

Agreements, Contracts and Leases, 1832-1948; 1 Fibredex box.

Attachments, Executions, Levies and Liens on Land, 1809-1938;
4 Fibredex boxes.

Probate of Deeds, 1885-1887; 1 volume.

Miscellaneous Land Records, 1809-1946; 2 Fibredex boxes.

MARRIAGE, DIVORCE AND VITAL STATISTICS

Marriage Bonds, 1808-1868; 5 Fibredex boxes.

Marriage Registers, 1868-1938; 4 volumes.

Divorce Records, 1829-1944; 19 Fibredex boxes.

MISCELLANEOUS RECORDS

Alien Registration, 1940-1943; 1 volume.

Petitions for Naturalization, 1906-1918; 4 volumes.

County Accounts, Claims and Correspondence, 1809-1938; 1 Fibredex box,
1 manuscript box.

Indian Records, 1821-1925; 1 Fibredex box.

Insolvent Debtors, 1814-1896; 7 Fibredex boxes.

Grand Jury Presentments and Reports, 1823-1966; 2 Fibredex boxes.

Orders and Decrees, 1870-1921; 1 volume.

Miscellaneous Records, 1815-1966; 5 Fibredex boxes.

Coroners' Inquests, 1822-1967; 2 Fibredex boxes.

Records of Slaves and Free Persons of Color, 1823-1868; 1 Fibredex box.

Records of Assignees, Receivers and Trustees, 1852-1942; 9 Fibredex boxes.

ROADS AND BRIDGES

Road Records, 1811-1927; 1 Fibredex box.

Roads, Cartways and Bridges, 1838-1932; 1 Fibredex box.

Railroad Records, 1869-1933; 5 Fibredex boxes.

SCHOOL RECORDS

School Records, 1830-1950; 1 Fibredex box.

TAX AND FISCAL RECORDS

Tax List, 1866-1868; 1 volume.

Miscellaneous Tax Records, 1820-1933; 2 Fibredex boxes.

WILLS

Wills, 1803-1937; 8 Fibredex boxes.

MICROFILM RECORDS

CORPORATIONS AND PARTNERSHIPS
Record of Corporations, 1885-1941; 1 reel.

COURT RECORDS
County Court of Pleas and Quarter Sessions
Minutes, 1809-1815, 1820-1868; 3 reels.
Superior Court
Minutes, 1869-1955; 14 reels.

ESTATES RECORDS
Record of Accounts, 1874-1966; 8 reels.

Appointment and Bonds of Administrators, 1902-1966; 6 reels.

Appointment of Executors, 1927-1966; 2 reels.

Appointment and Bonds of Guardians, 1909-1966; 3 reels.

Guardians' Bonds, 1909-1926; 1 reel.

Accounts of Indigent Orphans, 1921-1941; 1 reel.

Inheritance Tax Records, 1921-1966; 2 reels.

Record of Settlements, 1869-1966; 6 reels.

Qualification of Trustees Under Wills, 1963-1966; 1 reel.

Index to Estates, 1808-1939; 1 reel.

Cross Index to Administrators and Executors, 1870-1966; 1 reel.

Cross Index to Guardians, 1870-1966; 1 reel.

LAND RECORDS
Record of Deeds, 1809-1958; 99 reels.

Index to Real Estate Conveyances, Grantor, 1808-1966; 10 reels.

Index to Real Estate Conveyances, Grantee, 1808-1966; Index to Deeds of
Trust, 1959-1966; 10 reels.

Record of Land Entries, 1809-1887; 1 reel.

Record of Land Sold for Taxes, 1925-1927; 1 reel.

Federal Tax Lien Index, 1925-1966; 1 reel.

Record of Resales, 1924-1966; 3 reels.

MARRIAGE, DIVORCE AND VITAL STATISTICS
Marriage Licenses, 1857-1965; 27 reels.

Marriage Registers, 1868-1921, 1939-1965; 3 reels.

Index to Marriages, 1850-1939; 2 reels.

Maiden Names of Divorced Women, 1939-1966; 1 reel.

Index to Births, 1913-1978; 4 reels.

Index to Deaths, 1913-1972; 2 reels.

Index to Delayed Births, various years; 1 reel.

MILITARY AND PENSION RECORDS
Record of Armed Forces Discharges, various years, 1944-1966; 6 reels.

Index to Armed Forces Discharges, 1917-1966; 1 reel.

MISCELLANEOUS RECORDS
Clerk's Minute Dockets, 1921-1966; 3 reels.

Orders and Decrees, 1870-1921; 1 reel.

Special Proceedings, 1875-1951; 12 reels.
Cross Index to Special Proceedings, 1874-1966; 2 reels.

OFFICIALS, COUNTY
Minutes, Board of County Commissioners, 1868-1966; 4 reels.

SCHOOL RECORDS
Minutes, County Board of Education, 1885-1921; 1 reel.

TAX AND FISCAL RECORDS
Tax List, 1866-1868; 1 reel.

WILLS
Record of Wills and Inventories, 1808-1878; 1 reel.
Record of Wills, 1869-1966; 4 reels.
Index to Wills, 1829-1966; 1 reel.

HENDERSON COUNTY

Established in 1838 from Buncombe County.

ORIGINAL RECORDS

BONDS

 Apprentice Bonds, 1875-1885; 1 volume.

 Bastardy Bonds and Records, 1840-1936, 1953; 1 volume, 2 Fibredex boxes.

 Officials' Bonds and Records, 1839-1931; 8 Fibredex boxes.

CORPORATIONS AND PARTNERSHIPS

 Business, Corporation and Partnership Records, 1844-1959; 2 Fibredex boxes.

COURT RECORDS

 County Court of Pleas and Quarter Sessions

  Minutes, 1839-1868; 5 volumes.

  Execution Dockets, 1839-1859, 1866-1868; 3 volumes.

  State Docket, 1840-1868; 1 volume.

 Superior Court

  Minutes, 1841-1920; 18 volumes.

  Equity Minutes, 1841-1868; 1 volume.

  Equity Enrolling Docket, 1844-1868; 1 volume.

  Execution Docket, 1842-1846; 1 volume.

  State Docket, 1841-1856; 1 volume.

  Trial Dockets, 1851-1868; 2 volumes.

  Civil Action Papers, 1808-1959; 59 Fibredex boxes.

  Civil Action Papers Concerning Land, 1835-1933; 17 Fibredex boxes.

  Criminal Action Papers, 1839-1955; 38 Fibredex boxes.

  Miscellaneous Court Records, 1861-1966; 1 Fibredex box.

 Circuit Criminal Court/Western District Criminal Court

  Minutes, 1895-1901; 1 volume.

  Judgment Docket, 1895-1901; 1 volume.

ELECTION RECORDS

 Record of Elections, 1878-1924; 2 volumes.

 Election Records, 1844-1927; 1 Fibredex box.

ESTATES RECORDS

 Record of Accounts, 1870-1906; 2 volumes.

 Administrators' Bonds, 1871-1922; 2 volumes.

 Estates Records, 1838-1968; 119 Fibredex boxes.

 Guardians' Records, 1838-1968; 23 Fibredex boxes.

 Guardians' Bonds, 1872-1931; 2 volumes.

 Guardians' Docket, 1846-1869; 1 volume.

 Record of Settlements, 1869-1912; 1 volume.

 Record of Probate (Estates), 1868-1896; 1 volume.

LAND RECORDS

 Record of Deeds, 1839-1841; 1 volume.

 Record of Probate of Deeds, 1839-1876; 2 volumes.

Deeds of Sale, 1795-1959; 10 Fibredex boxes.

Deeds of Trust, 1848-1955; 1 Fibredex box.

Quitclaim Deeds, 1835-1959; 1 Fibredex box.

Miscellaneous Deeds, 1799-1949; 1 Fibredex box.

Ejectments, 1838-1957; 5 Fibredex boxes.

Levies on Land, 1840-1926; 5 Fibredex boxes.

Miscellaneous Land Records, 1847-1959; 2 Fibredex boxes.

MARRIAGE, DIVORCE AND VITAL STATISTICS

Marriage Records, 1838-1955; 1 Fibredex box.

Divorce Records, 1842-1931; 3 Fibredex boxes.

MILITARY AND PENSION RECORDS

Record of Confederate Pensions, 1885-1905; 1 volume.

Record of Medical Examinations, 1911-1927; 1 volume.

Pension Records, 1885-1939; 3 Fibredex boxes.

MISCELLANEOUS RECORDS

Alien Registration, 1927-1948; 1 volume.

Declaration of Intent, 1913-1925; 1 volume.

Petitions for Naturalization, 1910-1927; 1 volume.

County Accounts, 1909-1968; 1 volume.

Clerk of Court Correspondence, 1873-1962; 10 Fibredex boxes.

Homestead Records, 1867-1927; 1 Fibredex box.

Insolvent Debtors, 1838-1929; 1 Fibredex box.

Grand Jury Records, 1840-1954; 1 Fibredex box.

Justices of the Peace Records, 1853-1955; 2 Fibredex boxes.

Lunacy Records, 1849-1929; 1 Fibredex box.

Orders and Decrees, 1869-1885; 1 volume.

Miscellaneous Correspondence, 1846-1930; 2 Fibredex boxes.

Miscellaneous Records, 1840-1956; 4 Fibredex boxes.

Coroners' Inquests, 1863-1934; 1 volume, 1 Fibredex box.

Records of Assignees, Receivers and Trustees, 1857-1944; 1 Fibredex box.

ROADS AND BRIDGES

Road Records, 1842-1927; 3 Fibredex boxes.

Railroad Records, 1896-1909; 3 Fibredex boxes.

TAX AND FISCAL RECORDS

Tax Records, 1841-1955; 1 Fibredex box.

WILLS

Wills, 1797, 1817, 1835-1969; 62 Fibredex boxes.

Cross Index to Wills, 1841-1949; 1 volume.

MICROFILM RECORDS

CORPORATIONS AND PARTNERSHIPS

Record of Corporations, 1874-1957; 2 reels.

Partnership Records, 1913-1963; 1 reel.

COURT RECORDS
    County Court of Pleas and Quarter Sessions
        Minutes, 1839-1868; 3 reels.
    Superior Court
        Minutes, 1841-1949; 14 reels.
ELECTION RECORDS
    Record of Elections, 1928-1966; 1 reel.
ESTATES RECORDS
    Record of Accounts, 1871-1967; 9 reels.
    Administrators' and Executors' Bonds, 1917-1929; 1 reel.
    Record of Appointment of Administrators, 1895-1930; 1 reel.
    Record of Administrators, 1919-1968; 4 reels.
    Record of Administrators, Executors and Guardians, 1903-1928; 2 reels.
    Record of Executors, 1927-1967; 2 reels.
    Guardians' Bonds, 1928-1967; 1 reel.
    Record of Guardians, 1925-1967; 2 reels.
    Accounts of Indigent Orphans, 1910-1937; 1 reel.
    Inheritance Tax Records, 1915-1956; 1 reel.
    Record of Settlements, 1869-1968; 7 reels.
LAND RECORDS
    Record of Deeds, 1838-1959; 187 reels.
    Index to Real Estate Conveyances, Grantor, 1838-1968; 7 reels.
    Index to Real Estate Conveyances, Grantee, 1838-1962; 6 reels.
    Record of Surveys and Land Entries, 1921-1950; 1 reel.
    Record of Sales and Resales, 1916-1967; 4 reels.
MARRIAGE, DIVORCE AND VITAL STATISTICS
    Marriage Licenses, 1906-1967; 9 reels.
    Record of Marriage Licenses, 1921-1939; 2 reels.
    Marriage Registers, 1851-1967; 5 reels.
    Index to Births, 1914-1967; 1 reel.
    Index to Deaths, 1914-1967; 1 reel.
    Index to Delayed Births, various years; 1 reel.
MILITARY AND PENSION RECORDS
    Record of Armed Forces Discharges, 1944-1978; 8 reels.
MISCELLANEOUS RECORDS
    Orders and Decrees, 1869-1957; 2 reels.
    Special Proceedings, 1905-1957; 5 reels.
    Cross Index to Special Proceedings, 1869-1967; 1 reel.
    Record of Appointment of Receivers, 1916-1967; 1 reel.
OFFICIALS, COUNTY
    Minutes, Board of County Commissioners, 1868-1941; 5 reels.
SCHOOL RECORDS
    Minutes, County Board of Education, 1885-1967; 1 reel.

WILLS
Record of Wills, 1841-1967; 10 reels.
Index to Wills, 1843-1967; 1 reel.

HERTFORD COUNTY

Established in 1759 (effective 1760) from Chowan County.
Courthouse fires of 1830 and 1862 destroyed majority of county's records.

ORIGINAL RECORDS

BONDS

  Apprentice Bonds, 1861-1868; 1 Fibredex box.

  Bastardy Bonds, 1865-1898; 1 Fibredex box.

COURT RECORDS

  County Court of Pleas and Quarter Sessions

    Minutes, 1830-1868; 5 volumes.

    Execution Dockets, 1846-1868; 2 volumes.

    State Docket, 1845-1868; 1 volume.

    Trial and Appearance Dockets, 1830-1868; 3 volumes.

  Superior Court

    Minutes, 1868-1915; 5 volumes.

    Trial Docket, 1830-1836; Trial and Appearance Docket, 1842-1868;
      1 volume.

    Civil and Criminal Action Papers, 1802-1824, 1855-1914;
      11 Fibredex boxes.

    Supreme Court Opinions, 1859-1898; 1 manuscript box.

  Inferior Court/Criminal Court of Hertford County

    Minutes, Inferior Court, 1877-1891; Minutes, Criminal Court, 1891-
      1897; Minutes, Board of Justices of the Peace, 1878-1885;
      1 volume.

    Criminal Issues Docket, Inferior Court, 1879-1891; Criminal Issues
      Docket, Criminal Court, 1891-1897; 1 volume.

ELECTION RECORDS

  Record of Elections, 1880-1908, 1924-1932; 4 volumes.

ESTATES RECORDS

  Record of Estates, 1830-1866; 4 volumes.

  Record of Accounts, 1868-1896; 4 volumes.

  Administrators' Bonds, 1869-1915; 5 volumes.

  Estates Records, 1858-1914; 48 Fibredex boxes.

  Guardians' Records, 1858-1914; 1 Fibredex box.

  Guardians' Accounts, 1823-1866; 3 volumes.

  Guardians' Bonds, 1869-1915; 2 volumes.

  Record of Settlements, 1868-1910; 1 volume.

LAND RECORDS

  Deeds, 1775-1940; 9 Fibredex boxes.

  Deeds of Trust and Mortgage Deeds, 1871-1940; 2 Fibredex boxes.

  Cross Index to Real Estate Conveyances, 1862-1920; 9 volumes.

MARRIAGE, DIVORCE AND VITAL STATISTICS

  Divorce Records, 1871-1914; 2 Fibredex boxes.

MISCELLANEOUS RECORDS
>Miscellaneous Records, 1787-1939; 3 Fibredex boxes.

TAX AND FISCAL RECORDS
>Tax Lists, 1782, 1859-1860; 1 volume, 1 manuscript box.

WILLS
>Wills, 1763, 1861-1903; 4 Fibredex boxes.

MICROFILM RECORDS

CORPORATIONS AND PARTNERSHIPS
>Record of Corporations, 1878-1962; 1 reel.
>Partnership Records, 1918-1952; 1 reel.

COURT RECORDS
>County Court of Pleas and Quarter Sessions
>>Minutes, 1830-1868; 1 reel.
>Superior Court
>>Minutes, 1868-1950; 6 reels.

ELECTION RECORDS
>Record of Elections, 1880-1962; 1 reel.

ESTATES RECORDS
>Record of Accounts, 1830-1840, 1891-1963; 4 reels.
>Record of Accounts and Inventories, 1895-1963; 2 reels.
>Appointment of Administrators, Executors and Guardians, 1868-1933; 1 reel.
>Record of Administrators, 1918-1963; 2 reels.
>Administrators' Bonds, 1869-1915; Guardians' Bonds, 1869-1914; 1 reel.
>Record of Executors, 1933-1963; 1 reel.
>Guardians' Accounts, 1823-1845; 1 reel.
>Record of Guardians, 1931-1962; 1 reel.
>Record of Inheritance Tax Collections, 1920-1963; 1 reel.
>Record of Settlements, 1868-1963; 3 reels.

LAND RECORDS
>Record of Deeds, 1862-1946; 54 reels.
>Index to Real Estate Transfers, Grantor, 1862-1960; 2 reels.
>Index to Real Estate Transfers, Grantee, 1862-1960; 2 reels.
>Record of Taxes for Mortgagees, 1931-1934; 1 reel.
>Record of Resale of Land by Trustees and Mortgagees, 1920-1963; 2 reels.

MARRIAGE, DIVORCE AND VITAL STATISTICS
>Marriage Licenses, 1904-1961; 5 reels.
>Marriage Registers, 1868-1971; 1 reel.
>Maiden Names of Divorced Women, 1939-1962; 1 reel.
>Index to Vital Statistics, 1913-1954; 1 reel.

MILITARY AND PENSION RECORDS
>Record of Armed Forces Discharges, 1918-1986; 2 reels.
>Register of Confederate Soldiers, 1861-1865; 1 reel.

MISCELLANEOUS RECORDS
    Orders and Decrees, 1868-1950; 4 reels.
    Special Proceedings, 1881-1968; 3 reels.
    Index to Civil Actions and Special Proceedings, 1881-1968; 1 reel.
OFFICIALS, COUNTY
    Minutes, Board of County Commissioners, 1868-1939; 2 reels.
WILLS
    Record of Wills, 1829-1963; 3 reels.
    Cross Index to Wills, 1830-1963; 1 reel.

HOKE COUNTY

Established in 1911 from Cumberland and Robeson counties.

ORIGINAL RECORDS

COURT RECORDS
> Superior Court
>> Minutes, 1911-1949; 4 volumes.

ELECTION RECORDS
> Record of Elections, 1920-1966; 2 volumes.

ESTATES RECORDS
> Record of Amounts Paid for Indigent Children, 1912-1955; 1 volume.

LAND RECORDS
> Land Entries, 1913-1929; 1 volume, 1 manuscript box.

MARRIAGE, DIVORCE AND VITAL STATISTICS
> Maiden Names of Divorced Women, 1944-1965; 1 volume.

MISCELLANEOUS RECORDS
> Alien Registration, 1927; 1 volume.
> Dentists' Certificates of Registration, 1912-1943; 1 volume.
> Nurses' Certificates of Registration, 1918-1942; 1 volume.
> Optometrists' and Chiropractors' Certificates of Registration, 1911-1949; 1 volume.
> Physicians' and Surgeons' Certificates of Registration, 1911-1964; 1 volume.
> Clerk's Minute Dockets (Special Proceedings), 1921-1956; 3 volumes.

MICROFILM RECORDS

CORPORATIONS AND PARTNERSHIPS
> Record of Corporations, 1911-1970; 1 reel.
> Record of Partnerships, 1943-1970; 1 reel.

COURT RECORDS
> Superior Court
>> Minutes, 1911-1966; 4 reels.
>> Judgment Docket, Land Tax Sales, 1930-1942; 1 reel.

ELECTION RECORDS
> Minutes, Board of Elections, 1956-1970; 1 reel.
> Record of Elections, 1916-1966; 1 reel.

ESTATES RECORDS
> Record of Accounts, 1911-1966; 3 reels.
> Record of Administrators, Executors and Guardians, 1911-1953; 1 reel.
> Record of Administrators, 1921-1966; 2 reels.
> Record of Executors, 1953-1966; 1 reel.
> Cross Index to Administrators and Executors, 1911-1966; 1 reel.
> Record of Guardians, 1928-1966; 1 reel.
> Cross Index to Guardians, 1911-1966; 1 reel.

Record of Amounts Paid for Indigent Children, 1912-1955; 1 reel.
Inheritance Tax Records, 1919-1970; 1 reel.
Record of Settlements, 1911-1965; 3 reels.
Trustee Ledger for Minors, 1943-1966; 1 reel.

LAND RECORDS
Record of Deeds, 1911-1959; 21 reels.
General Index to Real Estate Conveyances, Grantor, 1911-1970; 2 reels.
General Index to Real Estate Conveyances, Grantee, 1911-1970; 2 reels.
Easements and Rights-of-Way, 1929-1966; 2 reels.
Federal Tax Lien Index, 1924-1969; 1 reel.
Report of Land Sales Under Foreclosures, 1923-1966; 1 reel.

MARRIAGE, DIVORCE AND VITAL STATISTICS
Marriage Registers, 1911-1970; 1 reel.
Maiden Names of Divorced Women, 1944-1965; 1 reel.
Index to Vital Statistics, 1913-1968; 1 reel.

MILITARY AND PENSION RECORDS
Record of Armed Forces Discharges, 1924-1983; 3 reels.

MISCELLANEOUS RECORDS
Lunacy Docket, 1911-1966; 1 reel.
Clerk's Minute Dockets, 1921-1966; 2 reels.
Orders and Decrees, 1911-1967; 3 reels.
Special Proceedings, 1911-1970; 2 reels.
Cross Index to Special Proceedings, 1911-1966; 1 reel.

OFFICIALS, COUNTY
Minutes, Board of County Commissioners, 1911-1970; 2 reels.

SCHOOL RECORDS
Minutes, County Board of Education, 1911-1970; 1 reel.

TAX AND FISCAL RECORDS
Tax Scrolls, 1915, 1925, 1965; 1 reel.

WILLS
Record of Wills, 1911-1966; 1 reel.

HYDE COUNTY

Established in 1705 as Wickham Precinct of Bath County.
Name changed to Hyde in 1712.

ORIGINAL RECORDS

BONDS
Apprentice Bonds and Records, 1771-1911; 1 volume, 2 Fibredex boxes.
Bastardy Bonds and Records, 1740-1896; 1 volume, 2 Fibredex boxes.
Officials' Bonds, 1794-1903; 1 volume, 3 Fibredex boxes.

COURT RECORDS
County Court of Pleas and Quarter Sessions
Minutes, 1736-1737, 1744-1868; 19 volumes, 1 manuscript box.
Appearance, Reference (Trial), Crown (State) and Execution Dockets, 1744-1797; 4 volumes, 1 manuscript box.
Appearance and Trial Dockets, 1790-1820; 3 volumes, 1 manuscript box.
Appearance Dockets, 1820-1868; 4 volumes.
State Docket, 1825-1828; 1 volume.
Trial Dockets, 1818-1868; 9 volumes, 1 manuscript box.
Superior Court
Minutes, 1807-1921; 10 volumes.
Equity Minutes, 1808-1868; 1 volume.
Equity Enrolling Docket, 1808-1852; 1 volume.
Equity Execution Docket, 1808-1868; 1 volume.
Equity Trial Dockets, 1816-1868; 2 volumes.
Appearance Docket, 1822-1860; 1 volume.
Execution Dockets, 1808-1852; 3 volumes.
State Dockets, 1813-1859; 3 volumes.
Trial and Appearance Docket, 1807-1822; 1 volume.
Trial Dockets, 1822-1869; 3 volumes.
Civil and Criminal Action Papers, 1713-1899; 18 Fibredex boxes.

ELECTION RECORDS
Record of Elections, 1878-1970; 6 volumes.

ESTATES RECORDS
Record of Estates, 1837-1868; 3 volumes.
Record of Accounts, 1869-1905; 3 volumes.
Administrators' Bonds, 1868-1919; 3 volumes.
Estates Records, 1745-1904; 68 Fibredex boxes.
Guardians' Records, 1745-1904; 5 Fibredex boxes.
Guardians' Accounts, 1850-1860; 1 volume.
Guardians' Bonds, 1884-1919; 1 volume.
Record of Settlements, 1869-1905; 1 volume.

LAND RECORDS
Record of Deeds, 1736-1840; 9 volumes.

Deeds and Land Records, 1757-1897; 1 Fibredex box.

Cross Index to Deeds, 1736-1840; 1 volume.

Land Entries, 1778-1795; 1 volume.

Land Grants, 1779-1857; 2 volumes.

MARRIAGE, DIVORCE AND VITAL STATISTICS

Marriage Bonds, 1742-1868; 1 Fibredex box.

Marriage Register, 1868-1873; 1 volume.

Cohabitation Records, 1866; 1 volume.

Divorce Records, 1829-1898; 1 Fibredex box.

MISCELLANEOUS RECORDS

Alien Registration, 1940; 1 volume.

County Accounts and Claims, 1853-1873; 1 volume.

Insolvent Debtors and Homestead and Personal Property Exemptions, 1811-1904; 1 Fibredex box.

Registry of Licenses to Trades, 1881-1903; 1 volume.

Licenses to Catch Oysters, 1895-1902; 2 volumes.

Receipts from Oyster License Tax, 1895-1904; 1 volume.

Minutes, Wardens of the Poor, 1837-1868; 1 volume.

Minutes, Franklin Society, 1861; 1 volume.

Lake Landing Township Minutes, 1869-1877; 1 volume.

Miscellaneous Records, 1735-1908; 4 Fibredex boxes.

OFFICIALS, COUNTY

Minutes (Rough), Board of County Commissioners, 1878-1885; 1 volume.

ROADS AND BRIDGES

Road Docket, 1855-1879, 1923; 1 volume.

Road Records, 1767-1888; 2 Fibredex boxes.

SCHOOL RECORDS

Minutes, Board of Superintendents of Common Schools, 1841-1861; 1 volume.

TAX AND FISCAL RECORDS

Lists of Taxables, 1837-1868; 4 volumes, 1 manuscript box.

WILLS

Record of Wills and Estates, 1755-1818; 9 volumes.

Wills, 1760-1906; 9 Fibredex boxes.

MICROFILM RECORDS

BONDS

Apprentice Bonds, 1868-1912; 1 reel.

COURT RECORDS

County Court of Pleas and Quarter Sessions

Minutes, 1736-1815, 1820-1868; 5 reels.

Appearance, Crown, Reference and Execution Dockets, 1744-1761; 1 reel.

Superior Court
>Minutes, 1869-1921; 3 reels.
>Equity Minutes, 1808-1868; 1 reel.
>Equity Enrolling Docket, 1808-1852; 1 reel.

ELECTION RECORDS
>Record of Elections, 1880-1956; 1 reel.

ESTATES RECORDS
>Record of Estates, 1845-1868; 2 reels.
>Record of Accounts, 1869-1921; 3 reels.
>Administrators' Bonds, 1869-1919; 1 reel.
>Appointment of Executors, 1868-1919; 1 reel.
>Cross Index to Administrators and Executors, 1870-1960; 1 reel.
>Guardians' Accounts, 1849-1860; 1 reel.
>Guardians' Bonds, 1884-1919; 1 reel.
>Guardians' Settlements, 1837-1845; 1 reel.
>Cross Index to Guardians, 1870-1960; 1 reel.
>Record of Settlements, 1856-1905; 1 reel.

LAND RECORDS
>Record of Deeds, 1736-1918; 34 reels.
>Record of Mortgages and Deeds of Trust, 1882-1915; 6 reels.
>Index to Real Estate Conveyances, Grantor, 1736-1937; 4 reels.
>Index to Real Estate Conveyances, Grantee, 1736-1937; 4 reels.
>Entry Takers' Book, 1891-1892; 1 reel.
>Grant Book, 1782-1787; 1 reel.

MARRIAGE, DIVORCE AND VITAL STATISTICS
>Marriage Bonds, 1741-1868; 2 reels.
>Marriage Registers, 1855-1975; 1 reel.
>Index to Vital Statistics, 1877-1958; 1 reel.

MILITARY AND PENSION RECORDS
>Record of Armed Forces Discharges, 1917-1987; 3 reels.

MISCELLANEOUS RECORDS
>Orders and Decrees, 1869-1941; 1 reel.
>Special Proceedings, 1885-1968; 8 reels.
>Cross Index to Special Proceedings, 1859-1960; 1 reel.
>Minutes, Wardens of the Poor, 1837-1868; 1 reel.

ROADFS AND BRIDGES
>Road Overseers' Book, 1858-1879; 1 reel.

TAX AND FISCAL RECORDS
>Lists of Taxables, 1837-1868; 2 reels.

WILLS
>Record of Wills, 1764-1968; 7 reels.
>Record of Wills, Inventories and Sales of Estates, 1756-1762, 1765-1802;
>>3 reels.
>Cross Index to Wills, 1764-1970; 1 reel.

IREDELL COUNTY

Established in 1788 from Rowan County.
Courthouse fire of 1854 destroyed many court records.

ORIGINAL RECORDS

BONDS

Bastardy Bonds and Records, 1855, 1860-1913; 1 volume, 2 Fibredex boxes.
Constables' Bonds, 1847-1866; 1 volume.
Officials' Bonds, 1868-1903; 1 volume.

COURT RECORDS

County Court of Pleas and Quarter Sessions

Minutes, 1789-1868; 7 volumes.
Appearance Dockets, 1810-1868; 4 volumes.
Execution Dockets, 1791-1801, 1835-1844; 4 volumes.
Levy Dockets, 1845-1858; 2 volumes.
Indictment and Recognizance Docket, 1802-1821; 1 volume.
State Docket, 1857-1868; 1 volume.
Trial Dockets, 1810-1841, 1855-1868; 5 volumes.

Superior Court

Minutes, 1807-1845, 1869-1909; 15 volumes.
Equity Minutes, 1828-1868; 2 volumes.
Equity Enrolling Dockets, 1837-1841, 1862-1868; 2 volumes.
Equity Trial Dockets, 1807-1827, 1854-1868; 2 volumes.
Appearance and Reference Docket, 1808-1825; 1 volume.
Execution Dockets, 1808-1833, 1841-1861; 4 volumes.
State and Recognizance Docket, 1808-1826; 1 volume.
Trial Dockets, 1808-1857; 3 volumes.
Civil Action Papers, 1808-1924; 22 Fibredex boxes.
Civil Action Papers Concerning Land, 1845-1932; 8 Fibredex boxes.
Criminal Action Papers, 1814-1913; 28 Fibredex boxes.

ELECTION RECORDS

Record of Elections, 1878-1928; 3 volumes.
Election Records, 1886-1926; 1 Fibredex box.

ESTATES RECORDS

Record of Estates, 1843-1868; 3 volumes.
Record of Accounts, 1868-1889; 3 volumes.
Administrators' Bonds, 1846-1899; 4 volumes.
Appointment of Administrators, Executors and Guardians, 1868-1876, 1888-1905; 3 volumes.
Record of Widows' Year's Support, 1871-1895; 1 volume.
Estates Records, 1790-1944; 142 Fibredex boxes.
Guardians' Records, 1803-1935, 1943; 11 Fibredex boxes.
Guardians' Accounts, 1894-1907; 1 volume.
Guardians' Bonds, 1846-1900; 3 volumes.

Petitions and Orders, 1901-1905, 1921; 1 volume.

Record of Settlements, 1868-1895; 2 volumes.

Fiduciary Account Book, 1833-1867; 1 volume.

LAND RECORDS

Deeds, 1811-1945; 6 Fibredex boxes.

Mortgage Deeds and Deeds of Trust, 1857-1948; 1 Fibredex box.

Probate of Deeds, 1868-1886; 3 volumes.

Ejectments, 1853-1906; 1 Fibredex box.

Land Entries, 1855-1905; 2 volumes.

Attachments, Executions, Liens and Levies on Land, 1843-1913;
3 Fibredex boxes.

Miscellaneous Land Records, 1856-1943; 1 Fibredex box.

MARRIAGE, DIVORCE AND VITAL STATISTICS

Marriage Bonds, 1788-1868; 1 Fibredex box.

Record of Marriage Certificates, 1851-1867, 1899; Record of Cohabitation,
1866; 1 volume.

Marriage Registers, 1867-1939; 5 volumes.

Divorce Records, 1855-1913; 3 Fibredex boxes.

MILITARY AND PENSION RECORDS

Court Martial Minutes, 1808-1862; 1 volume.

MISCELLANEOUS RECORDS

County Accounts and Buildings, 1815-1918; 1 Fibredex box.

County Home Account Books, 1903-1908, 1914-1916; 1 manuscript box.

Personal Accounts, 1854-1892; 1 Fibredex box.

Homestead and Personal Property Exemptions, 1869-1899, 1933;
1 Fibredex box.

Miscellaneous Records, 1808-1949; 5 Fibredex boxes.

Coroners' Inquests, 1854-1906; 1 Fibredex box.

Slave Records, 1823-1872; 1 Fibredex box.

Records of Assignees, Trustees and Receivers, 1843-1917; 5 Fibredex boxes.

ROADS AND BRIDGES

Railroad Records, 1860-1909; 4 Fibredex boxes.

TAX AND FISCAL RECORDS

List of Taxables, 1837-1842; 1 volume.

Miscellaneous Tax Records, 1790-1910; 1 Fibredex box.

WILLS

Wills, 1787-1917; 13 Fibredex boxes.

Cross Index to Wills, [1790-1868, 1894-1907]; 1 volume.

MICROFILM RECORDS

BONDS

Bastardy Bonds, 1870-1879; 1 reel.

Officials' Bonds, 1868-1903; 1 reel.

CORPORATIONS AND PARTNERSHIPS

Record of Corporations, 1888-1956; 4 reels.

Partnership Records, 1913-1965; 1 reel.

COURT RECORDS

County Court of Pleas and Quarter Sessions

Minutes, 1789-1868; 2 reels.

Superior Court

Minutes, 1807-1954; 14 reels.

Equity Minutes, 1828-1868; 1 reel.

ELECTION RECORDS

Record of Elections, 1908-1964; 1 reel.

ESTATES RECORDS

Record of Accounts, 1869-1965; 17 reels.

Administrators' Bonds, 1846-1965; 5 reels.

Appointment of Administrators, Executors and Guardians, 1888-1931; 4 reels.

Appointment of Administrators and Executors, 1931-1965; 4 reels.

Appointment of Executors, 1868-1876; 1 reel.

Guardians' Bonds, 1899-1939; 1 reel.

Appointment of Guardians, 1928-1964; 1 reel.

Appointment of Trustees and Guardians, 1962-1965; 1 reel.

Guardians' Accounts, 1894-1965; 5 reels.

Accounts of Indigent Orphans, 1913; 1 reel.

Dowers and Widows' Year's Support, 1895-1965; 2 reels.

Inheritance Tax Records, 1920-1965; 2 reels.

Record of Inventories, 1843-1867; 2 reels.

Record of Settlements, 1868-1894; 1 reel.

Index to Final Accounts, 1788-1970; 3 reels.

LAND RECORDS

Record of Deeds, 1788-1960; 181 reels.

Index to Deeds, Grantor, 1788-1965; 15 reels.

Index to Deeds, Grantee, 1788-1965; 14 reels.

Land Entries, 1789-1794, 1855-1905; 1 reel.

Record of Sales and Resales, 1921-1965; 3 reels.

MARRIAGE, DIVORCE AND VITAL STATISTICS

Marriage Bonds, 1790-1866; 1 reel.

Marriage Licenses, 1893-1964; 14 reels.

Marriage Registers, Female, 1851-1965; 2 reels.

Marriage Registers, Male, 1851-1972; 3 reels.

Record of Cohabitation, 1866; 1 reel.

Index to Births, 1913-1981; 5 reels.

Index to Deaths, 1913-1965; 3 reels.

Index to Delayed Births, various years; 1 reel.

MILITARY AND PENSION RECORDS

Record of Armed Forces Discharges, 1918-1981; 14 reels.

Index to Armed Forces Discharges, 1918-1965; 1 reel.

MISCELLANEOUS RECORDS
Orders and Decrees, 1869-1893; 1 reel.
Special Proceedings, 1887-1949; 16 reels.
Index to Special Proceedings, Plaintiff, 1868-1965; 2 reels.
Index to Special Proceedings, Defendant, 1868-1965; 1 reel.
Index to Special Proceedings, 1970-1981; 1 reel.
OFFICIALS, COUNTY
Minutes, Board of County Commissioners, 1868-1947; 6 reels.
SCHOOL RECORDS
Minutes, County Board of Education, 1885-1899, 1907-1950; 1 reel.
TAX AND FISCAL RECORDS
Land Valuations for Direct Tax, 1800; 1 reel.
WILLS
Record of Wills, 1790-1965; 9 reels.
Index to Wills, Devisor, 1788-1970; 1 reel.
Index to Wills, Devisee, 1788-1970; 2 reels.

JACKSON COUNTY

Established in 1851 from Haywood and Macon counties.
Many records missing; reason unknown.

ORIGINAL RECORDS

COURT RECORDS
> County Court of Pleas and Quarter Sessions
>> Minutes, 1853-1868; 2 volumes.
>> Execution Docket, 1860-1868; 1 volume.
> Superior Court
>> Minutes, 1869-1910; 9 volumes.
>> Equity Minutes, 1853-1864; 1 volume.

ELECTION RECORDS
> Record of Elections, 1878-1938; 4 volumes.

ESTATES RECORDS
> Record of Estates, 1853-1879, 1885; 1 volume.
> Appointment of Administrators, Executors, Guardians and Masters, 1868-
>> 1913; 1 volume.
> Record of Administrators, 1870-1914, 1924; 1 volume.
> Record of Guardians, 1871-1915; 1 volume.

LAND RECORDS
> Record of Deeds, 1853-1875; 4 volumes.
> Cross Index to Deeds, [1853-1891]; 2 volumes.
> Probate of Deeds, 1872-1894; 2 volumes.

MARRIAGE, DIVORCE AND VITAL STATISTICS
> Record of Maiden Names of Divorced Women, 1940-1971; 1 volume.

MISCELLANEOUS RECORDS
> Registry of Licenses to Trades, 1873-1904; 1 volume.
> Orders and Decrees, 1869-1908; 1 volume.

MICROFILM RECORDS

CORPORATIONS AND PARTNERSHIPS
> Record of Incorporations, 1891-1970; 1 reel.
> Partnership Records, 1913-1960; 1 reel.

COURT RECORDS
> County Court of Pleas and Quarter Sessions
>> Minutes, 1853-1868; 1 reel.
> Superior Court
>> Minutes, 1869-1957; 9 reels.
>> Equity Minutes, 1853-1864; 1 reel.

ELECTION RECORDS
> Record of Elections, 1878-1968; 1 reel.

ESTATES RECORDS

Record of Administrators, Executors and Guardians, 1870-1966; 3 reels.
Appointment of Executors, 1868-1914; 1 reel.
Index to Administrators and Executors, 1911-1966; 1 reel.
Record of Guardians, 1871-1915, 1930-1966; 2 reels.
Cross Index to Guardians, 1911-1966; 1 reel.
Inheritance Tax Records, 1923-1970; 1 reel.
Record of Inventories, 1863-1875; 1 reel.
Record of Settlements, 1868-1966; 3 reels.
Trust Fund Records, 1928-1966; 1 reel.
Qualification of Trustees Under Wills, 1964; 1 reel.

LAND RECORDS

Record of Deeds, 1853-1960; 68 reels.
Index to Real Estate Conveyances, Grantor, 1853-1970; 14 reels.
Index to Real Estate Conveyances, Grantee, 1853-1970; 14 reels.
Land Entry Books, 1853-1968; 1 reel.
Index to Land Entries, 1853-1968; 1 reel.

MARRIAGE, DIVORCE AND VITAL STATISTICS

Marriage Registers, 1853-1974; 1 reel.
Maiden Names of Divorced Women, 1940-1968; 1 reel.
Index to Births, 1913-1992; 2 reels.
Index to Deaths, 1913-1992; 1 reel.
Index to Delayed Births, 1877-1991; 1 reel.

MILITARY AND PENSION RECORDS

Record of Armed Forces Discharges, 1917-1979; 5 reels.

MISCELLANEOUS RECORDS

Orders and Decrees, 1869-1908; 1 reel.
Special Proceedings, 1885-1970; Index to Special Proceedings, 1885-1966;
        5 reels.
Receipts and Disbursements by Clerk for Special Proceedings, 1919-1931;
        1 reel.

WILLS

Record of Wills, 1868-1966; 2 reels.
Index to Wills, 1853-1966; 1 reel.

JOHNSTON COUNTY

Established in 1746 from Craven County.
No record of fires, but many records missing.

ORIGINAL RECORDS

BONDS

Apprentice Bonds, 1850-1911; 4 volumes.

Bastardy Bonds, 1850-1895; 2 volumes.

COURT RECORDS

County Court of Pleas and Quarter Sessions

Minutes, 1759-1868; 16 volumes.

Appearance Dockets, 1820-1868; 3 volumes.

Execution Dockets, 1790-1868; 6 volumes.

State Dockets, 1793-1868; 6 volumes.

Trial and Appearance Dockets, 1786-1820; 6 volumes.

Trial Dockets, 1820-1868; 6 volumes.

Witness Ticket Book, 1818-1840; 1 volume.

Superior Court

Minutes, 1807-1913; 11 volumes.

Equity Minutes, 1807-1868; 2 volumes.

Equity Trial and Appearance Docket, 1848-1868; 1 volume.

Appearance Docket, 1852-1869; 1 volume.

State Docket, 1861-1868; 1 volume.

Trial Docket, 1852-1868; 1 volume.

Civil Action Papers, 1771-1927; 13 Fibredex boxes.

Civil Action Papers Concerning Land, 1853-1930; 9 Fibredex boxes.

Criminal Action Papers, 1769-1936; 7 Fibredex boxes.

ELECTION RECORDS

Record of Elections, 1878-1921; 3 volumes.

ESTATES RECORDS

Record of Estates, 1781-1868; 27 volumes.

Record of Accounts, 1868-1913; 7 volumes.

Administrators' Bonds, 1849-1914; 8 volumes.

Appointment of Administrators, Executors and Guardians, 1868-1923;
2 volumes.

Estates Records, 1771-1962; 91 Fibredex boxes.

Guardians' Records, 1793-1939; 18 Fibredex boxes.

Guardians' Accounts, 1903-1914; 1 volume.

Guardians' Bonds, 1847-1868, 1898-1912; 3 volumes.

Guardians' Scire Facias Docket, 1817-1851; 1 volume.

Record of Settlements, 1868-1924; 4 volumes.

LAND RECORDS

Record of Deeds, 1759-1765, 1779-1782; 2 volumes.

Deeds, 1748-1939; 7 Fibredex boxes.

Deeds of Trust and Mortgage Deeds, 1830-1930; 2 Fibredex boxes.

Land Entry Books, 1778-1903; 3 volumes.

Record of Land Divisions, 1789-1883; 3 volumes.

Miscellaneous Land Records, 1772-1954; 2 Fibredex boxes.

Record of Probate, 1869-1880; 1 volume, 1 pamphlet.

MARRIAGE, DIVORCE AND VITAL STATISTICS

Marriage Bonds, 1746-1868; 12 Fibredex boxes.

Record of Cohabitation, 1866; 1 volume.

Divorce Records, 1853-1926; 5 Fibredex boxes.

MILITARY AND PENSION RECORDS

Court Martial Minutes, 1761-1779; 1 volume.

Record of Confederate Soldiers from Johnston County, 1861-1864; 1 volume.

List of Ex-Confederate Soldiers and Widows, 1900-1904; 1 volume.

Record of Pensions, 1903-1938; 1 volume.

MISCELLANEOUS RECORDS

Sheriffs' and Clerks' Settlement Book, 1825-1837; 1 volume.

Orders and Decrees, 1868-1918; 1 volume.

Special Proceedings, 1869-1883, 1895-1912; 2 volumes.

Miscellaneous Records, 1764-1930; 3 Fibredex boxes.

Records of Assignees, Receivers and Trustees, 1884-1952; 5 Fibredex boxes.

ROADS AND BRIDGES

Railroad Records, 1853-1921; 4 Fibredex boxes.

TAX AND FISCAL RECORDS

Lists of Taxables, 1809-1819, 1859-1868; 4 volumes.

Taxables, 1786-1863; 4 Fibredex boxes.

WILLS

Wills, 1760-1922; 11 Fibredex boxes.

Cross Index to Wills, 1760-1904; 1 volume.

MICROFILM RECORDS

BONDS

Apprentice Bonds, 1850-1911; 1 reel.

CORPORATIONS AND PARTNERSHIPS

Record of Incorporations, 1890-1962; 2 reels.

Partnership Records, 1914-1961; 1 reel.

COURT RECORDS

County Court of Pleas and Quarter Sessions

Minutes, 1759-1868; 5 reels.

Superior Court

Minutes, 1868-1929; 8 reels.

Equity Minutes, 1807-1866; 1 reel.

ELECTION RECORDS

Record of Elections, 1878-1926; 1 reel.

ESTATES RECORDS
>Record of Estates, 1781-1868; 11 reels.
>Record of Accounts, 1808-1946; 10 reels.
>Administrators' Bonds, 1849-1940; 6 reels.
>Appointment of Administrators, Executors and Guardians, 1868-1923; 1 reel.
>Guardians' Records, 1866-1868; 1 reel.
>Guardians' Bonds, 1898-1962; 3 reels.
>Guardians' Accounts, 1903-1924; 1 reel.
>Record of Dowers, 1902-1949; 1 reel.
>Record of Widows' Year's Support, 1902-1939; 1 reel.
>General Index to Estate Proceedings and Divisions of Land, 1923-1962; 1 reel.
>Record of Monies Paid into Court by Administrators, 1900-1942; 1 reel.
>Record of Settlements, 1868-1923; 2 reels.

LAND RECORDS
>Record of Deeds and Grants, 1759-1842; 13 reels.
>Record of Deeds, 1842-1926, 1944-1946; 141 reels.
>General Index to Real Estate Conveyances, Grantor, 1749-1979; 9 reels.
>General Index to Real Estate Conveyances, Grantee, 1749-1979; 7 reels.
>Land Division Books, 1789-1968; 7 reels.
>Index to Heirs' Land Divisions, 1789-1925; 1 reel.
>Land Entries, 1778-1926; 1 reel.
>Land Grants, 1779-1782; 1 reel.
>Plat Books, 1914-1962; 1 reel.
>Index to Plats, 1914-1979; 1 reel.
>Certificate Record of Land Sold for Taxes, 1933; 1 reel.
>Federal Tax Lien Index, 1925-1969; 1 reel.
>Accounts of Land Sales by Commissioners, 1907-1968; 1 reel.
>Record of Resale of Land by Mortgagees and Trustees, 1919-1962; 5 reels.
>Record of Foreclosures, 1927-1982; 3 reels.

MARRIAGE, DIVORCE AND VITAL STATISTICS
>Marriage Bonds, 1768-1868; 4 reels.
>Marriage Bond Abstracts, 1768-1868; 1 reel.
>Marriage Licenses, 1894-1961; 16 reels.
>Marriage Registers, 1760-1988; 5 reels.
>Maiden Names of Divorced Women, 1940-1968; 1 reel.
>Index to Births, 1913-1972; 3 reels.
>Index to Deaths, 1913-1988; 1 reel.
>Index to Delayed Births, 1941-1988; 1 reel.

MILITARY AND PENSION RECORDS
>Record of Armed Forces Discharges, 1918-1988; 9 reels.
>Index to Armed Forces Discharges, 1918-1979; 1 reel.

MISCELLANEOUS RECORDS
>Orders and Decrees, 1868-1939; 6 reels.
>Special Proceedings, 1869-1962; 3 reels.
>Index to Special Proceedings, 1869-1988; 4 reels.

Record of Assignments, 1894-1951; 1 reel.

Bonds of Trustees in Assignments, 1913-1916; 1 reel.

Receivers' Accounts, 1905-1953; 1 reel.

OFFICIALS, COUNTY

Minutes, Board of County Commissioners, 1868-1939; 3 reels.

SCHOOL RECORDS

Minutes, County Board of Education, 1885-1938; 1 reel.

TAX AND FISCAL RECORDS

Tax Lists, 1872-1905, 1915; 11 reels.

WILLS

Record of Wills, 1760-1968; 13 reels.

Index to Wills, Devisor, 1760-1968; 1 reel.

Index to Wills, Devisee, 1760-1968; 1 reel.

JONES COUNTY

Established in 1779 from Craven County.
In 1862, courthouse burned during Civil War battle;
many court records destroyed.

ORIGINAL RECORDS

BONDS

Apprentice Bonds, 1847-1902; 1 volume, 1 Fibredex box.

Bastardy Bonds, 1812-1914; 1 volume, 1 Fibredex box.

COURT RECORDS

County Court of Pleas and Quarter Sessions

Minutes, 1807-1868; 7 volumes.

Appearance Dockets, 1807-1868; 3 volumes.

Execution Dockets, 1847-1868; 4 volumes.

State Dockets, 1821-1868; 3 volumes.

Trial Dockets, 1807-1868; 3 volumes.

Clerk's Fee Book, 1858-1875; 1 volume.

Superior Court

Minutes, 1807-1932; 11 volumes.

Equity Minutes, 1826-1868; 2 volumes.

Equity Execution Docket, 1852-1868; 1 volume.

Equity Trial and Appearance Dockets, 1820-1868; 3 volumes.

Appearance Docket, 1861-1868; 1 volume.

Execution Dockets, 1842-1868; 2 volumes.

State Docket, 1847-1868; 1 volume.

Trial Docket, 1842-1865; 1 volume.

Civil Action Papers, 1853-1905, 1915, 1931; 7 Fibredex boxes.

Civil Action Papers Concerning Land, 1858-1944; 5 Fibredex boxes.

Criminal Action Papers, 1800, 1853-1905, 1938; 4 Fibredex boxes.

ELECTION RECORDS

Record of Elections, 1878-1922; 4 volumes.

ESTATES RECORDS

Record of Estates, 1780-1854; 6 volumes.

Record of Accounts, 1868-1925; 2 volumes.

Administrators' Bonds, 1869-1938; 3 volumes.

Estates Records, 1783-1939, 1949; 38 Fibredex boxes.

Guardians' Records, 1779-1935; 14 Fibredex boxes.

Guardians' Bonds, 1869-1913; 1 volume.

Record of Guardians, 1908-1933; 1 volume.

Record of Settlements and Divisions of Estates, 1830-1902; 5 volumes.

LAND RECORDS

Record of Deeds, 1779-1828; 12 volumes.

Index to Deeds, 1779-1810; 2 volumes.

Ejectments, 1853-1905, 1915; 1 Fibredex box.

Land Entries, 1841-1898; 1 volume.

Land Grants, 1788-1795; 1 volume.

Miscellaneous Land Records, 1796-1940; 4 Fibredex boxes.

MARRIAGE, DIVORCE AND VITAL STATISTICS

Record of Marriage Certificates, 1851-1874; 1 volume.

Marriage Registers, 1874-1941; 3 volumes.

Divorce Records, 1871-1905; 2 Fibredex boxes.

MISCELLANEOUS RECORDS

Lunacy Records, 1884-1934; 1 Fibredex box.

Registry of Licenses to Trades, 1874-1903; 1 volume.

Special Proceedings Docket, 1869-1912; 1 volume.

Miscellaneous Records, 1785-1935; 1 Fibredex box.

Records of Assignees, Receivers and Trustees, 1895-1934; 2 Fibredex boxes.

TAX AND FISCAL RECORDS

Record of Federal Direct Taxes Collected, 1866; 1 volume.

WILLS

Wills, 1779-1935; 10 Fibredex boxes.

MICROFILM RECORDS

BONDS

Bastardy Bonds, 1869-1892; 1 reel.

CORPORATIONS AND PARTNERSHIPS

Record of Corporations, 1891-1964; 1 reel.

Record of Partnerships, 1923-1949; 1 reel.

COURT RECORDS

County Court of Pleas and Quarter Sessions
Minutes, 1807-1868; 1 reel.

Superior Court
Minutes, 1820-1964; 5 reels.

ELECTION RECORDS

Record of Elections, 1878-1916, 1924-1964; 1 reel.

ESTATES RECORDS

Record of Estates, 1792-1868; 4 reels.

Record of Accounts, 1854-1964; 3 reels.

Bonds of Administrators, Executors and Guardians, 1915-1938; 1 reel.

Record of Administrators, Executors and Guardians, 1921-1964; Cross Index
to Administrators, Executors and Guardians, 1920-1964; 1 reel.

Appointment of Executors, 1868-1923; 1 reel.

Appointment of Receivers of Estates, 1905-1957; 1 reel.

Accounts of Indigent Orphans, 1908-1933; 1 reel.

Inheritance Tax Records, 1924-1964; 1 reel.

Inventories of Estates, 1809-1929; 1 reel.

Division and Settlement of Estates, 1809-1957; 3 reels.

LAND RECORDS

Record of Deeds, 1779-1964; 73 reels.

General Index to Real Estate Conveyances, Grantor, 1779-1964; 2 reels.

General Index to Real Estate Conveyances, Grantee, 1779-1964; 2 reels.

Land Entry Books, 1779-1795, 1841-1959; 1 reel.

Record of Grants, 1780-1783; 1 reel.

Record of Sales and Resales, 1924-1963; 1 reel.

MARRIAGE, DIVORCE AND VITAL STATISTICS

Marriage Licenses, 1867-1961; 4 reels.

Marriage Registers, 1851-1964; 1 reel.

Maiden Names of Divorced Women, 1946-1963; 1 reel.

Index to Vital Statistics, 1914-1961; 1 reel.

Index to Delayed Births, various years; 1 reel.

MILITARY AND PENSION RECORDS

Record of Armed Forces Discharges, 1918-1962, 1974-1981; 2 reels.

Record of Pensions, 1908-1926; 1 reel.

MISCELLANEOUS RECORDS

Orders and Decrees, 1869-1960; 1 reel.

Special Proceedings, 1869-1964; 3 reels.

OFFICIALS, COUNTY

Minutes, Board of County Commissioners, 1868-1964; 3 reels.

SCHOOL RECORDS

Minutes, County Board of Education, 1873-1879, 1885-1964; 1 reel.

TAX AND FISCAL RECORDS

Tax List, 1779; 1 reel.

WILLS

Record of Wills, 1779-1964; 2 reels.

Original Wills, 1760-1842; 1 reel.

Index to Wills, 1779-1964; 1 reel.

LEE COUNTY

Established in 1907 from Chatham and Moore counties.

ORIGINAL RECORDS
BONDS
> Apprentice Bonds, 1911-1923; 1 volume.

COURT RECORDS
> Superior Court
>> Minutes, 1908-1913; 1 volume.

ELECTION RECORDS
> Record of Elections, 1908-1924; 1 volume.

MILITARY AND PENSION RECORDS
> Record of Pensions, 1908, 1926-1940; 2 volumes.

MISCELLANEOUS RECORDS
> Alien Registration, 1928, 1940; 1 volume.
> Miscellaneous Records, 1928-1946; 1 manuscript box.

WILLS
> Cross Index to Wills, 1908-1923; 1 volume.

MICROFILM RECORDS

BONDS
> Apprentice Bonds, 1911-1923; 1 reel.

CORPORATIONS AND PARTNERSHIPS
> Record of Corporations, 1907-1966; 2 reels.
> Index to Corporations, Assumed Names and Partnerships, 1907-1970; 1 reel.

COURT RECORDS
> Superior Court
>> Minutes, 1908-1959; 6 reels.

ELECTION RECORDS
> Record of Elections, 1908-1946; 1 reel.

ESTATE RECORDS
> Record of Accounts, 1907-1934; 1 reel.
> Record of Administrators, Executors and Guardians, 1908-1922; 1 reel.
> Record of Administrators, 1914-1968; 8 reels.
> Record of Executors, 1952-1968; 1 reel.
> Record of Executors and Guardians, 1927-1936; 1 reel.
> Record of Guardians, 1935-1968; 2 reels.
> Guardians of World War Veterans, 1931-1948; 1 reel.
> Accounts of Indigent Orphans, 1909-1930; 1 reel.
> Record of Dowers, 1908-1951; 1 reel.
> Inheritance Tax Records, 1921-1968; 2 reels.
> Record of Settlements, 1912-1926; 1 reel.
> Cross Index to Administrators and Executors, 1908-1919; 1 reel.

Index to Administrators and Executors, 1908-1924; 1 reel.

Index to Guardians and Wards, 1912-1923; 2 reels.

LAND RECORDS

Record of Deeds, 1908-1962; 36 reels.

Index to Real Estate Conveyances, Grantor, 1908-1970; 10 reels.

Index to Real Estate Conveyances, Grantee, 1908-1970; 9 reels.

Index to Real Estate Conveyances, Trustee, 1953-1970; 2 reels.

Record of Surveys, 1908-1928; 1 reel.

Record of Taxes for Mortgagees, 1931-1934; 1 reel.

Federal Tax Lien Index, 1925-1970; 1 reel.

Record of Resale of Land by Trustees and Mortgagees, 1920-1962; 3 reels.

MARRIAGE, DIVORCE AND VITAL STATISTICS

Marriage Licenses, 1908-1970; 8 reels.

Index to Marriages, 1908-1969; 1 reel.

Maiden Names of Divorced Women, 1942-1968; 1 reel.

Index to Births, 1913-1969; 1 reel.

Index to Deaths and Delayed Births, 1913-1968; 1 reel.

Index to Delayed Births, various years; 1 reel.

MILITARY AND PENSION RECORDS

Record of Armed Forces Discharges, 1919-1988; 5 reels.

Index to Armed Forces Discharges, 1919-1970; 1 reel.

Record of Pensions, 1908-1940; 1 reel.

MISCELLANEOUS RECORDS

Record of Official Reports, 1908-1920; 1 reel.

Homestead Proceedings, 1927-1949; 1 reel.

Lunacy Dockets, 1908-1969; 3 reels.

Clerk's Minute Dockets, 1921-1968; 7 reels.

Orders and Decrees, 1908-1968; 7 reels.

Index to Clerk's Minute Dockets and Wills, 1908-1968; 3 reels.

Appointment of Receivers, 1908-1919; 1 reel.

OFFICIALS, COUNTY

Minutes, Board of County Commissioners, 1908-1970; 3 reels.

SCHOOL RECORDS

Minutes, County Board of Education, 1908-1970; 2 reels.

TAX AND FISCAL RECORDS

Tax Scrolls, 1965; 2 reels.

Minutes, Board of Equalization and Review, 1963-1970; 1 reel.

WILLS

Record of Wills, 1908-1968; 3 reels.

Index to Wills, 1908-1924; 1 reel. SEE ALSO Index to Clerk's Minute Dockets and Wills, 1908-1968.

LENOIR COUNTY

Established in 1791 from Dobbs County.
Most court records destroyed in fires of 1878 and 1880.

ORIGINAL RECORDS

BONDS

Apprentice Bonds and Records, 1879-1917; 2 volumes, 1 Fibredex box.

Officials' Bonds and Records, 1802-1937; 1 volume, 3 Fibredex boxes.

COURT RECORDS

Superior Court

Minutes, 1880-1916; 16 volumes.

Civil Action Papers, 1866-1939; 14 Fibredex boxes.

Civil Action Papers Concerning Land, 1878-1939; 4 Fibredex boxes.

Criminal Action Papers, 1901-1928; 1 Fibredex box.

Inferior Court

Minutes, 1878-1885; 1 volume.

ELECTION RECORDS

Record of Elections, 1880-1932; 3 volumes.

Election Records, 1880-1908; 2 Fibredex boxes.

ESTATES RECORDS

Record of Accounts, 1880-1904; 4 volumes.

Administrators' Bonds, 1879-1891, 1900-1905; 2 volumes.

Estates Records, 1830-1956; 94 Fibredex boxes.

Guardians' Records, 1868, 1874-1952; 26 Fibredex boxes.

Guardians' Bonds, 1879-1904; 2 volumes.

Record of Settlements, 1880-1904; 2 volumes.

LAND RECORDS

Deeds of Sale, 1792-1941; 4 Fibredex boxes.

Miscellaneous Deeds, 1816-1939; 1 Fibredex box.

Cross Index to Deeds, 1879-1893; 1 volume.

Land Entries, 1879-1915; 1 volume.

Record Book, 1738-1866; 1 volume.

Attachments, Executions, Levies and Liens on Land, 1873-1919;
1 Fibredex box.

Boundary Line Disputes, 1885-1938; 1 Fibredex box.

Foreclosures, 1890-1955; 3 Fibredex boxes.

Petitions for Partition of Land, 1877-1939; 2 Fibredex boxes.

Petitions for Sale of Land, 1884-1939; 3 Fibredex boxes.

Miscellaneous Land Records, 1879-1943; 1 Fibredex box.

MARRIAGE, DIVORCE AND VITAL STATISTICS

Marriage Bonds, 1791-1868; 1 Fibredex box.

Marriage Registers, 1873-1937; 2 volumes.

Record of Marriages Performed by K. F. Foscue, Justice of the Peace, 1924-
1935; 1 volume.

Divorce Records, 1880-1914, 1933; 1 Fibredex box.

Index to Vital Statistics, 1914-1928; 1 volume.

MISCELLANEOUS RECORDS

Alien Registration, 1927, 1940; 1 volume.

Assumed Business Names, Corporations and Partnership Records, 1878-1938; 1 Fibredex box.

Record of Proceedings of the Committee of Finance, 1855-1868; 1 volume.

Record of Official Reports, 1888-1914; 1 volume.

Lunacy Records, 1881-1934; 5 Fibredex boxes.

Canal Records, 1883-1927; 1 Fibredex box.

Timber Records, 1903-1929; 1 Fibredex box.

Miscellaneous Records, 1868-1949; 2 Fibredex boxes.

Records of Assignees, Receivers and Trustees, 1878-1942; 5 Fibredex boxes.

ROADS AND BRIDGES

Record of Appointment of Road Overseers, 1826-1862; 1 volume.

Road, Bridge and Ferry Records, 1878-1921; 2 Fibredex boxes.

Railroad Records, 1889-1937; 2 Fibredex boxes.

SCHOOL RECORDS

School Records, 1879-1935; 1 Fibredex box.

TAX AND FISCAL RECORDS

Tax Records, 1880-1937; 2 Fibredex boxes.

WILLS

Wills, 1824-1916; 1 Fibredex box.

Cross Index to Wills, 1868-1936; 1 volume.

MICROFILM RECORDS

CORPORATIONS AND PARTNERSHIPS

Record of Corporations, 1900-1935; 1 reel.

Partnership Records, 1916-1946; 1 reel.

COURT RECORDS

Superior Court

Minutes, 1880-1953; 17 reels.

ELECTION RECORDS

Record of Elections, 1924-1966; 1 reel.

ESTATES RECORDS

Record of Accounts, 1880-1966; 13 reels.

Administrators' Bonds, 1905-1955; 4 reels.

Appointment of Administrators, Executors and Guardians, 1894-1955; 1 reel.

Guardians' Bonds, 1905-1955; 2 reels.

Record of Amounts Paid for Indigent Children, 1913-1942; 1 reel.

Divisions, Dowers and Year's Provisions, 1868-1956; 2 reels.

Widows' Year's Allowance, 1927-1958; 1 reel.

Inheritance Tax Records, 1923-1966; 1 reel.

Record of Settlements, 1880-1966; 8 reels.

Index to Estates: Titles, 1870-1966; 3 reels.

Index to Estates: Wards, 1870-1966; 4 reels.

LAND RECORDS

Record of Deeds, 1880-1955; 89 reels.

Index to Real Estate Conveyances, Grantor, 1746-1964; 9 reels.

Index to Real Estate Conveyances, Grantee, 1746-1966; 9 reels.

Map Books, 1913-1966; 3 reels.

Index to Map Books, 1870-1966; 1 reel.

Record of Resale of Land, 1921-1966; 4 reels.

MARRIAGE, DIVORCE AND VITAL STATISTICS

Marriage Bonds, 1791-1868; 1 reel.

Marriage Registers, 1873-1966; 3 reels.

Index to Births, 1914-1981; 9 reels.

Index to Deaths, 1914-1966; 4 reels.

Index to Delayed Births, various years; 1 reel.

MILITARY AND PENSION RECORDS

Record of Armed Forces Discharges, 1918-1981; 8 reels.

Index to Armed Forces Discharges, 1945-1966; 1 reel.

MISCELLANEOUS RECORDS

Record of Burials, 1915-1966; Cemetery Lot Map, no date; 1 reel.

Record of Cemetery Lots, Kinston, 1848-1915; 1 reel.

Homestead Returns, 1937-1964; 1 reel.

Orders and Decrees, 1880-1942; 13 reels.

Special Proceedings, 1874-1941; 1 reel.

Index to Special Proceedings and Orders and Decrees, Plaintiff, 1874-1966; 3 reels.

Index to Special Proceedings and Orders and Decrees, Defendant, 1874-1966; 4 reels.

OFFICIALS, COUNTY

Minutes, Board of County Commissioners, 1873-1966; 4 reels.

SCHOOL RECORDS

Minutes, County Board of Education, 1884-1957; 1 reel.

WILLS

Record of Wills, 1869-1966; 6 reels.

Index to Wills, Devisor, 1869-1966; 1 reel.

Index to Wills, Devisee, 1869-1966; 1 reel.

LINCOLN COUNTY

Established in 1779 from Tryon County.
No known losses but many records are missing.

ORIGINAL RECORDS

BONDS

    Apprentice Bonds, 1783-1917; 2 volumes, 3 Fibredex boxes.

    Bastardy Bonds, 1784-1893; 3 Fibredex boxes.

    Officials' Bonds, 1769-1883; 5 Fibredex boxes.

COURT RECORDS

    County Court of Pleas and Quarter Sessions

        Minutes, 1781-1868; 15 volumes.

        Appearance Docket, 1843-1868; 1 volume.

        Execution Dockets, 1806-1868; 4 volumes.

        Levy Docket, 1838-1846; 1 volume.

        Recognizance Docket, 1817-1825; 1 volume.

        State Dockets, 1792-1806, 1835-1868; 3 volumes.

        Trial and Appearance Dockets, 1783-1843; 5 volumes,
            2 manuscript boxes.

        Trial Docket, 1843-1868; 1 volume.

    Superior Court

        Minutes, 1816-1911; 12 volumes, 1 manuscript box.

        Equity Minutes, 1830-1868; 2 volumes.

        Equity Enrolling Dockets, 1812-1867; 3 volumes.

        Equity Execution Docket, 1857-1868; 1 volume.

        Equity Trial and Appearance Dockets, 1810-1868; 3 volumes.

        Appearance Docket, 1843-1870; 1 volume.

        Execution Dockets, 1813-1871; 5 volumes.

        Lien Docket, 1893-1931; 1 volume.

        Recognizance Docket, 1817-1841; 1 volume.

        State Dockets, 1823-1869; 3 volumes.

        Trial and Appearance Dockets, 1807-1842; 2 volumes.

        Trial Dockets, 1843-1870; 3 volumes.

        Civil Action Papers, 1771-1917; 36 Fibredex boxes.

        Civil Action Papers Concerning Land, 1790-1918; 8 Fibredex boxes.

        Civil Action Papers Concerning Land and Gold Mining, Andrew Falls,
            Plaintiff, 1832; 1 Fibredex box.

        Civil Action Papers Concerning Gold, Iron and Railroads, 1831-1899;
            1 Fibredex box.

        Criminal Action Papers, 1782-1894; 9 Fibredex boxes.

ELECTION RECORDS

    Record of Elections, 1878-1934; 4 volumes.

    Election Records, 1798-1922; 6 Fibredex boxes.

    Permanent Roll of Registered Voters, 1902-1908; 1 volume.

ESTATES RECORDS

Record of Estates, 1812-1819, 1831-1868; 3 volumes.

Record of Accounts, 1868-1907; 6 volumes.

Administrators' Bonds, 1868-1913; 3 volumes.

Estates Records, 1779-1925; 138 Fibredex boxes.

Guardians' Records, 1777-1925; 15 Fibredex boxes.

Guardians' Bonds, 1868-1924; 3 volumes.

Record of Amounts Paid for Indigent Children, 1924-1930; 1 volume.

LAND RECORDS

Record of Deeds, 1770-1810; 8 volumes.

Deeds, 1777-1925; 2 Fibredex boxes.

Ejectments, 1800-1895; 2 Fibredex boxes.

Land Entries, 1788-1825; 2 volumes.

Land Grants, 1763-1813; 4 volumes.

MARRIAGE, DIVORCE AND VITAL STATISTICS

Marriage Bonds, 1779-1868; 20 Fibredex boxes.

Record of Marriage Certificates, 1851-1870; 1 volume.

Record of Cohabitation, 1866; 1 volume.

Divorce Records, 1811-1921; 2 Fibredex boxes.

MILITARY AND PENSION RECORDS

Civil War Records, 1864-1923; 1 Fibredex box.

Pension Records, 1885-1894, 1901-1907; 1 Fibredex box.

Record Book, Company A, 34th Regiment N. C. Troops, 1861-1865;
1 volume.

MISCELLANEOUS RECORDS

County Accounts and Claims, 1773-1891; 1 Fibredex box.

Insolvent Debtors and Homestead and Personal Property Exemptions, 1788-
1895; 1 Fibredex box.

Lists of Jurors, 1785-1919; 1 Fibredex box.

Minutes, Wardens of the Poor, 1820-1868; 1 volume.

Miscellaneous Records, 1764-1923; 10 Fibredex boxes.

Drainage Record, 1912-1925; 1 volume.

OFFICIALS, COUNTY

Minutes, Board of County Commissioners, 1868-1870; 1 volume.

ROADS AND BRIDGES

Minutes, Board of Road Commissioners, 1913-1915; 1 volume.

Road Records, 1781-1869; 4 Fibredex boxes.

SCHOOL RECORDS

Minutes, Board of Superintendents of Common Schools, 1845-1865;
1 volume.

Lists of School Children, 1845-1862, 1883, 1895; 10 manuscript boxes.

Public School Register, 1893-1897; 1 volume.

TAX AND FISCAL RECORDS

Tax Lists, 1784-1886; 3 volumes, 4 Fibredex boxes.

WILLS
        Wills, 1769-1926; 28 Fibredex boxes.
        Cross Index to Wills, 1765-1940; 1 volume.

MICROFILM RECORDS

BONDS
        Apprentice Bonds, 1869-1917; 1 reel.
        Officials' Bonds, 1874-1921; 2 reels.
CORPORATIONS AND PARTNERSHIPS
        Record of Incorporations, 1887-1941; 1 reel.
COURT RECORDS
        County Court of Pleas and Quarter Sessions
                Minutes, 1782-1868; 5 reels.
                Trial and Appearance Docket, 1799-1807; 1 reel.
        Superior Court
                Minutes, 1842-1960; 8 reels.
                Equity Minutes, 1816-1867; 2 reels.
                Equity Enrolling Dockets, 1830-1868; 2 reels.
ELECTION RECORDS
        Record of Elections, 1878-1962; 1 reel.
ESTATES RECORDS
        Record of Accounts, 1868-1964; 9 reels.
        Administrators' Bonds, 1868-1913; 1 reel.
        Record of Administrators and Executors, 1909-1937; 1 reel.
        Record of Administrators, 1936-1964; 2 reels.
        Record of Executors, 1869-1908, 1924-1964; 1 reel.
        Guardians' Bonds, 1868-1925; 1 reel.
        Record of Guardians, 1924-1964; 1 reel.
        Inheritance Tax Records, 1921-1964; 1 reel.
        Inventories and Accounts of Estates, 1831-1868; 1 reel.
        Record of Receivers of Estates, 1907-1930; 1 reel.
        Record of Settlements, 1869-1964; 5 reels.
        Index to Accounts and Settlements, 1868-1964; 1 reel.
LAND RECORDS
        Record of Deeds, 1769-1961; 117 reels.
        Index to Real Estate Conveyances, Grantor, 1769-1964; 4 reels.
        Index to Real Estate Conveyances, Grantee, 1769-1964; 4 reels.
        Land Entries, 1788-1853; 3 reels.
        Land Grants, 1763-1923; 4 reels.
        Index to Grants, 1763-1923; 1 reel.
        Levies on Land, 1838-1846; 1 reel.
        Record of Sales and Resales of Land, 1921-1964; 2 reels.
MARRIAGE, DIVORCE AND VITAL STATISTICS
        Marriage Bonds, 1779-1868; 8 reels.

Marriage Licenses, 1868-1961; 8 reels.

Record of Marriages, 1851-1869; 1 reel.

Marriage Index, 1869-1964; 1 reel.

Record of Cohabitation, 1866; 1 reel.

Maiden Names of Divorced Women, 1942-1964; 1 reel.

Index to Births, 1913-1964; 1 reel.

Index to Deaths, 1913-1964; 1 reel.

MILITARY AND PENSION RECORDS

Record of Armed Forces Discharges, 1923-1975; 6 reels.

Index to Armed Forces Discharges, 1918-1977; 1 reel.

Record Book, Company A, 34th Regiment N. C. Troops, 1861-1865; 1 reel.

MISCELLANEOUS RECORDS

Orders and Decrees, 1868-1954; 16 reels.

Index to Orders and Decrees, Special Proceedings and Lunacy, 1868-1964; 1 reel.

Index to Special Proceedings, 1968-1977; 1 reel.

OFFICIALS, COUNTY

Minutes, Board of County Commissioners, 1870-1964; 6 reels.

SCHOOL RECORDS

Minutes, County Board of Education, 1885-1964; 1 reel.

WILLS

Record of Wills, 1824-1964; 4 reels.

Index to Wills, 1772-1968; 2 reels.

MACON COUNTY

Established in 1828 from Haywood County.
No known losses but many records are missing.

ORIGINAL RECORDS

BONDS
> Bastardy Bonds and Records, 1838-1897; 1 volume, 1 Fibredex box.

COURT RECORDS
> County Court of Pleas and Quarter Sessions
>> Minutes, 1829-1868; 4 volumes.
>> Execution Dockets, 1838-1868; 2 volumes.
>> State Docket, 1829-1844; 1 volume.
>> Trial Docket, 1845-1868; 1 volume.
> Superior Court
>> Minutes, 1843-1914; 10 volumes.
>> Equity Minutes, 1833-1868; 2 volumes.
>> Equity Execution Docket, 1837-1868; 1 volume.
>> Equity Appearance Docket, 1835-1854; 1 volume.
>> Appearance Docket, 1840-1868; 1 volume.
>> Execution Dockets, 1846-1870; 2 volumes.
>> State Dockets, 1840-1869; 2 volumes.
>> Trial Dockets, 1840-1868; 2 volumes.
>> Civil Action Papers, 1822-1924; 31 Fibredex boxes.
>> Civil Action Papers Concerning Land, 1825-1926; 8 Fibredex boxes.
>> Criminal Action Papers, 1829-1902; 18 Fibredex boxes.

ELECTION RECORDS
> Minutes, Board of Elections, 1900-1928; 1 volume.
> Record of Elections, 1878-1914; 4 volumes.
> Election Records, 1829-1874; 1 Fibredex box.

ESTATES RECORDS
> Record of Estates, 1866-1868; 1 volume.
> Record of Accounts, 1868-1905; 2 volumes.
> Administrators' Bonds, 1870-1920; 3 volumes.
> Estates Records, 1831-1920; 27 Fibredex boxes.
> Guardians' Records, 1845-1937; 3 Fibredex boxes.
> Guardians' Bonds, 1870-1919; 2 volumes.
> Record of Settlements, 1870-1913; 1 volume.

LAND RECORDS
> Deeds, 1828-1920; 2 Fibredex boxes.
> Miscellaneous Deeds, 1843-1930; 1 Fibredex box.
> Ejectments, 1833-1890; 1 Fibredex box.
> Entry Takers' Books, 1836-1937; 10 volumes.
> Land Grants, 1836-1919; 1 Fibredex box.
> Cherokee Bond Account Books, 1820-1851; 3 volumes.

Cherokee Lands Surveyed, 1837; 1 volume.
Record of Probate, 1827-1875; 2 volumes.
Miscellaneous Land Records, 1837-1924; 1 Fibredex box.

MARRIAGE, DIVORCE AND VITAL STATISTICS
Marriage Bonds, 1828-1868; 4 Fibredex boxes.
Marriage Licenses, 1869-1891, 1908; 1 Fibredex box.
Marriage Registers, 1831-1943; 4 volumes.
Divorce Records, 1835-1913; 3 Fibredex boxes.

MILITARY AND PENSION RECORDS
Pension Roll, 1903-1910; 1 volume.

MISCELLANEOUS RECORDS
Alien Registration, 1940; 1 volume.
Insolvent Debtors, 1831-1860; 1 Fibredex box.
Clerk's Minute Docket (Special Proceedings), 1875-1884; 1 volume.
Orders and Decrees, 1869-1904; 2 volumes.
Miscellaneous Records, 1829-1922; 1 Fibredex box, 1 manuscript box.

ROADS AND BRIDGES
Road Records, 1829-1905; 2 Fibredex boxes.
Road Record (Overseers), 1838-1861; 1 volume.
Railroad Records, 1855-1914; 1 Fibredex box.

SCHOOL RECORDS
School Records, 1835-1928; 1 Fibredex box.
Public School Statistical Records, 1885-1896; 1 volume.

TAX AND FISCAL RECORDS
Tax Lists, 1857-1868; 1 volume.

WILLS
Wills, 1830-1905, 1933; 3 Fibredex boxes.

MICROFILM RECORDS

CORPORATIONS AND PARTNERSHIPS
Record of Incorporations, 1887-1966; 1 reel.
Partnership Records, 1916-1966; 1 reel.

COURT RECORDS
County Court of Pleas and Quarter Sessions
Minutes, 1829-1868; 1 reel.
Superior Court
Minutes, 1869-1963; 8 reels.
Cross Index to Minutes, 1869-1963; 2 reels.

ESTATES RECORDS
Record of Accounts, 1868-1966; 4 reels.
Appointment of Administrators, Executors and Guardians, 1868-1913; 1 reel.
Record of Administrators, Executors and Guardians, 1913-1930; 1 reel.
Record of Administrators, 1931-1966; 2 reels.
Record of Executors, 1930-1966; 1 reel.

Record of Guardians, 1927-1966; 1 reel.

Record of Amounts Paid for Indigent Children, 1903-1945; 1 reel.

Inheritance Tax Records, 1920-1966; 1 reel.

Record of Settlements, 1870-1966; 3 reels.

Index to Estates, 1868-1966; 1 reel.

LAND RECORDS

Record of Deeds, 1828-1960; 71 reels.

Index to Real Estate Conveyances, Grantor, 1829-1966; 11 reels.

Index to Real Estate Conveyances, Grantee, 1829-1966; 11 reels.

State Grant Index, 1826-1926; 1 reel.

Record of Surveys, 1905-1927; 1 reel.

Record of Sale of Land, 1925-1966; 2 reels.

MARRIAGE, DIVORCE AND VITAL STATISTICS

Marriage Bonds, 1828-1868; 5 reels.

Marriage Registers, 1829-1966; 2 reels.

Maiden Names of Divorced Women, 1940-1965; 1 reel.

Index to Births, 1913-1966; 1 reel.

Index to Deaths, 1913-1966; 1 reel.

Index to Delayed Births, various years; 1 reel.

MILITARY AND PENSION RECORDS

Record of Armed Forces Discharges, 1917-1979; 3 reels.

MISCELLANEOUS RECORDS

Orders and Decrees, 1869-1955; 10 reels.

Special Proceedings Dockets, 1875-1928; 1 reel.

Cross Index to Special Proceedings, 1869-1939; 1 reel.

Index to Special Proceedings, 1940-1966; 1 reel.

OFFICIALS, COUNTY

Minutes, Board of County Commissioners, 1868-1922; 4 reels.

SCHOOL RECORDS

Minutes, County Board of Education, 1885-1966; 1 reel.

WILLS

Record of Wills, 1830-1966; 3 reels.

Cross Index to Wills, 1830-1966; 1 reel.

Mountain school and students, date unknown. Photograph from the files of the State Archives.

MADISON COUNTY

Established in 1851 from Buncombe and Yancey counties.

ORIGINAL RECORDS

BONDS

    Apprentice Bonds, 1874-1914; 1 volume.

    Apprentice Bonds and Records, 1851-1907; Bastardy Bonds and Records, 1851-1910; 1 Fibredex box.

    Bastardy Bonds, 1874-1910; 1 volume.

    Officials' Bonds, 1851-1894; 1 Fibredex box.

COURT RECORDS

    County Court of Pleas and Quarter Sessions

        Minutes, 1865-1868; 1 volume.

        Appearance Docket, 1852-1867; 1 volume.

        Execution Docket, 1863-1868; 1 volume.

    Superior Court

        Minutes, 1851-1913; 11 volumes.

        Civil Action Papers, 1837-1925; 13 Fibredex boxes.

        Civil Action Papers Concerning Land, 1856-1940; 8 Fibredex boxes.

        Criminal Action Papers, 1849-1936; 12 Fibredex boxes.

    Inferior Court

        Minutes, 1883-1888, 1894-1895; 1 volume.

    Circuit Criminal Court/Western District Criminal Court

        Minutes, 1895-1899; 1 volume.

ELECTION RECORDS

    Record of Elections, 1878-1914, 1928-1936; 4 volumes.

    Voter Registration Books, 1932-1964; 22 volumes.

ESTATES RECORDS

    Record of Estates, 1852-1862; 1 volume.

    Record of Accounts, 1873-1909; 1 volume.

    Administrators' Bonds, 1874-1904; 2 volumes.

    Appointment of Administrators, Executors, Guardians and Masters, 1868-1913; 1 volume.

    Estates Records, 1833, 1851-1943; 37 Fibredex boxes.

    Guardians' Records, 1855-1928; 5 Fibredex boxes.

    Guardians' Bonds, 1874-1896; 2 volumes.

LAND RECORDS

    Record of Deeds, 1851-1858, 1862-1891; 2 volumes.

    Ejectments, 1851-1907; 1 Fibredex box.

    Levies on Land, 1851-1932; 1 Fibredex box.

    Probate of Deeds, 1894-1902; 1 volume.

    Miscellaneous Land Records, 1817-1932; 1 Fibredex box.

MARRIAGE, DIVORCE AND VITAL STATISTICS

Marriage Bonds, 1851-1868; 3 Fibredex boxes.

Marriage Licenses, 1868-1945, 1956; 33 Fibredex boxes.

Marriage Register, 1862-1895; 1 volume.

Divorce Records, 1854-1926; 6 Fibredex boxes.

MISCELLANEOUS RECORDS

Insolvents and Homestead and Personal Property Exemptions, 1852-1916; 1 Fibredex box.

Miscellaneous Records, 1851-1932; 4 Fibredex boxes.

Records of Assignees, Receivers and Trustees, 1851-1913; 1 Fibredex box.

ROADS AND BRIDGES

Minutes, County Highway Commission, 1915-1919; 2 volumes.

Road Reports and Records, 1854-1937; Railroad Records, 1855-1907; 1 Fibredex box.

WILLS

Wills, 1851-1915; 2 Fibredex boxes.

MICROFILM RECORDS

BONDS

Apprentice Bonds, 1874-1914; 1 reel.

Record of Officials' Bonds, 1894-1969; 1 reel.

CORPORATIONS AND PARTNERSHIPS

Record of Corporations, 1890-1969; 1 reel.

COURT RECORDS

Superior Court

Minutes, 1851-1900; 4 reels.

Minutes, Civil, 1900-1958; 4 reels.

Minutes, Criminal, 1899-1955; 5 reels.

ELECTION RECORDS

Record of Elections, 1878-1968; 1 reel.

ESTATES RECORDS

Record of Accounts, 1873-1968; 4 reels.

Administrators' Bonds, 1874-1904; 1 reel.

Appointment of Administrators, Executors and Guardians, 1868-1913; 1 reel.

Record of Administrators, 1904-1968; 2 reels.

Appointment and Record of Executors, 1914-1968; 1 reel.

Guardians' Bonds, 1874-1892, 1917-1968; 1 reel.

Record of Guardians, 1904-1968; 2 reels.

Accounts of Indigent Orphans, 1911-1915; 1 reel.

Inheritance Tax Records, 1924-1968; 1 reel.

Inventory Docket, 1852-1862; 1 reel.

Record of Settlements, 1868-1968; 3 reels.

Index to Administrators and Executors, 1851-1968; 1 reel.

Cross Index to Guardians, 1851-1968; 1 reel.

Index to Estates, 1968-1969; 1 reel.

LAND RECORDS

Record of Deeds, 1851-1967; 55 reels.

Index to Real Estate Conveyances, Grantor, 1851-1969; 4 reels.

Index to Real Estate Conveyances, Grantee, 1851-1969; 4 reels.

Record of Resale of Land by Trustees and Mortgagees, 1923-1969; 1 reel.

MARRIAGE, DIVORCE AND VITAL STATISTICS

Marriage Bonds, 1851-1868; 3 reels.

Marriage Registers, 1851-1966; 1 reel.

Maiden Names of Divorced Women, 1939-1967; 1 reel.

Index to Births, 1913-1993; 2 reels.

Index to Deaths, 1913-1993; 1 reel.

Index to Delayed Births, various years; 1 reel.

MILITARY AND PENSION RECORDS

Record of Armed Forces Discharges, 1917-1994; 4 reels.

MISCELLANEOUS RECORDS

Orders and Decrees, 1868-1928; 1 reel.

Special Proceedings, 1883-1968; 8 reels.

Index to Special Proceedings, 1899-1969; 1 reel.

OFFICIALS, COUNTY

Minutes, Board of County Commissioners, 1872-1943; 4 reels.

WILLS

Record of Wills, 1851-1968; 2 reels.

Cross Index to Wills, 1851-1969; 1 reel.

MARTIN COUNTY

Established in 1774 from Halifax and Tyrrell counties.
Courthouse fire of 1884 destroyed many court records.

ORIGINAL RECORDS

COURT RECORDS
 County Court of Pleas and Quarter Sessions
  Minutes, 1847; 1 volume.
  Execution Docket, 1844-1859; 1 volume.
  Trial and Appearance Docket, 1852-1860; 1 volume.
 Superior Court
  Minutes, 1838-1912; 8 volumes.
  Equity Minutes, 1809-1829; 1 volume.
  Equity Trial Docket, 1834-1861; 1 volume.
  Civil Action Papers, 1885-1903; 2 Fibredex boxes.
  Civil Action Papers Concerning Land, 1882-1903; 4 Fibredex boxes.
  Criminal Action Papers, 1884-1903; 1 Fibredex box.
 Inferior Court
  Minutes, 1877-1885; 1 volume.
  Criminal Issues Docket, 1878-1884; 1 volume.

ELECTION RECORDS
 Record of Elections, 1874-1922; 4 volumes.

ESTATES RECORDS
 Record of Accounts, 1869-1904; 3 volumes.
 Administrators' Bonds, 1867-1870, 1885-1913; 4 volumes.
 Appointment of Administrators, Executors, Guardians and Masters, 1869-
  1886; 1 volume.
 Record of Widows' Year's Support, 1885-1901; 1 volume.
 Estates Records, 1820-1906; 6 Fibredex boxes.
 Guardians' Records, 1887-1904; 4 Fibredex boxes.
 Guardians' Bonds, 1866-1870, 1885-1913; 3 volumes.
 Record of Settlements, 1869-1916; 2 volumes.

LAND RECORDS
 Record of Deeds, 1774-1787; 1 volume.
 Record of Land Entries, 1866-1900; 1 volume.
 Land Records, 1779-1917; 1 Fibredex box.

MARRIAGE, DIVORCE AND VITAL STATISTICS
 Divorce Records, 1882-1903; 2 Fibredex boxes.

MISCELLANEOUS RECORDS
 Alien Registration, 1940; 1 volume.
 Miscellaneous Records, 1774-1906; 1 Fibredex box.

WILLS
 Wills, 1885-1925; 10 Fibredex boxes.

MICROFILM RECORDS

CORPORATIONS AND PARTNERSHIPS

    Record of Incorporations, 1890-1963; 1 reel.

    Record of Partnerships, 1913-1963; 1 reel.

COURT RECORDS

    Superior Court

        Minutes, 1838-1939; 6 reels.

ELECTION RECORDS

    Record of Elections, 1922-1962; 1 reel.

ESTATES RECORDS

    Record of Accounts, 1869-1963; 4 reels.

    Accounts of Sale and Inventories, 1905-1963; 1 reel.

    Appointment of Administrators and Executors, 1887-1928; 1 reel.

    Record of Administrators, 1914-1963; 4 reels.

    Record of Guardians, 1914-1963; 2 reels.

    Guardians of World War Veterans, 1930-1956; 1 reel.

    Accounts of Indigent Orphans, 1907-1934; 1 reel.

    Record of Widows' Year's Support, 1885-1963; 1 reel.

    Record of Widows' Dowers, 1904-1924; 1 reel.

    Inheritance Tax Records, 1923-1962; 1 reel.

    Final Accounts, 1869-1963; 5 reels.

LAND RECORDS

    Record of Deeds, 1774-1941; 61 reels.

    Index to Real Estate Conveyances, Grantor, 1772-1963; 4 reels.

    Index to Real Estate Conveyances, Grantee, 1772-1963; 3 reels.

    Record of Land Entries, 1901-1933; 1 reel.

    Record of Land Divisions, 1885-1963; 1 reel.

    Record of Surveys, 1908-1923; 1 reel.

    Registration of Land Titles (Torrens Act), 1933-1962; 1 reel.

    Plat Books, 1890-1963; 1 reel.

    Index to Plats, 1890-1963; 1 reel.

    Federal Tax Lien Index, 1934-1963; 1 reel.

    Record of Resale by Trustees and Mortgagees, 1924-1963; 2 reels.

MARRIAGE, DIVORCE AND VITAL STATISTICS

    Marriage Licenses, 1882-1963; 10 reels.

    Marriage Registers, 1872-1963; 2 reels.

    Maiden Names of Divorced Women, 1937-1960; 1 reel.

    Index to Vital Statistics, 1913-1962; 2 reels.

    Index to Delayed Births, 1937-1985; 2 reels.

MILITARY AND PENSION RECORDS

    Record of Armed Forces Discharges, 1919-1990; 5 reels.

    Index to Armed Forces Discharges, 1918-1985; 2 reels.

MISCELLANEOUS RECORDS

    Record of Homesteads, 1886-1958; 1 reel.

Orders and Decrees, 1868-1963; 8 reels.

Special Proceedings Dockets, 1868-1963; 2 reels.

OFFICIALS, COUNTY

Minutes, Board of County Commissioners, 1876-1922; 2 reels.

Minutes, County Board of Social Services, 1937-1963; 1 reel.

SCHOOL RECORDS

Minutes, County Board of Education, 1884-1963; 1 reel.

TAX AND FISCAL RECORDS

Tax Scrolls, 1885-1894, 1900-1904, 1914-1915; 4 reels.

WILLS

Record of Wills, 1774-1963; 4 reels.

Cross Index to Wills, 1774-1963; 1 reel.

McDOWELL COUNTY

Established in 1842 from Burke and Rutherford counties.

ORIGINAL RECORDS

BONDS

Apprentice Bonds and Records, 1798, 1842-1917; 1 Fibredex box.

Bastardy Bonds and Records, 1842-1932; 2 Fibredex boxes.

Officials' Bonds and Records, 1843-1922; 3 Fibredex boxes.

COURT RECORDS

County Court of Pleas and Quarter Sessions

Minutes, 1843-1867; 2 volumes.

Execution Dockets, 1843-1868; 3 volumes.

State Docket, 1857-1868; 1 volume.

Trial and Appearance Dockets, 1844-1860; 2 volumes.

Superior Court

Minutes, 1845-1925; 18 volumes.

Equity Minutes, 1852-1866; 1 volume.

Equity Minutes (Rough), 1851-1855; 1 volume.

Equity Execution Docket, 1853-1868; 1 volume.

Equity Trial Docket, 1852-1868; 1 volume.

Execution Dockets, 1846-1862; 2 volumes.

State Docket, 1845-1867; 1 volume.

Trial, Appearance and Reference Dockets, 1845-1869; 4 volumes.

Civil Action Papers, 1822-1933; 29 Fibredex boxes.

Civil Action Papers Concerning Land, 1846-1935; 25 Fibredex boxes.

Criminal Action Papers, 1843-1936; 38 Fibredex boxes.

Circuit Criminal Court/Western District Criminal Court

Minutes, 1897-1901; 1 volume.

ELECTION RECORDS

Record of Elections, 1896-1901, 1920-1968; 5 volumes.

ESTATES RECORDS

Record of Estates, 1859-1879; 1 volume.

Record of Accounts, 1869-1900; 1 volume.

Appointment of Administrators, Executors and Guardians, 1868-1910;
1 volume.

Estates Records, 1830, 1832, 1842-1939; 88 Fibredex boxes.

Guardians' Records, 1843-1937; 14 Fibredex boxes.

Guardians' Accounts, 1910-1934; 2 volumes.

Record of Settlements, 1872-1925; 1 volume.

LAND RECORDS

Deeds, 1813-1916; 1 Fibredex box.

Cross Index to Deeds, 1843-1917; 5 volumes.

Ejectments, 1844-1909; 5 Fibredex boxes.

Land Entry Books, 1843-1915; 7 volumes.

Record of Surveys, 1905-1914; 1 volume.

Attachments, Executions, Levies and Liens on Land, 1843-1935;
    4 Fibredex boxes.

Mineral Lease Book, 1891-1892; 1 volume.

Index to Mineral Lease Book, 1891-1892; 1 volume.

Miscellaneous Land Records, 1797-1939; 3 Fibredex boxes.

MARRIAGE, DIVORCE AND VITAL STATISTICS

Marriage Bonds, 1842-1868; 2 Fibredex boxes.

Divorce Records, 1849-1941; 9 Fibredex boxes.

MILITARY AND PENSION RECORDS

Pension Records, 1852-1939; 2 Fibredex boxes.

MISCELLANEOUS RECORDS

Alien Registration, 1927, 1940, 1942; 1 volume.

County Accounts and Correspondence, 1843-1941; 1 Fibredex box.

Homestead and Personal Property Exemptions, 1858-1926; 1 Fibredex box.

Lunacy Records, 1848-1951; 1 Fibredex box.

Clerk's Minute Dockets (Special Proceedings), 1921-1968; 4 volumes.

Special Proceedings, 1870-1898; 4 volumes.

Miscellaneous Records, 1843-1938; 5 Fibredex boxes.

Records of Slaves and Free Persons of Color, 1843-1873; 1 Fibredex box.

Records of Assignees, Receivers and Trustees, 1844-1942; 8 Fibredex boxes.

ROADS AND BRIDGES

Road Records, 1843-1921; 2 Fibredex boxes.

Railroad Records, 1860-1925; 16 Fibredex boxes.

Railroad Bonds, 1867, 1887, 1907; 4 Fibredex boxes.

Miscellaneous Railroad Records, 1860-1917; 1 Fibredex box.

SCHOOL RECORDS

Minutes, County Board of Education, 1873-1885; 1 volume.

TAX AND FISCAL RECORDS

Lists of Taxables, 1842-1859; 2 volumes.

Tax Records, 1839-1917, 1927; 2 Fibredex boxes.

WILLS

Wills, 1841-1920; 6 Fibredex boxes.

Index to Wills, 1843-1868; 1 volume.

Cross Index to Wills, 1843-1905; 1 volume.

MICROFILM RECORDS

CORPORATIONS AND PARTNERSHIPS

Record of Corporations, 1886-1962; 1 reel.

Record of Partnerships, 1913-1966; 1 reel.

COURT RECORDS

County Court of Pleas and Quarter Sessions
    Minutes, 1843-1867; 1 reel.

Superior Court
>>> Minutes, 1845-1957; 12 reels.
>>> Equity Minutes, 1852-1866; 1 reel.

ELECTION RECORDS
>>> Record of Elections, 1896-1968; 1 reel.

ESTATES RECORDS
>>> Record of Accounts, 1869-1968; 6 reels.
>>> Record of Administrators, Executors and Guardians, 1913-1930; 1 reel.
>>> Record of Administrators, 1921-1968; 3 reels.
>>> Appointment of Executors, 1870-1910; 1 reel.
>>> Record of Executors, 1930-1968; 1 reel.
>>> Record of Guardians, 1926-1968; 1 reel.
>>> Record of Indigent Children and Lunacy Funds, 1934-1953; 1 reel.
>>> Record of Widows' Year's Allowance, 1923-1966; 1 reel.
>>> Inheritance Tax Records, 1923-1968; 1 reel.
>>> Inventories of Estates, 1859-1867; 1 reel.
>>> Record of Settlements, 1872-1968; 5 reels.
>>> Index to Estates, 1843-1968; 1 reel.

LAND RECORDS
>>> Record of Deeds, 1843-1956; 66 reels.
>>> Index to Real Estate Conveyances, Grantor, 1842-1961; 7 reels.
>>> Index to Real Estate Conveyances, Grantee, 1842-1961; 7 reels.
>>> Land Entry Books, 1843-1956; 2 reels.
>>> Record of Surveys, 1905-1913; 1 reel.
>>> Map Books, 1925-1968; 1 reel.
>>> Index to Map Books, 1925-1968; 1 reel.
>>> Record of Sales by Trustees and Mortgagees, 1921-1968; 2 reels.

MARRIAGE, DIVORCE AND VITAL STATISTICS
>>> Marriage Bonds, 1842-1868; 1 reel.
>>> Marriage Licenses, 1868-1961; 10 reels.
>>> Marriage Registers, 1851-1945; 2 reels.
>>> Index to Marriage Registers, 1851-1968; 1 reel.
>>> Maiden Names of Divorced Women, 1940-1965; 1 reel.
>>> Index to Births, 1914-1969; 2 reels.
>>> Index to Deaths and Delayed Births, 1913-1967; 1 reel.

MILITARY AND PENSION RECORDS
>>> Record of Armed Forces Discharges, 1919-1969; 7 reels.
>>> Index to Armed Forces Discharges, 1919-1969; 1 reel.

MISCELLANEOUS RECORDS
>>> Orders and Decrees, 1869-1957; 1 reel.
>>> Special Proceedings, 1870-1953; 8 reels.
>>> Index to Special Proceedings, 1870-1953, 1968-1980; 3 reels.

OFFICIALS, COUNTY
>>> Minutes, Board of County Commissioners, 1868-1968; 5 reels.

SCHOOL RECORDS
  Minutes, County Board of Education, 1885-1968; 1 reel.
TAX AND FISCAL RECORDS
  Tax Lists, 1842-1859; 1 reel.
WILLS
  Record of Wills, 1843-1968; 4 reels.
  Index to Wills, 1843-1968; 1 reel.

MECKLENBURG COUNTY

Established in 1762 (effective 1763) from Anson County.

ORIGINAL RECORDS

BONDS

        Apprentice Bonds, 1871-1920; 2 volumes.

        Officials' Bonds and Records, 1779-1954; 2 Fibredex boxes.

CORPORATIONS AND PARTNERSHIPS

        Partnership Records, 1871-1955; 2 Fibredex boxes.

COURT RECORDS

        County Court of Pleas and Quarter Sessions

                Minutes, 1774-1868; 12 volumes.

                Appeal Docket, 1810-1822; 1 volume.

                Appearance Dockets, 1824-1867; 5 volumes.

                Execution Dockets, 1774-1861; 19 volumes.

                Levy Docket, 1827-1830; 1 volume.

                State Dockets, 1828-1868; 3 volumes.

                Trial, Appearance and Reference Dockets, 1774-1810; 13 volumes.

                Trial Dockets, 1810-1866; 7 volumes.

        Superior Court

                Minutes, 1811-1885; 8 volumes.

                Equity Minutes, 1822-1852, 1859-1869; 2 volumes.

                Equity Trial Dockets, 1846-1868; 2 volumes.

                Appearance Docket, 1811-1838; 1 volume.

                Execution Dockets, 1811-1836, 1846-1854; 4 volumes.

                Receipt Docket, 1825-1828; 1 volume.

                Recognizance Docket, 1825-1852; 1 volume.

                Trial, Appearance and Reference Docket, 1807-1810; 1 volume.

                Trial Dockets, 1811-1843; 2 volumes.

                Civil Action Papers, 1784-1959, 1966; 146 Fibredex boxes.

                Civil Action Papers Concerning Land, 1784-1959, 1961, 1965; 64 Fibredex boxes.

                Civil Action Papers Concerning Occupational Licensing Boards, 1922-1953; 2 Fibredex boxes.

                Criminal Action Papers, 1778-1875, 1914, 1935, 1961; 1 Fibredex box.

        Inferior Court

        Minutes, 1877-1885; 2 volumes.

        Criminal Court

        Minutes, 1885-1890; 1 volume.

        Circuit Criminal Court

        Minutes, 1898; 1 volume.

        Eastern District Criminal Court

        Minutes, 1899-1901; 1 volume.

ELECTION RECORDS

Record of Elections, 1924-1932; 1 volume.

ESTATES RECORDS

Record of Accounts, 1785-1896; 12 volumes.

Administrators' Bonds, 1870-1911; 8 volumes.

Estates Records, 1762-1957; 282 Fibredex boxes.

Guardians' Records, 1779-1955; 11 Fibredex boxes.

Guardians' Bonds, 1870-1911; 5 volumes.

Record of Settlements, 1869-1904; 3 volumes.

Record of Probate (Estates), 1868-1907; 1 volume.

LAND RECORDS

Deeds of Sale and Miscellaneous Deeds, 1772-1938; 1 Fibredex box.

Ejectments, 1793-1954, 1977; 4 Fibredex boxes.

Land Entries, 1778-1855; 2 volumes.

Land Grants and Deeds, 1789-1845; 1 volume.

Land Sold for Taxes, 1893, 1896, 1931-1950; 1 Fibredex box.

Record of Probate of Deeds, 1858-1868; 1 volume.

Attachments, Executions and Liens on Land, 1855-1968; 17 Fibredex boxes.

Land Condemnations, 1892-1968; 2 Fibredex boxes.

Foreclosures of Mortgages and Deeds of Trust, 1870-1955;
    25 Fibredex boxes.

Miscellaneous Land Records, 1767-1953; 2 Fibredex boxes.

MARRIAGE, DIVORCE AND VITAL STATISTICS

Marriage Bonds, 1783-1868; 13 Fibredex boxes.

Marriage Register, 1868-1884; 1 volume.

Divorce Records, 1846-1969; 322 Fibredex boxes.

MISCELLANEOUS RECORDS

Alien, Naturalization and Citizenship Records, 1822, 1886-1927;
    1 Fibredex box.

County Accounts, 1868-1884; 2 volumes.

Insolvents and Homestead and Personal Property Exemptions, 1787-1919;
    1 Fibredex box.

Orders and Decrees, 1869-1902; 8 volumes.

Child Custody and Support Records, 1866-1956, 1964, 1975;
    3 Fibredex boxes.

Commissions to Hold Court, 1886-1937, 1951; 1 Fibredex box.

Promissory Notes and Personal Accounts, 1758-1897; 1 Fibredex box.

Miscellaneous Records, 1759-1959; 5 Fibredex boxes.

Records of Assignees, Receivers and Trustees, 1847-1958; 55 Fibredex boxes.

ROADS AND BRIDGES

Road, Bridge and Ferry Records, 1783-1921; 1 Fibredex box.

Railroad Records, 1856-1955; 33 Fibredex boxes.

SCHOOL RECORDS

School Records, 1798, 1863-1955; 3 Fibredex boxes.

TAX AND FISCAL RECORDS
List of Taxables, 1797-1824; 1 volume.
WILLS
Record of Wills, 1761-1854; 9 volumes.
Wills, 1749-1918; 25 Fibredex boxes.
Cross Index to Wills, 1763-1929; 2 volumes.

MICROFILM RECORDS

BONDS
Apprentice Bonds, 1871-1920; 1 reel.
Officials' Bonds, 1889-1930; 1 reel.
CORPORATIONS AND PARTNERSHIPS
Record of Corporations, 1884-1947; 12 reels.
Record of Partnerships, 1913-1937; 1 reel.
Record of Limited Partnerships, 1942-1965; 1 reel.
Index to Partnerships and Assumed Names, 1913-1971; 1 reel.
COURT RECORDS
County Court of Pleas and Quarter Sessions
Minutes, 1774-1857; 5 reels.
Superior Court
Minutes, 1811-1901; 6 reels.
Minutes, Civil, 1901-1952; 32 reels.
Minutes, Criminal, 1901-1946; 7 reels.
Equity Minutes, 1822-1852, 1859-1869; 2 reels.
Index to Judgments, Plaintiff, 1909-1956; 3 reels.
Index to Judgments, Defendant, 1909-1956; 4 reels.
Inferior Court
Minutes, 1877-1885; 1 reel.
Circuit Criminal Court
Minutes, 1898; 1 reel.
Criminal Court/Eastern District Criminal Court
Minutes, 1885-1901; 1 reel.
ELECTION RECORDS
Minutes, Board of Elections, 1936-1956; 1 reel.
Record of Elections, 1908-1932; 1 reel.
ESTATES RECORDS
Record of Accounts, 1785-1965; 38 reels.
Administrators' Bonds, 1870-1911; 2 reels.
Record of Administrators, Executors and Guardians, 1911-1928; 1 reel.
Record of Administrators, 1912-1955; 19 reels.
Record of Executors and Guardians, 1868-1964; 6 reels.
Record of Guardians, 1914-1963; 8 reels.
Record of Guardians of World War Veterans, 1930-1961; 1 reel.
Guardians' Bonds, 1870-1911; 1 reel.

Inheritance Tax Records, 1919-1964; 5 reels.

Record of Settlements, 1869-1965; 19 reels.

Index to Estates, 1765-1965; 9 reels.

LAND RECORDS

Record of Real Estate Conveyances, 1763-1959; 773 reels.

Index to Real Estate Conveyances, Grantor, 1763-1955; 48 reels.

Index to Real Estate Conveyances, Grantee, 1763-1955; 41 reels.

Index to Real Estate Conveyances, Grantee: Firms and Corporations, 1919-1936, 1948-1955; 3 reels.

Land Entries, 1778-1855, 1870-1937; 2 reels.

Land Grants, 1789-1848; 1 reel.

Plats, 1892, 1907-1951; 4 reels.

MARRIAGE, DIVORCE AND VITAL STATISTICS

Marriage Bonds, 1783-1868; 4 reels.

Marriage Licenses, 1851-1962; 47 reels.

Record of Marriages, Black, 1850-1867; Record of Cohabitation, 1866-1867; 1 reel.

Marriage Registers, 1850-1960; 3 reels.

Maiden Names of Divorced Women, 1937-1965; 1 reel.

Index to Births, 1913-1947; 4 reels.

Index to Deaths, 1909-1947; 2 reels.

Index to Delayed Births, various years; 1 reel.

MILITARY AND PENSION RECORDS

Record of Armed Forces Discharges, 1918-1977; 23 reels.

Index to Armed Forces Discharges, 1918-1976; 1 reel.

MISCELLANEOUS RECORDS

Record of Officials' Reports, 1875-1887; 1 reel.

Record of Lunacy, 1899-1953; 5 reels.

Orders and Decrees, 1869-1960; 27 reels.

Special Proceedings, 1869-1965; 6 reels.

Index to Special Proceedings and Orders and Decrees, Plaintiff, 1896-1968; 3 reels.

Index to Special Proceedings and Orders and Decrees, Defendant, 1896-1968; 2 reels.

OFFICIALS, COUNTY

Minutes, Board of County Commissioners, 1868-1956; 10 reels.

TAX AND FISCAL RECORDS

List of Taxables, 1797-1824; 1 reel.

Tax Scrolls, 1915; 1 reel.

WILLS

Record of Wills, 1763-1965; 25 reels.

Index to Wills, Devisor, 1763-1968; 2 reels.

Index to Wills, Devisee, 1763-1968; 2 reels.

MITCHELL COUNTY

Established in 1861 from Burke, Caldwell, McDowell, Watauga and Yancey counties. Several records believed destroyed during move into new courthouse in 1907.

ORIGINAL RECORDS

BONDS

> Apprentice Bonds and Records, 1863-1904; Bastardy Bonds and Records, 1867-1906; 2 Fibredex boxes.

COURT RECORDS

> County Court of Pleas and Quarter Sessions
>> Minutes, 1861-1868; 1 volume.
>
> Superior Court
>> Minutes, 1861-1910; 11 volumes.
>> Civil Action Papers, 1862-1913; 9 Fibredex boxes.
>> Civil Action Papers Concerning Land, 1869-1925; 11 Fibredex boxes.
>> Criminal Action Papers, 1861-1915; 21 Fibredex boxes.

ELECTION RECORDS

> Record of Elections, 1880-1924; 4 volumes.

ESTATES RECORDS

> Administrators' Bonds, 1907-1909; 1 volume.
>
> Appointment of Administrators, Executors, Guardians and Masters, 1871-1909; 1 volume.
>
> Estates Records, 1826-1946; 15 Fibredex boxes.
>
> Guardians' Records, 1866-1926; 3 Fibredex boxes.
>
> Guardians' Bonds, 1907-1911; 1 volume.

LAND RECORDS

> Deeds, 1846-1951; 2 Fibredex boxes.
>
> Miscellaneous Deeds, 1881-1951; 1 Fibredex box.
>
> Ejectments, 1862-1893; Levies, Executions and Attachments, 1867-1908; 2 Fibredex boxes.
>
> Miscellaneous Land Records, 1789-1936; 1 Fibredex box.
>
> Record of Probate of Deeds, 1861-1882; 2 volumes.

MISCELLANEOUS RECORDS

> Alien, Naturalization and Citizenship Records, 1927, 1940; 1 volume.
>
> Registry of Licenses to Trades, 1877-1902; 1 volume.
>
> Miscellaneous Records, 1861-1935; 2 Fibredex boxes.
>
> Records of Assignees, Receivers and Trustees, 1885-1910; 1 Fibredex box.

MARRIAGE, DIVORCE AND VITAL STATISTICS

> Divorce Records, 1867-1915; 5 Fibredex boxes.

ROADS AND BRIDGES

> Minutes, Board of Road Commissioners, 1915-1926; 1 volume.

TAX AND FISCAL RECORDS

> Tax List, 1861-1868; 1 volume.
>
> Tax Records, 1873-1911; 1 Fibredex box.

WILLS
Wills, 1823-1927; 2 Fibredex boxes.

MICROFILM RECORDS

CORPORATIONS AND PARTNERSHIPS
Record of Corporations, 1887-1962; 1 reel.
Record of Partnerships, 1913-1918; 1 reel.

COURT RECORDS
County Court of Pleas and Quarter Sessions
Minutes, 1861-1868; 1 reel.
Superior Court
Minutes, 1861-1966; 9 reels.
Minutes, Divorce Proceedings, 1948; 1 reel.
Judgment Docket, Land Tax Sales, 1931-1968; 1 reel.

ELECTION RECORDS
Record of Elections, 1880-1970; 1 reel.

ESTATES RECORDS
Record of Accounts, 1875-1968; 3 reels.
Administrators' Bonds, 1907-1909; 1 reel.
Appointment and Record of Administrators, 1871-1909; 1 reel.
Record of Administrators, Executors and Guardians, 1909-1943; 1 reel.
Record of Administrators, 1919-1968; 2 reels.
Record of Executors, 1943-1968; 1 reel.
Guardians' Bonds, 1907-1911; 1 reel.
Record of Guardians, 1919-1968; 1 reel.
Accounts of Indigent Orphans, 1909-1961; 1 reel.
Record of Dowers, 1908-1938; 1 reel.
Inheritance Tax Records, 1924-1970; 1 reel.
Record of Settlements, 1868-1969; 2 reels.
Index to Administrators and Executors, 1871-1968; 1 reel.
Cross Index to Guardians, 1871-1968; 1 reel.

LAND RECORDS
Record of Deeds, 1861-1958; 57 reels.
Record of Commissioners' Deeds, 1936-1951; 1 reel.
Index to Real Estate Conveyances, Grantor, 1861-1977; 4 reels.
Index to Real Estate Conveyances, Grantee, 1861-1977; 4 reels.
Land Entry Books, 1901-1950; 1 reel.
Severance of Subsurface Rights and Index, 1967; 1 reel.
Record of Taxes for Mortgagees, 1931-1947; 1 reel.
Federal Tax Lien Index, 1944-1951, 1957-1968; 1 reel.
Record of Sales by Trustees, Mortgagees and Executors, 1923-1968; 1 reel.

MARRIAGE, DIVORCE AND VITAL STATISTICS
Marriage Registers, 1861-1969; 1 reel.
Index to Marriage Licenses, 1860-1937; 1 reel.

Index to Births, 1913-1992; 1 reel.

Index to Deaths, 1913-1992; 1 reel.

Index to Delayed Births, 1913-1970; 1 reel.

MILITARY AND PENSION RECORDS

Record of Armed Forces Discharges, 1922-1993; 4 reels.

MISCELLANEOUS RECORDS

Record of Officials' Settlements, 1910-1968; 1 reel.

Record of Homesteads, 1907-1939; 1 reel.

Record of Lunacy, 1899-1964; 1 reel.

Clerk's Minute Docket, 1921-1951; 1 reel.

Orders and Decrees, 1870-1963; 1 reel.

Special Proceedings Dockets, 1902-1968; 4 reels.

Index to Special Proceedings and Orders and Decrees, 1869-1968; 1 reel.

Index to Special Proceedings, 1968-1977; 1 reel.

Appointment of Receivers, 1907-1932; 1 reel.

OFFICIALS, COUNTY

Minutes, Board of County Commissioners, 1868-1965; 4 reels.

ROADS AND BRIDGES

Road Commissioners' Docket, 1915-1926; 1 reel.

SCHOOL RECORDS

Minutes, County Board of Education, 1901-1928; 1 reel.

Index to School Deeds, 1946; 1 reel.

TAX AND FISCAL RECORDS

Tax List, 1861-1868; 1 reel.

WILLS

Record of Wills, 1887-1969; 2 reels.

Cross Index to Wills, 1887-1969; 1 reel.

MONTGOMERY COUNTY

Established in 1779 from Anson County.
Courthouse fire of 1835 destroyed many records.

ORIGINAL RECORDS

BONDS

      Apprentice Bonds and Records, 1840-1897; 1 Fibredex box.

      Bastardy Bonds and Records, 1843-1897; 1 Fibredex box.

      Officials' Bonds and Records, 1837-1918; 1 volume, 2 Fibredex boxes.

COURT RECORDS

      County Court of Pleas and Quarter Sessions

            Minutes, 1843-1868; 5 volumes.

            Partial Index to Minute Dockets, 1843-1868; 1 volume.

            Trial Dockets, 1843-1868; 2 volumes.

      Superior Court

            Minutes, 1843-1912; 9 volumes.

            Equity Enrolling Docket, 1807-1824; 1 volume.

            Bills and Answers Filed in Equity, 1827; 1 volume.

            Civil Execution Docket, 1843-1852; 1 volume.

            State Execution Docket, 1843-1860; 1 volume.

            Recognizance Docket, 1821-1845; 1 volume.

            State Docket, 1843-1859; 1 volume.

            Trial Dockets, 1855, 1865-1868; 2 volumes.

            Civil Action Papers, 1833-1940; 15 Fibredex boxes.

            Civil Action Papers Concerning County Commissioners, 1872-1904; 1 Fibredex box.

            Civil Action Papers Concerning Land, 1843-1916; 8 Fibredex boxes.

            Criminal Action Papers, 1833-1921; 13 Fibredex boxes.

ELECTION RECORDS

      Record of Elections, 1878-1924; 6 volumes.

      Election Records, 1779-1922; 2 Fibredex boxes.

ESTATES RECORDS

      Record of Estates, 1843-1868; 3 volumes.

      Record of Accounts, 1868-1900; 2 volumes.

      Administrators' Bonds, 1870-1891; 1 volume.

      Appointment of Administrators, Executors, Guardians and Masters, 1868-1901; 1 volume.

      Estates Records, 1818-1970; 56 Fibredex boxes.

      Guardians' Records, 1843-1933; 5 Fibredex boxes.

      Guardians' Accounts, 1843-1868; 1 volume.

      Guardians' Bonds, 1874-1904; 2 volumes.

      Record of Settlements, 1868-1924; 2 volumes.

LAND RECORDS

      Deeds of Sale, 1794-1920; 1 Fibredex box.

Miscellaneous Deeds, 1783-1924; 1 Fibredex box.

Ejectments, 1840-1892; 1 Fibredex box.

Land Entries, 1837-1858; 2 volumes.

Land Sales for Taxes, 1845-1870; 1 Fibredex box.

Tax Levies on Land, 1873-1880; 1 volume.

Condemnation of Land, 1877-1908; 1 Fibredex box.

Timber Records, 1867-1907; 1 Fibredex box.

Miscellaneous Land Records, 1769-1922; 1 Fibredex box.

MARRIAGE, DIVORCE AND VITAL STATISTICS

Marriage Bonds, 1779-1868; 3 Fibredex boxes.

Marriage Certificates, 1866-1867; 1 volume.

Divorce Records, 1856-1907; 1 Fibredex box.

MISCELLANEOUS RECORDS

Alien Registration, 1927, 1940; 1 volume.

County Accounts and Claims, 1844-1911; 2 volumes, 1 Fibredex box.

Insolvent Debtors, 1787-1920; 1 Fibredex box.

Orders and Decrees, 1868-1912; 3 volumes.

Minutes, Wardens of the Poor, 1831-1867; 1 volume.

Miscellaneous Records, 1785-1922; 3 Fibredex boxes.

Witness Tickets, 1844-1868; 1 Fibredex box.

Records of Assignees, Receivers and Trustees, 1843-1932; 1 Fibredex box.

OFFICIALS, COUNTY

Minutes, Board of County Commissioners, 1868; 1 volume.

ROADS AND BRIDGES

Road Orders, 1843-1868; 1 volume.

Road Records, 1839-1926; 2 Fibredex boxes.

Railroad Records, 1891-1910; 1 Fibredex box.

SCHOOL RECORDS

Minutes, County Board of Education, 1872-1883; 1 volume.

TAX AND FISCAL RECORDS

Lists of Taxables, 1843-1873; 5 volumes.

Tax Records, 1843-1890; 1 Fibredex box.

WILLS

Wills, 1785-1970; 8 Fibredex boxes.

MICROFILM RECORDS

COURT RECORDS

County Court of Pleas and Quarter Sessions

Minutes, 1843-1868; Partial Index to Minutes, 1843-1868; 2 reels.

Superior Court

Minutes, 1843-1964; 10 reels.

Equity Minutes, 1807-1824; 1 reel.

ELECTION RECORDS

Record of Elections, 1896-1962; 2 reels.

ESTATES RECORDS

Record of Estates, 1842-1858; 2 reels.

Record of Accounts, 1847-1964; 5 reels.

Administrators' Bonds, 1874-1891; 1 reel.

Record of Administrators, 1900-1964; 4 reels.

Appointment of Executors, 1868-1946; 1 reel.

Guardians' Bonds, 1894-1904; 1 reel.

Appointment of Guardians, 1901-1964; 1 reel.

Record of Amounts Paid for Indigent Children, 1913-1947; 1 reel.

Record of Estates Under $300, 1932-1958; 1 reel.

Inheritance Tax Records, 1923-1964; 1 reel.

Record of Settlements, 1868-1964; 3 reels.

LAND RECORDS

Record of Deeds, 1774-1807, 1838-1961; 47 reels.

Index to Real Estate Conveyances, Grantor, 1838-1964; 4 reels.

Index to Real Estate Conveyances, Grantee, 1838-1964; 4 reels.

Land Entries, 1837-1955; 1 reel.

Record of Surveys, 1904-1912; 1 reel.

Federal Tax Lien Index, 1925-1964; 1 reel.

Record of Resales, 1923-1964; 2 reels.

MARRIAGE, DIVORCE AND VITAL STATISTICS

Marriage Bonds, 1842-1868; 1 reel.

Marriage Bond Abstracts, 1842-1868; 1 reel.

Marriage Licenses, 1846-1964; 10 reels.

Marriage Registers, 1843-1981; 2 reels.

Index to Vital Statistics, 1913-1964; 2 reels.

Index to Delayed Births, various years; 2 reels.

MISCELLANEOUS RECORDS

County Accounts and Claims, 1841-1870; Minutes, Board of County Commissioners, 1868-1870; 1 reel.

Orders and Decrees, 1868-1962; 7 reels.

Special Proceedings and Index, 1869-1933; 2 reels.

OFFICIALS, COUNTY

Minutes, Board of County Commissioners, 1870-1931; 3 reels.

SCHOOL RECORDS

Minutes, County Board of Education, 1884-1926; 1 reel.

TAX AND FISCAL RECORDS

Tax Lists, 1873-1916; 10 reels.

WILLS

Record of Wills, 1843-1964; 4 reels.

Cross Index to Wills, 1848-1964; 1 reel.

MOORE COUNTY

Established in 1784 from Cumberland County.
Courthouse fire of 1889 destroyed most land records and many court records.

ORIGINAL RECORDS

BONDS
>   Apprentice Bonds, 1890-1903; 1 volume.

COURT RECORDS
>   County Court of Pleas and Quarter Sessions
>>   Minutes, 1784-1858; 7 volumes.
>>   Appearance Docket, 1841-1854; 1 volume.
>>   Execution Dockets, 1818-1867; 6 volumes.
>>   State Docket, 1834-1851; 1 volume.
>>   Trial and Appearance Dockets, 1798-1841; 3 volumes.
>>   Trial Docket, 1841-1845; 1 volume.
>>   Index to Trial Docket, 1785-1868; 1 volume.

>   Superior Court
>>   Minutes, 1869-1873; 1 volume.
>>   Equity Trial Docket, 1850-1868; 1 volume.
>>   Appearance Dockets, 1835-1869; 2 volumes.
>>   Execution Dockets, 1834-1881; 4 volumes.
>>   Recognizance Docket, 1836-1844, 1849; 1 volume.
>>   Civil Action Papers, 1829-1915; Criminal Action Papers, 1883-1916;
>>   12 Fibredex boxes.
>>   Civil Action Papers Concerning Land, 1874-1924; 16 Fibredex boxes.

ELECTION RECORDS
>   Record of Elections, 1878-1932; 4 volumes.

ESTATES RECORDS
>   Record of Estates, 1820-1862; 6 volumes.
>   Administrators' Bonds, 1864-1922; 4 volumes.
>   Record of Dowers, 1889-1921; 1 volume.
>   Record of Widows' Year's Support, 1889-1968; 2 volumes.
>   Estates Records, 1828-1921; 19 Fibredex boxes.
>   Guardians' Records, 1870-1912; 1 Fibredex box.
>   Guardians' Accounts, 1834-1857, 1889-1931; 3 volumes.
>   Guardians' Bonds, 1889-1929; 2 volumes.

LAND RECORDS
>   Deeds, 1797-1923; 1 Fibredex box.
>   Mortgage Deeds and Deeds of Trust, 1834-1926; 1 Fibredex box.
>   Ejectments, 1881-1913; 1 Fibredex box.
>   Attachments, Executions, Liens and Levies on Land, 1869-1915;
>   1 Fibredex box.
>   Miscellaneous Land Records, 1798-1926; 2 Fibredex boxes.

MARRIAGE, DIVORCE AND VITAL STATISTICS
Divorce Records, 1887-1915; 2 Fibredex boxes.
MILITARY AND PENSION RECORDS
List of Applications for Pensions, 1885-1888; 1 manuscript box.

Record of Pensions, 1890-1919; 2 volumes.
MISCELLANEOUS RECORDS
Record of Naturalization, 1887-1917; 1 volume.

County Accounts, 1796-1841; 1 volume.

Homestead and Personal Property Exemptions, 1864-1924; 4 Fibredex boxes.

Mining Records, 1882-1913; 1 Fibredex box.

Miscellaneous Records, 1784-1935; 5 Fibredex boxes.

Records of Assignees, Receivers and Trustees, 1869-1933; 4 Fibredex boxes.
ROADS AND BRIDGES
Appointment of Road Overseers, 1875-1895; 1 volume.

Railroad Records, 1889-1915; 3 Fibredex boxes.
TAX AND FISCAL RECORDS
Tax List, 1852-1860; 1 volume.
WILLS
Wills, 1831, 1859-1921; 3 Fibredex boxes.

MICROFILM RECORDS

CORPORATIONS AND PARTNERSHIPS
Record of Corporations, 1889-1944; 2 reels.

Partnership Records, 1913-1965; 1 reel.
COURT RECORDS
County Court of Pleas and Quarter Sessions
Minutes, 1784-1858; 3 reels.

Superior Court
Minutes, 1835-1956; 18 reels.

Index to Minutes, Plaintiff, 1786-1953; 2 reels.

Index to Minutes, Defendant, 1786-1953; 4 reels.

Criminal Judgment Docket, 1887-1896; 1 reel.
ELECTION RECORDS
Record of Elections, 1934-1964; 1 reel.
ESTATES RECORDS
Record of Estates, 1820-1831, 1837-1851, 1856-1861; 1 reel.

Record of Accounts, 1868-1965; 6 reels.

Administrators' Bonds, 1880-1897, 1923-1963; 5 reels.

Appointment of Executors, 1868-1902; 1 reel.

Record of Guardians, 1834-1857; 1 reel.

Guardians' Accounts, 1888-1965; 3 reels.

Guardians' Bonds, 1890-1909; 1 reel.

Appointment of Guardians, 1932-1968; 2 reels.

Record of Accounts for Indigent Orphans, 1909-1959; 1 reel.

Record of Dowers and Widows' Year's Support, 1889-1964; 1 reel.

Estates Not Exceeding $300, 1950-1965; 1 reel.

Inheritance Tax Records, 1923-1966; 1 reel.

Record of Settlements, 1869-1965; 6 reels.

Index to Administrators and Executors, 1787-1819, 1898-1916; 1 reel.

Index to Guardians, 1889-1915; 1 reel.

Index to Final Accounts: Administrators, 1868-1965; 1 reel.

Index to Final Accounts: Guardians, 1868-1965; 1 reel.

LAND RECORDS

Record of Deeds, 1889-1961; 124 reels.

Index to Real Estate Conveyances, Grantor, 1889-1966; 10 reels.

Index to Real Estate Conveyances, Grantee, 1889-1966; 10 reels.

Index to Real Estate Conveyances, Grantor and Grantee: Banks and Trustees, 1940-1966; 1 reel.

Entry Book, 1889-1958; 1 reel.

Record of Grants, 1787-1965; 2 reels.

Map Books, 1902-1965; Index to Maps, 1907-1965; 3 reels.

Record of Sales and Resales of Land, 1930-1966; 3 reels.

MARRIAGE, DIVORCE AND VITAL STATISTICS

Marriage Licenses, 1889-1961; 10 reels.

Marriage Record, 1851-1867; 1 reel.

Marriage Registers, 1889-1965; 2 reels.

Maiden Names of Divorced Women, 1939-1963; 1 reel.

Index to Births, 1913-1964; 2 reels.

Index to Deaths, 1913-1964; 1 reel.

Index to Delayed Births, 1879-1956; 1 reel.

MILITARY AND PENSION RECORDS

Record of Armed Forces Discharges, 1918-1965; 4 reels.

Index to Armed Forces Discharges, 1918-1965; 1 reel.

MISCELLANEOUS RECORDS

Orders and Decrees, 1868-1951; 11 reels.

Special Proceedings, 1901-1920; 1 reel.

Index to Special Proceedings, Plaintiff, 1869-1965; 3 reels.

Index to Special Proceedings, Defendant, 1869-1965; 2 reels.

Receivers' and Assignees' Accounts, 1896-1951; 1 reel.

OFFICIALS, COUNTY

Minutes, Board of County Commissioners, 1889-1945; 4 reels.

SCHOOL RECORDS

Minutes, County Board of Education, 1872-1941; 1 reel.

WILLS

Record of Wills, 1783-1965; 12 reels.

Index to Wills, Devisor, 1793-1965; 1 reel.

Index to Wills, Devisee, 1793-1965; 1 reel.

NASH COUNTY

Established in 1777 from Edgecombe County.

ORIGINAL RECORDS

BONDS

Apprentice Bonds, 1793-1868, 1900-1918; 1 volume, 3 Fibredex boxes.

Bastardy Bonds and Records, 1779-1883; 1 volume, 3 Fibredex boxes.

Clerks' Bonds, 1807-1885; 1 Fibredex box.

Constables' Bonds, 1779-1882; 3 Fibredex boxes.

Officials' Bonds, 1778-1888; 2 volumes, 2 Fibredex boxes.

COURT RECORDS

County Court of Pleas and Quarter Sessions

Minutes, 1778-1868; 14 volumes.

Appearance and Trial Dockets, 1779-1826; 2 volumes, 3 manuscript boxes.

Appearance Dockets, 1826-1868; 4 volumes, 1 manuscript box.

Execution Dockets, 1782-1867; 9 volumes.

State Dockets, 1779-1793, 1808-1868; 4 volumes, 1 manuscript box.

Trial Dockets, 1823-1868; 6 volumes.

Superior Court

Minutes, 1807-1915; 16 volumes.

Equity Trial Dockets, 1811-1868; 4 volumes.

Execution Dockets, 1825-1868; 2 volumes.

State Dockets, 1813-1853; 3 volumes.

Trial and Appearance Dockets, 1813-1859; 3 volumes.

Miscellaneous Dockets, 1779-1880; 1 Fibredex box.

Civil Action Papers, 1751-1908; 75 Fibredex boxes.

Criminal Action Papers, 1783-1897; 26 Fibredex boxes.

Criminal Action Papers Concerning Fornication and Adultery, 1789-1871; 1 Fibredex box.

Circuit Criminal Court/Eastern District Criminal Court

Minutes, 1897-1901; 1 volume.

ELECTION RECORDS

Record of Elections, 1878-1924; 5 volumes.

Election Records, 1830-1908; 2 Fibredex boxes.

ESTATES RECORDS

Record of Estates, 1818-1868; 8 volumes.

Record of Accounts, 1869-1915; 7 volumes.

Administrators' Bonds, 1857-1910; 5 volumes.

Record of Widows' Year's Support, 1883-1918; 1 volume.

Estates Records, 1770-1909; 83 Fibredex boxes.

Guardians' Records, 1784-1874; 13 Fibredex boxes.

Guardians' Accounts, 1820-1867; 4 volumes.

Guardians' Bonds, 1857-1915; 5 volumes.

Division of Slaves, 1830-1861; 1 volume. SEE ALSO Marriage, Divorce and
    Vital Statistics.
Record of Settlements, 1869-1915; 3 volumes.
Miscellaneous Estates Records, 1779-1881; 3 Fibredex boxes.

LAND RECORDS

Deeds of Sale, 1774-1913; 17 Fibredex boxes.
Deeds of Gift, 1797-1896; 2 Fibredex boxes.
Deeds of Trust, 1794-1917; 2 Fibredex boxes.
Mortgage Deeds, 1849-1912; 2 Fibredex boxes.
Leases and Bills of Sale, 1794-1911; 1 Fibredex box.
Miscellaneous Deeds and Liens on Land, 1825-1918; 1 Fibredex box.
Ejectments, 1787-1861; 1 Fibredex box.
Land Entries, 1838-1909; 1 volume.
Land Records, 1739-1911; 2 Fibredex boxes.

MARRIAGE, DIVORCE AND VITAL STATISTICS

Marriage Bonds, 1777-1868; 7 Fibredex boxes.
Record of Marriage Certificates, 1851-1867; 1 volume.
Miscellaneous Marriage Records, 1836-1887; 1 manuscript box.
Record of Cohabitation, 1866; Division of Slaves, 1862-1865; 1 volume.
Divorce Records, 1817-1878; 1 Fibredex box.

MISCELLANEOUS RECORDS

Alien Registration, 1927, 1940; 1 volume.
Naturalization Record, 1908; 1 volume.
County Accounts, 1778-1899; 1 volume, 3 Fibredex boxes.
Insolvent Debtors and Homestead and Personal Property Exemptions, 1829-
    1910; 1 Fibredex box.
Mill Records, 1782-1875; 1 Fibredex box.
Minutes, Wardens of the Poor, 1844-1869; 1 volume.
Miscellaneous Records, 1778-1909; 2 Fibredex boxes.
Powers of Attorney, 1788-1913; 1 Fibredex box.
Public Works, 1819-1884; 1 Fibredex box.
Slave Records, 1781-1864; 2 Fibredex boxes.

OFFICIALS, COUNTY

Lists of Magistrates, 1779-1861; 1 Fibredex box.
Officials' Appointments, 1784-1914; 1 Fibredex box.
Officials' Reports, 1815-1898; 1 Fibredex box.

ROADS AND BRIDGES

Bridge Records, 1779-1874; 2 Fibredex boxes.
Road Records, 1768-1887; 2 Fibredex boxes.

SCHOOL RECORDS

Minutes, Board of Superintendents of Common Schools, 1843-1864;
    1 volume.
School Records, 1844-1884; 2 Fibredex boxes.

TAX AND FISCAL RECORDS

Tax Records, 1787-1902; 2 Fibredex boxes.

WILLS

Record of Wills, 1778-1873; 4 volumes.
Wills, 1778-1922; 10 Fibredex boxes.
Index to Wills, 1779-1926; 1 volume.

MICROFILM RECORDS

BONDS

Apprentice Bonds, 1919-1931; 1 reel.

CORPORATIONS AND PARTNERSHIPS

Record of Incorporations, 1887-1945; 1 reel.

COURT RECORDS

County Court of Pleas and Quarter Sessions
Minutes, 1778-1868; 7 reels.
Superior Court
Minutes, 1807-1963; 17 reels.
Equity Minutes, 1811-1857, 1861-1867; 1 reel.

ELECTION RECORDS

Record of Elections, 1904, 1932-1962; 1 reel.

ESTATES RECORDS

Record of Accounts, 1869-1964; 17 reels.
Administrators' Bonds, 1910-1933; 1 reel.
Appointment of Administrators, Executors and Guardians, 1868-1923; 2 reels.
Appointment of Administrators, 1922-1964; 5 reels.
Appointment of Executors, 1923-1964; 1 reel.
Appointment of Guardians, 1906-1964; 2 reels.
Guardians' Accounts, 1820-1867; 2 reels.
Accounts of Indigent Orphans, 1909-1963; 1 reel.
Widows' Year's Support, 1883-1963; 1 reel.
Inheritance Tax Records, 1913-1964; 2 reels.
Inventories and Sale of Estates, 1818-1833; 1 reel.
Division of Slaves, 1829-1861; 1 reel.
Record of Settlements, 1869-1964; 9 reels.
Trust Fund Records, 1918-1958; 1 reel.
Index to Administrators, Executors and Guardians, 1868-1968; 2 reels.
Index to Guardians, 1868-1963; 2 reels.

LAND RECORDS

Record of Deeds, 1778-1964; 223 reels.
General Index to Deeds, Grantor, 1777-1963; 12 reels.
General Index to Deeds, Grantee, 1777-1963; 12 reels.
Land Entries, 1776-1794; 1 reel.
Plats, 1937-1960; 1 reel.
Record of Sales by Mortgagees, Trustees and Executors, 1919-1963; 2 reels.

MARRIAGE, DIVORCE AND VITAL STATISTICS

Marriage Bonds, 1777-1868; 2 reels.

Record of Marriages, 1851-1857; 1 reel.

Marriage Registers, 1872-1964; 4 reels.

Record of Cohabitation, 1866; 1 reel.

Maiden Names of Divorced Women, 1940-1964; 1 reel.

Index to Births, 1913-1962; 4 reels.

Index to Deaths, 1913-1987; 4 reels.

Index to Delayed Births, various years; 1 reel.

MILITARY AND PENSION RECORDS

Record of Armed Forces Discharges, 1919-1964; 3 reels.

Index to Armed Forces Discharges, no date; 1 reel.

MISCELLANEOUS RECORDS

Orders and Decrees, 1869-1963; 21 reels.

Index to Orders and Decrees, Plaintiff, 1869-1963; 2 reels.

Index to Orders and Decrees, Defendant, 1869-1963; 2 reels.

OFFICIALS, COUNTY

Minutes, Board of County Commissioners, 1868-1930; 3 reels.

SCHOOL RECORDS

Minutes, County Board of Education, 1896-1956; 1 reel.

Community School Register, District 22, 1878-1889; 1 reel.

TAX AND FISCAL RECORDS

Tax Scrolls, 1875; 1 reel.

WILLS

Record of Wills, 1778-1964; 5 reels.

Record of Unrecorded Wills, 1790-1922; 1 reel.

Index to Wills, 1778-1963; 4 reels.

NEW HANOVER COUNTY

Established in 1729 from Carteret Precinct as a precinct of Bath County.
Courthouse fires have destroyed a few records through the years.

ORIGINAL RECORDS

BONDS

Apprentice Bonds and Records, 1797-1899; 2 volumes, 2 Fibredex boxes.
Bastardy Bonds and Records, 1818-1906; 1 volume, 1 Fibredex box.
Constables' Bonds, 1846-1865; 1 volume.
Inspectors' Bonds, 1870-1893; 2 volumes.
Lumber Inspectors' Bonds, 1844-1868; 2 volumes.
Naval Stores Inspectors' Bonds, 1844-1868; 2 volumes.
Naval Stores and Lumber Inspectors' Bonds, 1841-1843; 1 volume.
Officials' Bonds and Records, 1766-1908; 2 volumes, 5 Fibredex boxes.
Sheriffs' Bonds, 1841-1867; 2 volumes.
Sheriffs' and Constables' Bonds, 1857-1858; 1 volume.

CORPORATIONS AND PARTNERSHIPS

Incorporations, 1879-1906; 2 Fibredex boxes.

COURT RECORDS

County Court of Pleas and Quarter Sessions
  Minutes, 1738-1868; 30 volumes.
  Appeal Dockets, 1841-1868; 2 volumes.
  Appearance Dockets, 1801-1814, 1827-1868; 6 volumes.
  Execution Dockets, 1758-1862; 24 volumes, 1 manuscript box.
  Magistrates' Dockets, 1832-1841; 2 volumes.
  Recognizance Docket, 1841-1860; 1 volume.
  State Dockets, 1808-1814, 1844-1867; 3 volumes.
  Reference (Trial) and Appearance Docket, 1750-1758; 2 volumes.
  Trial, Appearance and Reference Dockets, 1771-1786; 2 volumes.
  Trial Dockets, 1786-1797; 7 volumes.
  Trial and Reference Dockets, 1797-1860; 17 volumes.
  Record of Appointments and Orders, 1774-1868; 3 volumes.

Superior Court
  Minutes, 1806-1910; 22 volumes.
  Equity Minutes, 1860-1868; 1 volume.
  Equity Appearance Docket, 1848-1868; 1 volume.
  Equity Execution Docket, 1853-1866; 1 volume.
  Equity Trial Docket, 1848-1868; 1 volume.
  Appearance Dockets, 1807-1868; 3 volumes.
  Execution Dockets, 1810-1868; 6 volumes.
  Recognizance Docket, 1806-1821; 1 volume.
  State Dockets, 1824-1829, 1836-1875, 1891; 4 volumes.
  Trial and Reference Dockets, 1807-1868; 7 volumes.
  Civil Action Papers, 1758-1915; 52 Fibredex boxes.

Civil Action Papers Concerning Land, 1848-1940, 1955;
26 Fibredex boxes.

Criminal Action Papers, 1788-1907; 11 Fibredex boxes.

Criminal Court
Minutes, 1867-1868, 1877-1884, 1888-1895; 4 volumes.

Circuit Criminal Court/Eastern District Criminal Court
Minutes, 1895-1901; 1 volume.

ELECTION RECORDS

Election Records, 1832-1919; 4 Fibredex boxes.

Record of Elections, 1878-1928; 2 volumes.

ESTATES RECORDS

Record of Estates, 1830-1894; 7 volumes.

Record of Accounts, 1868-1915; 6 volumes.

Administrators' Bonds, 1844-1918; 12 volumes.

Appointment of Administrators, Executors, Guardians and Masters, 1868-1879; 1 volume.

Estates Records, 1741-1939; 118 Fibredex boxes.

Guardians' Records, 1763-1934; 18 Fibredex boxes.

Guardians' Accounts, 1867-1918; 3 volumes.

Guardians' Bonds, 1841-1911; 6 volumes.

Record of Inventories and Accounts of Assignees, 1894-1913; 1 volume.

Inventory of Estate of John Rowan, 1782; 1 volume.

Record of Settlements, 1869-1884; 1 volume.

LAND RECORDS

Record of Deeds, 1805-1810, 1813-1818; 2 volumes.

Deeds, 1757-1945; 13 Fibredex boxes.

Quit Claim Deeds, 1874-1945; 2 Fibredex boxes.

Mortgage Deeds, 1816-1945; 3 Fibredex boxes.

Deeds of Trust, 1846-1967; 1 Fibredex box.

General Index to Deeds, Vendor, 1729-1914; 11 volumes.

General Index to Deeds, Vendee, 1729-1914; 11 volumes.

Block Book, 1911-1922; 1 volume.

Ejectments, 1784-1898; 1 Fibredex box.

Land Entry Book, 1784-1796; 1 volume.

Lists of Deeds Proved, 1808-1863; 1 Fibredex box.

Attachments, Executions, Levies and Liens on Land, 1847, 1868-1917;
3 Fibredex boxes.

Decrees Concerning Land, 1875-1914; 1 volume.

Miscellaneous Land Records, 1748-1950; 2 Fibredex boxes.

MARRIAGE, DIVORCE AND VITAL STATISTICS

Marriage Bonds, 1741-1868; 4 Fibredex boxes.

Lists of Marriage Bonds, Certificates and Licenses, 1791-1867;
1 manuscript box.

Record of Marriage Licenses, 1843-1863; 1 volume.

Marriage Registers, 1867-1943; 9 volumes.

Record of Cohabitation, 1866-1868; 2 volumes.
Cohabitation Certificates, 1866-1868; 1 manuscript box.
Divorce Records, 1858-1945; 10 Fibredex boxes.

MILITARY AND PENSION RECORDS
Record of Pensions, 1926-1949; 2 volumes.

MISCELLANEOUS RECORDS
Alien Registration, 1927, 1940; 2 volumes.
Citizenship and Naturalization Records, 1842-1908; 4 Fibredex boxes.
County Accounts and Correspondence, 1783-1898; 1 Fibredex box.
Registry of Claims Allowed by Committee of Finance, 1843-1877; 1 volume.
Registry of County Bonds, 1877-1895; 1 volume.
Journal of Committee of Finance, 1846-1868; 1 volume.
Journal of County Trustee, 1866-1868; 1 volume.
Journals of County Treasurer, 1870-1873; 2 volumes.
Insolvent Debtors and Homestead and Personal Property Exemptions, 1809-1916; 4 Fibredex boxes.
Registry of Licenses to Trades, 1869-1894; 2 volumes.
Stock Marks, 1862-1917; 2 volumes.
Orders and Decrees, 1869-1918; 3 volumes.
Special Proceedings, 1877-1904; 5 volumes.
Minutes, Wardens of the Poor, 1850-1868; 1 volume.
Treasurers' Accounts with Wardens of the Poor, 1867-1868; 1 volume.
Miscellaneous Records, 1756-1945; 5 Fibredex boxes.
Coroners' Records, 1768-1880; 2 Fibredex boxes.
Records of Slaves and Free Persons of Color, 1786-1888; 1 Fibredex box.
Records of Assignees, Receivers and Trustees, 1861-1915; 14 Fibredex boxes.

OFFICIALS, COUNTY
Minutes, Board of Magistrates, 1878-1894; 1 volume.
Minutes, Board of County Commissioners, 1873-1878, 1887-1918; 4 volumes.
Minutes, County Board of Health, 1879-1895; 1 volume.

ROADS AND BRIDGES
Road Records, 1798-1868; 1 Fibredex box.
Railroad Records, 1858-1915; 8 Fibredex boxes.

SCHOOL RECORDS
School Fund Journals, 1882-1913; 3 volumes.
School Records, 1841-1913; 1 Fibredex box.
County Examiner Letterbook, 1869-1874; 1 volume.

TAX AND FISCAL RECORDS
Lists of Taxables, 1815-1846; 5 volumes.
Assessment for Taxes, 1847, no date [ca. 1874]; 2 volumes.
Tax Records, 1779-1909; 2 Fibredex boxes.

WILLS
Record of Wills, 1790-1816, 1830-1848; 3 volumes.
Wills, 1732-1961; 111 Fibredex boxes.

Cross Index to Wills, 1744-1943; 2 volumes.

MICROFILM RECORDS

BONDS

 Bastardy Bonds, 1877-1879; 1 reel.

COURT RECORDS

 County Court of Pleas and Quarter Sessions

  Minutes, 1738-1868; 9 reels.

  Magistrates' Docket, 1832-1837; 1 reel.

 Superior Court

  Minutes, 1806-1939; 17 reels.

  Minutes, Criminal, 1939-1943; 1 reel.

  Equity Minutes, 1860-1868; 1 reel.

ELECTION RECORDS

 Record of Elections, 1878-1960; 1 reel.

ESTATES RECORDS

 Record of Accounts, 1829-1832, 1835-1847, 1879-1940; 7 reels.

 Administrators' Bonds, 1844-1946; 9 reels.

 Appointment of Executors, 1868-1878; 1 reel.

 Guardians' Accounts, 1904-1934; 1 reel.

 Guardians' Bonds, 1856-1911; 2 reels.

 Record of Guardians, 1910-1946; 2 reels.

 Division of Land and Dowers, 1800-1934; 1 reel.

 Index to Administrators, Guardians and Wards, 1841-1856; 1 reel.

LAND RECORDS

 Record of Deeds, 1734-1941; 174 reels.

 Index to Real Estate Conveyances, Grantor, 1729-1954; 13 reels.

 Index to Real Estate Conveyances, Grantee, 1729-1954; 12 reels.

 Index to Real Estate Conveyances, Grantee: Carolina Building and Loan

  Association, 1926-1954; 1 reel.

 Land Entries, 1778-1948; Surveyors' Entry Book, 1905-1907; 1 reel.

 Map Books and Index, 1914-1961; 2 reels.

 Foreclosure Accounts, 1924-1960; 1 reel.

MARRIAGE, DIVORCE AND VITAL STATISTICS

 Marriage Bonds, 1740-1868; 2 reels.

 Record of Marriage Licenses Issued, 1843-1863; 1 reel.

 Marriage Licenses, 1867-1946; 36 reels.

 Marriage Registers, White, 1848-1961; 2 reels.

 Marriage Registers, Black, 1848-1939; 1 reel.

 Record of Cohabitation, 1866-1868; 1 reel.

 Record of Births in Wilmington, 1903-1910; 1 reel.

 Record of Deaths in Wilmington, 1903-1907; 1 reel.

 Index to Births, 1913-1961, 1971-1974; 4 reels.

 Index to Deaths, 1913-1961; 2 reels.

Index to Delayed Births, 1879-1928, various years; 2 reels.
MILITARY AND PENSION RECORDS
Record and Index of Armed Forces Discharges, 1918-1961; 5 reels.
MISCELLANEOUS RECORDS
Record of Homesteads, 1869-1933; 1 reel.
Orders and Decrees, 1869-1943; 3 reels.
Special Proceedings, 1877-1964; 14 reels.
Cross Index to Parties to Actions, 1935, no date; 1 reel.
TAX AND FISCAL RECORDS
Tax Lists, 1815-1819, 1836-1846, 1856-1900, 1905, 1915, 1925; 8 reels.
Assessment for Taxes, 1847; 1 reel.
WILLS
Record of Wills, 1747-1961; 9 reels.
Cross Index to Wills, 1735-1961; 2 reels.

NORTHAMPTON COUNTY

Established in 1741 from Bertie County.
A few records are missing; reason unknown.

ORIGINAL RECORDS

BONDS

    Apprentice Bonds and Records, 1797-1911; 1 volume, 1 Fibredex box.

    Bastardy Bonds and Records, 1783-1894; 6 Fibredex boxes.

    Constables' Bonds, 1787-1874; 3 Fibredex boxes.

    Officials' Bonds, 1787-1899; 2 Fibredex boxes.

COURT RECORDS

    County Court of Pleas and Quarter Sessions

        Minutes, 1792-1796, 1813-1868; 14 volumes.

        Appearance Docket, 1860-1868; 1 volume.

        Execution Dockets, 1818-1821, 1828-1868; 6 volumes.

        State Docket, 1857-1868; 1 volume.

        Trial, Appearance and State Dockets, 1802-1868; 10 volumes.

    Superior Court

        Minutes, 1818-1908; 15 volumes.

        Equity Minutes, 1807-1868; 3 volumes.

        Equity Trial and Appearance Docket, 1850-1861; 1 volume.

        Execution Docket, 1867-1869; 1 volume.

        Trial and Appearance Docket, 1833-1840, 1842-1864, 1866; 1 volume.

        Civil Action Papers, 1771-1926; 93 Fibredex boxes.

        Civil Action Papers Concerning Land, 1784-1925; 9 Fibredex boxes.

        Criminal Action Papers, 1779-1878; 22 Fibredex boxes.

    Inferior Court

        Minutes, 1877-1885; 1 volume.

    Eastern District Criminal Court

        Minutes, 1899-1901; 1 volume.

ELECTION RECORDS

    Record of Elections, 1878-1953; 3 volumes.

    Election Records, 1828-1897; 2 Fibredex boxes.

ESTATES RECORDS

    Record of Estates, 1781-1868; 14 volumes.

    Record of Accounts, 1868-1909; 9 volumes.

    Administrators' Bonds, 1868-1918; 4 volumes.

    Estates Records, 1785-1929; 229 Fibredex boxes.

    Guardians' Records, 1785-1926; 53 Fibredex boxes.

    Guardians' Accounts, 1781-1802, 1818-1868; 9 volumes.

    Guardians' Bonds, 1868-1891; 1 volume.

    Record of Guardians, 1821-1874; 1 volume.

    Record of Settlements, 1869-1907; 3 volumes.

LAND RECORDS

Deeds, 1743-1878; 26 Fibredex boxes.

Deeds of Gift, 1767-1866; 1 Fibredex box.

Deeds of Trust, 1798-1925; 4 Fibredex boxes.

Mortgage Deeds, 1741-1924; 2 Fibredex boxes.

Index to Deed Book 3, [1759-1766]; 1 pamphlet.

Ejectments, 1782-1869; 2 Fibredex boxes.

Levies on Land, 1805-1869; 2 Fibredex boxes.

Attachments, Executions and Liens on Land, 1833-1873; 2 Fibredex boxes.

Land Records, 1784-1924; 2 Fibredex boxes.

Miscellaneous Deeds and Land Records, 1774-1920; 1 Fibredex box.

MARRIAGE, DIVORCE AND VITAL STATISTICS

Marriage Bonds, 1811-1868; 7 Fibredex boxes.

Divorce Records, 1818-1951; 3 Fibredex boxes.

MILITARY AND PENSION RECORDS

Court Martial Minutes, 1824-1850; 1 volume.

MISCELLANEOUS RECORDS

Coroners' Reports, 1793-1905; 1 Fibredex box.

County Accounts, 1787-1879; 3 Fibredex boxes.

Mill Records, 1786-1859; 1 Fibredex box.

Minutes, Wardens of the Poor, St. George's Parish, 1773-1814; 1 volume.

Miscellaneous Records, 1774-1936; 6 Fibredex boxes.

Bills of Sale, 1779-1875; 2 Fibredex boxes.

Boundary Agreement, 1957; 1 manuscript box.

Powers of Attorney, 1740, 1808-1879; 1 Fibredex box.

Provisions Furnished Indigent Families, 1861-1865; 1 Fibredex box.

Slave Records, 1785-1867; 3 Fibredex boxes.

Witness Tickets, 1806-1868; 3 Fibredex boxes.

ROADS AND BRIDGES

Bridge Records, 1785-1867; 2 Fibredex boxes.

Road Records, 1789-1867; 5 Fibredex boxes.

Railroad Records, 1832-1916; 4 Fibredex boxes.

TAX AND FISCAL RECORDS

Lists of Taxables, 1823-1851; 3 volumes.

Tax Records, 1784-1879; 3 Fibredex boxes.

WILLS

Record of Wills, 1762-1791; 2 volumes.

Wills, 1764-1950; 46 Fibredex boxes.

MICROFILM RECORDS

BONDS

Apprentice Bonds, 1869-1918; 1 reel.

CORPORATIONS AND PARTNERSHIPS

Record of Corporations, 1887-1961; 1 reel.

Partnership Records, 1930-1958; 1 reel.

COURT RECORDS

County Court of Pleas and Quarter Sessions

Minutes, 1792-1796, 1813-1868; 6 reels.

Superior Court

Minutes, 1818-1834, 1845-1946; 9 reels.

Equity Minutes, 1807-1834, 1857-1868; 1 reel.

Inferior Court

Minutes, 1877-1885; 1 reel.

ELECTION RECORDS

Record of Elections, 1880-1917, 1924-1950; 1 reel.

ESTATES RECORDS

Record of Estates, 1781-1792, 1796-1868; 7 reels.

Record of Accounts, 1868-1961; 9 reels.

Administrators' Bonds, 1883-1918; 1 reel.

Record of Administrators, 1911-1961; 4 reels.

Record of Executors, 1923-1961; 1 reel.

Guardians' Bonds, 1868-1918; 1 reel.

Record of Guardians, 1908-1961; 1 reel.

Inventories and Accounts of Sale, 1864-1868; 1 reel.

Record of Settlements, 1861-1961; 5 reels.

LAND RECORDS

Record of Deeds, 1741-1933; 68 reels.

Index to Deeds and Mortgages, Grantor, 1741-1961; 5 reels.

Index to Deeds and Mortgages, Grantee, 1741-1961; 4 reels.

Record of Resale of Land by Mortgagees and Trustees, 1921-1961; 2 reels.

MARRIAGE, DIVORCE AND VITAL STATISTICS

Marriage Bonds, 1741-1868; 2 reels.

Marriage Licenses, 1863-1961; 9 reels.

Marriage Registers, 1851-1974; 4 reels.

Index to Marriages, 1865-1974; 1 reel.

Maiden Names of Divorced Women, 1946-1968; 1 reel.

Index to Births, 1913-1967; 1 reel.

Index to Deaths, 1913-1979; 1 reel.

Index to Delayed Births, various years; 1 reel.

MILITARY AND PENSION RECORDS

Record of Armed Forces Discharges, 1943-1981; 3 reels.

MISCELLANEOUS RECORDS

Clerk's Minute Dockets, 1924-1961; 1 reel.

Orders and Decrees, 1869-1934; 6 reels.

Cross Index to Special Proceedings, 1869-1961; 1 reel.

Minutes and Accounts, Wardens of the Poor, 1773-1814; 1 reel.

TAX AND FISCAL RECORDS

Lists of Taxables, 1823-1851; 2 reels.

WILLS

Record of Wills, 1759-1961; 5 reels.

Cross Index to Wills, 1760-1961; 1 reel.

ONSLOW COUNTY

Established in 1734 from New Hanover Precinct as a precinct of Bath County.
Storms of 1752 and 1786 destroyed many records. Later court
records are missing; reason unknown.

ORIGINAL RECORDS

BONDS

    Apprentice Bonds and Records, 1757-1907; 1 Fibredex box.

    Bastardy Bonds and Records, 1764-1909; 1 volume, 2 Fibredex boxes.

    Officials' Bonds and Records, 1779-1913; 4 Fibredex boxes.

COURT RECORDS

    County Court of Pleas and Quarter Sessions

        Minutes, 1732-1868; 20 volumes.

        Appeal Docket, 1787-1790; 1 volume.

        Appearance Dockets, 1801-1868; 4 volumes.

        Execution Dockets, 1762-1868; 15 volumes.

        Crown Dockets, 1763-1774; 2 volumes.

        State Dockets, 1795-1868; 2 volumes.

        Trial, Appearance and Crown Dockets, 1745-1763; 5 volumes.

        Trial and Appearance Dockets, 1763-1788; 4 volumes.

        Trial and Appeal Dockets, 1793-1800; 4 volumes.

        Trial Dockets, 1827-1868; 4 volumes.

    Superior Court

        Minutes, 1844-1909; 8 volumes.

        Equity Minutes, 1839-1850; 1 volume.

        Equity Trial and Appearance Docket, 1840-1852; 1 volume.

        Appearance Docket, 1834-1868; 1 volume.

        Execution Dockets, 1851-1868; 2 volumes.

        Presentments Docket, 1879-1893; 1 volume.

        State Docket, 1854-1869; 1 volume.

        Trial Dockets, 1834-1869; 3 volumes.

        Civil Transfer Docket, 1869-1877; 1 volume.

        Civil Action Papers, 1759-1919; 72 Fibredex boxes.

        Civil Action Papers Concerning Land, 1778-1929; 7 Fibredex boxes.

        Criminal Action Papers, 1765-1914; 22 Fibredex boxes.

ELECTION RECORDS

    Record of Elections, 1878-1932; 3 volumes.

ESTATES RECORDS

    Record of Accounts, 1830-1909; 5 volumes.

    Administrators' Bonds, 1870-1913; 4 volumes.

    Appointment of Administrators, Executors, Guardians and Masters, 1868-
        1912; 1 volume.

    Estates Records, 1735-1914; 83 Fibredex boxes.

    Guardians' Records, 1775-1909; 9 Fibredex boxes.

Guardians' Bonds, 1857-1912; 4 volumes.
Inventories of Estates, 1780-1785; 1 volume.
Inventories and Accounts of Sale, 1829-1862; 4 volumes.
Record of Settlements, 1869-1895; 1 volume.

LAND RECORDS

Record of Deeds, 1740-1807; 25 volumes.
Deeds of Sale, 1751-1900; 6 Fibredex boxes.
Mortgage Deeds, 1833-1908; 1 Fibredex box.
Miscellaneous Deeds, 1790-1862; 1 Fibredex box.
Ejectments, 1790-1901; 1 Fibredex box.
Entry Books, 1778-1889; 7 volumes.
Land Grant Books, 1781-1794; 3 volumes.
Miscellaneous Land Records, 1753-1908; 1 Fibredex box.
Petitions for Partition, 1870-1909; 1 Fibredex box.

MARRIAGE, DIVORCE AND VITAL STATISTICS

Marriage Bonds, 1745-1868; 4 Fibredex boxes.
Divorce Records, 1866-1906; 1 Fibredex box.

MILITARY AND PENSION RECORDS

Record of Pensions, 1911-1932; 1 volume.

MISCELLANEOUS RECORDS

Orders and Decrees, 1868-1926; 1 volume.
Miscellaneous Records, 1732-1950; 10 Fibredex boxes.

ROADS AND BRIDGES

Appointment of Road Overseers, 1827-1853; 1 volume.

TAX AND FISCAL RECORDS

Tax Records, 1774-1912; 4 Fibredex boxes.

WILLS

Record of Wills, 1757-1783; 1 volume.
Wills and Inventories of Estates, 1774-1790; 1 volume.
Wills, 1746-1934; 10 Fibredex boxes.
Cross Index to Wills, 1829-1939; 2 volumes.

MICROFILM RECORDS

COURT RECORDS

County Court of Pleas and Quarter Sessions
Minutes, 1734-1868; 6 reels.
Superior Court
Minutes, 1869-1926; 5 reels.

ESTATES RECORDS

Record of Accounts, 1868-1961; 3 reels.
Administrators' Bonds, 1870-1912; 2 reels.
Record of Administrators, 1913-1931; 1 reel.
Appointment of Executors, 1869-1912; 1 reel.
Guardians' Bonds, 1857-1912; 1 reel.

Inventories and Accounts of Sale, 1845-1861; 1 reel.

Record of Final Settlements, 1869-1961; 3 reels.

LAND RECORDS

Record of Deeds, 1740-1925; 52 reels.

Index to Real Estate Conveyances, Grantor, 1734-1965; 7 reels.

Index to Real Estate Conveyances, Grantee, 1734-1965; 8 reels.

Land Entries, 1781-1955; 2 reels.

Land Grants, 1712-1839, 1877-1928; 5 reels.

Reports of Sales, 1921-1961; 1 reel.

MARRIAGE, DIVORCE AND VITAL STATISTICS

Marriage Bonds, 1745-1868; 1 reel.

Marriage Licenses, 1893-1947; 8 reels.

Marriage Registers, 1851-1947; 1 reel.

Index to Births, 1914-1960; 2 reels.

Index to Deaths, 1912-1959; 2 reels.

Index to Delayed Births, various years; 1 reel.

MILITARY AND PENSION RECORDS

Index to Armed Forces Discharges, 1915-1981; 1 reel.

MISCELLANEOUS RECORDS

Homestead Returns, 1869-1922; 1 reel.

Orders and Decrees, 1868-1926; 1 reel.

Special Proceedings, 1882-1923; 3 reels.

Index to Special Proceedings, Plaintiff, 1869-1968; 1 reel.

Index to Special Proceedings, Defendant, 1869-1968; 1 reel.

OFFICIALS, COUNTY

Minutes, Board of County Commissioners, 1868-1924; 2 reels.

TAX AND FISCAL RECORDS

Tax Lists, 1769-1771, 1774-1790; 2 reels.

WILLS

Wills, 1790-1961; 5 reels.

Index to Wills, Devisor, 1790-1970; 1 reel.

Index to Wills, Devisee, 1790-1970; 1 reel.

ORANGE COUNTY

Established in 1752 from Bladen, Granville and Johnston counties.
Many court records are missing; reason unknown.

ORIGINAL RECORDS

BONDS

Apprentice Bonds and Records, 1780-1905; 1 volume, 3 Fibredex boxes.
Bastardy Bonds and Records, 1782-1908; 9 Fibredex boxes.
Constables' Bonds, 1786-1915; 3 Fibredex boxes.
Officials' Bonds, 1782-1939; 2 volumes, 2 Fibredex boxes.
Sheriffs' Bonds, 1782-1928; 1 Fibredex box.

COURT RECORDS

County Court of Pleas and Quarter Sessions
Minutes, 1752-1766, 1777-1868; 34 volumes, 1 manuscript box.
Execution Dockets, 1807-1820, 1853-1861; 1 volume,
1 manuscript box.
State Docket, 1772-1797; 1 volume.
Trial, Appearance and Reference Docket, 1782-1786; 1 volume.
Trial and Appearance Docket, 1848-1857; 1 volume.

Superior Court
Minutes, 1807-1881; 5 volumes.
Equity Minutes, 1834-1864; 2 volumes.
Equity Fee Books, 1797-1843; 2 volumes.
Equity Prosecution Bond Docket, 1789-1817; 1 volume.
Execution Docket, 1829-1839; 1 volume.
Civil Action Papers, 1771-1943; 135 Fibredex boxes.
Civil Action Papers Concerning Land, 1778-1934; 8 Fibredex boxes.
Criminal Action Papers, 1778-1909; 78 Fibredex boxes.

ELECTION RECORDS

Record of Elections, 1878-1922; 3 volumes.
Election Records, 1783-1910; 11 Fibredex boxes.
Voter Registration Book, Cole Store Precinct, 1896-1898; 1 volume.

ESTATES RECORDS

Administrators' Bonds, 1868-1913; 7 volumes.
Estates Records, 1754-1944; 135 Fibredex boxes.
Guardians' Records, 1782-1941; 26 Fibredex boxes.
Guardians' Accounts, 1819-1910; 4 volumes.
Guardians' Bonds, 1868-1899; 2 volumes.
Inventories, Sales and Accounts of Estates, 1758-1785, 1800-1912;
24 volumes.

LAND RECORDS

Deeds, 1755-1927; 8 Fibredex boxes.
Deeds of Trust and Mortgage Deeds, 1797-1930; 2 Fibredex boxes.
Miscellaneous Deeds, 1764-1925; 1 Fibredex box.

Index to Deeds, 1755-1869; 3 volumes, 1 manuscript box.

Registration of Deeds, 1752-1793; 2 volumes.

Ejectments, 1782-1902; 4 Fibredex boxes.

Land Entry Book, 1830-1908; 1 volume.

Land Grant Book, 1779-1794; 1 volume.

Levies on Land and/or Personal Property, 1784-1886; 4 Fibredex boxes.

Land Records, 1752-1940; 2 Fibredex boxes.

MARRIAGE, DIVORCE AND VITAL STATISTICS

Marriage Bonds, 1779-1868; 19 Fibredex boxes.

Marriage License Applications, 1929-1930; 1 volume.

Record of Marriage Certificates, 1860-1861, 1865-1867; 1 volume.

Cohabitation Certificates, 1866-1868; 1 volume.

Divorce Records, 1824-1908; 3 Fibredex boxes.

MISCELLANEOUS RECORDS

Alien Registration, 1940; 1 volume.

County Accounts, 1767-1893; 3 Fibredex boxes.

Account Book, County Jail, 1837-1843; 1 volume.

Account Book, County Trustee, 1834-1848, 1864-1875; 1 volume.

Record of Official Reports, 1874-1908; 1 volume.

Astray Book, 1831-1847; 1 volume.

Bills of Sale, 1778-1886; 1 Fibredex box.

Coroners' Reports, 1785-1911; 1 Fibredex box.

Grand Jury Presentments, 1781-1887; 1 Fibredex box.

Jury Records, 1772-1878; 2 Fibredex boxes.

Homestead and Personal Property Exemptions, 1821-1918; 1 Fibredex box.

Insolvents, 1773-1887; 8 Fibredex boxes.

Account Book, Wardens of the Poor, 1842-1868; 1 volume.

Minutes, Wardens of the Poor, 1832-1879; 2 volumes.

Miscellaneous Records, 1768-1942; 5 Fibredex boxes.

Personal Accounts, 1773-1862; 1 Fibredex box.

Powers of Attorney, 1781-1909; 1 Fibredex box.

Promissory Notes, 1773-1869; 2 Fibredex boxes.

Provisions for Families of Soldiers, 1863-1865; 1 Fibredex box.

Slave Records, 1783-1865; 1 Fibredex box.

OFFICIALS, COUNTY

Minutes, Board of County Commissioners, 1868-1936; 9 volumes.

ROADS AND BRIDGES

Bridge Records, 1787-1868; 1 Fibredex box.

Road Records, 1786-1909; 4 Fibredex boxes.

TAX AND FISCAL RECORDS

Lists of Taxable Property, 1780-1827; 6 volumes.

Tax List, 1915; 1 volume.

Poll Tax Register, 1902-1914; 1 volume.

Record of Federal Direct Taxes Collected, 1866; 1 volume.

WILLS
Wills, 1753-1937; 17 Fibredex boxes.

MICROFILM RECORDS

CORPORATIONS AND PARTNERSHIPS
Record of Incorporations, 1878-1952; 1 reel.
Partnership Records and Index, 1930-1962; 1 reel.
COURT RECORDS
County Court of Pleas and Quarter Sessions
Minutes, 1752-1766, 1777-1800, 1805-1868; 11 reels.
Superior Court
Minutes, 1807-1955; 10 reels.
Equity Minutes, 1789-1864; 2 reels.
Equity Account Book, 1833-1843; 1 reel.
Equity Partitions, 1859-1938; 1 reel.
ELECTION RECORDS
Record of Elections, 1897-1960; 1 reel.
ESTATES RECORDS
Record of Estates, 1758-1785, 1800-1912; 11 reels.
Record of Accounts, 1869-1949; 2 reels.
Administrators' Bonds, 1891-1913; 1 reel.
Record of Administrators, Executors and Guardians, 1915-1929; 1 reel.
Record of Administrators, 1918-1962; 4 reels.
Appointment of Executors, 1870-1915; 1 reel.
Record of Executors, 1929-1962; 1 reel.
Guardians' Accounts, 1819-1853, 1909-1951; 2 reels.
Guardians' Bonds, 1880-1891; 1 reel.
Record of Guardians, 1929-1962; 1 reel.
Inheritance Tax Records, 1921-1962; 1 reel.
Inventories, Sales and Settlements of Estates, 1837-1843; 1 reel.
Record of Inventories, 1912-1951; 1 reel.
Record of Settlements, 1868-1954; 4 reels.
LAND RECORDS
Record of Deeds, 1755-1961; 112 reels.
Index to Deeds, Grantor, 1755-1962; 4 reels.
Index to Deeds, Grantee, 1755-1962; 3 reels.
Land Entry Book, 1830-1908; 1 reel.
Registration of Deeds, 1752-1793; 1 reel.
Federal Tax Lien Index, 1928-1962; 1 reel.
Record of Sales and Resales, 1917-1962; 3 reels.
MARRIAGE, DIVORCE AND VITAL STATISTICS
Marriage Bonds, 1752-1868; 10 reels.
Marriage Bond Abstracts, 1752-1868; 1 reel.
Marriage Licenses, 1866-1962; 8 reels.

Marriage Registers, 1851-1962; 2 reels.
Record of Marriage, 1866-1867; 1 reel.
Cohabitation Certificates, 1866-1868; 1 reel.
Maiden Names of Divorced Women, 1941-1969; 1 reel.
Index to Births, 1913-1961; 1 reel.
Index to Deaths, 1913-1961; 1 reel.

MILITARY AND PENSION RECORDS

Record of Armed Forces Discharges, 1918-1954; Index, 1918-1962; 2 reels.

MISCELLANEOUS RECORDS

County Trustees' Account Books, 1834-1875; 1 reel.
Jail Account Book, 1831-1847; 1 reel.
Record of Officials' Reports, 1874-1908; 1 reel.
Clerk's Minute Docket, 1919-1953; 1 reel.
Orders and Decrees, 1868-1952; 5 reels.
Cross Index to Special Proceedings, 1878-1962; 1 reel.
Wardens of the Poor, 1832-1879; 2 reels.
Poor House Book, 1842-1868; 1 reel.
Astray Book, 1831-1847; 1 reel.

OFFICIALS, COUNTY

Minutes, Board of County Commissioners, 1868-1962; 4 reels.

SCHOOL RECORDS

Minutes, County Board of Education, 1872-1962; 1 reel.

TAX AND FISCAL RECORDS

Tax Lists, 1779-1827; 4 reels.

WILLS

Record of Wills, 1752-1946; 7 reels.
Cross Index to Wills, 1756-1962; 1 reel.

PAMLICO COUNTY

Established in 1872 from Beaufort and Craven counties.

ORIGINAL RECORDS

BONDS

  Bastardy Bonds and Records, 1874-1910; .5 Fibredex box.

  Officials' Bonds and Records, 1872-1928; 1.5 Fibredex boxes.

COURT RECORDS

  Superior Court

    Minutes, 1872-1913; 3 volumes.

    Civil Action Papers, 1873-1921; 1 Fibredex box.

    Civil Action Papers Concerning Land, 1872-1935; 2 Fibredex boxes.

    Criminal Action Papers, 1875-1914; 1 Fibredex box.

ESTATES RECORDS

  Record of Accounts, 1872-1931; 1 volume.

  Estates Records, 1872-1939; 10 Fibredex boxes.

  Guardians' Records, 1875-1920; 1 Fibredex box.

  Record of Settlements, 1881-1927; 1 volume.

LAND RECORDS

  Deeds and Miscellaneous Land Records, 1869-1919; 2 Fibredex boxes.

MARRIAGE, DIVORCE AND VITAL STATISTICS

  Divorce Records, 1874-1915; 1 Fibredex box.

MISCELLANEOUS RECORDS

  Miscellaneous Records, 1874-1937; 2 Fibredex boxes.

WILLS

  Wills, 1872-1921; 2 Fibredex boxes.

MICROFILM RECORDS

CORPORATIONS AND PARTNERSHIPS

  Record of Incorporations, 1887-1968; 1 reel.

COURT RECORDS

  Superior Court

    Minutes, 1872-1947; 3 reels.

ESTATES RECORDS

  Record of Accounts, 1872-1935; 1 reel.

  Accounts, Inventories and Sales of Estates, 1930-1968; 2 reels.

  Record of Administrators, Executors and Guardians, 1907-1948; 1 reel.

  Record of Administrators, 1927-1968; 1 reel.

  Cross Index to Administrators and Executors, 1872-1968; 1 reel.

  Record of Guardians, 1942-1968; 1 reel.

  Cross Index to Guardians, 1872-1968; 1 reel.

  Clerk's Receiver Accounts, 1901-1920; 1 reel.

  Widows' Year's Support, 1899-1945; 1 reel.

Inheritance Tax Records, 1923-1968; 1 reel.

Record of Settlements, 1881-1968; 2 reels.

LAND RECORDS

Record of Deeds, 1872-1950; 57 reels.

General Index to Deeds and Mortgages, Grantor, 1872-1968; 4 reels.

General Index to Deeds and Mortgages, Grantee, 1872-1968; 3 reels.

Land Entry Book, 1872-1961; 1 reel.

Record of Land Registration, 1916-1967; 1 reel.

Record of Sale of Land by Trustees and Mortgagees, 1921-1968; 1 reel.

MARRIAGE, DIVORCE AND VITAL STATISTICS

Marriage Licenses, 1872-1968; 6 reels.

Marriage Registers, 1872-1968; 1 reel.

Maiden Names of Divorced Women, 1928-1966; 1 reel.

Index to Vital Statistics, 1913-1968; 1 reel.

MILITARY AND PENSION RECORDS

Record of Armed Forces Discharges, 1943-1968; 1 reel.

Record of Confederate Veterans, 1889-1918; 1 reel.

MISCELLANEOUS RECORDS

Orders and Decrees, 1873-1962; 1 reel.

Special Proceedings, 1872-1954; 3 reels.

OFFICIALS, COUNTY

Minutes, Board of County Commissioners, 1872-1944; 4 reels.

SCHOOL RECORDS

Minutes, County Board of Education, 1885-1893, 1922-1968; 1 reel.

WILLS

Record of Wills, 1872-1968; 2 reels.

Cross Index to Wills, 1872-1968; 1 reel.

PASQUOTANK COUNTY

Established by 1670 as a precinct of Albemarle County.
Many early records are missing; reason unknown.

ORIGINAL RECORDS

BONDS

Apprentice Bonds and Records, 1716-1898; 10 volumes, 2 Fibredex boxes.

Bastardy Bonds and Records, 1740-1917; 3 Fibredex boxes.

Constables' Bonds, 1737, 1785-1880; 1 volume, 2 Fibredex boxes.

Officials' Bonds, 1741-1882; 1 Fibredex box.

Ordinary Bonds, 1766-1867; 1 Fibredex box.

Sheriffs' Bonds, 1741-1882; 1 Fibredex box.

COURT RECORDS

County Court of Pleas and Quarter Sessions

Minutes, 1737-1868; 19 volumes.

Appearance Dockets, 1845-1868; 3 volumes.

Execution Dockets, 1755-1862, 1866-1868; 23 volumes.

Petition Docket, 1856-1868; 1 volume.

State Dockets, 1785-1791, 1798-1868; 4 volumes.

Reference (Trial) and Appearance Dockets, 1700, 1755-1765;
3 volumes.

Trial, Appearance and Reference Dockets, 1765-1824; 11 volumes.

Trial, Appearance, Reference and Petition Dockets, 1819-1857;
12 volumes.

Trial Dockets, 1856-1862, 1866-1868; 2 volumes.

Clerk's Account Book, 1790-1808; 1 volume.

Superior Court

Minutes, 1807-1861, 1866-1922; 10 volumes.

Equity Minutes, 1822-1868; 2 volumes.

Equity Execution Docket, 1824-1831; 1 volume.

Equity Trial Docket, 1822-1850; 1 volume.

Execution Dockets, 1822-1868; 2 volumes.

State Dockets, 1807-1869; 3 volumes.

Trial and Appearance Dockets, 1807-1881; 5 volumes.

Civil Action Papers, 1712-1925; 89 Fibredex boxes.

Civil Action Papers Concerning Land, 1756-1922; 14 Fibredex boxes.

Criminal Action Papers, 1729-1919; 13 Fibredex boxes.

Miscellaneous Court Records, 1721-1897; 1 Fibredex box.

ELECTION RECORDS

Record of Elections, 1878-1920; 3 volumes.

Voter Registration Books, 1892, 1900; 15 volumes.

Voter Registration Challenge Book, no date; 1 volume.

ESTATES RECORDS

Record of Estates (Accounts and Settlements), 1795-1868; 14 volumes.

Record of Accounts, 1868-1919; 6 volumes.

Accounts of Sale of Estates, 1797-1868; 8 volumes.

Administrators' Bonds, 1798-1868, 1881-1907; 17 volumes.

Estates Records, 1712-1931; 202 Fibredex boxes.

Guardians' Records, 1719-1931; 25 Fibredex boxes.

Guardians' Accounts (Orphans' Court), 1757-1797; 2 volumes.

Guardians' Bonds, 1798-1896; 18 volumes.

Inventories of Estates, 1797-1854; 2 volumes.

Record of Settlements, 1868-1920; 3 volumes.

Fiduciary Account Book, 1808-1828; 1 volume.

LAND RECORDS

Record of Deeds, 1700-1786; 7 volumes.

Deeds, 1666-1947; 11 Fibredex boxes.

Miscellaneous Deeds, 1723-1948; 6 Fibredex boxes.

Ejectments, 1746-1901; 2 Fibredex boxes.

Land Entry Books, 1778-1793, 1831-1838; 2 volumes.

Tax Levies on Land, 1874-1899; 1 volume.

Attachments, Executions, Levies and Liens on Land, 1801-1917;
        2 Fibredex boxes.

Land Drainage Records, 1765-1878; 1 Fibredex box.

Miscellaneous Land Records, 1694-1946; 2 Fibredex boxes,
        1 oversized manuscript box.

Petitions to Divide and Sell Land and Reports of Sale, 1744-1904;
        2 Fibredex boxes.

Record of Probate of Deeds and Mortgages, 1903-1915; 1 volume.

MARRIAGE, DIVORCE AND VITAL STATISTICS

Marriage Bonds, 1741-1868; 3 Fibredex boxes.

Record of Cohabitation, 1866-1867; 1 volume.

Births, Deaths, Marriages, Brands and Flesh Marks, 1691-1822; 2 volumes.

Divorce Records, 1838-1919; 10 Fibredex boxes.

MISCELLANEOUS RECORDS

County Accounts, Buildings and Correspondence, 1752-1896;
        2 Fibredex boxes.

Insolvent Debtors, 1744-1877; 8 Fibredex boxes.

Loyalty Oaths, 1865; 2 volumes.

Orders and Decrees, 1869-1911; 4 volumes.

Minutes, Wardens of the Poor, 1807-1868; 2 volumes.

Personal Accounts, 1730-1899; 1 Fibredex box.

Powers of Attorney, 1711-1907; 1 Fibredex box.

Promissory Notes, 1720-1920; 2 Fibredex boxes.

Miscellaneous Records, 1703-1940; 7 Fibredex boxes.

Records of Slaves and Free Persons of Color, 1733-1892; 2 Fibredex boxes.

Records Concerning Elizabeth City, 1828-1918; 5 Fibredex boxes.

Records of Assignees, Receivers and Trustees, 1801-1922; 4 Fibredex boxes.

OFFICIALS, COUNTY
>Records of Justices of the Peace, 1720-1896; 1 Fibredex box.
>Minutes, Board of Justices of the Peace, 1878-1882; 1 volume.

ROADS AND BRIDGES
>Road Records, 1734-1920; 4 Fibredex boxes.
>Railroad Records, 1875-1921; 6 Fibredex boxes.

SCHOOL RECORDS
>Minutes, County Board of Education, 1872-1885; 1 volume.
>School Records, 1757-1914; 3 Fibredex boxes.

TAX AND FISCAL RECORDS
>Tax Lists, 1735-1882; 7 volumes, 3 Fibredex boxes.
>Miscellaneous Tax Records, 1785-1912; 2 Fibredex boxes.
>Poll Tax Record, 1914-1918; 1 volume.

WILLS
>Record of Wills, 1752-1792; 3 volumes.
>Wills, 1709-1917; 20 Fibredex boxes.

MICROFILM RECORDS

BONDS
>Apprentice Bonds, 1798-1898; 2 reels.
>Apprentice Bonds for Negroes, 1842-1861; 1 reel.

CORPORATIONS AND PARTNERSHIPS
>Record of Partnerships, 1917-1960; 1 reel.

COURT RECORDS
>County Court of Pleas and Quarter Sessions
>>Minutes, 1737-1868; 5 reels.
>Superior Court
>>Minutes, 1807-1908; 3 reels.
>>Equity Minutes, 1822-1868; 1 reel.

ELECTION RECORDS
>Record of Elections, 1878-1960; 1 reel.

ESTATES RECORDS
>Accounts of Sale of Estates, 1797-1868; 4 reels.
>Administrators' and Guardians' Accounts, 1803-1834; 2 reels.
>Record of Accounts, 1868-1919; 3 reels.
>Administrators' Bonds, 1865-1868, 1881-1904; 1 reel.
>Record of Administrators, 1913-1943; 1 reel.
>Record of Executors, 1915-1960; 1 reel.
>Guardians' Accounts, 1757-1866; 6 reels.
>Guardians' Bonds, 1798-1896; 5 reels.
>Widows' Year's Support, 1881-1960; 1 reel.
>Inventories of Estates, 1795-1854; 1 reel.
>Record of Settlements, 1868-1928, 1956-1960; 2 reels.

LAND RECORDS

Record of Deeds, 1700-1910; 35 reels.

Index to Deeds, Grantor, 1700-1915; 2 reels.

Index to Deeds, Grantee, 1700-1915; 1 reel.

Land Entry Books, 1778-1793, 1831-1838; 1 reel.

Record of Land Division, 1793-1885; 1 reel.

Map Book, 1940-1960; 1 reel.

MARRIAGE, DIVORCE AND VITAL STATISTICS

Marriage Bonds, 1741-1868; 2 reels.

Marriage Licenses, 1867-1960; 29 reels.

Marriage Registers, 1865-1960; 3 reels.

General Index to Marriages, 1865-1960; 4 reels.

Record of Cohabitation, 1866-1867; 1 reel.

Maiden Names of Divorced Women, 1937-1959; 1 reel.

Births, Deaths, Marriages, Brands and Flesh Marks, 1691-1822; 1 reel.

Record of Deaths, 1903-1911; 1 reel.

Index to Deaths, 1903-1982; 2 reels.

MILITARY AND PENSION RECORDS

Index to Armed Forces Discharges, 1920-1982; 1 reel.

MISCELLANEOUS RECORDS

Orders and Decrees, 1869-1915; 3 reels.

Index to Orders and Decrees, Plaintiff, 1869-1960; 1 reel.

Index to Orders and Decrees, Defendant, 1869-1960; 1 reel.

Minutes, Wardens of the Poor, 1807-1868; 1 reel.

OFFICIALS, COUNTY

Minutes, Board of County Commissioners, 1868-1906; 2 reels.

TAX AND FISCAL RECORDS

Tax Lists, 1797-1897, 1905, 1915, 1925; 15 reels.

Tax Levies, 1874-1899; 1 reel.

WILLS

Record of Wills, 1752-1966; 7 reels.

Original Wills, 1720-1804; 3 reels.

Cross Index to Wills, 1766-1966; 1 reel.

PENDER COUNTY

Established in 1875 from New Hanover County.

ORIGINAL RECORDS

BONDS

Officials' Bonds, 1875-1886; 1 volume.

COURT RECORDS

Superior Court

Civil Action Papers, 1878-1949; 3 Fibredex boxes.

Civil Action Papers Concerning Land, 1877-1955; 15 Fibredex boxes.

ESTATES RECORDS

Administrators' Bonds, 1875-1903; 1 volume.

Record of Dowers, 1875-1922; 1 volume.

Estates Records, 1866-1969; 16 Fibredex boxes.

Guardians' Records, 1856-1945; 2 Fibredex boxes.

Guardians' Bonds, 1875-1903; 1 volume.

LAND RECORDS

Deeds, 1819-1946; 4 Fibredex boxes.

Mortgage Deeds and Deeds of Trust, 1874-1945; 2 Fibredex boxes.

Index to Deeds, 1875-1900; 2 volumes.

Ejectments, 1877-1941; 1 Fibredex box.

Land Grants, 1784-1954; 1 Fibredex box.

Attachments, Executions, Levies and Liens on Land, 1870-1940;
1 Fibredex box.

Miscellaneous Land Records, 1873-1966; 4 Fibredex boxes.

MARRIAGE, DIVORCE AND VITAL STATISTICS

Marriage Registers, 1875-1936; 6 volumes.

Divorce Records, 1877-1950; 5 Fibredex boxes.

MISCELLANEOUS RECORDS

Registry of Licenses to Trades, 1875-1879; 1 volume.

Stock Marks, 1875-1925; 2 volumes.

Coroners' Inquests, 1876-1968; 9 Fibredex boxes.

Miscellaneous Records, 1856-1965; 3 Fibredex boxes.

Records of Assignees, Receivers and Trustees, 1882-1964; 2 Fibredex boxes.

ROADS AND BRIDGES

Railroad Records, 1881-1946; 3 Fibredex boxes.

WILLS

Wills, 1832, 1875-1969; 27 Fibredex boxes.

MICROFILM RECORDS

BONDS

Officials' Bonds, 1875-1886; 1 reel.

CORPORATIONS AND PARTNERSHIPS

Record of Corporations and Partnerships, 1903-1976; 2 reels.

Index to Corporations and Partnerships, 1903-1982; 1 reel.

COURT RECORDS

Superior Court

Minutes, 1875-1961; 6 reels.

Index to Minutes, Plaintiff, 1875-1968; 1 reel.

Index to Minutes, Defendant, 1875-1968; 3 reels.

Index to Judgments, Liens and Special Proceedings, Plaintiff, 1875-1968; 3 reels.

Index to Judgments, Liens and Special Proceedings, Defendant, 1875-1968; 3 reels.

ELECTION RECORDS

Record of Elections, 1918-1966; 1 reel.

ESTATES RECORDS

Administrators' Bonds, 1875-1903; 1 reel.

Record of Administrators, Executors and Guardians, 1903-1968; 4 reels.

Record of Executors and Guardians, 1939-1967; 1 reel.

Guardians' Bonds, 1913-1926; 1 reel.

Record of Amounts Paid for Indigent Children, 1913-1926; 1 reel.

Record of Dowers, 1875-1922; 1 reel.

Inheritance Tax Records, 1923-1959; 1 reel.

Record of Inventories, 1875-1968; 4 reels.

Record of Final Accounts, 1875-1968; 3 reels.

Index to Final Accounts, 1875-1968; 1 reel.

LAND RECORDS

Record of Deeds, 1875-1955; 92 reels.

Index to Real Estate Conveyances, Grantor, 1875-1977; 8 reels.

Index to Real Estate Conveyances, Grantee, 1875-1977; 8 reels.

Record of Land Entry, 1875-1963; 1 reel.

Registration of Land Titles, 1916-1962; 2 reels.

Federal Tax Lien Index, 1928-1968; 2 reels.

Plat Books, 1881-1957; 1 reel.

Index to Plats, 1920-1982; 1 reel.

Record of Resale of Land by Trustees and Mortgagees, 1923-1968; 3 reels.

MARRIAGE, DIVORCE AND VITAL STATISTICS

Marriage Licenses, 1886-1968; 11 reels.

Marriage Registers, 1875-1971; 2 reels.

Maiden Names of Divorced Women, 1937-1943; 1 reel.

Index to Births, 1913-1971; 2 reels.

Index to Deaths, 1913-1971; 2 reels.

Index to Delayed Births, various years; 1 reel.

MILITARY AND PENSION RECORDS

Record of Armed Forces Discharges, 1942-1960; 1 reel.

Record of Confederate Pensions, 1927-1934; 1 reel.

MISCELLANEOUS RECORDS
Record of Lunacy, 1903-1960; 1 reel.
Orders and Decrees, 1875-1947; 1 reel.
Special Proceedings, 1875-1968; 7 reels.
Cross Index to Special Proceedings, 1875-1900; 1 reel.
SCHOOL RECORDS
Minutes, County Board of Education, 1875-1954; 3 reels.
WILLS
Record of Wills, 1875-1968; 4 reels.
Cross Index to Wills, 1875-1931; 1 reel.
Index to Wills, Devisor, 1875-1968; 1 reel.
Index to Wills, Devisee, 1875-1968; 1 reel.

PERQUIMANS COUNTY

Established by 1670 as a precinct of Albemarle County.
A few of the early records are missing; reason unknown.

ORIGINAL RECORDS

BONDS

Apprentice Bonds and Records, 1737-1892; 3 volumes, 4 Fibredex boxes.

Bastardy Bonds and Records, 1756-1905; 2 volumes, 4 Fibredex boxes.

Constables' Bonds, 1777-1907; 1 Fibredex box.

Officials' Bonds, 1720-1908; 3 Fibredex boxes.

COURT RECORDS

County Court of Pleas and Quarter Sessions

Minutes (Precinct Court), 1688-1738; 3 volumes.

Minutes, 1738-1868; 11 volumes.

Execution Dockets, 1784-1864; 6 volumes.

Levy Docket, 1840-1853, 1857; 1 volume.

State Dockets, 1835-1868; 2 volumes.

Trial, Appearance and Reference Dockets, 1777-1852; 11 volumes.

Trial and Appearance Dockets, 1852-1862; 2 volumes.

Executions Returned by Sheriff, 1842-1843; 1 volume.

Superior Court

Minutes, 1807-1908; 5 volumes.

Equity Minutes, 1819-1868; 2 volumes.

Equity Enrolling Docket, 1838-1867; 1 volume.

Equity Execution Docket, 1825-1850; 1 volume.

Execution Dockets, 1808-1869; 3 volumes.

State Dockets, 1840-1868; 2 volumes.

Trial and Appearance Dockets, 1807-1852; 2 volumes.

Civil Action Papers, 1709-1912; 53 Fibredex boxes.

Civil Action Papers Concerning Land, 1838-1911; 4 Fibredex boxes.

Criminal Action Papers, 1740-1905; 21 Fibredex boxes.

ELECTION RECORDS

Record of Elections, 1878-1936; 2 volumes.

Election Records, 1790-1868; 1 Fibredex box.

ESTATES RECORDS

Record of Estates (Audited Accounts), 1804-1868; 3 volumes.

Record of Accounts, 1869-1909; 3 volumes.

Administrators' Bonds, 1842-1911; 9 volumes.

Appointment of Administrators, Executors, Guardians and Masters, 1868-1911; 1 volume.

Divisions of Estates, 1841-1861; 1 volume.

Estates Records, 1714-1930; 147 Fibredex boxes.

Guardians' Records, 1709-1925; 21 Fibredex boxes.

Guardians' Accounts, 1808-1870; 4 volumes.

Guardians' Bonds, 1842-1911; 4 volumes.

Inventories and Accounts of Sale, 1806-1868; 5 volumes.

Orphans' Docket, 1806-1820; 1 volume.

Record of Settlements, 1868-1904; 1 volume.

LAND RECORDS

Record of Deeds, 1739-1824; 10 volumes.

Record of Deeds and Grants, 1780-1791; 2 volumes.

Record of Deeds and Wills, 1744-1794; 3 volumes.

Deeds, 1709-1938; 6 Fibredex boxes.

Index to Deeds, 1814-1819; 1 pamphlet.

Grantor Index to Deeds and Deeds of Trust, 1879-1893; 1 volume.

Grantee Index to Deeds and Deeds of Trust, 1879-1893; 1 volume.

Ejectments, 1737-1887; 1 Fibredex box.

Land Records, 1709-1907; 2 Fibredex boxes.

Record of Probate of Deeds, 1878-1884; 1 volume.

MARRIAGE, DIVORCE AND VITAL STATISTICS

Marriage Bonds, 1742-1868; 7 Fibredex boxes.

Record of Marriage Licenses and Certificates, 1860-1867; 1 volume.

Marriage Registers, 1867-1940; 3 volumes.

Births, Marriages and Flesh Marks, 1659-1820; 2 volumes.

Divorce Records, 1824-1912; 3 Fibredex boxes.

MILITARY AND PENSION RECORDS

Record of Pensions, 1907-1918; 1 volume.

MISCELLANEOUS RECORDS

Alien Registration, 1905, 1907; 1 volume.

County Accounts, 1756-1869; 3 Fibredex boxes.

Settlement of County Accounts, Committee of Finance, 1845-1872; 1 volume.

Record of Official Reports, 1875-1927; 1 volume.

Coroners' Reports, 1794-1892; 1 Fibredex boxes.

Insolvent Debtors, 1789-1861; 1 Fibredex box.

Jury Lists, 1709-1868; 1 Fibredex box.

Jury Tickets, 1791-1867; 1 Fibredex box.

Registry of Licenses to Trades, 1869-1879; 1 volume.

Orders and Decrees, 1868-1914; 2 volumes.

Minutes, Wardens of the Poor, 1818-1874; 1 volume.

Miscellaneous Records, 1710-1933; 6 Fibredex boxes.

Personal Accounts, 1714-1930; 3 Fibredex boxes.

Promissory Notes, 1712-1863; 1 Fibredex box.

Slave Records, 1759-1864; 1 Fibredex box.

ROADS AND BRIDGES

Road Records, 1711-1910; 5 Fibredex boxes.

Railroad Records, 1881-1912; 1 Fibredex box.

TAX AND FISCAL RECORDS

Lists of Taxables, 1742-1849; 1 volume, 5 Fibredex boxes.

Tax Receipts, 1875; 1 volume.

Tax Records, 1795-1868; 1 Fibredex box.

Record of Federal Direct Taxes Collected, 1866; 1 volume.

WILLS

Wills, 1711-1909; 15 Fibredex boxes.

MICROFILM RECORDS

BONDS

Apprentice Bonds, 1852-1890; 1 reel.

COURT RECORDS

County Court of Pleas and Quarter Sessions

Minutes, 1688-1706, 1735-1868; 6 reels.

Superior Court

Minutes, 1807-1915; 3 reels.

ESTATES RECORDS

Record of Accounts, 1864-1960; 4 reels.

Administrators' Bonds, 1842-1911; 1 reel.

Appointment of Administrators, Executors and Guardians, 1868-1911; 1 reel.

Record of Administrators, Executors and Guardians, 1911-1966; 2 reels.

Record of Administrators, 1919-1960; 2 reels.

Guardians' Accounts, 1808-1865; 2 reels.

Guardians' and Administrators' Accounts, 1809-1837; 1 reel.

Guardians' Bonds, 1842-1911; 1 reel.

Orphans' Docket, 1806-1820, 1864-1870; 1 reel.

Divisions of Estates, 1841-1861; 1 reel.

Inheritance Tax Records, 1923-1959; 1 reel.

Inventories and Accounts of Sale, 1804-1864; 3 reels.

Record of Settlements, 1796-1827, 1867-1965; 5 reels.

Cross Index to Executors and Guardians, 1806-1960; 1 reel.

Cross Index to Guardians, 1806-1960; 1 reel.

LAND RECORDS

Record of Deeds, 1681-1919; 29 reels.

Index to Real Estate Conveyances, Grantor, 1681-1968; 4 reels.

Index to Real Estate Conveyances, Grantee, 1681-1968; 4 reels.

Land Entries, 1838-1876; 1 reel.

Plat Books, 1808-1947; 1 reel.

Record of Town Lot Sales, 1759-1824; 1 reel.

Record of Sale and Resale Under Mortgagees and Trustees, 1935-1959; 1 reel.

MARRIAGE, DIVORCE AND VITAL STATISTICS

Marriage Bonds, 1740-1868; 2 reels.

Record of Marriage Bonds, 1847-1859; 1 reel.

Record of Marriage Licenses, 1851-1867; 1 reel.

Marriage Registers, 1852-1995; 3 reels.

Record of Marriages by Freedmen, 1866-1867; 1 reel.

Births, Marriages, Deaths and Flesh Marks, 1659-1820; 1 reel.

Index to Vital Statistics, 1913-1995; 1 reel.

Index to Delayed Births, 1882-1985; 1 reel.

MILITARY AND PENSION RECORDS

Record of Armed Forces Discharges, 1918-1995; 2 reels.

MISCELLANEOUS RECORDS

Clerk's Minute Docket, 1923-1944; 1 reel.

Orders and Decrees, 1868-1921; 2 reels.

Cross Index to Special Proceedings, 1880-1964; 1 reel.

OFFICIALS, COUNTY

Minutes, Board of County Commissioners, 1868-1902; 1 reel.

TAX AND FISCAL RECORDS

Tax Book, 1866; 1 reel.

WILLS

Record of Wills, 1761-1966; 4 reels.

Wills, 1711-1800; 2 reels.

Index to Wills, 1761-1966; 1 reel.

PERSON COUNTY

Established in 1791 (effective 1792) from Caswell County.

ORIGINAL RECORDS

BONDS

    Apprentice Bonds and Records, 1801-1925; 1 volume, 1 Fibredex box.

    Bastardy Bonds and Records, 1793-1891; 1 Fibredex box.

    Constables' Bonds and Records, 1792-1854; 1 Fibredex box.

    Officials' Bonds and Records, 1792-1903; 2 volumes, 1 Fibredex box.

CENSUS RECORDS (County Copy)

    Census, 1880; 2 volumes.

COURT RECORDS

    County Court of Pleas and Quarter Sessions

        Minutes, 1792-1868; 14 volumes.

        Rough Minutes and Dockets, 1803-1866; 1 Fibredex box.

        Execution Dockets, 1813-1825, 1838-1868; 5 volumes.

        Levy Dockets, 1795-1826, 1837; 2 volumes.

        State Dockets, 1792-1868; 4 volumes.

        Trial and Appearance Dockets, 1792-1814, 1824-1868; 5 volumes.

        Summons Docket (Writs Issued), 1793-1807; 1 volume.

        Witness Fee Docket, 1822-1853; 1 volume.

    Superior Court

        Minutes, 1807-1864, 1869-1909; 8 volumes.

        Equity Minutes, 1808-1854; 2 volumes.

        Equity Trial and Execution Docket, 1807-1853; 1 volume.

        Equity Trial and Appearance Docket, 1854-1868; 1 volume.

        Execution Dockets, 1808-1857; 3 volumes.

        State Dockets, 1808-1838, 1851-1868; 2 volumes.

        Trial and Appearance Dockets, 1807-1868; 3 volumes.

        Summons Docket, 1869-1870; 1 volume.

        Civil Action Papers, 1813-1924; 8 Fibredex boxes.

        Civil Action Papers Concerning Board of County Commissioners, 1871-1906; 1 Fibredex box.

        Civil Action Papers Concerning Land, 1775-1914; 2 Fibredex boxes.

ELECTION RECORDS

    Election Records, 1804-1918; 1 Fibredex box.

ESTATES RECORDS

    Record of Accounts, 1868-1908; 4 volumes.

    Administrators' Bonds, 1870-1882, 1889-1898; 2 volumes.

    Estates Records, 1795-1920; 44 Fibredex boxes.

    Guardians' Records, 1800-1920; 4 Fibredex boxes.

    Guardians' Accounts, 1810-1865; 4 volumes.

    Guardians' Bonds, 1870-1899; 1 volume.

    Record of Settlements, 1869-1898; 1 volume.

LAND RECORDS
>Deeds, 1778-1912; 4 Fibredex boxes.
>Deeds of Trust, 1774-1923; 1 Fibredex box.
>Miscellaneous Deeds, 1796-1904; 1 Fibredex box.
>Land Entry Book, 1873-1887, 1899; 1 volume.
>Miscellaneous Land Records, 1792-1906; 1 Fibredex box.

MARRIAGE, DIVORCE AND VITAL STATISTICS
>Marriage Bonds, 1791-1868; 10 Fibredex boxes.
>Record of Cohabitation, 1866; 1 volume.
>Divorce Records, 1829-1913; 2 Fibredex boxes.

MISCELLANEOUS RECORDS
>Alien Registration, 1927, 1940; 1 volume.
>County Accounts, 1881-1885; 2 volumes.
>List of Jurors, 1893-1915; 1 volume.
>Registry of Licenses to Trades, 1877-1901; 1 volume.
>Minutes, Wardens of the Poor, 1792-1868; 2 volumes.
>Miscellaneous Records, 1792-1932; 2 Fibredex boxes.
>Powers of Attorney, 1785-1900; 1 Fibredex box.
>Tobacco and Snuff Manufacturer's Record, 1869-1871; 1 volume.
>Records of Assignees, Receivers and Trustees, 1842-1923; 3 Fibredex boxes.

OFFICIALS, COUNTY
>Minutes, Board of Magistrates, 1880-1894; 1 volume.
>Record of Magistrates, 1893-1922; 1 volume.
>Record of Magistrates and Notaries Public, 1923-1943; 1 volume.

ROADS AND BRIDGES
>Appointment of Road Overseers, 1823-1868; 2 volumes.
>Road Records, 1797-1888; 1 Fibredex box.
>Railroad Records, 1886-1921; 1 Fibredex box.

SCHOOL RECORDS
>School Records, 1832-1930; 1 Fibredex box.
>School Registers, 1887-1904; 8 volumes.

TAX AND FISCAL RECORDS
>Lists of Taxables, 1915, 1925; 3 volumes.
>List of Insolvents, 1892-1898; 1 volume.
>Schedule B Taxes, 1869-1883; 1 volume.
>Tax Records, 1792-1910; 2 Fibredex boxes.
>Tax Receipt Book, 1871; 1 volume.

WILLS
>Record of Wills, Inventories, Sales of Estates and Taxables, 1792-1844;
>>15 volumes.
>Wills, 1790-1943; 17 Fibredex boxes.

MICROFILM RECORDS

CORPORATIONS AND PARTNERSHIPS

> Record of Corporations, 1895-1966; 1 reel.
>
> Partnership Records, 1913-1966; 1 reel.

COURT RECORDS

> County Court of Pleas and Quarter Sessions
>> Minutes, 1792-1868; 4 reels.
>
> Superior Court
>> Minutes, 1821-1864, 1869-1966; 8 reels.

ELECTION RECORDS

> Record of Elections, 1906-1964; 1 reel.

ESTATES RECORDS

> Record of Accounts, 1868-1966; 7 reels.
>
> Administrators' Bonds, 1870-1966; 5 reels.
>
> Appointment of Executors, 1868-1894; Record of Executors, 1925-1966;
>> 1 reel.
>
> Guardians' Accounts, 1810-1944; 1 reel.
>
> Guardians' Bonds, 1870-1899; 1 reel.
>
> Appointment of Guardians, 1899-1966; 1 reel.
>
> Clerk's Receiver Accounts, 1894-1903; 1 reel.
>
> Inheritance Tax Records, 1919-1961; 1 reel.
>
> Record of Settlements, 1869-1966; 5 reels.
>
> Index to Estates, 1947-1966; 1 reel.

LAND RECORDS

> Record of Deeds, 1789-1959; 56 reels.
>
> Index to Real Estate Conveyances, Grantor, 1790-1974; 6 reels.
>
> Index to Real Estate Conveyances, Grantee, 1790-1974; 4 reels.
>
> Index to Real Estate Conveyances, Grantee: Trustees, 1900-1974; 2 reels.
>
> Entry Book, 1872-1899; 1 reel.
>
> Record of Resale of Land by Trustees and Mortgagees, 1920-1960; 1 reel.

MARRIAGE, DIVORCE AND VITAL STATISTICS

> Marriage Bonds, 1791-1868; 6 reels.
>
> Record of Marriage Certificates, 1851-1867; Marriage Registers, 1867-1966;
>> 1 reel.
>
> Maiden Names of Divorced Women, 1938-1966; 1 reel.
>
> Index to Births, 1913-1979; 2 reels.
>
> Index to Deaths, 1913-1986; 1 reel.

MILITARY AND PENSION RECORDS

> Record of Armed Forces Discharges, 1918-1966; 3 reels.

MISCELLANEOUS RECORDS

> Orders and Decrees, 1868-1962; 9 reels.
>
> Index to Special Proceedings, 1954-1966; 1 reel.

OFFICIALS, COUNTY

> Minutes, Board of County Commissioners, 1868-1947; 3 reels.

SCHOOL RECORDS
> Minutes, Board of Superintendents of Common Schools, 1841-1864; Minutes,
> County Board of Education, 1872-1886, 1909-1953; 1 reel.

TAX AND FISCAL RECORDS
> Tax Scrolls, 1876-1925; 4 reels.

WILLS
> Wills, Inventories, Sales of Estates and Taxables, 1792-1844; 7 reels.
> Record of Wills, 1847-1968; 5 reels.
> Original Wills, 1791-1900; 3 reels.
> Cross Index to Wills, 1792-1956; 1 reel.
> Index to Wills, Devisee, 1970-1986; 1 reel.

PITT COUNTY

Established in 1760 (effective 1761) from Beaufort County.
Courthouse fire of 1857 destroyed most of the court records.

ORIGINAL RECORDS

BONDS
> Bastardy Bonds and Records, 1858-1926; 2 Fibredex boxes.

COURT RECORDS
> County Court of Pleas and Quarter Sessions
>> Minutes, 1858-1868; 4 volumes.
>> Execution Docket, 1858-1868; 1 volume.
>> Trial Dockets, 1850-1868; 3 volumes.
>> Bench Docket (Civil and Criminal), 1858-1863, 1866; 1 volume.
>
> Superior Court
>> Minutes, 1858-1913, 1915-1921; 21 volumes.
>> Equity Minutes, 1858-1868; 1 volume.
>> Execution Docket, 1858-1864, 1867; 1 volume.
>> State Docket, 1858-1863, 1866-1870; 1 volume.
>> Trial Docket, 1858-1873; 1 volume.
>> Bench Docket (Civil and Criminal), 1858-1867; 1 volume.
>> Civil Action Papers, 1850-1907; 19 Fibredex boxes.
>> Civil Action Papers Concerning Land, 1859-1921; 15 Fibredex boxes.
>> Civil Action Papers Concerning Canals and Land Drainage, 1857-1902; 2 Fibredex boxes.
>> Criminal Action Papers, 1771, 1857-1931; 31 Fibredex boxes.
>
> Inferior Court
>> Minutes, 1877-1885; 1 volume.

ELECTION RECORDS
> Record of Elections, 1896-1903; 1 volume.

ESTATES RECORDS
> Record of Accounts, 1868-1926; 6 volumes.
> Record of Dowers and Widows' Year's Support, 1858-1885; 1 volume.
> Estates Records, 1791, 1827-1947; 77 Fibredex boxes.
> Guardians' Records, 1858-1919, 1923; 19 Fibredex boxes.
> Guardians' Accounts, 1858-1916; 5 volumes.
> Inventories and Accounts of Sale, 1857-1872; 2 volumes.
> Record of Settlements, 1858-1923; 7 volumes.

LAND RECORDS
> Record of Deeds, 1817-1818; 1 volume.
> Deeds, Deeds of Trust and Mortgage Deeds, 1763-1892; 1 Fibredex box.
> Entry Book, 1858-1941; 1 volume.
> Land Grant Books, 1779-1800; 2 volumes.
> Miscellaneous Land Records, 1778-1923; 2 Fibredex boxes.

Steamboat, probably the <u>Greenville</u>, on the Tar River, date unknown. Photograph from the files of the State Archives.

MARRIAGE, DIVORCE AND VITAL STATISTICS

Marriage Bonds, 1826-1833; 1 folder in Fibredex box.

Marriage Registers, 1867-1875; 3 volumes.

Record of Cohabitation, 1866; 1 volume.

Divorce Records, 1861, 1866, 1870-1906; 4 Fibredex boxes.

MILITARY AND PENSION RECORDS

Record of Pensions, 1920-1969; 1 volume.

MISCELLANEOUS RECORDS

Alien Registration, 1940; 1 volume.

Homestead and Personal Property Exemptions, 1870-1916; 1 Fibredex box.

Coroners' Inquests, 1861-1960; 14 Fibredex boxes.

Miscellaneous Records, 1763-1924; 3 Fibredex boxes.

Records of Slaves and Free Persons of Color, 1858-1870; 1 Fibredex box.

Records of Assignees, Receivers and Trustees, 1870-1925; 2 Fibredex boxes.

OFFICIALS, COUNTY

Minutes, Board of Justices of the Peace, 1877-1894; 1 volume.

ROADS AND BRIDGES

Railroad Records, 1893-1906; 2 Fibredex boxes.

WILLS

Wills, 1805, 1808, 1817, 1836-1930, 1938; 18 Fibredex boxes.

MICROFILM RECORDS

BONDS

Apprentice Bonds, 1911-1926; 1 reel.

CORPORATIONS AND PARTNERSHIPS

Record of Corporations, 1885-1948; 2 reels.

Record of Limited Partnerships, 1943-1962; 1 reel.

Index to Partnerships, 1915-1963; 1 reel.

COURT RECORDS

County Court of Pleas and Quarter Sessions

Minutes, 1858-1868; 1 reel.

Superior Court

Minutes, 1858-1915; 10 reels.

Minutes, Civil, 1915-1945; 7 reels.

Minutes, Criminal, 1914-1941; 3 reels.

Inferior Court

Minutes, 1877-1885; 1 reel.

ELECTION RECORDS

Record of Elections, 1878-1962; 1 reel.

ESTATES RECORDS

Record of Accounts, 1868-1951; 6 reels.

Appointment of Administrators, Executors and Guardians, 1868-1916; 1 reel.

Record of Administrators, 1912-1950; 5 reels.

Record of Executors, 1916-1963; 1 reel.

Guardians' Accounts, 1896-1950; 3 reels.

Record of Guardians' Qualifications, 1913-1950; 2 reels.

Dowers and Widows' Year's Allowance, 1858-1946; 1 reel.

Inheritance Tax Records, 1923-1963; 1 reel.

Record of Settlements, 1868-1952; 7 reels.

Index to Final Accounts and Administrators, 1868-1963; 2 reels.

LAND RECORDS

Record of Deeds, 1762-1946; 152 reels.

Index to Real Estate Conveyances, Grantor, 1762-1952; 7 reels.

Index to Real Estate Conveyances, Grantee, 1762-1962; 7 reels.

Entry Takers' Book, 1858-1941; 1 reel.

Land Divisions, 1858-1936; 2 reels.

Map Book and Index, 1911-1963; 1 reel.

Record of Sales by Trustees and Mortgagees, 1920-1938; 3 reels.

MARRIAGE, DIVORCE AND VITAL STATISTICS

Marriage Bonds, 1826, 1829, 1833; 1 reel.

Marriage Licenses, 1890-1961; 17 reels.

Record of Marriages, 1851-1867; 1 reel.

Marriage Registers, 1868-1961; 3 reels.

Maiden Names of Divorced Women, 1942-1963; 1 reel.

Index to Births, 1913-1957; 2 reels.

Index to Deaths, 1916-1961; 1 reel.

Index to Delayed Births, various years; 1 reel.

MILITARY AND PENSION RECORDS

Record of Armed Forces Discharges, 1918-1951; 9 reels.

Index to Armed Forces Discharges, 1918-1963; 1 reel.

MISCELLANEOUS RECORDS

Inquisition of Lunacy, 1899-1947; 1 reel.

Orders and Decrees, 1869-1947, 1962-1963; 14 reels.

Special Proceedings Dockets, 1872-1949; 4 reels.

General Index to Civil Actions and Special Proceedings, 1869-1963; 6 reels.

OFFICIALS, COUNTY

Minutes, Board of County Commissioners, 1868-1963; 8 reels.

Index to Minutes, Board of County Commissioners, 1936-1950; 1 reel.

SCHOOL RECORDS

Minutes, County Board of Education, 1885-1956; 2 reels.

WILLS

Record of Wills, 1858-1963; 5 reels.

Index to Wills, Devisor, 1858-1968; 1 reel.

POLK COUNTY

Established in 1847 from Henderson and Rutherford counties; act repealed in 1848. Reestablished in 1855.

ORIGINAL RECORDS

BONDS

> Apprentice Bonds, 1877-1912; 2 volumes.
>
> Officials' Bonds, 1865-1866; Record of Deeds, 1862, 1865-1867; 1 volume.

COURT RECORDS

> County Court of Pleas and Quarter Sessions
>> Minutes, 1847-1848, 1855-1868; 2 volumes.
>> Execution Docket, 1855-1868; 1 volume.
>> State Docket, 1855-1868; 1 volume.
>> Trial and Appearance Docket, 1855-1868; 1 volume.
>
> Superior Court
>> Minutes, 1855-1912; 5 volumes. SEE ALSO Guardians' Accounts, Rutherford County.
>> Equity Execution Docket, 1858-1868; 1 volume.
>> Equity Trial and Appearance Docket, 1848, 1856-1868; 1 volume.
>> Appearance Docket, 1856-1869; 1 volume.
>> Execution Docket, 1855-1869; 1 volume.
>> State Docket, 1855-1868; 1 volume.
>> Trial Docket, 1855-1868, 1870; 1 volume.
>> Civil Action Papers, 1852-1909; 7 Fibredex boxes.
>> Civil Action Papers Concerning County Officials, 1870-1908; 1 Fibredex box.
>> Civil Action Papers Concerning Land, 1853-1917; 5 Fibredex boxes.
>> Criminal Action Papers, 1854-1911; 21 Fibredex boxes.

ELECTION RECORDS

> Record of Elections, 1878-1946; 3 volumes.

ESTATES RECORDS

> Record of Accounts, 1869-1909; 1 volume.
>
> Administrators' Bonds, 1876-1911; 1 volume.
>
> Appointment of Administrators, Executors, Guardians and Masters, 1869-1918; 1 volume.
>
> Cross Index to Executors and Administrators, 1869-1939; 1 volume.
>
> Estates Records, 1851-1913; 17 Fibredex boxes.
>
> Guardians' Records, 1852-1915; 1 Fibredex box.
>
> Guardians' Bonds, 1872-1911; 1 volume.
>
> Cross Index to Guardians, 1869-1939; 1 volume.
>
> Record of Settlements, 1869-1922; 1 volume.

LAND RECORDS

> Record of Deeds, 1863-1865; 1 volume.
>
> Deeds, 1830-1925; 2 Fibredex boxes.

General Index to Deeds, 1855-1900; 1 volume.
Ejectments, 1854-1897; 1 Fibredex box.
Land Entries, 1870-1950; 1 volume.
Levies on Land for Taxes, 1887-1894; 1 volume.
Record of Probate, 1855-1902; 3 volumes.

MARRIAGE, DIVORCE AND VITAL STATISTICS
Marriage Bonds, 1855-1868; 2 Fibredex boxes.
Divorce Records, 1856-1909; 1 Fibredex box.

MILITARY AND PENSION RECORDS
Record of Pensions, 1911-1913; 1 volume.

MISCELLANEOUS RECORDS
Alien Registration, 1927, 1940, 1948; 1 volume.
Declaration of Intent (to Become a Citizen), 1912; 1 volume.
Registry of Licenses to Trades, 1872-1902; 1 volume.
Special Proceedings, 1878-1909; 1 volume.
Minutes, Wardens of the Poor, 1861-1864; 1 volume.
Miscellaneous Records, 1856-1921; 4 Fibredex boxes.
Records of Assignees, Receivers and Trustees, 1855-1909; 1 Fibredex box.

ROADS AND BRIDGES
Railroad Records, 1872-1909; 1 Fibredex box.

WILLS
Record of Wills, 1855-1867; 1 volume.
Wills, 1855-1916; 2 Fibredex boxes.
Cross Index to Wills, 1855-1939; 1 volume.

MICROFILM RECORDS

BONDS
Apprentice Bonds, 1877-1912; 1 reel.

CORPORATIONS AND PARTNERSHIPS
Record of Corporations, 1884-1969; 1 reel.
Record of Partnerships and Assumed Names, 1945-1969; 1 reel.

COURT RECORDS
County Court of Pleas and Quarter Sessions
Minutes, 1847-1848, 1855-1868; 1 reel.
Superior Court
Minutes, 1847-1848, 1855-1958; 5 reels.
General Index to Civil Minutes, 1855-1968; 1 reel.
General Index to Criminal Minutes, 1855-1968; 1 reel.

ELECTION RECORDS
Record of Elections, 1878-1950; 1 reel.

ESTATES RECORDS
Record of Accounts, 1869-1966; 4 reels.
Administrators' Bonds, 1876-1911; 1 reel.
Appointment of Administrators, Executors and Guardians, 1869-1918; 1 reel.

Record of Administrators, Executors and Guardians, 1911-1939; 1 reel.
Record of Administrators, 1923-1968; 2 reels.
Record of Executors, 1939-1968; 1 reel.
Guardians' Bonds, 1872-1911; 1 reel.
Record of Guardians, 1928-1968; 1 reel.
Record of Amounts Paid for Indigent Children, 1913-1948; 1 reel.
Inheritance Tax Records, 1923-1968; 1 reel.
Record of Settlements, 1870-1968; 3 reels.
Trust Fund Record, 1931-1935; 1 reel.
Index to Annual Accounts and Final Settlements, 1869-1968; 1 reel.
Index to Estates, 1868-1969; 1 reel.
Index to Estates, Administrators, Executors and Guardians, 1868-1968; 1 reel.

LAND RECORDS
Record of Deeds, 1848-1967; 29 reels.
Index to Real Estate Conveyances, Grantor, 1855-1969; 2 reels.
Index to Real Estate Conveyances, Grantee, 1855-1969; 2 reels.
Land Entries, 1870-1950; 1 reel.

MARRIAGE, DIVORCE AND VITAL STATISTICS
Marriage Bonds, 1855-1868; 1 reel.
Marriage Licenses, 1868-1969; 2 reels.
Marriage Registers, 1866-1969; 1 reel.
Maiden Names of Divorced Women, 1942-1968; 1 reel.
Index to Vital Statistics, 1913-1976; 1 reel.
Index to Delayed Births, 1868-1994; 1 reel.

MILITARY AND PENSION RECORDS
Record of Armed Forces Discharges, 1917-1969; 2 reels.
Record of Soldiers in World War I, 1917-1919; 1 reel.

MISCELLANEOUS RECORDS
Orders and Decrees, 1931-1949; 1 reel.
Special Proceedings, 1878-1966; 5 reels.
Index to Special Proceedings, 1878-1968; 1 reel.
Appointment of Receivers, 1927-1959; 1 reel.

OFFICIALS, COUNTY
Minutes, Board of County Commissioners, 1871-1963; 4 reels.

SCHOOL RECORDS
Minutes, County Board of Education, 1936-1969; 1 reel.

TAX AND FISCAL RECORDS
Tax Scrolls, 1945; 1 reel.

WILLS
Record of Wills, 1855-1968; 5 reels.
Index to Wills, 1855-1968; 1 reel.

RANDOLPH COUNTY

Established in 1779 from Guilford County.
Many court records are missing; reason unknown.

ORIGINAL RECORDS

BONDS
 Apprentice Bonds and Records, 1779-1923; 1 volume, 4 Fibredex boxes.
 Bastardy Bonds and Records, 1770, 1780-1930; 1 volume, 9 Fibredex boxes.
 Officials' Bonds, 1784-1888; 6 Fibredex boxes.

CENSUS RECORDS (County Copy)
 Census, 1880; 2 pamphlets.

CORPORATIONS AND PARTNERSHIP
 Articles of Incorporation, 1877-1898; 1 Fibredex box.

COURT RECORDS
 County Court of Pleas and Quarter Sessions
  Minutes, 1794-1868; 17 volumes.
  Execution Dockets, 1784-1868; 13 volumes.
  Levy Docket, 1820-1839; 1 volume.
  Recognizance Dockets, 1813-1841; 3 volumes.
  State Dockets, 1783-1868; 7 volumes.
  Trial, Appearance and Reference Dockets, 1779-1845; 9 volumes.
  Trial and Appearance Dockets, 1845-1868; 3 volumes.
  Clerk's Fee and Receipt Books, 1851-1867; 2 volumes.
  Witness Fee Docket, 1800-1809; 1 volume.
 Superior Court
  Minutes, 1833-1900; 12 volumes.
  Equity Minutes, 1825-1868; 3 volumes.
  Equity Execution Docket, 1860-1868; 1 volume.
  Equity Trial and Appearance Dockets, 1827-1868; 3 volumes.
  Execution Dockets, 1815-1827, 1841-1867; 5 volumes.
  State Dockets, 1821-1868; 3 volumes.
  Trial, Appearance and Reference Dockets, 1813-1852; 4 volumes.
  Trial and Appearance Dockets, 1853-1868; 2 volumes.
  Clerk's Fee and Receipt Book, 1854-1860; 1 volume.
  Civil Action Papers, 1772-1930; 88 Fibredex boxes.
  Civil Action Papers Concerning Land, 1787-1931; 11 Fibredex boxes.
  Criminal Action Papers, 1780-1920; 65 Fibredex boxes.

ELECTION RECORDS
 Record of Elections, 1880-1936, 1944-1968; 6 volumes.
 Election Records, 1791-1902; 6 Fibredex boxes.
 Voter Registration Book, 1902-1908; 1 volume.

ESTATES RECORDS
 Administrators' Bonds, 1870-1886; 2 volumes.

Widows' Dowers and Year's Support, 1872-1887; 1 volume.
Estates Records, 1781-1928; 153 Fibredex boxes.
Guardians' Records, 1793-1928; 15 Fibredex boxes.
Guardians' Accounts, 1833-1868; 2 volumes.
Guardians' Bonds, 1878-1918; 5 volumes.
Record of Settlements, 1911-1918; 1 volume.

LAND RECORDS

Deeds, 1788-1920; 1 Fibredex box.
Deeds of Trust, Mortgage Deeds and Bills of Sale, 1784-1917;
    1 Fibredex box.
Ejectments, 1792-1897, 1930; 3 Fibredex boxes.
Land Entries, 1802-1833; 2 volumes.
Levies on Land, 1790-1905; 5 Fibredex boxes.
Miscellaneous Land Records, 1782-1929; 1 Fibredex box.
Lists of Deeds and Bills of Sale Proved, 1784-1832; 1 Fibredex box.

MARRIAGE, DIVORCE AND VITAL STATISTICS

Marriage Bonds, 1779-1868; 14 Fibredex boxes.
Divorce Records, 1804-1927; 4 Fibredex boxes.

MILITARY AND PENSION RECORDS

Civil War Records, 1861-1865, 1870; 1 Fibredex box.

MISCELLANEOUS RECORDS

County Accounts and Claims, 1784-1887; 2 Fibredex boxes.
Insolvent Debtors, 1792-1878; 5 Fibredex boxes.
Jury Lists and Excuses, 1779-1869; 2 Fibredex boxes.
Special Proceedings Dockets, 1906-1927; 3 volumes.
Miscellaneous Records, 1781-1922; 6 Fibredex boxes.
Records of Slaves and Free Persons of Color, 1788-1887; 2 Fibredex boxes.
Record of Strays, 1800-1845; 1 volume.
Records of Assignees, Receivers and Trustees, 1843-1929; 3 Fibredex boxes.

OFFICIALS, COUNTY

Minutes, Board of County Commissioners, 1874-1946; 10 volumes.

ROADS AND BRIDGES

Appointment of Overseers of Roads, 1817-1833; 2 volumes.
Road Orders, 1783-1868; 13 Fibredex boxes.
Road Petitions, 1791-1868; 3 Fibredex boxes.
Road, Railroad and Bridge Records, 1784-1898; 2 Fibredex boxes.

TAX AND FISCAL RECORDS

Lists of Taxables, 1784-1867; 1 volume, 4 Fibredex boxes.
Assessment of Land for Taxation, 1855; 1 volume.
Miscellaneous Tax Records, 1782-1886; 1 Fibredex box.

WILLS

Wills, 1775-1902; 14 Fibredex boxes.
Index to Wills, Settlements and Sales, 1794-1832; 1 manuscript box.

MICROFILM RECORDS

BONDS
>Apprentice Bonds, 1890-1923; 1 reel.

COURT RECORDS
>County Court of Pleas and Quarter Sessions
>>Minutes, 1779-1868; 6 reels.
>Superior Court
>>Minutes, 1807-1833, 1850-1946; 11 reels.
>>Equity Minutes, 1825-1868; 1 reel.

ESTATES RECORDS
>Record of Accounts, 1868-1964; 12 reels.
>Administrators' Bonds, 1870-1953; 7 reels.
>Record of Administrators, 1953-1964; 2 reels.
>Appointment of Executors, 1868-1913; 1 reel.
>Guardians' Accounts, 1812-1851; 2 reels.
>Guardians' Settlements, 1852-1868; 1 reel.
>Guardians' Bonds, 1885-1918; 2 reels.
>Record of Guardians, 1916-1964; 2 reels.
>Accounts for Indigent Orphans, 1904-1958; 1 reel.
>Record of Widows' Year's Allowance, 1888-1964; 1 reel.
>Inheritance Tax Records, 1923-1964; 1 reel.
>Distribution Dockets, 1885-1958; 2 reels.
>Record of Settlements, 1867-1964; 7 reels.
>Cross Index to Administrators, Executors and Guardians, 1868-1964; 1 reel.

LAND RECORDS
>Record of Deeds, 1779-1963; 249 reels.
>Index to Real Estate Conveyances, Grantor, 1779-1964; 22 reels.
>Index to Real Estate Conveyances, Grantee, 1779-1964; 24 reels.
>Land Entries, 1794-1801, 1833-1837; 1 reel.
>Federal Tax Lien Index, 1933; 1 reel.
>Record of Resale of Land, 1931-1940; 1 reel.

MARRIAGE, DIVORCE AND VITAL STATISTICS
>Marriage Bonds, 1779-1868; 10 reels.
>Marriage Bond Abstracts, 1779-1868; 1 reel.
>Marriage Registers, 1851-1981; 3 reels.
>Index to Marriages, Female, 1851-1964; 1 reel.
>Index to Marriages, Male, 1851-1981; 1 reel.
>Maiden Names of Divorced Women, 1945-1970; 1 reel.
>Index to Births, 1913-1981; 3 reels.
>Index to Deaths, 1913-1980; 2 reels.
>Index to Delayed Births, various years; 1 reel.

MILITARY AND PENSION RECORDS
>Record and Index of Armed Forces Discharges, 1919-1964; 6 reels.

MISCELLANEOUS RECORDS
      Orders and Decrees, 1869-1951; 9 reels.

      Special Proceedings, 1901-1964; 3 reels.

      Cross Index to Special Proceedings, 1915-1957; 1 reel.

      Miscellaneous Historical Records, 1779-1838; 1 reel.

OFFICIALS, COUNTY
      Minutes, Board of County Commissioners, 1874-1964; 3 reels.

ROADS AND BRIDGES
      Appointment of Road Overseers, 1817-1833; 1 reel.

SCHOOL RECORDS
      Report of the Board of Superintendents of Common Schools, 1840-1864; 1 reel.

      Minutes, County Board of Education, 1881-1885, 1910-1964; 1 reel.

WILLS
      Record of Wills, 1773-1964; 9 reels.

      Cross Index to Wills, 1773-1964; 1 reel.

RICHMOND COUNTY

Established in 1779 from Anson County.
A few of the court records are missing; reason unknown.

ORIGINAL RECORDS

BONDS

Apprentice Bonds and Records, 1782-1912; 1 volume, 1 Fibredex box.

Bastardy Bonds and Records, 1783-1880; 1 volume, 1 Fibredex box.

Officials' Bonds and Records, 1794-1924; 2 Fibredex boxes.

Sheriffs' Bonds and Records, 1785-1912; 3 Fibredex boxes.

COURT RECORDS

County Court of Pleas and Quarter Sessions

Minutes, 1779-1797, 1800-1868; 14 volumes, 1 manuscript box.

Allowance Dockets, 1830-1841, 1848-1868; 2 volumes.

Execution Dockets, 1783-1863; 2 volumes, 2 manuscript boxes.

Recognizance Docket, 1797-1815; 1 manuscript box.

State Dockets, 1784-1823; 2 volumes.

Trial, Appearance and Reference Dockets, 1785-1814;
2 manuscript boxes.

Trial Docket, 1855-1868; 1 volume.

Superior Court

Minutes, 1823-1913; 15 volumes.

Equity Minutes, 1829-1868; 3 volumes.

Equity Enrolling Docket, 1851-1868; 1 manuscript box.

Equity Execution Dockets, 1830-1868; 2 volumes.

Equity Trial Docket, 1860-1868; 1 volume.

Appearance Docket, 1831-1867; 1 volume.

Execution Dockets, 1809-1824, 1845-1868; 4 volumes.

Recognizance Docket, 1807-1834; 1 manuscript box.

State Dockets, 1831-1868; 4 volumes.

Trial and Appearance Docket, 1807-1823; 1 volume.

Trial Dockets, 1831-1868; 2 volumes.

Miscellaneous Dockets, 1782-1934; 1 Fibredex box.

Civil Action Papers, 1772-1928; 37 Fibredex boxes.

Civil Action Papers Concerning County Commissioners and
Municipalities, 1838-1910; 1 Fibredex box.

Civil Action Papers Concerning Land, 1773-1926; 6 Fibredex boxes.

Criminal Action Papers, 1777-1941; 31 Fibredex boxes.

ELECTION RECORDS

Record of Elections, 1878-1936; 5 volumes.

Election Records, 1786-1936; 2 Fibredex boxes.

ESTATES RECORDS

Record of Estates, 1778-1833, 1848-1863; 4 volumes.

Record of Accounts, 1869-1916; 5 volumes.

Administrators' Bonds, 1870-1911; 3 volumes.

Appointment of Administrators, Executors, Guardians and Masters, 1868-1915; 2 volumes.

Estates Records, 1772-1933; 69 Fibredex boxes.

Guardians' Records, 1784-1913; 13 Fibredex boxes.

Guardians' Accounts, 1858-1868; 1 volume.

Guardians' Bonds, 1870-1915; 3 volumes.

Record of Settlements, 1869-1904; 1 volume.

Fiduciary Account Book, 1834; 1 volume.

LAND RECORDS

Deeds of Sale, 1794-1930; 7 Fibredex boxes.

Mortgage Deeds, 1822-1926, 1936; 2 Fibredex boxes.

Miscellaneous Deeds, 1820-1934; 1 Fibredex box.

Ejectments, 1786-1887; 2 Fibredex boxes.

Land Entries, 1780-1798, 1849-1890; 3 volumes.

Levies on Land, 1779-1894; 1 Fibredex box.

Petitions for Partition, 1847-1912; 1 Fibredex box.

Miscellaneous Land Records, 1762-1931; 1 Fibredex box.

MARRIAGE, DIVORCE AND VITAL STATISTICS

Marriage Bonds, 1791-1868; 1 Fibredex box.

Cohabitation Certificates, 1866-1868; 1 manuscript box.

Divorce Records, 1816-1910; 3 Fibredex boxes.

MISCELLANEOUS RECORDS

County Accounts, 1783-1923; 2 Fibredex boxes.

Record of Homestead and Personal Property Exemptions, 1869-1874; 1 volume.

Registry of Licenses to Trades, 1875-1885; 1 volume.

Miscellaneous Records, 1779-1939; 5 Fibredex boxes.

Slave Records, 1778-1866; 2 Fibredex boxes.

Records of Assignees, 1782-1911; 2 Fibredex boxes.

Records of Receivers and Trustees, 1784-1929; 1 Fibredex box.

ROADS AND BRIDGES

Bridge Records, 1790-1897; 1 Fibredex box.

Road Dockets, 1850-1866, 1877-1879; 2 volumes.

Road Records, 1778-1909; 3 Fibredex boxes.

Railroad Records, 1867-1914; 3 Fibredex boxes.

SCHOOL RECORDS

School Records, 1839-1903; 2 Fibredex boxes.

TAX AND FISCAL RECORDS

Tax Records, 1783-1898; 1 Fibredex box.

Assessment of Land and Cost Docket, 1855, 1868-1869; 1 volume.

WILLS

Record of Wills and Inventories, 1789-1807; 1 pamphlet.

Record of Wills, 1848-1864; 1 volume.

Wills, 1779-1915; 10 Fibredex boxes.
Cross Index to Wills, 1779-1934; 1 volume.

MICROFILM RECORDS

CORPORATIONS AND PARTNERSHIPS
Record of Incorporations, 1887-1964; 2 reels.
Record of Partnerships, 1915-1964; 1 reel.

COURT RECORDS
County Court of Pleas and Quarter Sessions
Minutes, 1779-1797, 1800-1868; 4 reels.
Superior Court
Minutes, 1823-1964; 15 reels.
Equity Minutes, 1829-1868; 1 reel.

ELECTION RECORDS
Record of Elections, 1878-1964; 1 reel.

ESTATES RECORDS
Record of Accounts, 1869-1964; 7 reels.
Appointment of Administrators, Executors and Guardians, 1865-1935; 1 reel.
Record of Administrators, 1911-1964; 4 reels.
Appointment of Executors, 1926-1964; 1 reel.
Appointment of Guardians, 1935-1964; 2 reels.
Amounts Paid for Indigent Children, 1912-1927, 1955-1963; 1 reel.
Record of Accounts and Receivership of Minors, 1925-1953; 1 reel.
Widows' Year's Allowance, 1927-1963; 1 reel.
Inheritance Tax Records, 1923-1964; 1 reel.
Record of Settlements, 1854-1964; 5 reels.
Qualification of Trustees Under Wills, 1963; 1 reel.
Index to Administrators, Executors and Guardians, 1911-1964; 1 reel.

LAND RECORDS
Record of Deeds, 1777-1962; 183 reels.
Index to Real Estate Conveyances, Grantor, 1784-1961; 5 reels.
Index to Real Estate Conveyances, Grantee, 1784-1961; 4 reels.
Land Entries, 1780-1795, 1849-1945; 1 reel.
Land Grants, 1854-1929; 1 reel.
Federal Tax Lien Index, 1935-1951; 1 reel.
Record of Resale by Trustees and Mortgagees, 1921-1964; 4 reels.

MARRIAGE, DIVORCE AND VITAL STATISTICS
Marriage Bonds, 1779-1868; 1 reel.
Marriage Licenses, 1870-1964; 8 reels.
Marriage Registers, 1851-1964; 2 reels.
Cohabitation Certificates, 1866-1868; 1 reel.
Index to Births, 1914-1972; 2 reels.
Index to Deaths, 1913-1967; 1 reel.
Index to Delayed Births, various years; 1 reel.

MILITARY AND PENSION RECORDS
  Record of Armed Forces Discharges, 1918-1972; 8 reels.
  Index to Armed Forces Discharges, 1918-1964; 1 reel.
MISCELLANEOUS RECORDS
  Homesteads and Exemptions, 1869-1874; 1 reel.
  Clerk's Minute Dockets, 1916-1960; 2 reels.
  Orders and Decrees, 1869-1964; 12 reels.
  Special Proceedings, 1883-1964; 1 reel.
  Appointment of Receivers, 1955-1964; 1 reel.
OFFICIALS, COUNTY
  Minutes, Board of County Commissioners, 1868-1964; 9 reels.
SCHOOL RECORDS
  Minutes, Board of Superintendents of Common Schools, 1839-1840; Minutes,
    County Board of Education, 1877-1925; 1 reel.
TAX AND FISCAL RECORDS
  Tax List, 1915; 1 reel.
WILLS
  Record of Wills, 1779-1964; 5 reels.
  Cross Index to Wills, 1779-1968; 2 reels.

ROBESON COUNTY

Established in 1787 from Bladen County.
Many of the court records are missing; reason unknown.

ORIGINAL RECORDS

BONDS
>Apprentice Bonds and Records, 1820-1904; 1 Fibredex box.
>Bastardy Bonds and Records, 1813-1911, 1935-1966; 5 Fibredex boxes.
>Officials' Bonds and Records, 1795-1914; 2 Fibredex boxes.

COURT RECORDS
>County Court of Pleas and Quarter Sessions
>>Minutes, 1797-1813, 1830-1868; 11 volumes.
>>Execution Dockets, 1855-1867; 2 volumes.
>>Trial Docket, 1858-1868; 1 volume.
>Superior Court
>>Minutes, 1844-1912; 19 volumes.
>>Minutes, Criminal, 1909-1966; 19 volumes.
>>Cross Index to Minutes, 1873-1912; 7 volumes.
>>Equity Minutes, 1847-1868; 1 volume.
>>Equity Execution Docket, 1850-1868; 1 volume.
>>Appearance Docket, 1859-1868; 1 volume.
>>Execution Dockets, 1836-1867; 3 volumes.
>>Recognizance Docket, 1841-1847; 1 volume.
>>State Dockets, 1841-1869; 2 volumes.
>>Trial Docket, 1846-1851, 1862; 1 volume.
>>Index to Judgments, 1867-1891; 2 volumes.
>>Civil Action Papers, 1801-1921; 33 Fibredex boxes.
>>Civil Action Papers Concerning Land, 1816-1926; 28 Fibredex boxes.
>>Criminal Action Papers, 1803-1966; 183 Fibredex boxes.
>Inferior Court
>>Minutes, 1883-1885; 1 volume.
>Circuit Criminal Court/Eastern District Criminal Court
>>Minutes, 1895-1900; 1 volume.

ELECTION RECORDS
>Record of Elections, 1910-1938; 3 volumes.

ESTATES RECORDS
>Record of Estates, 1829-1870; 7 volumes.
>Record of Accounts, 1870-1910; 5 volumes.
>Administrators' Bonds, 1880-1891, 1899-1903; 2 volumes.
>Estates Records, 1801-1935; 90 Fibredex boxes.
>Guardians' Records, 1821-1928; 8 Fibredex boxes.
>Guardians' Accounts, 1857-1902; 1 volume.
>Cross Index to Guardians' Accounts, [1857-1902]; 1 volume.

Guardians' Bonds, 1900-1902; 1 volume.

Record of Settlements, 1869-1914; 1 volume.

Cross Index to Settlements, [1869-1914]; 1 volume.

Record of Probate (Estates) and Appointment, 1868-1936; 1 volume.

LAND RECORDS

Record of Deeds, 1792-1826; 6 volumes.

Ejectments, 1824-1900; 5 Fibredex boxes.

Attachments, Executions, Levies and Liens on Land, 1821-1914;
2 Fibredex boxes.

Miscellaneous Land Records, 1782-1926; 3 Fibredex boxes.

MARRIAGE, DIVORCE AND VITAL STATISTICS

Marriage Bonds, 1803-1868; 7 Fibredex boxes.

Divorce Records, 1841-1920; 5 Fibredex boxes.

MILITARY AND PENSION RECORDS

Record of Pensions, 1908-1939; 1 volume.

MISCELLANEOUS RECORDS

Alien Registration, 1927; 1 volume.

Petitions for Naturalization, 1911-1913; 1 volume.

County Accounts, Buildings and Correspondence, 1810-1910; 1 Fibredex box.

Insolvents and Homestead and Personal Property Exemptions, 1793-1904;
2 Fibredex boxes.

Orders and Decrees, 1869-1904; 5 volumes.

Miscellaneous Records, 1817-1939; 5 Fibredex boxes.

Coroners' Inquests, 1857-1965; 27 Fibredex boxes.

Records Concerning Lumber, Timber and Mills, 1835-1911; 1 Fibredex box.

Records Concerning Slaves and Free Persons of Color, 1814-1867;
4 Fibredex boxes.

Assignment Books, 1893-1905; 2 volumes.

Records of Assignees, Receivers and Trustees, 1877-1927; 5 Fibredex boxes.

ROADS AND BRIDGES

Appointment of Road Overseers, 1833-1868; 1 Fibredex box.

Road and Bridge Records, 1833-1924; 1 Fibredex box.

Railroad Records, 1857-1914; 7 Fibredex boxes.

TAX AND FISCAL RECORDS

List of Taxables, 1837-1845; 1 volume.

Tax Records, 1788-1910; 2 Fibredex boxes.

WILLS

Wills, 1783-1918, 1930, 1933, 1935; 13 Fibredex boxes.

MICROFILM RECORDS

CORPORATIONS AND PARTNERSHIPS

Record of Corporations, 1890-1946; 2 reels.

Record of Partnerships, 1915-1966; 1 reel.

Index to Corporations and Partnerships, 1890-1966; 1 reel.

COURT RECORDS
County Court of Pleas and Quarter Sessions
Minutes, 1797-1868; 4 reels.
Superior Court
Minutes, 1844-1899; 6 reels.
Minutes, Civil, 1899-1960; 23 reels.
Minutes, Criminal, 1901-1955; 7 reels.
Cross Index to Minutes, 1872-1966; 5 reels.
Equity Minutes, 1847-1868; 1 reel.
ELECTION RECORDS
Record of Elections, 1878-1922, 1940-1965; 1 reel.
ESTATES RECORDS
Record of Estates, 1829-1870; 3 reels.
Record of Accounts, 1870-1961; 17 reels.
Record of Administrators, Executors, Justices of the Peace and Notaries,
1869-1936; 1 reel.
Record of Administrators, 1907-1966; 8 reels.
Record of Executors, 1911-1966; 3 reels.
Record of Guardians, 1907-1966; 4 reels.
Record of Amounts Paid for Indigent Children, 1912-1966; 1 reel.
Inheritance Tax Records, 1923-1958; 1 reel.
Record of Settlements, 1869-1914; Cross Index to Settlements, 1869-1914;
1 reel.
Qualification of Trustees Under Wills, 1962-1965; 1 reel.
LAND RECORDS
Record of Deeds, 1787-1960; 161 reels.
Index to Real Estate Conveyances, Grantor, 1787-1966; 10 reels.
Index to Real Estate Conveyances, Grantee, 1787-1966; 12 reels.
Entry Takers' Book, 1854-1945; 1 reel.
Record of Land Grants, 1788-1797; 1 reel.
Record of Land Sold for Taxes, 1925; 1 reel.
Federal Tax Lien Index, 1928-1966; 1 reel.
Registration of Land Titles, 1914-1923; 1 reel.
Record of Resale of Land, 1931-1966; 3 reels.
MARRIAGE, DIVORCE AND VITAL STATISTICS
Marriage Bonds, 1786-1868; 7 reels.
Marriage Registers, 1867-1966; 7 reels.
Record of Marriage and Cohabitation, 1850-1866; 1 reel.
Maiden Names of Divorced Women, 1940-1966; 1 reel.
Index to Births, 1913-1965; 3 reels.
Index to Deaths, 1911-1963; 1 reel.
Index to Delayed Births, various years; 1 reel.
MILITARY AND PENSION RECORDS
Record of Armed Forces Discharges, 1917-1966; 9 reels.
Index to Armed Forces Discharges, 1917-1966; 1 reel.

MISCELLANEOUS RECORDS

Record of Homestead Allotments, 1941-1961; 1 reel.

Orders and Decrees, 1869-1960; 27 reels.

Special Proceedings Dockets, 1868-1951; 6 reels.

Index to Special Proceedings, Plaintiff, 1868-1966; 1 reel.

Index to Special Proceedings, Defendant, 1868-1966; 1 reel.

OFFICIALS, COUNTY

Minutes, Board of County Commissioners, 1868-1936; 9 reels.

SCHOOL RECORDS

Minutes, County Board of Education, 1885-1911; 1 reel.

Boundaries of School Districts and Record of Elections, 1904-1927; 1 reel.

TAX AND FISCAL RECORDS

List of Taxables, 1837-1845; 1 reel.

WILLS

Record of Wills, 1787-1966; 10 reels.

Original Wills, 1783-1851; 2 reels.

Cross Index to Wills, 1787-1966; 2 reels.

ROCKINGHAM COUNTY

Established in 1785 from Guilford County.
A few of the court records are missing; reason unknown.

ORIGINAL RECORDS

BONDS

    Apprentice Bonds, 1871-1919; 2 volumes.

    Bastardy Bonds, 1873-1878; 1 volume.

    Officials' Bonds and Records, 1803-1925; 1 Fibredex box.

COURT RECORDS

    County Court of Pleas and Quarter Sessions

        Minutes, 1786-1868; 17 volumes.

        Execution Dockets, 1788-1868; 13 volumes.

        State Dockets, 1800-1868; 6 volumes.

        Trial and Appearance Dockets, 1786-1861; 10 volumes.

    Superior Court

        Minutes, 1807-1856; 3 volumes.

        Equity Minutes, 1807-1868; 4 volumes.

        Equity Proceeding, 1822-1828; 1 volume.

        Equity Trial and Appearance Dockets, 1807-1868; 3 volumes.

        Equity Bills of Cost, 1860-1874; 1 volume.

        Execution Dockets, 1814-1868; 5 volumes.

        Recognizance Docket, 1811-1845; 1 volume.

        State Docket, 1809-1821; 1 volume.

        Trial and Appearance Dockets, 1807-1850; 2 volumes.

        Civil Action Papers, 1804-1923; 14 Fibredex boxes.

        Civil Action Papers Concerning Land, 1827-1928; 5 Fibredex boxes.

        Criminal Action Papers, 1807-1925; 8 Fibredex boxes.

ELECTION RECORDS

    Record of Elections, 1878-1922; 4 volumes.

ESTATES RECORDS

    Record of Estates, 1829-1868; 9 volumes.

    Administrators' Bonds, 1870-1880; 1 volume.

    Estates Records, 1780-1926; 58 Fibredex boxes.

    Guardians' Records, 1804-1925; 6 Fibredex boxes.

    Guardians' Accounts, 1855-1868; 1 volume.

    Guardians' Bonds, 1872-1893, 1906-1919; 2 volumes.

    Record of Settlements, 1817-1868; 5 volumes.

LAND RECORDS

    Deeds of Sale, 1786-1899; 18 Fibredex boxes.

    Deeds of Gift, 1797-1895; 1 Fibredex box.

    Deeds of Mortgage, 1821-1913; 1 Fibredex box.

    Deeds of Trust, 1808-1914; 3 Fibredex boxes.

Deeds of Warranty and Quit Claim, 1788-1913; 1 Fibredex box.

Ejectments, 1808-1909; 1 Fibredex box.

Attachments, Executions, Liens and Levies on Land, 1806-1924;
4 Fibredex boxes.

Miscellaneous Land Records, 1789-1926; 1 Fibredex box.

Processioners' Book, 1836-1842; 1 volume.

MARRIAGE, DIVORCE AND VITAL STATISTICS

Marriage Bonds, 1785-1868; 9 Fibredex boxes.

Record of Marriage Certificates, 1851-1867; 1 volume.

Index to Marriages, 1790-1868; 1 volume.

Miscellaneous Marriage Records, 1812-1925; 1 Fibredex box.

Divorce Records, 1824-1921; 2 Fibredex boxes.

MISCELLANEOUS RECORDS

Homestead Records, 1871-1927; 1 Fibredex box.

Miscellaneous Business Records, 1852-1925; 1 Fibredex box.

Jury Lists and Tickets, 1819-1851; 1 Fibredex box.

Miscellaneous Records, 1786-1925; 2 Fibredex boxes.

Powers of Attorney, 1784-1923; 1 Fibredex box.

Records of Slaves and Free Persons of Color, 1795-1867; 2 Fibredex boxes.

Records of Assignees, Receivers and Trustees, 1861-1925; 9 Fibredex boxes.

ROADS AND BRIDGES

Road and Bridge Records, 1822-1899; 1 Fibredex box.

Record of Appointment of Road Overseers, 1811-1829; 1 volume.

Railroad Records, 1867-1901; 3 Fibredex boxes.

SCHOOL RECORDS

Minutes, Board of Superintendents of Common Schools, 1841-1864;
1 volume.

TAX AND FISCAL RECORDS

Miscellaneous Tax Records, 1857-1899; 2 Fibredex boxes.

WILLS

Wills, 1772-1915; 2 Fibredex boxes.

MICROFILM RECORDS

BONDS

Apprentice Bonds, 1871-1919; 1 reel.

Bastardy Bonds, 1873-1878; 1 reel.

CORPORATIONS AND PARTNERSHIPS

Record of Corporations, 1884-1967; 4 reels.

Record of Partnership, 1913-1972; 1 reel.

COURT RECORDS

County Court of Pleas and Quarter Sessions
Minutes, 1786-1868; 5 reels.

Superior Court
Minutes, 1807-1948; 10 reels.

Equity Minutes, 1807-1868; 1 reel.

Index to Judgments, Plaintiff, 1921-1970; 2 reels.

Index to Judgments, Defendant, 1921-1970; 2 reels.

ELECTION RECORDS

Record of Elections, 1878-1968; 2 reels.

ESTATES RECORDS

Record of Estates, 1829-1868; 3 reels.

Record of Accounts, 1868-1966; 15 reels.

Administrators' Bonds, 1870-1880; 1 reel.

Appointment of Administrators, Executors and Guardians, 1895-1970; 3 reels.

Record of Administrators, 1926-1954; 2 reels.

Appointment of Executors, 1868-1895; 1 reel.

Record of Executors, 1931-1954; 1 reel.

Guardians' Bonds, 1872-1919; 1 reel.

Accounts for Indigent Orphans, 1908-1937; 1 reel.

Estates Not Exceeding $300, 1929-1937; 1 reel.

Inheritance Tax Records, 1922-1965; 2 reels.

Record of Renunciations, 1964-1970; 1 reel.

Record of Settlements, 1817-1965; 12 reels.

Index to Guardians and Trustees, 1868-1970; 1 reel.

LAND RECORDS

Record of Deeds, 1785-1957; 103 reels.

Index to Real Estate Conveyances, Grantor, 1785-1962; 10 reels.

Index to Real Estate Conveyances, Grantee, 1785-1962; 9 reels.

Record of Land Entries, 1904-1929; 1 reel.

Index to Federal Tax Liens, 1929-1965; 1 reel.

Record of Sales by Mortgagees, Trustees and Executors, 1918-1923; 1 reel.

Record of Resales by Mortgagees and Trustees, 1919-1923; 1 reel.

Record of Foreclosures Under Deeds of Trust, 1924-1965; 1 reel.

MARRIAGE, DIVORCE AND VITAL STATISTICS

Marriage Bonds, 1785-1868; 9 reels.

Record of Marriages, 1851-1867; 1 reel.

Record of Marriages, 1865-1867; Processioners' Book, 1836-1842; 1 reel.

Marriage Registers, 1867-1979; 6 reels.

Index to Marriage Licenses, Bonds and Certificates, 1790-1868; 1 reel.

Maiden Names of Divorced Women, 1937-1970; 1 reel.

Index to Births, 1913-1968; 2 reels.

Index to Deaths, 1913-1978; 2 reels.

Index to Delayed Births, various years; 1 reel.

MILITARY AND PENSION RECORDS

Record of Armed Forces Discharges, 1917-1966; 7 reels.

Index to Armed Forces Discharges, 1918-1972; 1 reel.

MISCELLANEOUS RECORDS

Record of Lunacy, 1899-1952; 1 reel.

Orders and Decrees, 1869-1952; 8 reels.

Index to Special Proceedings, Plaintiff, 1869-1969; 1 reel.

Index to Special Proceedings, Defendant, 1869-1969; 1 reel.

Record of Receivers' Accounts, 1902-1957; 1 reel.

OFFICIALS, COUNTY

Minutes, Board of County Commissioners, 1870-1979; 5 reels.

Minutes, County Board of Health, 1911-1925, 1946-1965; 1 reel.

ROADS AND BRIDGES

Overseers of Roads, 1811-1829; 1 reel.

SCHOOL RECORDS

Minutes, Board of Superintendents of Common Schools, 1841-1868; Minutes, County Board of Education, 1868-1876; 1 reel.

Minutes, County Board of Education, 1877-1885, 1909-1965; 1 reel.

TAX AND FISCAL RECORDS

Tax Lists, 1887, 1888, 1890, 1899, 1904, 1912, 1915; 3 reels.

WILLS

Record of Wills, 1785-1966; 7 reels.

Cross Index to Wills, 1804-1965; 1 reel.

ROWAN COUNTY

Established in 1753 from Anson County.
A few records were destroyed by Federal troops in 1865.

ORIGINAL RECORDS

BONDS
 Apprentice Bonds and Records, 1777-1904; 1 volume, 1 Fibredex box.
 Bastardy Bonds and Records, 1757-1925; 2 volumes, 2 Fibredex boxes.
 Officials' Bonds and Records, 1768-1900; 1 Fibredex box.
CORPORATIONS AND PARTNERSHIPS
 Corporation Records, 1871-1903; 1 Fibredex box.
COURT RECORDS
 County Court of Pleas and Quarter Sessions
  Minutes, 1753-1868; 24 volumes.
  Rough Minutes, 1767-1859; 2 Fibredex boxes.
  Appearance Dockets, 1809-1868; 5 volumes.
  Argument and Petition Docket, 1807-1832; 1 volume.
  Execution Dockets, 1761-1833, 1845-1868; 11 volumes.
  Recognizance Docket, 1811-1818; 1 volume.
  Reference Dockets, 1814-1849; 2 volumes.
  State Dockets, 1791-1818, 1830-1868; 4 volumes.
  Trial, Appearance and Reference Dockets, 1753-1810; 9 volumes.
  Trial Dockets, 1810-1868; 8 volumes.
  Minutes, Probate Court, 1819-1822; 1 volume.
  Clerk's Receipt Book, 1811-1826; 1 volume.
 Superior Court
  Minutes, 1811-1904, 1909-1910; 22 volumes.
  Equity Minutes, 1818-1864; 3 volumes.
  Equity Enrolling Dockets, 1805-1806, 1820-1844; 5 volumes.
  Equity Trial and Appearance Dockets, 1806-1868; 2 volumes,
   1 pamphlet.
  Appearance and Reference Docket, 1808-1835; 1 volume.
  Appearance Dockets, 1835-1869; 2 volumes.
  Execution Dockets, 1809-1828, 1848-1869; 5 volumes.
  Recognizance Docket, 1823-1827; 1 volume.
  Reference Docket, 1820-1838; 1 volume.
  State Dockets, 1821-1869; 3 volumes.
  Trial Dockets, 1807-1869; 5 volumes.
  Clerk's Receipt Book, 1823-1838; 1 volume.
  Clerk's Cashbook, 1876-1901; 1 volume.
  Clerk's Fee Book, 1932-1935; 1 volume.
  Civil Action Papers, 1755-1915; 5 Fibredex boxes.
  Civil Action Papers Concerning Land, 1758-1912; 6 Fibredex boxes.

Criminal Action Papers, 1756-1913; 6 Fibredex boxes.
Inferior Court
Minutes, 1877-1885; 2 volumes.
Criminal Issues Docket, 1877-1885; 1 volume.
Judgment Docket, 1877-1885; 1 volume.

ELECTION RECORDS

Record of Elections, 1878-1932; 3 volumes.
Election Records, 1796-1944; 3 Fibredex boxes.

ESTATES RECORDS

Record of Accounts, 1869-1928; 7 volumes.
Administrators' Bonds, 1870-1930; 12 volumes.
Appointment of Administrators, Executors, Guardians and Masters, 1868-1879; 1 volume.
Division of Estates, 1807-1868; 2 volumes.
Estates Records, 1753-1929; 166 Fibredex boxes.
Guardians' Records, 1769-1928; 10 Fibredex boxes.
Guardians' Accounts, 1849-1860; 1 volume.
Guardians' Bonds, 1870-1883, 1893-1952; 8 volumes.
Inventories and Accounts of Sale, 1849-1864; 4 volumes.
Clerk's Receiver Accounts, 1902-1919; 1 volume.
Record of Settlements, 1849-1903; 7 volumes.
Record of Probate (Estates), 1868-1896; 1 volume.
Fiduciary Account Book (Estate of Daniel Cress), 1823; 1 volume.

LAND RECORDS

Deeds and Land Records, 1753-1881; 1 Fibredex box.
Index to Deeds, Grantor, 1753-1921; 5 volumes.
Index to Deeds, Grantee, 1753-1921; 4 volumes.
Ejectments, 1791-1881; 1 Fibredex box.
Miscellaneous Land Records, 1753-1921; 1 Fibredex box.
Record of Probate of Deeds and Mortgages, 1884-1885; 1 volume.
Processioners' Returns, 1803-1824, 1879-1893; 2 volumes.

MARRIAGE, DIVORCE AND VITAL STATISTICS

Marriage Bonds, 1758-1868; 23 Fibredex boxes.
Register of Marriage Bonds, 1758-1866; 1 volume.
Divorce Records, 1805-1900; 4 Fibredex boxes.

MILITARY AND PENSION RECORDS

Military Records, 1781-1919; 2 Fibredex boxes.

MISCELLANEOUS RECORDS

Alien Registration, 1927, 1940; 1 volume.
Alien and Naturalization Records, 1823-1915; 1 Fibredex box.
Petitions for Naturalization, 1910-1914; 1 volume.
County Claims Allowed, 1805-1836; 1 volume.
County Trustees' Account Book, 1805-1826; 1 volume.
Treasurers' Account of General Fund, 1918-1920; 1 volume.

Minutes, Farmers Educational and Co-operative Union of America, 1915-1929; 1 volume.

Record of Jurors, 1905-1914; 1 volume.

Jury Lists, 1779-1913; 1 Fibredex box.

Orders and Decrees, 1896-1911; 1 volume.

Special Proceedings Docket, 1873-1909; 1 volume.

Minutes, Wardens of the Poor, 1818-1865; 2 volumes.

Wardens of the Poor, 1771-1871; 1 Fibredex box.

Miscellaneous Records, 1740-1940; 4 Fibredex boxes.

Mining Records, 1833-1909; 2 Fibredex boxes.

Persons Convicted and Sentenced to Chain Gang and Jail, 1908-1909; 1 volume.

OFFICIALS, COUNTY

Records of Justices of the Peace, 1778-1924; 1 volume, 1 Fibredex box.

ROADS AND BRIDGES

Record of Appointment of Road Overseers, 1824-1831; 1 volume.

Road Records and Reports, 1757-1913; 2 Fibredex boxes.

Treasurers' Account of Township Road Fund, 1919-1920; 1 volume.

Railroad Records, 1855-1915; 1 Fibredex box.

SCHOOL RECORDS

Treasurer's Account of Public School Fund, 1918-1919; 1 volume.

School Records, 1812-1906; 4 Fibredex boxes.

TAX AND FISCAL RECORDS

Lists of Taxables, 1802-1849; 4 volumes.

Tax Records, 1758-1910; 5 Fibredex boxes.

WILLS

Wills, 1743-1900; 27 Fibredex boxes.

Cross Index to Wills, 1761-1953; 3 volumes.

MICROFILM RECORDS

BONDS

Commissioners' Bonds, 1937-1944; 1 reel.

CORPORATIONS AND PARTNERSHIPS

Record of Corporations, 1904-1959; 3 reels.

Partnership Records, 1913-1962; 1 reel.

Index to Corporations, 1959-1968; 1 reel.

COURT RECORDS

County Court of Pleas and Quarter Sessions

Minutes, 1753-1868; 7 reels.

Abstracts of Minutes, 1753-1795; 1 reel.

Index to Abstracts of Minutes, 1753-1795; 1 reel.

Minutes, Probate Court, 1819-1822; 1 reel.

Superior Court

Minutes, 1820-1871, 1904-1942; 10 reels.

Equity Minutes, 1815-1820; 1 reel.

Equity Records, 1820-1844; 2 reels.

Index to Judgments, 1879-1927; 1 reel.

Clerk's Receipt Book, 1823-1861; 1 reel.

ELECTION RECORDS

Record of Elections, 1880-1948; 2 reels.

ESTATES RECORDS

Record of Accounts, 1908-1959; 9 reels.

Administrators' Bonds, 1823-1830, 1908-1914, 1927-1959; 3 reels.

Appointment of Administrators, Executors and Guardians, 1879; 1 reel.

Appointment of Administrators and Guardians, 1889-1909; 1 reel.

Record of Administrators, 1879-1959; 7 reels.

Record of Executors, 1926-1934; 1 reel.

Guardians' Bonds, 1764-1830, 1911-1918; 5 reels.

Record of Guardians, 1909-1959; 4 reels.

Division of Estates and Processioners' Returns, 1803-1842; 1 reel.

Record of Settlements, 1902-1959; 10 reels.

Record of Qualification of Trustees Under Wills, 1933-1956; 1 reel.

Index to Estates, 1952-1962; 1 reel.

LAND RECORDS

Record of Deeds, 1753-1962; 207 reels.

Index to Real Estate Conveyances, Grantor, 1753-1962; 18 reels.

Index to Real Estate Conveyances, Grantee, 1753-1962; 18 reels.

Land Entries, 1778-1925; 1 reel.

Federal Tax Lien Index, 1925-1962; 1 reel.

Processioners' Returns, 1803-1824; 1 reel.

Record of Sales by Mortgagees, Trustees and Executors, 1915-1959; 3 reels.

MARRIAGE, DIVORCE AND VITAL STATISTICS

Marriage Bonds, 1753-1868; 6 reels.

Marriage Bond Abstracts, 1753-1868; 2 reels.

Marriage Records, 1759-1867; 2 reels.

Marriage Registers, 1895-1962; 2 reels.

Record of Cohabitation, 1866; 1 reel.

Maiden Names of Divorced Women, 1937-1963; 1 reel.

Index to Births, 1913-1972; 3 reels.

Index to Deaths, 1913-1972; 2 reels.

MILITARY AND PENSION RECORDS

Record of Armed Forces Discharges, 1922-1968; 12 reels.

Index to Roster of Soldiers in the War of 1812, no date; 1 reel.

MISCELLANEOUS RECORDS

Alien Registration, 1927-1940; 1 reel.

Record of Lunacy, 1957-1970; 1 reel.

Orders and Decrees, 1935-1959; 2 reels.

Special Proceedings, 1879-1906, 1911-1959; 17 reels.

Index to Special Proceedings, Plaintiff, 1938-1970; 1 reel.

Index to Special Proceedings, Defendant, 1938-1970; 1 reel.

Wardens of the Poor, 1818-1865, 1878-1908; 1 reel.

Miscellaneous Historical Records, various dates; 1 reel.

OFFICIALS, COUNTY

Minutes, Board of County Commissioners, 1872-1958; 5 reels.

ROADS AND BRIDGES

Record of Road Overseers, 1824-1831; 1 reel.

SCHOOL RECORDS

Minutes, Board of Superintendents of Common Schools, 1847-1865; Minutes,
County Board of Education, 1877-1962; 2 reels.

TAX AND FISCAL RECORDS

Tax Lists, 1778, 1802-1892; 9 reels.

WILLS

Record of Wills, 1762-1951; 7 reels.

Cross Index to Wills, 1761-1959; 1 reel.

RUTHERFORD COUNTY

Established in 1779 from Tryon County.
Courthouse fire of 1907 destroyed many court records.

ORIGINAL RECORDS

BONDS
>Apprentice Bonds, 1872-1919; 2 volumes.
>
>Bastardy Bonds, 1872-1878; 1 volume.
>
>Officials' Bonds, 1880-1920; 1 Fibredex box.

COURT RECORDS
>County Court of Pleas and Quarter Sessions
>
>>Minutes, 1779-1868; 18 volumes, 1 manuscript box.
>>
>>Appearance Dockets, 1786-1792, 1843-1868; 1 volume,
>>>1 manuscript box.
>>
>>Execution Dockets, 1796-1868; 8 volumes.
>>
>>Levy Docket, 1844-1862; 1 volume.
>>
>>State Dockets, 1783-1793, 1800-1868; 4 volumes, 1 manuscript box.
>>
>>Trial Dockets, 1785-1792, 1843-1868; 3 volumes, 2 manuscript boxes.
>>
>>Trial and Appearance Dockets, 1792-1843; 6 volumes,
>>>2 manuscript boxes.
>
>Superior Court
>
>>Minutes, 1807-1911; 12 volumes.
>>
>>Equity Minutes (Orders and Decrees), 1839-1868; 1 volume.
>>
>>Equity Execution Docket, 1843-1868; 1 volume.
>>
>>Equity Trial and Appearance Docket, 1839-1868; 1 volume.
>>
>>Appearance Docket, 1855-1870; 1 volume.
>>
>>Execution Dockets, 1843-1860; 2 volumes.
>>
>>State Dockets, 1808-1821, 1831-1868; 4 volumes.
>>
>>Trial and Appearance Dockets, 1807-1859; 7 volumes.
>>
>>Trial Docket, 1860-1868; 1 volume.
>>
>>Civil Action Papers, 1783-1940; 23 Fibredex boxes.
>>
>>Civil Action Papers Concerning Land, 1870-1938; 20 Fibredex boxes.
>>
>>Civil Action Papers Concerning Mines, 1894-1917; 2 Fibredex boxes.
>>
>>Criminal Action Papers, 1868-1946; 8 Fibredex boxes.

ELECTION RECORDS
>Record of Elections, 1878-1917; 2 volumes.

ESTATES RECORDS
>Record of Estates, 1831-1868; 6 volumes.
>
>Administrators' Bonds, 1871-1896; 2 volumes.
>
>Estates Records, 1802-1968; 109 Fibredex boxes.
>
>Guardians' Records, 1851-1968; 24 Fibredex boxes.
>
>Guardians' Accounts, 1824-1868; 4 volumes.
>
>Guardians' Bonds, 1872-1911; 3 volumes.

LAND RECORDS

Record of Deeds, 1776-1810, 1817-1829; 20 volumes.

Deeds, 1794-1934; 3 Fibredex boxes.

Index to Deeds, [1776-1853]; 1 volume.

Land Entries, 1778-1898; 8 volumes.

Tax Levies on Land, 1896-1965; 6 Fibredex boxes.

Attachments, Executions, Liens and Levies on Land, 1858-1940;
1 Fibredex box.

Miscellaneous Land Records, 1768-1940; 2 Fibredex boxes.

MARRIAGE, DIVORCE AND VITAL STATISTICS

Marriage Bonds, 1774-1868; 11 Fibredex boxes.

Divorce Records, 1870-1940; 10 Fibredex boxes.

MILITARY AND PENSION RECORDS

Military Records, 1854-1937; 1 Fibredex box.

MISCELLANEOUS RECORDS

Alien Registration, 1940; 1 volume.

County Accounts, Claims and Correspondence, 1814, 1901-1938;
1 Fibredex box.

Homestead and Personal Property Exemptions, 1869-1934; 1 Fibredex box.

Inmate Register, County Home, 1914-1961; 1 volume.

Miscellaneous Records, 1784-1950; 4 Fibredex boxes.

Records of Assignees, Trustees and Receivers, 1888-1956; 5 Fibredex boxes.

ROADS AND BRIDGES

Road Dockets, 1803-1868; 3 volumes.

Railroad Records, 1876-1930; 6 Fibredex boxes.

SCHOOL RECORDS

School Records, 1880-1948; 1 Fibredex box.

WILLS

Wills, 1784-1968; 41 Fibredex boxes.

MICROFILM RECORDS

CORPORATIONS AND PARTNERSHIPS

Assumed Business Names, 1960-1963; 1 reel.

Record of Corporations, 1887-1965; 2 reels.

Partnership Records, 1908-1965; 1 reel.

COURT RECORDS

County Court of Pleas and Quarter Sessions
Minutes, 1779-1868; 5 reels.

Superior Court
Minutes, 1869-1939; 9 reels.

Minutes, Civil, 1939-1964; 3 reels.

Minutes, Criminal, 1939-1964; General Index to Criminal Minutes,
1939-1964; 2 reels.

ELECTION RECORDS
>Record of Elections, 1878-1964; 1 reel.

ESTATES RECORDS
>Record of Estates, 1831-1868; 2 reels.
>Record of Accounts, 1868-1964; 7 reels.
>Record of Administrators, 1896-1963; 5 reels.
>Appointment of Executors, 1868-1964; 1 reel.
>Record of Appointment of Receivers, Trustees and Executors, 1922-1934; 1 reel.
>Guardians' Bonds, 1872-1911; 1 reel.
>Record of Guardians, 1911-1964; 2 reels.
>Record of Widows' Year's Allowance, 1884-1964; 1 reel.
>Inheritance Tax Records, 1922-1964; 1 reel.
>Record of Settlements, 1868-1964; 5 reels.
>Index to Final Accounts, 1835-1964; 1 reel.

LAND RECORDS
>Record of Deeds, 1779-1965; 105 reels.
>Record of Deeds and Grants, 1796-1797; 1 reel.
>Index to Real Estate Conveyances, Grantor, 1779-1965; 10 reels.
>Index to Real Estate Conveyances, Grantee, 1779-1965; 10 reels.
>Record of Land Entries, 1898-1949; 1 reel.
>Federal Tax Lien Index, 1926-1949; 1 reel.
>Record of Sales by Mortgagees, 1921-1926; 1 reel.

MARRIAGE, DIVORCE AND VITAL STATISTICS
>Marriage Bonds, 1779-1868; 7 reels.
>Marriage Registers, 1851-1976; 3 reels.
>Maiden Names of Divorced Women, 1937-1964; 1 reel.
>Index to Births, 1914-1976; 2 reels.
>Index to Deaths, 1914-1976; 1 reel.
>Index to Delayed Births, various years; 1 reel.

MILITARY AND PENSION RECORDS
>Record of Armed Forces Discharges, 1918-1971; 9 reels.
>Index to Armed Forces Discharges, 1918-1965; 1 reel.

MISCELLANEOUS RECORDS
>Special Proceedings, 1868-1950; 10 reels.
>Index to Special Proceedings, Plaintiff, 1868-1964; 2 reels.
>Index to Special Proceedings, Defendant, 1868-1964; 2 reels.
>Index to Special Proceedings, 1968-1977; 1 reel.

OFFICIALS, COUNTY
>Minutes, Board of County Commissioners, 1868-1944; 7 reels.

SCHOOL RECORDS
>Minutes, County Board of Education, 1880-1922; 1 reel.

WILLS
>Record of Wills, 1782-1964; 6 reels.
>Cross Index to Wills, 1782-1964; 1 reel.

SAMPSON COUNTY

Established in 1784 from Duplin County.
Early court records are missing; losses may have been caused by
Federal sympathizers in 1865 and clerk's office fire of 1921.
Early deed books of Duplin County prior to 1784 are listed herein.

ORIGINAL RECORDS

BONDS
>   Bastardy Bonds and Records, 1835-1924; 2 Fibredex boxes.

COURT RECORDS
>   County Court of Pleas and Quarter Sessions
>>   Minutes, 1794-1868; 15 volumes.
>>   Appearance Dockets, 1821-1842, 1853-1868; 4 volumes.
>>   Execution Dockets, 1800-1868; 4 volumes.
>>   State Dockets, 1806-1868; 7 volumes.
>>   Trial and Appearance Dockets, 1784-1791, 1808-1814; 2 volumes.
>>   Trial Dockets, 1820-1868; 7 volumes.

>   Superior Court
>>   Minutes, 1814-1925; 23 volumes.
>>   Equity Minutes, 1807-1868; 2 volumes.
>>   Equity Execution Dockets, 1823-1868; 2 volumes.
>>   Equity Trial Dockets, 1816-1862; 2 volumes.
>>   Appearance Docket, 1858-1868; 1 volume.
>>   Execution Dockets, 1819-1832, 1858-1869; 2 volumes.
>>   State Dockets, 1832-1868; 3 volumes.
>>   Trial and Appearance Docket, 1809-1831; 1 volume.
>>   Trial Dockets, 1845-1869; 2 volumes.
>>   Civil Action Papers, 1790-1924; 20 Fibredex boxes.
>>   Civil Action Papers Concerning Land, 1791-1932; 13 Fibredex boxes.
>>   Criminal Action Papers, 1823-1934; 26 Fibredex boxes.

>   Inferior Court
>>   Minutes, 1881-1885; 1 volume.

ELECTION RECORDS
>   Record of Elections, 1878-1926; 3 volumes.

ESTATES RECORDS
>   Record of Estates, 1830-1849, 1855-1868; 8 volumes.
>   Record of Accounts, 1868-1909; 6 volumes.
>   Administrators' Bonds, 1854-1908; 4 volumes.
>   Estates Records, 1784-1923; 74 Fibredex boxes.
>   Guardians' Records, 1803-1918, 1929; 6 Fibredex boxes.
>   Guardians' Bonds, 1854-1907; 2 volumes.
>   Record of Settlements, 1869-1910; 2 volumes.

LAND RECORDS

Land Divisions, 1811-1927; 1 volume.

Record of Surveys, 1895-1911; 1 volume.

Attachments, Executions, Liens and Levies on Land, 1825-1920; 3 Fibredex boxes.

Miscellaneous Land Records, 1810-1928; 1 Fibredex box.

MARRIAGE, DIVORCE AND VITAL STATISTICS

Divorce Records, 1869-1921; 4 Fibredex boxes.

MISCELLANEOUS RECORDS

Alien Registration, 1927, 1940; 1 volume.

Petitions for Naturalization, 1911-1914; 1 volume.

County Claims Allowed, 1828-1852; 1 volume.

Homestead and Personal Property Exemptions, 1869-1923; 2 Fibredex boxes.

Special Proceedings, 1867-1906; 23 Fibredex boxes.

Minutes, Wardens of the Poor, 1785-1824; 1 volume.

Miscellaneous Records, 1798-1928; 4 Fibredex boxes.

Records of Assignees, Trustees and Receivers, 1856-1927; 5 Fibredex boxes.

ROADS AND BRIDGES

Record of Appointment of Road Overseers, 1829-1868; 3 volumes.

Railroad Records, 1869-1921; 4 Fibredex boxes.

TAX AND FISCAL RECORDS

Miscellaneous Tax Records, 1789-1922; 1 Fibredex box.

WILLS

Wills, 1778-1953; 20 Fibredex boxes.

MICROFILM RECORDS

COURT RECORDS

County Court of Pleas and Quarter Sessions
Minutes, 1794-1868; 5 reels.

Superior Court
Minutes, 1814-1944; 12 reels.

ELECTION RECORDS

Record of Elections, 1920-1964; 1 reel.

ESTATES RECORDS

Record of Estates, 1830-1849, 1855-1868; 3 reels.

Record of Accounts, 1868-1958; 10 reels.

Administrators' Bonds, 1908-1950; 5 reels.

Guardians' Bonds, 1907-1965; 3 reels.

Amounts Paid for Indigent Children, 1930-1937; 1 reel.

Inheritance Tax Records, 1924-1965; 1 reel.

Record of Settlements, 1869-1961; 7 reels.

Cross Index to Divisions and Sales of Estates, 1848-1927; 1 reel.

Cross Index to Guardians, 1854-1965; Index to Estates, various dates; 1 reel.

Index to Annual and Final Accounts, 1924-1937; 1 reel.

Index to Estates, 1925-1965; 1 reel.
LAND RECORDS
Record of Deeds, 1752-1958; 302 reels.

Cross Index to Real Estate Conveyances, 1754-1940; 15 reels.

Index to Real Estate Conveyances, Grantor, 1941-1965; 7 reels.

Index to Real Estate Conveyances, Grantee, 1941-1965; 7 reels.

Index to Real Estate Conveyances, Grantee: Trustees, 1962-1965; 1 reel.

Land Grants, 1770-1814; 2 reels.

Land Grants and Entries, 1789-1874; 1 reel.

Record of Surveys, 1895-1911; 1 reel.

Record of Resale, 1922-1957; 5 reels.

MARRIAGE, DIVORCE AND VITAL STATISTICS
Marriage Registers, 1867-1968; 2 reels.

Maiden Names of Divorced Women, 1939-1964; 1 reel.

Index to Births, 1913-1964; 2 reels.

Index to Deaths, 1913-1964; 1 reel.

Index to Delayed Births, various years; 1 reel.

MILITARY AND PENSION RECORDS
Record of Armed Forces Discharges, 1919-1989; 7 reels.

Index to Armed Forces Discharges, 1919-1965; 1 reel.

MISCELLANEOUS RECORDS
Orders and Decrees, 1867-1956; 18 reels.

Special Proceedings, 1868-1950; 2 reels.

Miscellaneous Orders and Decrees, and Appointment of Notaries Public and
    Railroad Policemen, 1913-1961; 1 reel.

Index to Special Proceedings, Plaintiff, 1867-1965; 1 reel.

Index to Special Proceedings, Defendant, 1867-1965; 1 reel.

Minutes, Wardens of the Poor, 1785-1824; 1 reel.

OFFICIALS, COUNTY
Minutes, Board of County Commissioners, 1868-1943; 5 reels.

SCHOOL RECORDS
Minutes, County Board of Education, 1895-1965; 1 reel.

TAX AND FISCAL RECORDS
Tax Lists, 1877-1893; 3 reels.

WILLS
Record of Wills, 1821-1965; 8 reels.

Record of Wills Not Probated, 1782-1964; 1 reel.

Index to Wills, 1820-1965; 2 reels.

SCOTLAND COUNTY

Established in 1899 from Richmond County.

ORIGINAL RECORDS

COURT RECORDS
    Superior Court
        Civil Action Papers, 1887-1955; 29 Fibredex boxes.
        Civil Action Papers Concerning Land, 1893-1951; 12 Fibredex boxes.
        Criminal Action Papers, 1891-1952; 9 Fibredex boxes.

ESTATES RECORDS
    Estates Records, 1887-1951; 43 Fibredex boxes.
    Guardians' Records, 1901-1951; 10 Fibredex boxes.

LAND RECORDS
    Deeds, 1903-1940; 1 Fibredex box.
    Land Sales for Taxes, 1923-1949; 2 Fibredex boxes.
    Petitions for Partition of Land, 1906-1943; 2 Fibredex boxes.
    Petitions for Sale of Land, 1901-1948; 1 Fibredex box.
    Miscellaneous Land Records, 1901-1955; 1 Fibredex box.

MARRIAGE, DIVORCE AND VITAL STATISTICS
    Marriage and Family Records, 1901-1951; 1 Fibredex box.
    Divorce Records, 1901-1948; 11 Fibredex boxes.

MISCELLANEOUS RECORDS
    Coroners' Inquests, 1902-1946; 5 Fibredex boxes.
    Miscellaneous Records, 1901-1955; 2 Fibredex boxes.
    Records of Assignees, Receivers and Trustees, 1901-1951; 5 Fibredex boxes.

ROADS AND BRIDGES
    Railroad Records, 1901-1939; 4 Fibredex boxes.

WILLS
    Wills, 1893, 1896, 1900-1937; 6 Fibredex boxes.

MICROFILM RECORDS

COURT RECORDS
    Superior Court
        Minutes, 1901-1959; 4 reels.

ELECTION RECORDS
    Record of Elections, 1904-1968; 1 reel.

ESTATES RECORDS
    Record of Accounts, 1901-1966; 4 reels.
    Appointment of Administrators and Guardians, 1901-1913; 1 reel.
    Record of Administrators, Executors and Guardians, 1913-1935; 1 reel.
    Record of Administrators, 1930-1966; 4 reels.
    Record of Executors and Guardians, 1935-1965; 1 reel.

Record of Executors, 1963-1966; 1 reel.

Record of Guardians and Trustees, 1965-1966; 1 reel.

Record of Accounts for Indigent Orphans, 1913-1941; 1 reel.

Orphans' Trust Fund, 1943-1965; 1 reel.

Inheritance Tax Records, 1920-1966; 2 reels.

Appointment of Receivers of Estates, 1928-1934; 1 reel.

Record of Settlements, 1901-1966; 5 reels.

Index to Estates, 1966-1970; 1 reel.

LAND RECORDS

Record of Deeds, 1900-1962; 32 reels.

Index to Deeds and Mortgages, Grantor, 1900-1970; 5 reels.

Index to Deeds and Mortgages, Grantee, 1900-1970; 3 reels.

Land Entry Books, 1900-1955; 1 reel.

Record of Grants, 1900-1950; 1 reel.

Index to Grants, 1900-1950; 1 reel.

Record of Resale of Land by Trustees and Mortgagees, 1916-1967; 1 reel.

MARRIAGE, DIVORCE AND VITAL STATISTICS

Marriage Licenses, 1900-1970; 4 reels.

Marriage Registers, 1900-1970; 1 reel.

Miscellaneous Marriage and Birth Records, various dates; 1 reel.

Maiden Names of Divorced Women, 1939-1966; 1 reel.

Index to Vital Statistics, 1913-1970; 3 reels.

Index to Delayed Births, various years; 1 reel.

MILITARY AND PENSION RECORDS

Record of Armed Forces Discharges, 1921-1978; 4 reels.

MISCELLANEOUS RECORDS

Clerk's Minute Dockets, 1907-1931; 1 reel.

Orders and Decrees, 1901-1966; 10 reels.

Special Proceedings, 1900-1966; 2 reels.

Index to Special Proceedings, 1900-1970; 1 reel.

Funeral Register, 1904-1914; 1 reel.

Record of Assignments, 1904-1918; 1 reel.

OFFICIALS, COUNTY

Minutes, Board of County Commissioners, 1900-1970; 4 reels.

ROADS AND BRIDGES

Minutes, County Board of Public Roads, 1904-1905; 1 reel.

TAX AND FISCAL RECORDS

Tax Scrolls, 1905, 1915, 1925, 1935, 1945, 1955, 1965; 2 reels.

WILLS

Record of Wills, 1898-1966; 3 reels.

Index to Wills, 1899-1966; 1 reel.

STANLY COUNTY

Established in 1841 from Montgomery County.
A few early court records are missing; reason unknown.

ORIGINAL RECORDS

BONDS
>   Apprentice Bonds, 1872-1938; 2 volumes.
>   Bastardy Bonds and Records, 1843-1923; 1 volume, 1 Fibredex box.
>   Officials' Bonds, 1848-1918; 2 volumes, 2 Fibredex boxes.

COURT RECORDS
>   County Court of Pleas and Quarter Sessions
>>   Minutes, 1841-1868; 5 volumes.
>>   Appearance (and Trial) Docket, 1841-1861; 1 volume.
>>   Execution Dockets, 1841-1868; 4 volumes.
>>   Trial Dockets, 1846-1868; 3 volumes.
>   Superior Court
>>   Minutes, 1841-1912; 8 volumes.
>>   Equity Minutes, 1841-1868; 1 volume.
>>   Equity Execution Docket, 1849-1869; 1 volume.
>>   Equity Trial and Appearance Docket, 1841-1868; 1 volume.
>>   Appearance Dockets, 1841-1883; 2 volumes.
>>   Execution Docket, 1842-1854; 1 volume.
>>   State Docket, 1856-1868; 1 volume.
>>   Criminal Issues Docket, 1869-1894; 1 volume.
>>   Trial Docket, 1868-1869; 1 volume.
>>   Civil Issues Docket, 1870-1899; 1 volume.
>>   Civil Action Papers, 1842-1917; 12 Fibredex boxes.
>>   Civil Action Papers Concerning Land, 1845-1941; 5 Fibredex boxes.
>>   Criminal Action Papers, 1841-1925; 18 Fibredex boxes.

ELECTION RECORDS
>   Record of Elections, 1878-1922; 4 volumes.

ESTATES RECORDS
>   Record of Estates, 1842-1869; 2 volumes.
>   Record of Accounts, 1868-1908; 3 volumes.
>   Administrators' Bonds, 1870-1917; 4 volumes.
>   Appointment of Administrators, Executors and Guardians, 1868-1903;
>>   1 volume.
>   Record of Administrators, 1899-1916; 1 volume.
>   Cross Index to Administrators, Executors and Guardians, 1868-1903;
>>   1 volume.
>   Estates Records, 1820, 1839-1952; 49 Fibredex boxes.
>   Guardians' Records, 1841-1941; 6 Fibredex boxes.
>   Guardians' Accounts and Returns, 1841-1870; 1 volume.

Guardians' Bonds, 1887-1912; 2 volumes.

Record of Settlements, 1868-1908; 1 volume.

LAND RECORDS

Record of Deeds, 1841-1847, 1854-1870; 3 volumes.

Deeds, 1857-1968; 6 Fibredex boxes.

Index to Deeds, [1841-1877]; 1 volume.

Ejectments, 1840-1866; 1 Fibredex box.

Land Entry Book, 1841-1932; 1 volume.

Record of Sales of Land, 1875-1899; 1 volume.

Attachments, Executions, Liens and Levies on Land, 1841-1927;
2 Fibredex boxes.

Miscellaneous Land Records, 1844-1963; 1 Fibredex box.

MARRIAGE, DIVORCE AND VITAL STATISTICS

Record of Marriage Licenses Issued, 1859-1905; 2 volumes.

Record of Marriages Performed by Ministers and Justices of the Peace, 1850-
1867; 1 volume.

Divorce Records, 1854-1920; 2 Fibredex boxes.

MISCELLANEOUS RECORDS

Alien Registration, 1959; 1 volume.

Petitions for Naturalization, 1921-1928; 1 volume.

County Accounts, 1841-1882; 1 volume.

County Claims Allowed, 1842-1861; 1 volume.

Registry of Licenses to Trades, 1874-1904; 1 volume.

Loyalty Oaths, 1865; 2 volumes.

Clerk's Minute Docket (Special Proceedings), 1869-1900; 1 volume.

Orders and Decrees, 1868-1887; 1 volume.

Minutes, Wardens of the Poor, 1849-1873; 2 volumes.

Miscellaneous Records, 1841-1965; 4 Fibredex boxes.

Records of Slaves and Free Persons of Color, 183_, 1843 -1868;
1 Fibredex box.

Records of Assignees, Trustees and Receivers, 1855-1913; 1 Fibredex box.

ROADS AND BRIDGES

Record of Appointment of Road Overseers, 1841-1860; 1 volume.

Road Records, 1842-1921; 1 Fibredex box.

Railroad Records, 1891-1917; 2 Fibredex boxes.

SCHOOL RECORDS

Common School Registers, 1858-1863; 2 volumes.

Report of the County Superintendent of Public Instruction, 1882-1891;
1 volume.

County School Account Book, 1894-1905; 1 volume.

School Fund Ledgers, 1910-1920; 3 volumes.

TAX AND FISCAL RECORDS

Lists of Taxables, 1840-1869; 3 volumes.

Poll Tax Record, 1912-1918; 1 volume.

Miscellaneous Tax Records, 1857-1912; 1 Fibredex box.

WILLS
    Wills, 1839-1927; 3 Fibredex boxes.

MICROFILM RECORDS

BONDS
    Apprentice Bonds, 1872-1938; 1 reel.
CORPORATIONS AND PARTNERSHIPS
    Record of Corporations, 1906-1948; 1 reel.
COURT RECORDS
    County Court of Pleas and Quarter Sessions
        Minutes, 1841-1868; 2 reels.
    Superior Court
        Minutes, 1841-1955; 12 reels.
        Equity Minutes, 1841-1868; 1 reel.
ELECTION RECORDS
    Record of Elections, 1878-1922, 1928-1964; 2 reels.
ESTATES RECORDS
    Record of Estates, 1841-1869; 1 reel.
    Record of Accounts, 1868-1968; 9 reels.
    Administrators' Bonds, 1870-1917; 1 reel.
    Appointment of Administrators, Executors and Guardians, 1914-1920; 1 reel.
    Record of Administrators, 1899-1968; 6 reels.
    Record of Executors, 1931-1967; 1 reel.
    Guardians' Accounts and Returns, 1841-1870; 1 reel.
    Guardians' Bonds, 1887-1912; 1 reel.
    Record of Guardians' Oaths and Bonds, 1930-1938, 1967-1968; 1 reel.
    Record of Guardians, 1924-1967; 2 reels.
    Clerk's Record of Monies Received for Payment to Minors, 1905-1921;
        1 reel.
    Inheritance Tax Records, 1923-1947; 1 reel.
    Accounts of Receivers of Estates, 1910-1927; 1 reel.
    Record of Settlements, 1841-1967; 10 reels.
    Cross Index to Administrators and Executors, 1868-1903; 1 reel.
    Index to Administrators, Executors and Guardians, 1915-1968; 1 reel.
LAND RECORDS
    Record of Deeds, 1841-1955; 89 reels.
    Index to Deeds, Grantor, 1841-1955; 6 reels.
    Index to Deeds, Grantee, 1841-1955; 7 reels.
    Land Entry Books, 1841-1939; 1 reel.
    Record of Resale of Land by Trustees and Mortgagees, 1920-1967; 2 reels.
MARRIAGE, DIVORCE AND VITAL STATISTICS
    Marriage Licenses, 1867-1967; 24 reels.
    Record of Marriages Performed by Ministers and Justices of the Peace, 1850-
        1867; 1 reel.

Marriage Registers, 1867-1968; 3 reels.

Maiden Names of Divorced Women, 1945-1968; 1 reel.

Index to Births and Delayed Births, 1913-1993; 3 reels.

Index to Deaths, 1913-1993; 2 reels.

MILITARY AND PENSION RECORDS

Record of Armed Forces Discharges, 1918-1920, 1943-1992; 10 reels.

Index to Armed Forces Discharges, 1918-1968; 1 reel.

MISCELLANEOUS RECORDS

Orders and Decrees, 1868-1950; 9 reels.

Special Proceedings, 1899-1961; 2 reels.

Index to Special Proceedings, Plaintiff, 1840-1967; 1 reel.

Index to Special Proceedings, Defendant, 1840-1967; 1 reel.

OFFICIALS, COUNTY

Minutes, Board of County Commissioners, 1868-1933; 3 reels.

ROADS AND BRIDGES

Road Overseers, 1841-1860; 1 reel.

SCHOOL RECORDS

Minutes, County Board of Education, 1885-1961; 1 reel.

TAX AND FISCAL RECORDS

Tax Lists, 1841-1869; 1 reel.

Tax Scrolls, 1872-1900, 1905, 1915; 6 reels.

WILLS

Record of Wills, 1841-1968; 5 reels.

Cross Index to Wills, 1841-1967; 1 reel.

STOKES COUNTY

Established in 1789 from Surry County.
A few court records are missing; reason unknown.

ORIGINAL RECORDS

BONDS

    Apprentice Bonds and Records, 1790-1909; 5 Fibredex boxes.

    Record of Apprentices and Masters, 1790-1817; 1 volume.

    Bastardy Bonds and Records, 1790-1932; 6 Fibredex boxes.

    Officials' Bonds and Records, 1790-1932; 8 Fibredex boxes.

    Tavern Bonds, 1795-1818; 1 Fibredex box.

COURT RECORDS

    County Court of Pleas and Quarter Sessions

        Minutes, 1790-1843, 1847-1868; 19 volumes.

        Appearance Dockets, 1804-1868; 8 volumes.

        Execution Dockets, 1790-1858; 18 volumes.

        Recognizance Dockets, 1824-1867; 5 volumes.

        State Dockets, 1790-1868; 12 volumes.

        Trial, Appearance and Reference Dockets, 1790-1804; 2 volumes,
            1 manuscript box.

        Trial and Reference Dockets, 1804-1847; 9 volumes.

        Trial Dockets, 1848-1868; 2 volumes.

        Clerk's Fee Docket, 1790-1811; 1 volume.

        Clerk's Receipt Book, 1859-1861; 1 volume.

    Superior Court

        Minutes, 1807-1846, 1878-1912; 10 volumes.

        Equity Minutes, 1849-1868; 1 volume.

        Equity Trial and Appearance Docket, 1849-1868; 1 volume.

        Equity Fee and Receipt Book, 1857-1871; 1 volume.

        Appearance Dockets, 1807-1834, 1855-1868; 2 volumes.

        Execution Dockets, 1815-1869, 1888-1899; 4 volumes,
            1 manuscript box.

        Recognizance Dockets, 1816-1858; 4 volumes.

        State Dockets, 1807-1815, 1835-1869; 3 volumes, 1 manuscript box.

        Trial and Reference Dockets, 1807-1857; 5 volumes.

        Clerk's Fee and Receipt Book, 1808-1828; 1 volume.

        Clerk's Account Book, 1905-1918; 1 volume.

        Civil Action Papers, 1782-1942; 69 Fibredex boxes.

        Civil Action Papers Concerning Land, 1791-1942; 16 Fibredex boxes.

        Criminal Action Papers, 1790-1944; 17 Fibredex boxes.

    Inferior Court

        Minutes, 1878-1885; 1 volume.

ELECTION RECORDS
> Election Records, 1790-1932; 7 Fibredex boxes.

ESTATES RECORDS
> Record of Estates, 1790-1849, 1861-1869; 15 volumes.
>
> Administrators' Bonds, 1886-1908; 2 volumes.
>
> Record of Administrators, 1790-1817; 1 volume.
>
> Estates Records, 1753-1941; 118 Fibredex boxes.
>
> Guardians' Records, 1790-1933; 6 Fibredex boxes.
>
> Record of Guardians, 1790-1821; 1 volume.
>
> Guardians' Bonds, 1872-1894; 1 volume.
>
> Record of Inheritance Tax, 1920-1925; 1 volume.
>
> Clerk's Receiver Accounts, 1886-1902; 1 volume.
>
> Record of Settlements, 1869-1912; 2 volumes.

LAND RECORDS
> Deeds, 1760-1929; 1 Fibredex box.
>
> Ejectments, 1791-1915, 1936; 3 Fibredex boxes.
>
> Land Entries, 1790-1798, 1809-1926; 3 volumes.
>
> Land Grants and Entries, 1779-1924; 1 Fibredex box.
>
> Clerk's Deed Book (Land Sold for Taxes), 1813-1816; 1 volume.
>
> Land Sold for Taxes, 1828, 1927-1941; 7 Fibredex boxes.
>
> Attachments, Executions, Levies and Liens on Land, Personal Property and Slaves, 1790-1934; 27 Fibredex boxes.
>
> Miscellaneous Land Records, 1784-1932; 1 Fibredex box.
>
> Petitions for Partition and to Sell Land, 1861, 1873-1911, 1935; 1 Fibredex box.
>
> Sales of Land Under Deeds of Trust, 1916-1925; 1 volume.

MARRIAGE, DIVORCE AND VITAL STATISTICS
> Marriage Bonds, 1790-1868; 38 manuscript boxes.
>
> Record of Marriage Certificates, 1851-1873; 2 volumes.
>
> Marriage Registers, 1873-1909; 2 volumes.
>
> Index to Marriage Licenses, 1868-1869; 1 volume.
>
> Record of Cohabitation and Negro Marriages, 1866-1873; 1 volume.
>
> Divorce Records, 1816-1941; 8 Fibredex boxes.

MILITARY AND PENSION RECORDS
> Military and Pension Records, 1779-1913; 1 Fibredex box.

MISCELLANEOUS RECORDS
> County Claims, 1790-1868; 4 volumes, 7 Fibredex boxes.
>
> County Claims Allowed, 1822-1844, 1866, 1910-1927; 3 volumes.
>
> County Trustee Account Books, 1811-1868; 3 volumes.
>
> Record of Bills of Sale, Powers of Attorney and Bonds, 1801-1841; 1 volume.
>
> Grand Jury Records and Presentments, 1790-1915; 1 Fibredex box.
>
> Insolvent Debtors and Homestead and Personal Property Exemptions, 1790-1931; 2 Fibredex boxes.
>
> Jury Records, 1790-1868; 1 Fibredex box.
>
> Lunacy Records, 1794-1931; 2 Fibredex boxes.

Marks, Brands and Strays, 1789-1861; 1 volume, 1 Fibredex box.
Merchants' Purchase Returns, 1873-1899; 3 Fibredex boxes.
Miscellaneous Records, 1781-1932; 4 Fibredex boxes.
Coroners' Inquests and Records, 1805-1916; 1 Fibredex box.
Personal Accounts, 1791-1864; 1 Fibredex box.
Returns of Fees, Fines and Forfeitures, 1810-1851, 1879-1927; 4 volumes.
Slave Records, 1806-1860; 1 Fibredex box.
Records of Assignees, Receivers and Trustees, 1896-1942; 3 Fibredex boxes.

OFFICIALS, COUNTY
Minutes, Board of County Commissioners, 1871-1909; 4 volumes.

ROADS AND BRIDGES
Record of Appointment of Road Overseers, 1806-1867; 4 volumes.
Minutes, Board of Road Commissioners of Quaker Gap Township, 1919-
1921; 1 volume.
Road and Bridge Records, 1790-1943; 1 volume, 10 Fibredex boxes.
Railroad Records, 1887-1934; 1 Fibredex box.

SCHOOL RECORDS
Minutes, County Board of Education and Accounts of School Fund, 1872-
1903; 2 volumes.
School Records, 1840-1939; 6 Fibredex boxes.

TAX AND FISCAL RECORDS
Lists of Taxables, 1790-1863; 9 volumes.
Tax Scrolls, 1929, 1931; 2 volumes.
Tax Records, 1790-1927; 10 Fibredex boxes.
Assessment of Real Property for Taxation, 1799; 1 volume.

WILLS
Wills, 1775-1925; 18 Fibredex boxes.

MICROFILM RECORDS

BONDS
Apprentice Bonds, 1790-1817; 1 reel.

CORPORATIONS AND PARTNERSHIPS
Record of Corporations, 1887-1965; 1 reel.
Partnership Records, 1913-1965; 1 reel.

COURT RECORDS
County Court of Pleas and Quarter Sessions
Minutes, 1790-1868; 5 reels.
Superior Court
Minutes, 1807-1846, 1878-1940; 6 reels.

ELECTION RECORDS
Record of Elections, 1926-1964; 1 reel.

ESTATES RECORDS
Record of Estates, 1790-1849, 1861-1869; 5 reels.
Record of Accounts, 1914-1965; 4 reels.

Appointment of Administrators, Executors and Guardians, 1868-1935; 1 reel.
Record of Administrators and Guardians, 1919-1939; 1 reel.
Record of Administrators, 1929-1965; 2 reels.
Record of Executors, 1936-1965; 2 reels.
Record of Guardians, 1941-1945; 1 reel.
Guardians' Accounts, 1930-1965; 1 reel.
Estates Not Exceeding $300, 1932-1959; 1 reel.
Inheritance Tax Records, 1931-1965; 1 reel.
Record of Settlements, 1846-1857, 1869-1960; 3 reels.
Index to Administrators, 1790-1817; 1 reel.
Index to Final Accounts, 1869-1965; 2 reels.

LAND RECORDS
Record of Deeds, 1788-1960; 94 reels.
Index to Real Estate Conveyances, Grantor, 1787-1962; 4 reels.
Index to Real Estate Conveyances, Grantee, 1787-1962; 4 reels.

MARRIAGE, DIVORCE AND VITAL STATISTICS
Marriage Bonds, 1790-1868; 10 reels.
Marriage Bond Abstracts, 1790-1868; 1 reel.
Marriage Licenses, 1839-1961; 9 reels.
Marriage Registers, 1851-1955; 3 reels.
Index to Marriages, 1956-1965; 1 reel.
Maiden Names of Divorced Women, 1937-1965; 1 reel.
Index to Births, 1913-1994; 2 reels.
Index to Deaths, 1913-1995; 1 reel.
Index to Delayed Births, various years; 1 reel.

MILITARY AND PENSION RECORDS
Record of Armed Forces Discharges, 1942-1970; 1 reel.
Index to Armed Forces Discharges, 1919-1981; 1 reel.

MISCELLANEOUS RECORDS
Orders and Decrees, 1869-1952; 8 reels.

OFFICIALS, COUNTY
Minutes, Board of County Commissioners, 1871-1943; 4 reels.

TAX AND FISCAL RECORDS
Lists of Taxables, 1790-1863; 3 reels.
Tax Lists, 1933, 1945; 2 reels.
Property Valuations, 1799; 1 reel.

WILLS
Record of Wills, 1790-1965; 4 reels.
Index to Wills, Devisor, 1790-1970; 1 reel.
Index to Wills, Devisee, 1790-1970; 1 reel.

SURRY COUNTY

Established in 1770 (effective 1771) from Rowan County.

ORIGINAL RECORDS

BONDS

 Apprentice Bonds and Records, 1779-1921; 1 Fibredex box.

 Bastardy Bonds and Records, 1782-1928; 1 Fibredex box.

 Officials' Bonds and Records, 1777-1893; 1 Fibredex box.

COURT RECORDS

 County Court of Pleas and Quarter Sessions

  Minutes, 1778-1867; 21 volumes, 6 manuscript boxes.

  Appearance Dockets, 1811-1868; 5 volumes.

  Execution Dockets, 1772-1857; 14 volumes.

  State Dockets, 1786-1796, 1808-1855; 6 volumes.

  Trial, Appearance and Reference Dockets, 1774-1805; 6 volumes.

  Trial and Reference Dockets, 1811-1827, 1836-1861; 7 volumes.

  Trial Docket, 1861-1868; 1 volume.

  Prosecution Bond Docket, 1788-1801; 1 volume.

 Superior Court

  Minutes, 1807-1863, 1866-1910; 14 volumes.

  Equity Minutes, 1855-1867; 1 volume.

  Equity Trial Dockets, 1819-1867; 2 volumes.

  Appearance Dockets, 1807-1867; 2 volumes.

  Execution Dockets, 1808-1844; 2 volumes.

  Recognizance Dockets, 1815-1841; 2 volumes.

  State Dockets, 1807-1848; 4 volumes.

  Trial and Reference Dockets, 1807-1867; 3 volumes,
   1 manuscript box.

  Witness Docket, 1827-1839; 1 volume.

  Miscellaneous Dockets, 1806-1872; 1 manuscript box.

  Civil Action Papers, 1770-1929; 16 Fibredex boxes.

  Civil Action Papers Concerning Land, 1778-1928; 7 Fibredex boxes.

  Criminal Action Papers, 1770-1928; 21 Fibredex boxes.

ELECTION RECORDS

 Record of Elections, 1878-1920; 4 volumes.

 Poll Books, 1878-1894, 1916-1950; 4 manuscript boxes.

 Voter Registration Books, 1896-1950; 3 manuscript boxes.

ESTATES RECORDS

 Record of Estates, 1784-1868; 10 volumes.

 Record of Accounts, 1868-1909; 5 volumes.

 Administrators' Bonds, 1876-1915; 1 volume, 2 manuscript boxes.

 Estates Records, 1771-1943; 75 Fibredex boxes.

 Guardians' Records, 1784-1935; 5 Fibredex boxes.

Guardians' Bonds, 1879-1903; 1 volume, 1 manuscript box.

Record of Settlements, 1868-1913; 2 volumes.

Record of Probate (Estates), 1868-1902, 1918; 1 volume.

LAND RECORDS

Record of Deeds, 1774-1780; 1 volume.

Deeds, 1774-1902; 5 Fibredex boxes.

Deeds of Trust, 1791-1910; 2 Fibredex boxes.

Ejectments, 1798-1905; 1 Fibredex box.

Land Entries, 1778-1875; 4 volumes.

Land Grants, 1782-1877; 1 Fibredex box.

Levies, Executions and Attachments, 1772-1930; 3 Fibredex boxes.

Miscellaneous Land Records, 1778-1922; 1 Fibredex box.

Record of Processioners, 1801-1887; 1 volume.

MARRIAGE, DIVORCE AND VITAL STATISTICS

Marriage Bonds, 1778-1868; 34 manuscript boxes.

Record of Marriage Certificates, 1853-1867; 1 volume.

Marriage Registers, 1867-1940; 8 volumes.

Divorce Records, 1826-1927; 2 Fibredex boxes.

MISCELLANEOUS RECORDS

Alien Registration, 1927, 1940; 1 volume.

Declaration of Intent (to Become a Citizen), 1911-1925; 1 volume.

Petitions for Naturalization, 1910-1928; 1 volume.

Insolvent Debtors and Homestead and Personal Property Exemptions, 1784-
1911; 2 Fibredex boxes.

Clerk's Minute Dockets (Special Proceedings), 1869-1874, 1877-1908;
3 volumes.

Orders and Decrees, 1868-1914; 2 volumes.

Cross Index to Special Proceedings, no date; 2 volumes.

Minutes, Wardens of the Poor, 1852-1877; 1 volume.

Miscellaneous Records, 1771-1928; 6 Fibredex boxes.

Record of Assignments, 1894-1897; 1 volume.

Record of Trustees, 1897-1901; 1 volume.

OFFICIALS, COUNTY

Minutes, Board of County Commissioners, 1881-1884; 1 Fibredex box.

ROADS AND BRIDGES

Appointment of Road Overseers, 1807-1869; 4 volumes.

Road Records, 1772-1931; 2 Fibredex boxes.

TAX AND FISCAL RECORDS

Lists of Taxables, 1815-1866; 5 volumes.

Tax Records, 1775-1888; 6 Fibredex boxes.

WILLS

Record of Wills, 1789-1901; 7 volumes.

Wills, 1770-1922; 9 Fibredex boxes.

Cross Index to Wills, 1772-1934; 1 volume.

MICROFILM RECORDS

CORPORATIONS AND PARTNERSHIPS
  Record of Corporations, 1886-1953; 2 reels.
COURT RECORDS
  County Court of Pleas and Quarter Sessions
    Minutes, 1779-1867; 4 reels.
    Prosecution Bond Docket, 1788-1801; 1 reel.
  Superior Court
    Minutes, 1807-1849, 1870-1940; 9 reels.
    Equity Minutes, 1855-1867; 1 reel.
ELECTION RECORDS
  Record of Elections, 1878-1898; 1 reel.
ESTATES RECORDS
  Record of Estates, 1792-1831, 1845-1868; 2 reels.
  Record of Accounts, 1868-1959; 8 reels.
  Administrators' Bonds, 1876-1958; 5 reels.
  Guardians' Bonds, 1879-1963; 3 reels.
  Accounts of Indigent Orphans, 1907-1937; 1 reel.
  Inheritance Tax Records, 1923-1963; 1 reel.
  Record of Inventories and Accounts of Sale, 1784-1845; 2 reels.
  Record of Inventories and Guardians' Returns, 1845-1883; 1 reel.
  Record of Petitions for Dower and Partition of Land, 1830-1874; 1 reel.
  Record of Settlements, 1869-1963; 6 reels.
  Index to Inventories, Accounts and Settlements, 1868-1970; 1 reel.
LAND RECORDS
  Record of Deeds, 1771-1939; 72 reels.
  Cross Index to Real Estate Conveyances, 1771-1879; 1 reel.
  Index to Real Estate Conveyances, Grantor, 1878-1957; 5 reels.
  Index to Real Estate Conveyances, Grantee, 1878-1957; 5 reels.
  Land Entries, 1778-1795, 1817-1883; 2 reels.
  Processioners' Book, 1801-1877; 1 reel.
  Federal Tax Lien Index, 1928-1963; 1 reel.
  Plat Books, 1920-1959; 2 reels.
  Resale of Land Sold by Mortgagees and Trustees, 1924-1944; 1 reel.
MARRIAGE, DIVORCE AND VITAL STATISTICS
  Marriage Bonds, 1780-1868; 5 reels.
  Marriage Licenses, 1868-1961; 11 reels.
  Marriage Registers, 1853-1940; 3 reels.
  Index to Marriage Registers, 1853-1977; 2 reels.
  Maiden Names of Divorced Women, 1939-1963; 1 reel.
  Index to Births, 1913-1994; 2 reels.
  Index to Deaths, 1909-1994; 2 reels.
  Index to Delayed Births, various years; 1 reel.

MILITARY AND PENSION RECORDS

Record of Armed Forces Discharges, 1919-1977; 8 reels.

Index to Armed Forces Discharges, 1901-1994; 1 reel.

MISCELLANEOUS RECORDS

Lunacy Records, 1899-1963; 2 reels.

Orders and Decrees, 1868-1970; 8 reels.

Special Proceedings, 1877-1970; 3 reels.

Special Proceedings Judgments, 1915-1963; 1 reel.

Index to Special Proceedings, Orders and Decrees, and Special Proceedings Judgments, Plaintiff, 1868-1970; 1 reel.

Index to Special Proceedings, Orders and Decrees, and Special Proceedings Judgments, Defendant, 1868-1970; 1 reel.

Record of Assignments, 1894-1906; 1 reel.

OFFICIALS, COUNTY

Minutes, Board of County Commissioners, 1869-1951; 4 reels.

Minutes, County Board of Health, 1944-1963; 1 reel.

Minutes, County Board of Social Services, 1937-1963; 1 reel.

ROADS AND BRIDGES

Appointment of Road Overseers, 1833-1858; 1 reel.

SCHOOL RECORDS

Minutes, County Board of Education, 1941-1963; 1 reel.

WILLS

Record of Wills, 1771-1961; 6 reels.

Index to Wills, Devisor, 1771-1970; 1 reel.

Index to Wills, Devisee, 1771-1970; 1 reel.

SWAIN COUNTY

Established in 1871 from Jackson and Macon counties.
Courthouse fire of 1879 destroyed many records.

ORIGINAL RECORDS

BONDS
>Apprentice Bonds, 1873-1918; 2 volumes.
>Bastardy Bonds, 1871-1880; 1 volume.

COURT RECORDS
>Superior Court
>>Minutes, 1871-1907; 7 volumes.

ELECTION RECORDS
>Record of Elections, 1878-1912; 2 volumes.

ESTATES RECORDS
>Administrators' Bonds, 1873-1908; 1 volume.
>Guardians' Bonds, 1871-1910; 1 volume.

LAND RECORDS
>Record of Deeds and Grants, 1872-1878; 2 volumes.
>Cross Index to Deeds, 1872-1913; 5 volumes.
>Land Entries, 1871-1944; 1 volume.
>Probate of Deeds, 1885-1891; 1 volume.

MISCELLANEOUS RECORDS
>Citizenship Records, 1894; 1 manuscript box.
>Record of Strays, 1885-1937; 1 volume.

MICROFILM RECORDS

BONDS
>Apprentice Bonds, 1873-1918; 1 reel.

CORPORATIONS AND PARTNERSHIPS
>Record of Incorporations, 1884-1970; 1 reel.
>Record of Partnerships, 1913-1915; 1 reel.

COURT RECORDS
>Superior Court
>>Minutes, 1871-1949; 8 reels.
>>Judgment Docket, Tax Suits, 1932-1933; 1 reel.

ELECTION RECORDS
>Record of Elections, 1878-1968; 1 reel.

ESTATES RECORDS
>Record of Accounts, 1877-1970; 2 reels.
>Administrators' Bonds, 1873-1908; 1 reel.
>Record of Administrators, Executors and Guardians, 1908-1927; 1 reel.
>Record of Administrators, 1919-1966; 1 reel.

Guardians' Bonds, 1871-1910; 1 reel.

Record of Guardians, 1925-1966; 1 reel.

Inheritance Tax Records, 1925-1967; 1 reel.

Record of Settlements, 1920-1937; 1 reel.

LAND RECORDS

Record of Deeds, 1872-1958; 39 reels.

Index to Deeds, Grantor, 1872-1970; 4 reels.

Index to Deeds, Grantee, 1872-1970; 5 reels.

Land Entry Books, 1872-1944; 1 reel.

Cross Index to Grants, 1872-1917; 1 reel.

Record of Surveys, 1905-1924; 1 reel.

Right-of-Way Easements, 1953-1961; 1 reel.

State Highway Commission Right-of-Way Plans, 1968; 1 reel.

Record of Sales by Mortgagees, Trustees and Executors, 1921-1966; 1 reel.

Land Sales Book, 1931-1932; 1 reel.

Record of Taxes for Mortgagees, 1931-1932; 1 reel.

MARRIAGE, DIVORCE AND VITAL STATISTICS

Marriage Registers, 1871-1959; 2 reels.

Maiden Names of Divorced Women, 1940-1966; 1 reel.

Index to Delayed Births, various years; 1 reel.

MILITARY AND PENSION RECORDS

Record of Armed Forces Discharges, 1917-1970, various years; 3 reels.

MISCELLANEOUS RECORDS

Record of Lunacy, 1909-1917; 1 reel.

Clerk's Minute Docket, 1908-1909; 1 reel.

Orders and Decrees, 1873-1908; 1 reel.

Special Proceedings, 1883-1966; 3 reels.

Cross Index to Special Proceedings, 1913-1966; 1 reel.

OFFICIALS, COUNTY

Minutes, Board of County Commissioners, 1871-1970; 5 reels.

SCHOOL RECORDS

Minutes, County Board of Education, 1908-1970; 2 reels.

TAX AND FISCAL RECORDS

Tax List, 1915; 1 reel.

WILLS

Record of Wills, 1873-1966; 1 reel.

Cross Index to Wills, 1873-1966; 1 reel.

TRANSYLVANIA COUNTY

Established in 1861 from Henderson and Jackson counties.

ORIGINAL RECORDS

BONDS
>   Apprentice Bonds, 1879-1906; 1 volume.
>   Bastardy Bonds, 1879-1880; 1 volume.

COURT RECORDS
>   County Court of Pleas and Quarter Sessions
>> Minutes, 1861-1868; 1 volume.
>> State Docket, 1861-1868; 1 volume.
>> Trial and Appearance Docket, 1861-1868; 1 volume.
>   Superior Court
>> Minutes, 1867-1910; 8 volumes.
>> Equity Minutes, 1864-1867; 1 volume.
>> State Docket, 1862-1867; 1 volume.
>> Civil Action Papers, 1850-1932; 1 Fibredex box.
>> Civil Action Papers Concerning Land, 1862-1932; 3 Fibredex boxes.
>> Criminal Action Papers, 1862-1921; 1 Fibredex box.

ELECTION RECORDS
>   Record of Elections, 1874-1926; 3 volumes.
>   Registration Books, 1902-1934; 17 volumes.

ESTATES RECORDS
>   Record of Estates, 1861-1916, 1931; 2 volumes.
>   Administrators' Bonds, 1876-1916; 2 volumes.
>   Estates Records, 1810-1951; 20 Fibredex boxes.
>   Guardians' Records, 1852-1925; 11 Fibredex boxes.
>   Guardians' Bonds, 1876-1917; 2 volumes.
>   Record of Guardians, 1863-1918; 3 volumes.
>   Record of Settlements, 1880-1936; 2 volumes.
>   Record of Probate (Estates), 1875-1899; 1 volume.

LAND RECORDS
>   Record of Deeds, 1861-1885; 4 volumes.
>   Deeds, 1827-1923; 2 Fibredex boxes.
>   Land Entry Books, 1865-1883, 1888-1917; 2 volumes.
>   Record of Probate of Chattel Mortgages and Mortgage Deeds, 1882-1889;
>>   1 volume.
>   Record of Probate of Deeds, 1861-1889; 2 volumes.
>   Attachments, Executions, Levies and Liens on Land, 1863-1931;
>>   3 Fibredex boxes.
>   Miscellaneous Land Records, 1854-1925; 2 Fibredex boxes.

MARRIAGE, DIVORCE AND VITAL STATISTICS
>   Marriage Bonds, 1861-1868; 1 manuscript box.

314

Record of Marriages, 1861-1872; 1 volume.
Marriage Registers, 1872-1934; 2 volumes.
Divorce Records, 1866-1921; 2 Fibredex boxes.

MISCELLANEOUS RECORDS
Miscellaneous Records, 1864-1926; 3 Fibredex boxes.

ROADS AND BRIDGES
Railroad Records, 1900-1918; 1 Fibredex box.

SCHOOL RECORDS
School Records, 1881-1927; 1 Fibredex box.

WILLS
Wills, 1838-1926; 2 Fibredex boxes.
Cross Index to Wills, 1879-1949; 1 volume.

MICROFILM RECORDS

BONDS
Apprentice Bonds, 1879-1906; 1 reel.
Bastardy Bonds, 1879-1880; 1 reel.

CORPORATIONS AND PARTNERSHIPS
Record of Corporations, 1903-1945; 1 reel.
Record of Partnerships, 1913-1970; 1 reel.

COURT RECORDS
County Court of Pleas and Quarter Sessions
Minutes, 1861-1868; Minutes, Board of County Commissioners, 1868-
1874; 1 reel.
Superior Court
Minutes, 1867-1950; 9 reels.
Equity Minutes, 1864-1867; 1 reel.
General Index to Minutes, Defendant, 1920-1968; 2 reels.
General Index to Minutes, Plaintiff, 1920-1950; 1 reel.
Tax Judgment Dockets, 1929-1948, 1962-1969; 2 reels.
General County Court
Minutes, 1913-1932; 1 reel.

ELECTION RECORDS
Record of Elections, 1874-1904, 1938-1968; 2 reels.

ESTATES RECORDS
Record of Estates, 1861-1888; 1 reel.
Record of Accounts, 1861-1968; 4 reels.
Record of Accounts and Probate Matters, 1875-1899; 1 reel.
Administrators' Bonds, 1876-1916; 1 reel.
Record of Administrators, Executors and Guardians, 1916-1941; 1 reel.
Record of Administrators, 1929-1968; 2 reels.
Record of Executors, 1941-1968; 1 reel.
Guardians' Bonds, 1876-1917; 1 reel.
Record of Guardians, 1863-1968; 2 reels.

Record of Amounts Paid for Indigent Children, 1916-1964; 1 reel.

Inheritance Tax Records, 1923-1968; 1 reel.

Record of Settlements, 1880-1968; 3 reels.

Cross Index to Administrators and Executors, 1862-1968; 1 reel.

Cross Index to Guardians, 1866-1968; 1 reel.

Index to Estates, 1960-1970; 1 reel.

LAND RECORDS

Record of Deeds, 1861-1958; 53 reels.

General Index to Deeds, Grantor, 1861-1970; 14 reels.

General Index to Deeds, Grantee, 1861-1970; 13 reels.

Land Entry Books, 1865-1959; 1 reel.

Record of Surveys, 1906-1959; 1 reel.

Record of Sales and Resales, 1921-1968; 2 reels.

MARRIAGE, DIVORCE AND VITAL STATISTICS

Marriage Bonds, 1861-1865; 1 reel.

Marriage Licenses, 1901-1970; 3 reels.

Marriage Registers, 1861-1970; 1 reel.

Maiden Names of Divorced Women, 1954-1968; 1 reel.

Index to Births, 1913-1969; 1 reel.

Index to Deaths, 1913-1969; 1 reel.

MILITARY AND PENSION RECORDS

Record of Armed Forces Discharges, 1918-1979; 5 reels.

MISCELLANEOUS RECORDS

Orders and Decrees, 1878-1966; 1 reel.

Special Proceedings, 1884-1956; 6 reels.

Cross Index to Special Proceedings, 1884-1968; 1 reel.

OFFICIALS, COUNTY

Minutes, Board of County Commissioners, 1868-1970; Minutes, Court of
Pleas and Quarter Sessions, 1861-1868; 5 reels.

TAX AND FISCAL RECORDS

Tax Scrolls, 1876, 1877, 1889, 1897, 1905; 1 reel.

WILLS

Record of Wills, 1879-1968; 3 reels.

Cross Index to Wills, 1879-1968; 1 reel.

TRYON COUNTY

Established in 1768 (effective 1769) from Mecklenburg County.
Divided into Lincoln and Rutherford counties in 1779.

ORIGINAL RECORDS

COURT RECORDS
> County Court of Pleas and Quarter Sessions
>> Minutes, 1769-1779; 2 volumes.
>> Trial, Appearance and Reference Docket, 1772-1778; 1 volume.

LAND RECORDS
> Record of Deeds, 1769-1779; 8 volumes.

MISCELLANEOUS RECORDS
> Miscellaneous Records, 1765-1783; 1 manuscript box.

MICROFILM RECORDS

COURT RECORDS
> County Court of Pleas and Quarter Sessions
>> Minutes, 1769-1782; 1 reel.
>> Trial, Appearance and Reference Docket, 1772-1778; 1 reel.

LAND RECORDS
> Record of Deeds, 1769-1779; 2 reels.

MISCELLANEOUS RECORDS
> Miscellaneous Records, 1765-1788; 1 reel.

TYRRELL COUNTY

Established in 1729 from Bertie, Chowan, Currituck and
Pasquotank precincts as a precinct of Albemarle County.
A few of the early records are missing; reason unknown.

ORIGINAL RECORDS

BONDS
>Apprentice Bonds and Records, 1742, 1780-1886; 1 volume,
>>2 Fibredex boxes.
>Bastardy Bonds and Records, 1793-1879; 2 Fibredex boxes.
>Officials' Bonds and Records, 1756-1900; 4 Fibredex boxes.

COURT RECORDS
>County Court of Pleas and Quarter Sessions
>>Minute Dockets, 1735-1834, 1841-1868; 17 volumes,
>>>1 manuscript box.
>>Appearance Dockets, 1852-1868; 2 volumes.
>>Execution Dockets, 1756-1866; 9 volumes, 1 manuscript box.
>>Levy Docket, 1838-1844; 1 volume.
>>State Dockets, 1762-1828, 1856-1859; 1 manuscript box.
>>Trial, Appearance and Reference Dockets, 1754-1798;
>>>2 manuscript boxes.
>>Trial and Appearance Dockets, 1798-1855; 7 volumes,
>>>1 manuscript box.
>>Trial Dockets, 1855-1868; 2 volumes, 1 manuscript box.
>>Clerk's Recording Docket, 1756-1762; 1 volume.
>Superior Court
>>Minute Dockets, 1807-1883; 4 volumes, 1 manuscript box.
>>Equity Minute Docket, 1852-1859, 1866-1868; 1 volume.
>>Execution Dockets, 1808-1862, 1867, 1869; 2 volumes.
>>State Dockets, 1815-1864, 1867-1869, 1874-1895, 1899-1905;
>>>3 volumes.
>>Trial and Appearance Dockets, 1816-1864; 2 volumes.
>>Bench Docket, 1816-1840; 1 volume.
>>Civil Action Papers, 1741-1899; 37 Fibredex boxes.
>>Criminal Action Papers, 1736-1898; 17 Fibredex boxes.

ELECTION RECORDS
>Record of Elections, 1878-1968; 5 volumes.

ESTATES RECORDS
>Record of Estates, 1802-1869; 4 volumes.
>Administrators' Bonds, 1904-1924; 1 volume.
>Appointment of Administrators, Executors, Guardians and Masters, 1868-
>>1878; 1 manuscript box.
>Estates Records, 1739-1895; 38 Fibredex boxes.

Guardians' Records, 1754-1895; 3 Fibredex boxes.

Guardians' Bonds, 1859-1868; 1 manuscript box.

Fiduciary Account Book, 1758-1775; Account Book of Dr. J. H. Ellis, 1819-1828; 1 volume.

LAND RECORDS

Record of Deeds, 1736-1819; 12 volumes.

Deeds, 1744-1897; 2 Fibredex boxes.

Ejectments, 1787-1898; 2 Fibredex boxes.

Land Entry Books, 1778-1796, 1887-1924; 1 volume, 1 manuscript box.

Miscellaneous Land Records, 1748, 1792-1895, 1981; 1 Fibredex box.

MARRIAGE, DIVORCE AND VITAL STATISTICS

Marriage Bonds, 1742-1868; 14 manuscript boxes.

MILITARY AND PENSION RECORDS

Minutes, Confederate Veterans Association, 1889-1917; 1 volume.

MISCELLANEOUS RECORDS

Insolvent Debtors, 1821-1868; 3 Fibredex boxes.

Jury Records, 1785-1898; 1 Fibredex box.

Miscellaneous Records, 1769-1908; 2 Fibredex boxes.

Record of Stock Marks, 1763-1819; 1 pamphlet.

Record of Strays, 1918, 1923; School Records, 1893; 1 volume.

ROADS AND BRIDGES

Road Records, 1788-1898; 2 Fibredex boxes.

TAX AND FISCAL RECORDS

Lists of Taxables, 1782, 1850; Sale of Land for Taxes, 1807-1808; 1 manuscript box.

WILLS

Wills, 1744-1922; 5 Fibredex boxes.

MICROFILM RECORDS

COURT RECORDS

County Court of Pleas and Quarter Sessions

Minutes, 1735-1868; 4 reels.

Superior Court

Minutes, 1807-1868; 5 reels.

Equity Minutes, 1852-1868; 1 reel.

ELECTION RECORDS

Record of Elections, 1880-1968; 3 reels.

ESTATES RECORDS

Record of Estates, 1802-1868; 3 reels.

Record of Accounts, 1868-1961; 2 reels.

Administrators' Bonds, 1904-1924; 1 reel.

Record of Administrators, Executors and Guardians, 1915-1961; 1 reel.

Record of Administrators, 1929-1961; 1 reel.

Appointment of Executors, 1905-1916; 1 reel.

Guardians' Bonds, 1859-1868; 1 reel.

Record of Dowers, 1939; 1 reel.

Record of Settlements, 1867-1961; 1 reel.

Wyriott Ormond Estate Records and Miscellaneous Accounts, 1758-1828; 1 reel.

Cross Index to Administrators and Executors, 1942-1944; 1 reel.

LAND RECORDS

Record of Deeds, 1736-1920; 33 reels.

Index to Real Estate Conveyances, Grantor, 1729-1960; 2 reels.

Index to Real Estate Conveyances, Grantee, 1729-1960; 2 reels.

Land Entries, 1887-1924; 1 reel.

Record of Grants, 1779-1780; 1 reel.

Registration of Land Titles, 1918-1960; 1 reel.

Record of Resale of Land by Mortgagees and Trustees, 1932-1956; 1 reel.

MARRIAGE, DIVORCE AND VITAL STATISTICS

Marriage Bonds, 1741-1868; 3 reels.

Marriage Bond Abstracts, 1741-1868; 1 reel.

Marriage Records, 1851-1868; 1 reel.

Marriage Registers, 1877-1975; 2 reels.

Index to Vital Statistics, 1913-1961; 1 reel.

Index to Delayed Births, various years; 1 reel.

MILITARY AND PENSION RECORDS

Record of Armed Forces Discharges, 1917-1986; 2 reels.

Index to Armed Forces Discharges, 1917-1986; 1 reel.

Minutes, Confederate Veterans Association, 1889-1917; 1 reel.

MISCELLANEOUS RECORDS

Record of Inquisition of Lunacy, 1900-1914; 1 reel.

Clerk's Minute Docket, 1925-1929; 1 reel.

Orders and Decrees, 1868-1961; 2 reels.

Special Proceedings, 1907-1968; 4 reels.

Cross Index to Special Proceedings, 1907-1968; 1 reel.

OFFICIALS, COUNTY

Minutes, Board of County Commissioners, 1878-1981; 5 reels.

Minutes, County Board of Social Services, 1937-1986; 2 reels.

Minutes, County Planning Board, 1970-1986; 1 reel.

SCHOOL RECORDS

Minutes, County Board of Education, 1911-1975; 2 reels.

TAX AND FISCAL RECORDS

Lists of Taxables, 1782, 1850; 1 reel.

Tax Lists, 1877-1899, 1901, 1915; 2 reels.

WILLS

Record of Wills, 1750-1961; 2 reels.

Cross Index to Wills, 1750-1968; 1 reel.

Court day in Monroe, Union County, circa 1900. The courthouse, built in 1886, is unusual in that it is adorned by a cross atop the cupola. Photograph from the files of the State Archives.

UNION COUNTY

Established in 1842 from Anson and Mecklenburg counties.
A few of the court records are missing; reason unknown.

ORIGINAL RECORDS

BONDS
> Apprentice Bonds, 1871-1910; 1 manuscript box.
> Bastardy Bonds, 1871-1882; 1 volume.

COURT RECORDS
> County Court of Pleas and Quarter Sessions
>> Minutes, 1843-1868; 5 volumes.
>> Appearance Docket, 1843-1868; 1 volume.
>> Execution Dockets, 1843-1868; 7 volumes.
>> State Dockets, 1843-1868; 2 volumes.
>> Trial Dockets, 1843-1868; 3 volumes.
> Superior Court
>> Minutes, 1844-1894; 6 volumes.
>> Equity Minutes, 1843-1868; 1 volume.
>> Equity Execution Docket, 1847-1868; 1 volume.
>> Equity Trial Docket, 1844-1868; 1 volume.
>> Appearance Docket, 1844-1870; 1 volume.
>> Execution Dockets, 1844-1862; 3 volumes.
>> State Docket, 1844-1869; 1 volume.
>> Trial Docket, 1844-1867; 1 volume.
>> Civil Action Papers, 1843-1969; 40 Fibredex boxes.
>> Civil Action Papers Concerning Land, 1853-1968; 23 Fibredex boxes.
>> Civil Action Papers Concerning Mines, 1844-1967; 3 Fibredex boxes.
>> Criminal Action Papers, 1844-1965; 1 Fibredex box.

ESTATES RECORDS
> Record of Estates, 1843-1870; 7 volumes.
> Record of Accounts, 1876-1904; 7 volumes.
> Administrators' Bonds, 1871-1909; 6 volumes.
> Estates Records, 1818-1969; 236 Fibredex boxes.
> Guardians' Records, 1846-1968; 38 Fibredex boxes.
> Guardians' Bonds, 1871-1910; 3 volumes.
> Index to Record of Estates, [1855-1870]; 1 volume.

LAND RECORDS
> Ejectments, 1848-1965; 1 Fibredex box.
> Partitions and Sales of Land, 1869-1969; 6 Fibredex boxes.
> Record of Probate, 1852-1881; 2 volumes.
> Attachments, Executions, Liens and Levies on Land, 1844-1968;
> 5 Fibredex boxes.
> Miscellaneous Land Records, 1796-1964; 1 Fibredex box.

MARRIAGE, DIVORCE AND VITAL STATISTICS
Divorce Records, 1865-1968; 46 Fibredex boxes.
MISCELLANEOUS RECORDS
Record of Declaration of Intent (to Become a Citizen), 1915-1928; 1 volume.
Settlement of County Accounts, Committee of Finance, 1850-1873; 1 volume.
Minutes and Accounts, Wardens of the Poor, 1858-1881; 1 volume.
Miscellaneous Records, 1844-1967; 3 Fibredex boxes.
Records of Assignees, Trustees and Receivers, 1883-1974; 6 Fibredex boxes.
ROADS AND BRIDGES
Road Docket, 1849-1868, 1877; 1 volume.
Road and Bridge Records, 1848-1959; 1 Fibredex box.
Railroad Records, 1875-1968; 6 Fibredex boxes.
SCHOOL RECORDS
School Records, 1896-1959; 1 Fibredex box.
TAX AND FISCAL RECORDS
Lists of Taxables, 1842-1853; 2 volumes.
WILLS
Wills, 1837-1968, 1977, 1978; 56 Fibredex boxes.

MICROFILM RECORDS

BONDS
Apprentice Bonds, 1871-1882; 1 reel.
Officials' Bonds, 1872-1892; 1 reel.
CORPORATIONS AND PARTNERSHIPS
Record of Corporations, 1885-1971; 4 reels.
Record of Partnerships and Assumed Names, 1913-1947; 1 reel.
Record of Limited Partnerships, 1944-1974; 1 reel.
COURT RECORDS
County Court of Pleas and Quarter Sessions
Minutes, 1843-1868; 3 reels.
Superior Court
Minutes, 1858-1863, 1895-1961; 15 reels.
Equity Minutes, 1843-1865; 1 reel.
Index to Civil Actions, 1932-1961; 1 reel.
Index to Judgments, Plaintiff, 1917-1960; 1 reel.
Index to Judgments, Defendant, 1917-1960; 1 reel.
ELECTION RECORDS
Record of Elections, 1878-1968; 2 reels.
Permanent Registrations, 1902-1908; 1 reel.
ESTATES RECORDS
Record of Estates, 1841-1876; 4 reels.
Record of Accounts, 1868-1967; 11 reels.
Accounts and Sales of Estates, 1916-1962; 3 reels.
Administrators' Bonds, 1871-1909; 2 reels.

Record of Administrators, Executors and Guardians, 1908-1968; 10 reels.

Appointment of Executors, 1868-1907; 1 reel.

Record of Executors and Guardians, 1940-1968; 2 reels.

Guardians' Bonds, 1871-1910; 1 reel.

Record of Guardians, 1908-1968; 3 reels.

Record of Amounts Paid for Indigent Children, 1926-1953; 1 reel.

Inheritance Tax Records, 1923-1972; 3 reels.

Record of Settlements, 1867-1970; 13 reels.

Index to Administrators and Executors, 1872-1914; 1 reel.

LAND RECORDS

Record of Deeds, 1843-1958; 97 reels.

Index to Deeds, Grantor, 1842-1972; 6 reels.

Index to Deeds, Grantee, 1842-1972; 6 reels.

Record of Land Sold for Taxes, 1930-1934; 2 reels.

MARRIAGE, DIVORCE AND VITAL STATISTICS

Marriage Bonds and Certificates, 1843-1871; 2 reels.

Marriage Licenses, 1872-1967; 12 reels.

Marriage Registers, 1843-1938; 2 reels.

Index to Marriage Registers, 1843-1965; 4 reels.

Maiden Names of Divorced Women, 1938-1968; 1 reel.

Index to Births, 1913-1971; 3 reels.

Index to Deaths, 1913-1981; 2 reels.

Index to Delayed Births, various years; 1 reel.

MILITARY AND PENSION RECORDS

Record of Armed Forces Discharges, 1918-1982; 7 reels.

Index to Armed Forces Discharges, 1918-1982; 1 reel.

Register of Confederate Soldiers of Monroe, 1903-1933; 1 reel.

Roster of Confederate and Revolutionary Soldiers, 1958; 1 reel.

MISCELLANEOUS RECORDS

Alien Registration Records, 1924-1940; 1 reel.

Record of Naturalization, 1914-1928; 1 reel.

Record of Lunacy, 1899-1946; 1 reel.

Orders and Decrees, 1881-1957; 12 reels.

Special Proceedings Dockets, 1887-1969; 5 reels.

Special Proceedings Costs Docket, 1938-1968; 1 reel.

Index to Special Proceedings, 1927-1960; 4 reels.

Index to Special Proceedings Files, 1869-1968; 2 reels.

Minutes, Wardens of the Poor, 1851-1881; 1 reel.

Minutes, Board of Trustees of Monroe Township, 1878-1901; 1 reel.

Reports of Receivers, 1927-1931; 1 reel.

OFFICIALS, COUNTY

Minutes, Board of County Commissioners, 1868-1955; 4 reels.

ROADS AND BRIDGES

Record of Road Overseers, 1849-1868; 1 reel.

Commissioners' Road Docket, 1869-1905; 1 reel.

SCHOOL RECORDS
    Minutes, County Board of Education, 1885-1967; 2 reels.
TAX AND FISCAL RECORDS
    Tax Lists, 1842-1869; 1 reel.
    Minutes, County Board of Equalization and Review, 1976-1982; 1 reel.
WILLS
    Record of Wills, 1842-1968; 7 reels.
    Cross Index to Wills, 1842-1968; 1 reel.

VANCE COUNTY

Established in 1881 from Franklin, Granville and Warren counties.

ORIGINAL RECORDS

BONDS
Officials' Bonds, 1881-1925; 1 volume.
LAND RECORDS
Cross Index to Deeds, 1849-1934; 5 volumes.
TAX AND FISCAL RECORDS
Tax Records, 1882-1884; 1 manuscript box.

MICROFILM RECORDS

BONDS
Apprentice Bonds, 1882-1922; 1 reel.
CORPORATIONS AND PARTNERSHIPS
Record of Corporations, 1888-1948; 1 reel.
COURT RECORDS
Superior Court
Minutes, 1881-1963; 14 reels.
ELECTION RECORDS
Record of Elections, 1884-1966; 1 reel.
ESTATES RECORDS
Record of Accounts, 1881-1968; 11 reels.
Administrators' Bonds, 1906-1913, 1922-1925; 1 reel.
Record of Administrators and Executors, 1925-1929; 1 reel.
Record of Administrators, 1930-1968; 4 reels.
Guardians' Bonds, 1926-1938; 1 reel.
Record of Guardians, 1938-1968; 1 reel.
Inheritance Tax Records, 1923-1958, 1968-1969; 1 reel.
Record of Settlements, 1883-1968; 6 reels.
Qualification of Trustees Under Wills, 1960-1968; 1 reel.
Index to Estates, 1968-1969; 1 reel.
LAND RECORDS
Record of Deeds, 1881-1963; 42 reels.
Index to Real Estate Conveyances, Grantor, 1881-1969; 4 reels.
Index to Real Estate Conveyances, Grantee, 1881-1969; 2 reels.
Record of Surveys, 1886-1907; 1 reel.
Record of Resale, 1925-1969; 2 reels.
MARRIAGE, DIVORCE AND VITAL STATISTICS
Marriage Licenses, 1897, 1902, 1911-1968; 9 reels.
Marriage Registers, 1881-1962; 1 reel.
Index to Marriage Register, 1963-1969; 1 reel.

Maiden Names of Divorced Women, 1937-1968; 1 reel.
Index to Vital Statistics, 1913-1968; 2 reels.
Index to Delayed Births, various years; 1 reel.

MILITARY AND PENSION RECORDS
Record of Armed Forces Discharges, 1924-1977; 6 reels.
Index to Armed Forces Discharges, 1918-1969; 1 reel.

MISCELLANEOUS RECORDS
Orders and Decrees, 1881-1953; 8 reels.
Index to Special Proceedings, Plaintiff, 1881-1969; 1 reel.
Index to Special Proceedings, Defendant, 1881-1969; 1 reel.

OFFICIALS, COUNTY
Minutes, Board of County Commissioners, 1883-1955; 4 reels.

SCHOOL RECORDS
Minutes, County Board of Education, 1899-1967; 1 reel.

TAX AND FISCAL RECORDS
Tax Scrolls, 1883-1899, 1903, 1925, 1935, 1945, 1955, 1956, 1965; 7 reels.

WILLS
Record of Wills, 1881-1968; 5 reels.
Cross Index to Wills, 1903-1969; 1 reel.

WAKE COUNTY

Established in 1771 from Cumberland, Johnston and Orange counties.
A few early court records are missing; reason unknown.
Several deed books were destroyed in register's office fire in 1832.

ORIGINAL RECORDS

BONDS
>Apprentice Bonds and Records, 1770-1903; 1 Fibredex box.
>Bastardy Bonds and Records, 1772-1937; 2 volumes, 2 Fibredex boxes.
>Constables' Bonds, 1787-1867; 1 Fibredex box.
>Officials' Bonds, 1878-1898; 2 volumes.

CENSUS RECORDS (County Copy)
>Census, 1880; 6 volumes.

COURT RECORDS
>County Court of Pleas and Quarter Sessions
>>Minutes, 1777-1868; 24 volumes.
>>Appearance Dockets, 1783-1818, 1838-1868; 6 volumes.
>>Execution Dockets, 1772-1830, 1840-1868; 13 volumes.
>>Levy Dockets, 1805-1819; 2 volumes.
>>Recognizance Docket, 1820-1837; 1 volume.
>>Reference Docket, 1799-1832; 1 volume.
>>Scire Facias Docket, 1799-1813; 1 volume.
>>State Dockets, 1795-1868; 7 volumes.
>>Trial Dockets, 1778-1868; 9 volumes.

>Superior Court
>>Minutes, 1818-1928; 48 volumes.
>>Minutes (Rough), 1859-1866, 1915-1930; 10 volumes.
>>Equity Minutes, 1818-1836, 1851-1868; 2 volumes.
>>Equity Appearance Dockets, 1818-1868; 3 volumes.
>>Equity Execution Dockets, 1820-1868; 2 volumes.
>>Equity Trial Dockets, 1818-1866; 3 volumes.
>>Appearance Dockets, 1835-1869; 2 volumes.
>>Execution Dockets, 1808-1871; 6 volumes.
>>State Dockets, 1814-1868; 4 volumes.
>>Criminal Issues Dockets, 1869-1915; 16 volumes.
>>Summons Dockets, 1868-1913; 7 volumes.
>>Trial, Appearance and Reference Dockets, 1814-1824; 2 volumes.
>>Trial and Reference Dockets, 1825-1863; 3 volumes.
>>Trial Docket, 1864-1868; 1 volume.
>>Civil Issues Docket, 1868-1886; 1 volume.
>>Clerk's Record of Fines and Penalties, 1879-1898; 1 volume.
>>Clerk's Fee Book, 1889-1912; 1 volume.
>>Costs Dockets (Criminal), 1839-1844, 1902-1903; 3 volumes.

Rural bridge in Wake County, date unknown. Note the primitive form of advertisement on the side rail. Photograph from the files of the State Archives.

Special Civil Order Docket, 1884; 1 volume.

Tax Judgment Dockets, 1878-1887; 2 volumes.

Civil Action Papers, 1770-1942; 92 Fibredex boxes.

Civil Action Papers Concerning Land, 1773-1947; 55 Fibredex boxes.

Criminal Action Papers, 1771-1946; 3 Fibredex boxes.

Criminal Court

Minutes, 1877-1879; 2 volumes.

Criminal Issues Docket, 1877-1879; 1 volume.

Judgment Docket, 1877-1879; 1 volume.

ELECTION RECORDS

Record of Elections, 1896-1920, 1928; 4 volumes.

Election Records, 1790-1938; 5 Fibredex boxes.

Voter Registration Book, 1904-1906; 1 volume.

ESTATES RECORDS

Record of Accounts, 1868-1916; 8 volumes.

Administrators' Bonds, 1868-1892; 3 volumes.

Administrators' Bonds and Appointments, 1892-1911; 5 volumes.

Record of Appointment of Administrators and Executors, 1858-1891;
3 volumes.

Appointment of Administrators, Executors, Guardians and Masters, 1868-
1893; 2 volumes.

Record of Administrators, Executors and Guardians, 1892-1914; 5 volumes.

Index to Executors and Administrators, 1858-1934; 2 volumes.

Index to Administrators' and Guardians' Accounts, no date; 1 volume.

Widows' Year's Support, 1878-1912; 1 volume.

Estates Records, 1771-1952, 1962, 1968; 383 Fibredex boxes.

Guardians' Records, 1772-1948; 44 Fibredex boxes.

Guardians' Accounts, 1878-1913; 5 volumes.

Guardians' Bonds, 1868-1892; 3 volumes.

Guardians' Bonds and Appointments, 1892-1910; 2 volumes.

Guardians' Dockets, 1817-1818, 1822-1828; 2 volumes.

Index to Guardians, 1858-1934; 1 volume.

Record of Amounts Paid for Indigent Orphans, 1899-1918, 1921-1935;
2 volumes.

Clerk's Receiver Accounts, 1913, 1917-1918; 1 volume.

Inventories and Accounts of Sale, 1878-1913; 5 volumes.

Record of Settlements, 1868-1918; 10 volumes.

LAND RECORDS

Deeds, 1774-1940; 2 Fibredex boxes.

Deeds of Trust, 1824-1940; 1 Fibredex box.

Mortgage Deeds, 1859-1935; 2 Fibredex boxes.

Ejectments, 1789-1937; 2 Fibredex boxes.

Land Divisions, 1820-1854, 1871-1937; 1 volume, 1 Fibredex box.

Land Entries, 1778-1846; 1 volume.

Attachments, Executions, Levies and Liens on Land, 1806, 1814, 1841-1942; 7 Fibredex boxes.

Index to Liens and Mortgages, 1934; 1 volume.

Condemnation Proceedings for Land, 1891-1940; 3 Fibredex boxes.

Miscellaneous Land Records, 1800-1939; 1 Fibredex box.

Probate Court Dockets, 1878-1883; 3 volumes.

Index to Probate Court Docket, 1878-1880; 1 volume.

MARRIAGE, DIVORCE AND VITAL STATISTICS

Marriage Bonds, 1790-1865; 58 manuscript boxes.

Record of Marriages, 1851-1857, 1862-1866; 1 volume.

Marriage Registers, 1868-1901; 3 volumes.

Record of Cohabitation, 1866; 1 volume.

Divorce Records, 1831-1952; 56 Fibredex boxes.

Register of Births, 1925-1938; 1 volume.

Registers of Deaths, 1887-1937; 4 volumes.

Death Certificates, 1900-1909; 9 volumes.

MILITARY AND PENSION RECORDS

Roster of Wake County Confederate Soldiers Association, 1886-1914; 1 volume.

MISCELLANEOUS RECORDS

Alien Registration, 1927, 1940; 1 volume.

Naturalization Records, 1821-1908, 1937; 1 Fibredex box.

Commissions from Governors to hold Court, 1929, 1938-1940; 1 Fibredex box.

County Accounts, 1890-1894; 1 volume.

General County Accounts, 1911-1915; 2 volumes.

County Home Accounts, 1911-1915; 1 volume.

Fraternal Organizations, 1895-1940; 3 Fibredex boxes.

Homestead and Personal Property Exemptions, 1869-1945; 1 volume, 9 Fibredex boxes.

Insolvent Debtors, 1800-1868; 3 Fibredex boxes.

Grand Jury Reports, 1826-1949; 1 Fibredex box.

Lists of Jurors, 1893-1929; 2 volumes.

Lists of Empaneled Jurors, 1895-1911; 2 volumes.

Jury Tickets, 1927-1931, 1939; 5 volumes.

Registry of Licenses to Trades, 1876-1877; 1 volume.

Architects' Certificates of Registration, 1915-1967; 2 volumes.

Chiropractors' Certificates of Registration, 1917-1956; 1 volume.

Dentists' Certificates of Registration, 1947-1960; 1 volume.

Nurses' Certificates of Registration, 1946-1953; 1 volume.

Opticians' Certificates of Registration, 1952-1966; 2 volumes.

Optometrists' Certificates of Registration, 1950-1965; 1 volume.

Osteopaths' Certificates of Registration, 1931-1947; 1 volume.

Physicians' and Surgeons' Certificates of Registration, 1939-1967; 5 volumes.

Clerk's Minute Dockets (Special Proceedings), 1921-1940, 1966-1968;
6 volumes.
Orders and Decrees, 1875-1916; 18 volumes.
Special Proceedings Dockets, 1870-1889; 2 volumes.
Miscellaneous Records, 1772-1952; 6 Fibredex boxes.
Personal Accounts, 1770-1913; 3 Fibredex boxes.
Southern Bell Telephone & Telegraph Co. Rate Hearings, 1932-1934;
2 Fibredex boxes.
Minutes, Board of Directors of County Workhouse, 1866-1874; 1 volume.
Records of Assignees, Receivers and Trustees, 1867-1959; 43 Fibredex boxes.
Record of Assignments, 1894-1921; 3 volumes.
Receivers' Accounts, 1895-1918; 1 volume.

OFFICIALS, COUNTY
Minutes, Board of County Commissioners, 1869-1910; 6 volumes.

ROADS AND BRIDGES
Road Records, 1800-1938; 2 Fibredex boxes.
Railroad Records, 1837-1940; 34 Fibredex boxes.

SCHOOL RECORDS
Minutes, County Board of Education, 1872-1885; 1 volume.
School Census, Raleigh Township, 1897-1910; 7 volumes.
School Records, 1856-1939; 4 Fibredex boxes.

TAX AND FISCAL RECORDS
Tax Lists, 1781-1867; 11 volumes, 2 Fibredex boxes.
Tax Records, 1870-1939; 4 Fibredex boxes.
Lists of Persons Paying Poll Taxes, 1904-1917; 6 volumes.
Record of Federal Direct Taxes Collected, 1865; 1 volume.

WILLS
Record of Wills, Inventories and Estates, 1771-1782; 1 volume.
Wills, 1771-1966; 119 Fibredex boxes.
Cross Index to Wills, 1774-1935; 2 volumes.
General Index to Wills, 1771-1952; 2 volumes.

MICROFILM RECORDS

CORPORATIONS AND PARTNERSHIPS
Record of Corporations, 1883-1913; 1 reel.

COURT RECORDS
County Court of Pleas and Quarter Sessions
Minutes, 1771-1868; 10 reels.
Superior Court
Minutes, 1818-1871, 1881-1884; 3 reels.
Equity Minutes, 1818-1866; 1 reel.

ESTATES RECORDS
Record of Estates, 1868-1888; 2 reels.
Record of Dowers, 1868-1953; 1 reel.

Frank Page's Mill, or Company Mill, on Crabtree Creek, near Cary Road, Wake County; built about 1810. Photograph from the files of the State Archives.

Index to Dowers, 1804-1946; 1 reel.

Inventories of Estates, 1891-1940; 3 reels.

Record of Final Settlements, 1883-1938; 7 reels.

General Index to Administrators, Executors, Guardians and Trustees, to 1941; 1 reel.

Index to Administrators, Executors and Inventories, 1891-1959; 1 reel.

Index to Guardians, 1858-1932; 1 reel.

General Index to Minors and Decedents, to 1941; 1 reel.

LAND RECORDS

Record of Deeds, 1785-1936; 229 reels.

Index to Real Estate Conveyances, Grantor, 1785-1958; 15 reels.

Index to Real Estate Conveyances, Grantor: Firms and Corporations, 1771-1971; 8 reels.

Index to Real Estate Conveyances, Grantee, 1785-1958; 13 reels.

Index to Real Estate Conveyances, Grantee: Firms and Corporations, 1771-1971; 7 reels.

Record of Land Divisions, 1820-1854; 1 reel.

Record of Partition of Land, 1879-1966; 3 reels.

General Index to Divisions of Land, 1792-1940; 1 reel.

Record of Sales and Resales by Mortgagees and Trustees, 1934-1936; 1 reel.

MARRIAGE, DIVORCE AND VITAL STATISTICS

Marriage Bonds, 1770-1868; 5 reels.

Marriage Licenses, 1851-1990; 63 reels.

Marriage Registers, 1839-1967; 18 reels.

Record of Cohabitation, 1866; 1 reel.

Maiden Names of Divorced Women, 1938-1968; 1 reel.

Death Certificates, 1900-1909; 4 reels.

MILITARY AND PENSION RECORDS

Record of Armed Forces Discharges, 1917-1971; 17 reels.

Index to Armed Forces Discharges, various years; 1 reel.

MISCELLANEOUS RECORDS

Orders and Decrees, 1878-1965; 22 reels.

Special Proceedings, 1879-1968; 9 reels.

Index to Special Proceedings, 1879-1968; 7 reels.

Record of Wardens of the Poor, 1846-1872; 1 reel.

OFFICIALS, COUNTY

Minutes, Board of County Commissioners, 1868-1935; 6 reels.

SCHOOL RECORDS

Minutes, County Board of Education, 1873-1959; 3 reels.

TAX AND FISCAL RECORDS

Lists of Taxables, 1781-1817; 1 reel.

Tax Lists, 1809-1904, 1925, 1934; 14 reels.

WILLS

Record of Wills, Inventories and Settlements of Estates, 1771-1868; 16 reels.
Record of Wills, 1868-1966; 20 reels.
Index to Wills, Devisor, 1771-1968; 1 reel.
Index to Wills, Devisee, 1771-1967; 2 reels.

WARREN COUNTY

Established in 1779 from Bute County.
Some court records are missing; reason unknown.

ORIGINAL RECORDS

BONDS
 Apprentice Bonds, 1779-1867, 1901; 1.5 Fibredex boxes.
 Bastardy Bonds, 1784-1895; .5 Fibredex box.
 Officials' Bonds, 1800-1875; 3 Fibredex boxes.
 Tavern Bonds, 1800-1859; 1 Fibredex box.

COURT RECORDS
 County Court of Pleas and Quarter Sessions
  Minutes, 1780-1813, 1823-1868; 20 volumes.
  Appearance Dockets, 1834-1868; 2 volumes.
  Execution Dockets, 1793-1868; 5 volumes.
  State Docket, 1851-1857; 1 volume.
  Trial, Appearance and State Dockets, 1794-1807; 7 volumes.
  Trial and Appearance Dockets, 1807-1825; 3 volumes.
  Trial Dockets, 1827-1868; 3 volumes.
  Judgment Dockets, 1787-1813; 2 volumes.
  Prosecution Bond Docket, 1826-1834; 1 volume.
 Superior Court
  Minutes, 1822-1931; 12 volumes.
  Equity Minutes, 1819-1868; 3 volumes.
  Appearance Docket, 1823-1867; 1 volume.
  Execution Docket, 1807-1839; 1 volume.
  State Docket, 1857-1868; 1 volume.
  Trial Dockets, 1823-1868; 2 volumes.
  Civil Action Papers, 1769-1896; 10 Fibredex boxes.
  Civil Action Papers Concerning Land, 1870-1905; 3 Fibredex boxes.
  Criminal Action Papers, 1790-1869; 1 Fibredex box.
 Inferior Court
  Minutes, 1877-1895; 1 volume.
 Circuit Criminal Court/Eastern District Criminal Court
  Minutes, 1895-1901; 1 volume.

ELECTION RECORDS
 Record of Elections, 1878-1933; 4 volumes.
 Election Records, 1821-1856; 1 Fibredex box.

ESTATES RECORDS
 Record of Accounts, 1868-1929; 4 volumes.
 Estates Records, 1768-1920; 60 Fibredex boxes.
 Guardians' Records, 1791-1929; 17 Fibredex boxes.
 Record of Settlements, 1879-1930; 2 volumes.

LAND RECORDS
>Bills of Sale, Deeds, Mortgages and Miscellaneous Land Records, 1778-1897;
>>2 Fibredex boxes.

MARRIAGE, DIVORCE AND VITAL STATISTICS
>Marriage Bonds, 1779-1868; 26 manuscript boxes.
>Register of Marriage Certificates, 1851-1867; 1 volume.

MILITARY AND PENSION RECORDS
>Court Martial Proceedings, 1791-1815; 1 volume.

MISCELLANEOUS RECORDS
>Alien Registration, 1940; 1 volume.
>Petitions for Naturalization, 1906-1914, 1957; 1 volume.
>County Buildings, Accounts and Claims, 1788-1908; 2 Fibredex boxes.
>County Claims Allowed, 1806-1814; 1 volume.
>Grand Jury Presentments and Jury Lists, 1795-1893; 1 Fibredex box.
>Miscellaneous Records, 1785-1929; 3 Fibredex boxes.

ROADS AND BRIDGES
>Bridge Records, 1800-1858; 1 Fibredex box.
>Record of Appointment of Road Overseers, 1805-1815, 1848-1866;
>>3 volumes.

SCHOOL RECORDS
>Minutes, Board of Superintendents of Common Schools, 1853-1860;
>>1 volume.
>Common School Registers, 1858-1864, 1882-1884; 12 volumes.

TAX AND FISCAL RECORDS
>Lists of Taxables, 1781-1801, 1824-1828, 1866-1868; 4 volumes.
>Record of Federal Direct Taxes Collected, 1866; 1 volume.
>Tax Records, 1780-1877; 2 Fibredex boxes.

WILLS
>Wills, 1780-1931; 23 Fibredex boxes.

MICROFILM RECORDS

CORPORATIONS AND PARTNERSHIPS
>Record of Corporations, 1892-1964; 1 reel.
>Partnership Records, 1913-1964; Index to Assumed Business Names, 1936-
>>1964; 1 reel.

COURT RECORDS
>County Court of Pleas and Quarter Sessions
>>Minutes, 1777-1813, 1823-1868; 6 reels.
>>Minutes (Rough), 1801-1805; 1 reel.
>Superior Court
>>Minutes, 1822-1964; 7 reels.
>>Equity Minutes, 1819-1838, 1855-1868; 1 reel.
>>Index to Criminal Minutes, 1823-1968; 1 reel.
>>Judgment Dockets, 1894-1925; 1 reel.

Index to Judgments, Plaintiff, 1904-1968; 1 reel.

Index to Judgments, Defendant, 1904-1968; 1 reel.

ELECTION RECORDS

Record of Elections, 1880-1964; 1 reel.

ESTATES RECORDS

Record of Accounts, 1868-1964; 5 reels.

Record of Administrators and Guardians, 1905-1906; 1 reel.

Record of Administrators, 1912-1964; Cross Index to Administrators, 1866-1965; 3 reels.

Record of Executors, 1919-1964; Cross Index to Administrators and Executors, 1927-1936; 1 reel.

Record of Guardians, 1926-1964; Cross Index to Guardians, 1926-1936; 1 reel.

Division of Estates, 1820-1821; 1 reel.

Inheritance Tax Records, 1923-1964; 1 reel.

Record of Settlements, 1878-1964; 3 reels.

LAND RECORDS

Record of Deeds, 1764-1958; 96 reels.

Cross Index to Real Estate Conveyances, 1764-1918; 1 reel.

General Index to Real Estate Conveyances, 1918-1925; 1 reel.

Index to Real Estate Conveyances, Grantor, 1860-1964; 4 reels.

Index to Real Estate Conveyances, Grantee, 1860-1964; 3 reels.

Record of Land Sold for Taxes, 1931; County Tax Lien, 1933-1934; 1 reel.

Federal Tax Lien Index, 1926-1964; 1 reel.

Record of Resale of Land, 1921-1964; 2 reels.

MARRIAGE, DIVORCE AND VITAL STATISTICS

Marriage Bonds, 1779-1868; 4 reels.

Marriage Bond Abstracts, 1779-1868; 1 reel.

Marriage Licenses, 1861-1964; 13 reels.

Marriage Registers, 1851-1978; 4 reels.

Cohabitation Records, 1866; 1 reel.

Maiden Names of Divorced Women, 1937-1968; 1 reel.

Index to Births, 1914-1991; 1 reel.

Index to Deaths, 1914-1991; 1 reel.

Index to Delayed Births, various years; 1 reel.

MILITARY AND PENSION RECORDS

Record of Armed Forces Discharges, 1918-1977; Index to Armed Forces Discharges, 1918-1964; 4 reels.

MISCELLANEOUS RECORDS

Orders and Decrees, 1877-1955; 8 reels.

Special Proceedings, 1918-1947; Index to Special Proceedings, 1870-1965; 1 reel.

Record of Assignments, 1898-1939; 1 reel.

OFFICIALS, COUNTY
Minutes, Board of County Commissioners, 1868-1879, 1907-1965; 2 reels.
Minutes, County Board of Health, 1946-1964; 2 reels.

SCHOOL RECORDS
Minutes, Board of Superintendents of Common Schools, 1853-1858; Minutes, County Board of Education, 1872-1964; 2 reels.

TAX AND FISCAL RECORDS
Tax Lists, 1779-1808; 1 reel.

WILLS
Record of Wills, Accounts, Inventories and Settlements, 1764-1863; 16 reels.
Record of Wills, 1863-1964; 3 reels.
Index to Wills, 1763-1968; 1 reel.

WASHINGTON COUNTY

Established in 1799 from Tyrrell County.
Courthouse destroyed in Federal bombardment of 1862.
Courthouse fires of 1869 and 1881, along with the destruction of 1862,
destroyed most of the court records and many of the land records.

ORIGINAL RECORDS

COURT RECORDS
> Superior Court
>> Minutes, 1822-1921; 9 volumes.
>> Civil Action Papers, 1815-1930; 3 Fibredex boxes.
>> Civil Action Papers Concerning Land, 1876-1932; 4 Fibredex boxes.
>> Criminal Action Papers, 1855, 1873-1918; 7 Fibredex boxes.

ELECTION RECORDS
> Record of Elections, 1878-1952; 2 volumes.

ESTATES RECORDS
> Estates Records, 1795-1933; 9 Fibredex boxes.
> Guardians' Records, 1870-1930; 3 Fibredex boxes.

LAND RECORDS
> Record of Deeds, 1800-1801; 1 volume.
> Deeds, 1830-1931; 1 Fibredex box.
> Deeds of Trust and Mortgage Deeds, 1878-1928; 1 Fibredex box.
> Land Records, 1856-1944; 1 Fibredex box.

MARRIAGE, DIVORCE AND VITAL STATISTICS
> Record of Freedmen's Marriages, 1866-1872; 1 volume.
> Divorce Records, 1851, 1873-1903; 1 Fibredex box.

MISCELLANEOUS RECORDS
> Registry of Licenses to Trades, 1883-1902; 1 volume.
> Record of Stock Marks, 1869-1930; 1 volume.
> Miscellaneous Records, 1867-1933; 2 Fibredex boxes.

WILLS
> Wills, 1856-1964; 5 Fibredex boxes.

MICROFILM RECORDS

CORPORATIONS AND PARTNERSHIPS
> Record of Corporations, 1932-1967; 1 reel.
> Partnership Records, 1917-1967; 1 reel.

COURT RECORDS
> Superior Court
>> Minutes, 1822-1959; 8 reels.

ESTATES RECORDS
> Record of Accounts, 1873-1951; 2 reels.

Record of Administrators, Executors and Guardians, 1911-1929; 1 reel.
Record of Administrators, 1919-1967; 2 reels.
Record of Executors, 1944-1967; 1 reel.
Record of Guardians, 1929-1967; 1 reel.
Inheritance Tax Records, 1935-1967; 1 reel.
Record of Settlements, 1873-1950; 2 reels.

LAND RECORDS

Record of Deeds, 1800-1960; 62 reels.
Index to Real Estate Conveyances, Grantor, 1779-1967; 2 reels.
Index to Real Estate Conveyances, Grantee, 1779-1967; 2 reels.
Registration of Land Titles, 1915-1962; 7 reels.
Record of Resale of Land by Trustees and Mortgagees, 1919-1967; 2 reels.

MARRIAGE, DIVORCE AND VITAL STATISTICS

Record of Marriages, 1851-1884; Marriage Registers, 1885-1920; 1 reel.
Marriage Registers, 1918-1967; 1 reel.
Maiden Names of Divorced Women, 1944-1967; 1 reel.
Index to Births, 1912-1985; 1 reel.
Index to Deaths, 1912-1986; 1 reel.

MILITARY AND PENSION RECORDS

Record of Armed Forces Discharges, 1918-1985; 2 reels.

MISCELLANEOUS RECORDS

Orders and Decrees, 1873-1964; 1 reel.
Special Proceedings Dockets, 1873-1954; 2 reels.
Cross Index to Special Proceedings, 1909-1967; 1 reel.

OFFICIALS, COUNTY

Minutes, Board of County Commissioners, 1868-1950; 3 reels.

SCHOOL RECORDS

Minutes, Board of Superintendents of Common Schools, 1841-1862; Minutes, County Board of Education, 1872-1926; 1 reel.

WILLS

Record of Wills, 1873-1967; 2 reels.
Cross Index to Wills, 1873-1967; 1 reel.

WATAUGA COUNTY

Established in 1849 from Ashe, Caldwell, Wilkes and Yancey counties.
Courthouse fire of 1873 destroyed all of the land records
and most of the court records.

ORIGINAL RECORDS

BONDS
>Apprentice Bonds, 1874-1906; 2 volumes.
>Apprentice Bonds, 1899-1900; Bastardy Bonds, 1874-1935; 1 Fibredex box.
>Bastardy Bonds, 1873-1878; 1 volume.
>Officials' Bonds, 1873-1958; 3 Fibredex boxes.

COURT RECORDS
>Superior Court
>>Minutes, 1873-1924; 9 volumes.
>>Civil Action Papers, 1873-1953; 12 Fibredex boxes.
>>Civil Action Papers Concerning Land, 1874-1948; 21 Fibredex boxes.
>>Criminal Action Papers, 1873-1962; 10 Fibredex boxes.

ELECTION RECORDS
>Record of Elections, 1878-1938; 3 volumes.

ESTATES RECORDS
>Record of Accounts, 1873-1914; 2 volumes.
>Administrators' Bonds, 1873-1911; 2 volumes.
>Appointment of Administrators, Executors, Guardians and Masters, 1873-1926; 1 volume.
>Estates Records, 1858-1948; 40 Fibredex boxes.
>Guardians' Records, 1873-1955; 7 Fibredex boxes.
>Guardians' Bonds, 1888-1910; 1 volume.
>Record of Settlements, 1873-1925; 1 volume.

LAND RECORDS
>Deeds, 1858-1976; 12 Fibredex boxes.
>Deeds of Trust, 1882-1976; 4 Fibredex boxes.
>Mortgage Deeds, 1877-1957; 1 Fibredex box.
>Cross Index to Deeds, 1873-1949; 10 volumes.
>Ejectments (Summary Proceedings), 1915-1947; 1 Fibredex box.
>Tax Levies on Land, 1874-1939; 1 Fibredex box.
>Attachments, Executions, Levies and Liens on Land, 1876-1947; 1 Fibredex box.
>Miscellaneous Land Records, 1830-1962; 1 Fibredex box.
>Record of Probate, 1873-1885; 1 volume.

MARRIAGE, DIVORCE AND VITAL STATISTICS
>Marriage Licenses, 1873-1894; 1 Fibredex box.
>Marriage Registers, 1873-1954; 3 volumes.
>Divorce Records, 1874-1948; 13 Fibredex boxes.

MISCELLANEOUS RECORDS
>Alien Registration, 1940; 1 volume.
>Homestead and Personal Property Exemptions, 1874-1933; 1 Fibredex box.
>Miscellaneous Records, 1858-1974; 3 Fibredex boxes.
>Records of Assignees, Receivers and Trustees, 1911-1936; 2 Fibredex boxes.

OFFICIALS, COUNTY
>Minutes, Board of County Commissioners, 1913-1921; 2 volumes.

ROADS AND BRIDGES
>Road and Bridge Records, 1867-1946; 5 Fibredex boxes.

SCHOOL RECORDS
>School Census, 1869-1896; 2 Fibredex boxes.
>School Vouchers and Miscellaneous School Records, 1870-1936;
>>3 Fibredex boxes.

TAX AND FISCAL RECORDS
>Miscellaneous Tax Records, 1873-1936; 1 Fibredex box.

WILLS
>Wills, 1859, 1872-1947; 7 Fibredex boxes.

MICROFILM RECORDS

BONDS
>Apprentice Bonds, 1874-1906; 1 reel.

CORPORATIONS AND PARTNERSHIPS
>Record of Corporations, 1889-1969; 1 reel.

COURT RECORDS
>Superior Court
>>Minutes, 1873-1959; 8 reels.

ELECTION RECORDS
>Record of Elections, 1878-1968; 1 reel.

ESTATES RECORDS
>Record of Accounts, 1873-1968; 4 reels.
>Administrators' Bonds, 1873-1911; 1 reel.
>Appointment of Administrators and Guardians, 1873-1926; 1 reel.
>Record of Administrators, 1911-1968; 2 reels.
>Record of Executors, 1925-1968; 1 reel.
>Record of Guardians, 1911-1968; 1 reel.
>Trust Funds and Accounts for Indigent Children, 1915-1968; 1 reel.
>Inheritance Tax Records, 1920-1969; 1 reel.
>Record of Settlements, 1873-1968; 3 reels.
>Index to Administrators and Executors, 1873-1968; 1 reel.
>Index to Guardians, 1873-1968; 1 reel.

LAND RECORDS
>Record of Deeds, 1870-1958; 53 reels.
>Index to Real Estate Conveyances, Grantor, 1872-1969; 5 reels.
>Index to Real Estate Conveyances, Grantee, 1872-1969; 5 reels.

Record of Surveys, 1904-1953; 1 reel.

Plat Books, 1922-1967; 1 reel.

Record of Resale of Land, 1922-1968; 1 reel.

MARRIAGE, DIVORCE AND VITAL STATISTICS

Marriage Registers, 1873-1969; 2 reels.

Index to Births, 1914-1969; 2 reels.

Index to Deaths, 1914-1968; 1 reel.

MILITARY AND PENSION RECORDS

Record of Armed Forces Discharges, 1922-1980; 5 reels.

MISCELLANEOUS RECORDS

Orders and Decrees, 1872-1967; 6 reels.

Cross Index to Orders and Decrees, 1873-1968; 1 reel.

Special Proceedings Docket, 1902-1921; 1 reel.

Index to Special Proceedings, 1968-1980; 1 reel.

Record of Assignees and Receivers, 1910-1920; 1 reel.

OFFICIALS, COUNTY

Minutes, Board of County Commissioners, 1873-1938; 4 reels.

TAX AND FISCAL RECORDS

Tax Lists, 1918, 1921; 1 reel.

Tax Scrolls, 1888-1926; 2 reels.

WILLS

Record of Wills, 1902-1968; 2 reels.

Cross Index to Wills, 1873-1969; 1 reel.

Atlantic and North Carolina Railroad train crossing the Little River trestle, near Goldsboro, Wayne County, circa 1865. Photograph from the files of the State Archives.

WAYNE COUNTY

Established in 1779 from Dobbs County.
A few early court records are missing; reason unknown.

ORIGINAL RECORDS

BONDS

    Apprentice Bonds and Records, 1800-1917; 3 volumes, 5 Fibredex boxes.

    Bastardy Bonds and Records, 1786-1879, 1889; Constables' Bonds, 1862-1865; 2 volumes, 5 Fibredex boxes.

    Officials' Bonds and Records, 1786-1925; 7 volumes, 6 Fibredex boxes.

    Tax Collectors' Bonds, 1892-1894; 1 volume.

COURT RECORDS

    County Court of Pleas and Quarter Sessions

        Minutes, 1787-1794, 1823-1867; 11 volumes.

        Appearance Docket, 1857-1868; 1 volume.

        Execution Dockets, 1802-1868; 9 volumes.

        State Dockets, 1785-1802, 1811-1868; 5 volumes.

        Trial and Appearance Docket, 1820-1822; 1 volume.

        Trial Dockets, 1823-1841, 1855-1868; 4 volumes.

    Superior Court

        Minutes, 1807-1910; 18 volumes.

        Equity Minutes, 1839-1843, 1851-1868; 3 volumes.

        Equity Execution Docket, 1858-1868; 1 volume.

        Equity Trial and Appearance Dockets, 1807-1861; 3 volumes.

        State Docket, 1834-1843; 1 volume.

        Trial and Appearance Dockets, 1807-1832; 2 volumes.

        Civil Action Papers, 1782-1924; 76 Fibredex boxes.

        Civil Action Papers Concerning Land, 1785-1930; 13 Fibredex boxes.

        Criminal Action Papers, 1785-1929; 39 Fibredex boxes.

    Inferior Court

        Minutes, 1877-1885; 1 volume.

ELECTION RECORDS

    Record of Elections, 1878-1930; 4 volumes.

    Election Records, 1792-1913; 2 Fibredex boxes.

ESTATES RECORDS

    Record of Estates, 1782-1868; 21 volumes.

    Record of Accounts, 1869-1914; 7 volumes.

    Administrators' Bonds, 1861-1896; 6 volumes.

    Appointment of Administrators, Executors, Guardians and Masters, 1868-1903; 1 volume.

    Record of Administrators, Executors and Guardians, 1874-1882; 1 volume.

    Estates Records, 1786-1937; 173 Fibredex boxes.

    Guardians' Records, 1787-1937; 19 Fibredex boxes.

Guardians' Bonds, 1824-1900; 9 volumes.

Record of Settlements, 1878-1919; 3 volumes.

LAND RECORDS

Deeds, 1785-1920; 4 Fibredex boxes.

Ejectments, 1788-1874, 1935; 3 Fibredex boxes.

Land Divisions and Sales of Land, 1814-1930; 1 Fibredex box.

Levies on Land, 1788-1889; 9 Fibredex boxes.

Miscellaneous Land Records, 1790-1927; 1 Fibredex box.

MARRIAGE, DIVORCE AND VITAL STATISTICS

Marriage Bonds, 1790-1859; 1 manuscript box.

Marriage Licenses, 1851-1861, 1863; 2 volumes.

Divorce Records, 1822-1930; 7 Fibredex boxes.

MISCELLANEOUS RECORDS

Alien Registration, 1927, 1933, 1935, 1940, 1954; 1 volume.

Declaration of Intent (to Become a Citizen), 1908, 1910; 1 volume.

County Accounts and Court Orders, 1785-1868; 3 Fibredex boxes.

Record of Official Reports, 1875-1919; 2 volumes.

Homestead and Personal Property Exemptions, 1849, 1867-1933;
    1.5 Fibredex boxes.

Insolvent Debtors, 1800-1863; 2.5 Fibredex boxes.

Jury Lists, 1797-1867; 1 Fibredex box.

Registry of Licenses to Trades, 1884-1903; 1 volume.

Minutes and Accounts, Wardens of the Poor, 1819-1841; 1 volume.

Minutes, Goldsboro Township Board of Trustees, 1869-1877; 1 volume.

Miscellaneous Records, 1783-1936; 1 volume, 5 Fibredex boxes.

Records of Slaves and Free Persons of Color, 1789-1869; 4 Fibredex boxes.

Records of Assignees, Receivers and Trustees, 1875-1935; 1 Fibredex box.

ROADS AND BRIDGES

Bridge Records, 1794-1886; 1 Fibredex box.

Appointment of Road Overseers, 1857-1879; 1 volume.

Minutes, County Highway Commission, 1916-1931; 2 volumes.

Road Records, 1791-1914; 4 Fibredex boxes.

Railroad Records, 1837-1912; 3 Fibredex boxes.

SCHOOL RECORDS

School Fund Ledger, 1884-1885; 1 volume.

TAX AND FISCAL RECORDS

Record of Tax Collections, 1935-1936; 2 volumes.

Tax Levies Under the Stock Law of 1885, 1885-1886; 1 volume.

Schedule "B" Tax Lists, 1896-1899; 3 volumes.

Tax Records, 1780-1920; 2 Fibredex boxes.

WILLS

Wills, 1776-1927; 18 Fibredex boxes.

Cross Index to Wills, 1782-1939; 2 volumes.

MICROFILM RECORDS

BONDS

    Apprentice Bonds, 1861-1889; 1 reel.

    Bastardy Bonds, 1861-1878, 1889; Constables' Bonds, 1862-1865; 1 reel.

CORPORATIONS AND PARTNERSHIPS

    Record of Corporations, 1869-1965; 3 reels.

    Partnership Records, 1914-1965; Limited Partnerships, 1945-1965; 1 reel.

COURT RECORDS

    County Court of Pleas and Quarter Sessions

        Minutes, 1823-1868; 3 reels.

    Superior Court

        Minutes, 1826-1942; 13 reels.

        Equity Minutes, 1819-1868; 1 reel.

        Index to Civil Actions, Plaintiff, no date; 1 reel.

ELECTION RECORDS

    Record of Elections, 1932-1964; 1 reel.

ESTATES RECORDS

    Record of Accounts, 1869-1953; 9 reels.

    Index to Accounts, 1907-1920; 1 reel.

    Administrators' Bonds, 1861-1892; 1 reel.

    Record of Administrators, 1897-1940; 5 reels.

    Record of Appointment of Administrators and Guardians, 1940-1957; 5 reels.

    Appointment of Executors, 1869-1903; 1 reel.

    Record of Executors and Guardians, 1899-1914; 1 reel.

    Record of Executors, 1914-1940; 1 reel.

    Guardians' Bonds, 1824-1878; 1 reel.

    Record of Guardians, 1916-1941; Cross Index to Guardians, 1903-1919; 1 reel.

    Divisions and Dowers, 1867-1950; 4 reels.

    Inheritance Tax Collections, 1914-1965; 2 reels.

    Record and Index of Receivers of Estates, 1937-1964; 1 reel.

    Record of Settlements, 1878-1953; 5 reels.

    Index to Final Accounts, 1877-1936; 1 reel.

    General Index to Estates: Decedents and Minors, 1788-1965; 1 reel.

    General Index to Estates: Executors, Administrators, Guardians and Trustees, 1820-1965; 1 reel.

    Cross Index to Administrators and Executors, 1903-1919; 1 reel.

LAND RECORDS

    Record of Deeds, 1779-1958; 242 reels.

    Index to Real Estate Conveyances, Grantor, 1780-1963; 10 reels.

    Index to Real Estate Conveyances, Grantee, 1780-1963; 11 reels.

    Record of Grants, 1826-1892; 1 reel.

    Cross Index to Land Divisions, 1786-1938; 1 reel.

    Federal Tax Lien Index, 1928-1969; 1 reel.

Plat Books and Index to Plats, 1847-1965; 4 reels.

Processioners' Record, 1819-1820; 1 reel.

Record of Resale Under Trustees and Mortgagees, 1921-1965; 5 reels.

Trustees' and Commissioners' Accounts of Land Sales, 1926-1965; 1 reel.

MARRIAGE, DIVORCE AND VITAL STATISTICS

Marriage Bonds, 1814-1868; 1 reel.

Marriage Licenses, 1877-1964; 20 reels.

Certificates of Marriage, 1851-1868; 1 reel.

Marriage Registers, 1861-1961; 4 reels.

Maiden Names of Divorced Women, 1939-1968; 1 reel.

Index to Births, 1913-1986; 5 reels.

Index to Deaths, 1913-1987; 3 reels.

Index to Delayed Births, various years; 1 reel.

MILITARY AND PENSION RECORDS

Record of Armed Forces Discharges, 1895-1988; 20 reels.

Index to Armed Forces Discharges, 1918-1988; 1 reel.

MISCELLANEOUS RECORDS

Record of Inebriates, 1942-1965; Record of Lunacy, 1899-1965; 2 reels.

Orders and Decrees, 1869-1948; 10 reels.

Special Proceedings, 1884-1952; 1 reel.

Index to Special Proceedings, Plaintiff, 1884-1965; 1 reel.

Index to Special Proceedings, Defendant, 1884-1965; 1 reel.

OFFICIALS, COUNTY

Minutes, Board of County Commissioners, 1868-1950; 5 reels.

Minutes, County Board of Health, 1930-1965; 1 reel.

SCHOOL RECORDS

Minutes, County Board of Education, 1921-1965; 1 reel.

TAX AND FISCAL RECORDS

Tax Lists, 1882-1883, 1891-1900, 1905; 4 reels.

WILLS

Record of Wills, Accounts, Inventories and Sales of Estates, 1782-1868; 8 reels.

Record of Wills, 1868-1957; 5 reels.

Index to Wills, Devisor, 1782-1968; 1 reel.

Index to Wills, Devisee, 1782-1968; 1 reel.

WILKES COUNTY

Established in 1777 (effective 1778) from Surry County and the
District of Washington.
A few early records are missing; reason unknown.

ORIGINAL RECORDS

BONDS

    Apprentice Bonds and Records, 1778-1916; 2 volumes, 1 Fibredex box.

    Bastardy Bonds and Records, 1773-1911; 1 volume, 5 Fibredex boxes.

    Officials' Bonds and Records, 1777-1914; 5 Fibredex boxes.

COURT RECORDS

    County Court of Pleas and Quarter Sessions

        Minutes, 1778-1868; 11 volumes, 3 manuscript boxes.

        Appearance Docket, 1840-1853; 1 volume.

        Execution Docket, 1837-1851; 1 volume.

        State Docket, 1778-1792; 1 manuscript box.

        Trial and Appearance Docket, 1824-1827; 1 volume.

        Trial Docket, 1837-1859; 1 volume.

        Witness Dockets, 1807-1837; 2 volumes.

        Miscellaneous Dockets, 1778-1859; 1 manuscript box.

    Superior Court

        Minutes, 1807-1912; 19 volumes, 2 manuscript boxes, 1 Fibredex box.

        Equity Minutes, 1819-1860; 1 manuscript box.

        Equity Enrolling Dockets, 1813-1857; 2 volumes.

        Equity Execution Docket, 1814-1861; Equity Appearance Docket,
            1815-1830; 1 manuscript box.

        Appearance Docket, 1823-1846; 1 volume.

        Execution Dockets, 1807-1860; 6 volumes.

        Recognizance Docket, 1812-1832; 1 volume.

        State Dockets, 1807-1822, 1837-1866; 3 volumes.

        Criminal Issues Dockets, 1873, 1879-1884; 3 volumes.

        Trial and Appearance Docket, 1807-1822; 1 volume.

        Trial Docket, 1822-1844; 1 volume.

        Witness Docket, 1824-1833; 1 volume.

        Miscellaneous Dockets, 1807-1855; 1 Fibredex box.

        Civil Action Papers, 1771-1936; 58 Fibredex boxes.

        Civil Action Papers Concerning Land, 1778-1928; 19 Fibredex boxes.

        Criminal Action Papers, 1761, 1778-1945; 62 Fibredex boxes.

ESTATES RECORDS

    Record of Accounts, 1868-1915; 3 volumes.

    Administrators' Bonds, 1890-1919; 2 volumes.

    Appointment of Administrators, Executors, Guardians and Masters, 1868-
        1903; 1 volume.

Record of Widows' Year's Allowance, 1871-1907; 1 volume.

Estates Records, 1777-1945; 49 Fibredex boxes.

Guardians' Records, 1780-1939; 4 Fibredex boxes.

Guardians' Bonds, 1910-1921; 1 volume.

Record of Settlements, 1805-1834, 1869-1905; 2 volumes.

LAND RECORDS

Record of Deeds and Grants, 1779-1796; 3 volumes.

Record of Deeds, 1789-1851; 11 volumes.

Deeds, 1741-1944; 4 Fibredex boxes.

Ejectments, 1799-1907; 2 Fibredex boxes.

Land Entries, 1783-1851; 5 volumes, 2 manuscript boxes.

List of Land Entries, 1808-1828; 1 volume.

Record of Sale of Land for Taxes, 1870-1887; 1 volume.

Petitions for Partition and Sale of Land, 1892-1912, 1932; 1 Fibredex box.

Processioners' Record, 1883-1884; 1 volume.

Miscellaneous Land Records, 1778-1925; 2 Fibredex boxes.

MARRIAGE, DIVORCE AND VITAL STATISTICS

Marriage Bonds, 1778-1868; 25 manuscript boxes.

Marriage and Family Records, 1788-1912; 1 Fibredex box.

Divorce Records, 1820-1912; 5 Fibredex boxes.

MILITARY AND PENSION RECORDS

Record of Pensions, no date; 1 volume.

Pension Records, 1814-1927; 1 Fibredex box.

MISCELLANEOUS RECORDS

Alien Registration, 1940; 1 volume.

County Accounts, 1773-1903; 1 Fibredex box.

Homestead Records, 1871-1917; 1 Fibredex box.

Insolvents' Records, 1780-1896; 1 Fibredex box.

Orders and Decrees, 1869-1913; 1 volume.

Miscellaneous Records, 1775-1946; 5 Fibredex boxes.

Record of Strays, 1822-1839; 1 volume.

Records of Assignees, Receivers and Trustees, 1872-1915; 1 Fibredex box.

ROADS AND BRIDGES

Road Dockets, 1822-1833, 1850-1856; 2 volumes.

Road Records, 1776-1911; 4 Fibredex boxes.

SCHOOL RECORDS

School Records, 1840-1904; 4 Fibredex boxes.

TAX AND FISCAL RECORDS

Tax Lists, 1778-1888; 4 Fibredex boxes.

Tax Records, 1781-1908; 1 Fibredex box.

WILLS

Record of Wills, Bonds, Inventories and Bills of Sale, 1778-1799; 2 volumes.

Wills, 1778-1948; 8 Fibredex boxes.

MICROFILM RECORDS

BONDS
>
> Bastardy Bonds, 1871-1883; 1 reel.

CORPORATIONS AND PARTNERSHIPS
>
> Record of Corporations, 1891-1964; 2 reels.
>
> Record of Partnerships, 1914-1964; 1 reel.

COURT RECORDS
>
> County Court of Pleas and Quarter Sessions
>> Minutes, 1778-1868; 3 reels.
>
> Superior Court
>> Minutes, 1830-1948; 18 reels.
>>
>> Equity Minutes, 1819-1860; 1 reel.
>>
>> Equity Enrolling Dockets, 1813-1857; 1 reel.
>>
>> Criminal Issues Docket (Solicitor), 1879-1883; 1 reel.

ELECTION RECORDS
>
> Record of Elections, 1904-1922, 1938-1954; 1 reel.

ESTATES RECORDS
>
> Record of Accounts, 1868-1963; 5 reels.
>
> Administrators' and Guardians' Bonds, 1890-1921; 1 reel.
>
> Appointment of Administrators, Executors and Guardians, 1868-1964; 7 reels.
>
> Widows' Annual Allowance, 1871-1963; 1 reel.
>
> Accounts of Indigent Orphans, 1913-1935; 1 reel.
>
> Inheritance Tax Records, 1919-1923, 1963-1964; 1 reel.
>
> Record of Settlements, 1869-1963; 4 reels.

LAND RECORDS
>
> Record of Deeds, 1779-1964; 214 reels.
>
> Record of Deeds and Bonds, 1784-1854; 1 reel.
>
> Index to Real Estate Conveyances, Grantor, 1779-1980; 15 reels.
>
> Index to Real Estate Conveyances, Grantee, 1779-1964; 15 reels.
>
> Record of Land Entries, 1783-1962; 5 reels.
>
> Record of Surveys, 1906-1931; 1 reel.

MARRIAGE, DIVORCE AND VITAL STATISTICS
>
> Marriage Bonds, 1778-1868; 5 reels.
>
> Marriage Registers, 1870-1965; 2 reels.
>
> Maiden Names of Divorced Women, 1945-1962; 1 reel.
>
> Index to Births, 1913-1994; 2 reels.
>
> Index to Deaths, 1913-1994; 1 reel.
>
> Index to Delayed Births, various years; 1 reel.

MILITARY AND PENSION RECORDS
>
> Record of Armed Forces Discharges, 1918-1983; 8 reels.
>
> Index to Armed Forces Discharges, 1918-1980; 1 reel.

MISCELLANEOUS RECORDS
>
> Orders and Decrees, 1869-1938; 1 reel.
>
> Special Proceedings, 1880-1964; 2 reels.

Index to Special Proceedings, 1970-1980; 1 reel.

OFFICIALS, COUNTY

Minutes, Board of County Commissioners, 1868-1964; 6 reels.

SCHOOL RECORDS

Minutes, Board of Superintendents of Common Schools, 1841-1853; 1 reel.

Minutes, County Board of Education, 1885-1963; 4 reels.

TAX AND FISCAL RECORDS

Tax Lists, 1778-1823, 1904; 1 reel.

WILLS

Record of Wills, 1778-1963; 7 reels.

Record of Wills, Inventories and Sales of Estates, 1779-1852; 1 reel.

Cross Index to Wills, 1780-1948; 1 reel.

WILSON COUNTY

Established in 1855 from Edgecombe, Johnston, Nash and Wayne counties.
A few early court records are missing; reason unknown.

ORIGINAL RECORDS

BONDS
>Apprentice Bonds, 1869-1919; 2 volumes.
>
>Bastardy Bonds and Records, 1855-1908; 3 Fibredex boxes.
>
>Constables' Bonds, 1857-1868; 1 volume.
>
>Officials' Bonds and Records, 1855-1958; 1 Fibredex box.
>
>Register of Officials' Bonds, 1868-1922; 1 volume.

COURT RECORDS
>County Court of Pleas and Quarter Sessions
>>Minutes, 1855-1868; 1 volume.
>>
>>Execution Dockets, 1855-1868; 3 volumes.
>>
>>State Docket, 1855-1868; 1 volume.
>>
>>Trial and Appearance Docket, 1855-1867; 1 volume.
>
>Superior Court
>>Minutes, 1855-1914; 9 volumes.
>>
>>Equity Minutes, 1855-1866; 2 volumes.
>>
>>Equity Trial Docket, 1861-1868; 1 volume.
>>
>>Trial and Appearance Docket, 1855-1868; 1 volume.
>>
>>Civil Action Papers, 1850-1922; 64 Fibredex boxes.
>>
>>Civil Action Papers Concerning Land, 1854-1916; 5 Fibredex boxes.
>>
>>Criminal Action Papers, 1855-1919; 52 Fibredex boxes.
>
>Inferior Court
>>Minutes, 1877-1885; 1 volume.
>
>Circuit Criminal Court/Eastern District Criminal Court
>>Minutes, 1897-1901; 1 volume.

ELECTION RECORDS
>Record of Elections, 1878-1936; 4 volumes.

ESTATES RECORDS
>Record of Accounts, 1868-1968; 24 volumes.
>
>Record of Accounts (Branch Banking and Trust Co.), 1933-1968; 12 volumes.
>
>Administrators' Bonds, 1882-1896; 3 volumes.
>
>Record of Land Divisions, Dowers and Widows' Year's Support, 1855-1868, 1879, 1914-1915; 1 volume.
>
>Index to Dowers and Land Partitions and Sales, [1855-1937]; 1 volume.
>
>Estates Records, 1854-1959; 65 Fibredex boxes.
>
>Guardians' Records, 1855-1915; 19 Fibredex boxes.
>
>Guardians' Accounts, 1855-1868; 1 volume.
>
>Guardians' Bonds, 1869-1939; 5 volumes.
>
>Inventories and Accounts of Sale, 1855-1868; 3 volumes.

Record of Settlements, 1868-1968; 18 volumes.

Record of Settlements (Branch Banking and Trust Co.), 1936-1968; 2 volumes.

Cross Index to Administrators, Executors and Guardians, 1897-1925; 1 volume.

LAND RECORDS

Deeds of Sale, 1836-1962; 10 Fibredex boxes.

Mortgage Deeds, 1855-1955; 5 Fibredex boxes.

Deeds of Release, 1861-1962; 1 Fibredex box.

Deeds of Trust, 1848-1961; 1 Fibredex box.

Miscellaneous Deeds, 1850-1963; 2 Fibredex boxes.

Miscellaneous Land Records, 1856-1962; 4 Fibredex boxes.

MARRIAGE, DIVORCE AND VITAL STATISTICS

Indexed Registers of Marriage, 1855-1903; 2 volumes.

Marriage Records, 1874-1957; 1 Fibredex box.

Divorce Records, 1859-1912; 5 Fibredex boxes.

Maiden Names of Divorced Women, 1937-1969; 1 volume.

MISCELLANEOUS RECORDS

Alien Registration, 1924-1944; 1 volume.

Petitions for Naturalization, 1909-1910; 1 volume.

Homestead Records, 1867-1930; 1 Fibredex box.

Orders and Decrees, 1868-1904; 1 volume.

Cross Index to Special Proceedings, [1868-1927]; 1 volume.

Adultery Records, 1855-1915; 2 Fibredex boxes.

Chattel Mortgages, 1858-1889; 1 Fibredex box.

Coroners' Reports, 1859-1915; 2 Fibredex boxes.

Powers of Attorney, 1859-1961; 1 Fibredex box.

Minutes, Board of Directors of Farmers' Banking and Trust Company, 1920-1927; 1 volume.

Minutes, Tobacco Board of Trade of the City of Wilson, 1904-1922; 1 volume.

Miscellaneous Records, 1786-1961; 3 Fibredex boxes.

Slave Records, 1855-1864; 1 Fibredex box.

Records of Assignees, Receivers and Trustees, 1855-1958; 8 Fibredex boxes.

OFFICIALS, COUNTY

Officials' Oaths, 1868-1924; 1 volume.

ROADS AND BRIDGES

Road Docket, 1855-1858; 1 volume.

Road Orders, Board of County Commissioners, 1898-1914; 1 volume.

Road Records, 1856-1911; 2 Fibredex boxes.

TAX AND FISCAL RECORDS

Tax Scrolls, 1915, 1920, 1921; 3 volumes.

Tax Records, 1858-1935; 1 Fibredex box.

WILLS

Wills, 1840-1925; 7 Fibredex boxes.

Cross Index to Wills, 1857-1926; 1 volume.

MICROFILM RECORDS

COURT RECORDS

County Court of Pleas and Quarter Sessions

Minutes, 1855-1868; 1 reel.

Superior Court

Minutes, 1855-1868, 1886-1908; 3 reels.

ESTATES RECORDS

Record of Accounts, 1868-1924; 6 reels.

Administrators' Bonds, 1869-1897, 1908-1916; 2 reels.

Record of Administrators, Executors and Guardians, 1897-1909; 1 reel.

Record of Administrators, 1917-1926; 2 reels.

Record of Executors, 1912-1960; 2 reels.

Guardians' Bonds, 1855-1885; 2 reels.

Record of Guardians, 1908-1919; 1 reel.

Division of Land, Record of Dowers and Widows' Year's Support, 1855-1923; 1 reel.

Record of Settlements, 1868-1959; 3 reels.

Index to Appointment of Administrators and Executors, 1900-1968; 1 reel.

Cross Index to Executors and Guardians, 1908-1924; 1 reel.

Index to Appointment of Guardians, 1900-1960; 1 reel.

LAND RECORDS

Record of Deeds, 1855-1901; 28 reels.

Index to Deeds and Mortgages, Grantor, 1855-1916; 1 reel.

Index to Deeds and Mortgages, Grantee, 1855-1916; 2 reels.

MARRIAGE, DIVORCE AND VITAL STATISTICS

Marriage Licenses, 1864-1957; 15 reels.

Record of Marriages, 1855-1866; 1 reel.

Marriage Registers, 1867-1954; 2 reels.

Record of Cohabitation, 1866; 1 reel.

Maiden Names of Divorced Women, 1937-1960; 1 reel.

Index to Births, 1913-1958; 2 reels.

Index to Deaths, 1913-1976; 2 reels.

Index to Delayed Births, various years; 1 reel.

MILITARY AND PENSION RECORDS

Record of Armed Forces Discharges, 1945-1989; 16 reels.

Index to Armed Forces Discharges, 1945-1974; 1 reel.

MISCELLANEOUS RECORDS

Lunacy Docket, 1956-1960; 1 reel.

Orders and Decrees, 1868-1920; 3 reels.

Index to Orders and Decrees, Plaintiff, 1897-1960; 2 reels.

Index to Orders and Decrees, Defendant, 1897-1960; 2 reels.
Special Proceedings, 1868-1917, 1934-1960; 5 reels.
Index to Special Proceedings, Plaintiff, 1868-1960; 1 reel.
Index to Special Proceedings, Defendant, 1868-1960; 1 reel.

OFFICIALS, COUNTY
Minutes, Board of County Commissioners, 1868-1914; 2 reels.

SCHOOL RECORDS
Minutes, County Board of Education, 1885-1916; 1 reel.

TAX AND FISCAL RECORDS
Tax Scrolls, 1915, 1920-1921; 1 reel.

WILLS
Record of Wills, 1855-1960; 6 reels.
Index to Wills, 1855-1971; 1 reel.

YADKIN COUNTY

Established in 1850 from Surry County.

ORIGINAL RECORDS

BONDS

Apprentice Bonds and Records, 1850-1937; 2 volumes, 1 Fibredex box.

Bastardy Bonds and Records, 1851-1934; 2 volumes, 4 Fibredex boxes.

Officials' Bonds, 1851-1902; 1 Fibredex box.

COURT RECORDS

County Court of Pleas and Quarter Sessions

Minutes, 1851-1868; 2 volumes.

Appearance Docket, 1851-1868; 1 volume.

Execution Dockets, 1852-1868; 2 volumes.

State Docket, 1851-1868; 1 volume.

Trial Docket, 1851-1868; 1 volume.

Superior Court

Minutes, 1851-1898; 6 volumes.

Equity Minutes, 1851-1868; 1 volume.

Civil Action Papers, 1845-1940; 19 Fibredex boxes.

Civil Action Papers Concerning Land, 1846-1934; 9 Fibredex boxes.

Criminal Action Papers, 1851-1926; 12 Fibredex boxes.

Miscellaneous Letters, Court Papers and Documents, 1853-1878;
1 manuscript box.

Inferior Court

Minutes, 1877-1886; 1 volume.

ELECTION RECORDS

Record of Elections, 1878-1932; 4 volumes.

Election Records, 1852-1881; 4 Fibredex boxes.

ESTATES RECORDS

Record of Estates, 1851-1871; 2 volumes.

Record of Accounts, 1868-1903; 4 volumes.

Administrators' Bonds, 1868-1917; 5 volumes.

Appointment of Administrators, Executors, Guardians and Masters, 1868-
1905; 1 volume.

Estates Records, 1850-1920; 54 Fibredex boxes.

Guardians' Records, 1851-1927; 4 Fibredex boxes.

Guardians' Accounts, 1856-1868; 1 volume.

Guardians' Bonds, 1868-1913; 3 volumes.

Record of Settlements, 1872-1912; 2 volumes.

LAND RECORDS

Deeds, 1793-1951; 4 Fibredex boxes.

Deeds of Trust, 1842-1951; 1 Fibredex box.

Cross Index to Deeds, 1850-1945; 3 volumes.

Miscellaneous Land Records, 1851-1953; 1 Fibredex box.
Record of Probate, 1874-1885; 1 volume.

MARRIAGE, DIVORCE AND VITAL STATISTICS

Marriage Bonds, 1850-1868; 9 manuscript boxes.
Divorce Records, 1851-1931; 2 Fibredex boxes.

MISCELLANEOUS RECORDS

County Accounts, 1843-1879; 1 Fibredex box.
Homestead and Personal Property Exemptions, 1860-1958; 1 Fibredex box.
Insolvent Debtors, 1851-1874; 1 Fibredex box.
Miscellaneous Records, 1843-1952; 2 Fibredex boxes.
Paupers' Book, 1885-1888; 1 volume.

ROADS AND BRIDGES

Road Records, 1839-1922; 3 Fibredex boxes.

SCHOOL RECORDS

School Records, 1853-1878; 1 Fibredex box.

WILLS

Wills, 1836-1942; 7 Fibredex boxes.

MICROFILM RECORDS

BONDS

Apprentice Bonds, 1870-1939; 1 reel.

CORPORATIONS AND PARTNERSHIPS

Record of Corporations, 1891-1969; 1 reel.

COURT RECORDS

County Court of Pleas and Quarter Sessions
Minutes, 1851-1868; 1 reel.
Superior Court
Minutes, 1851-1961; 7 reels.
Equity Minutes, 1851-1868; 1 reel.

ELECTION RECORDS

Record of Elections, 1878-1968; 2 reels.

ESTATES RECORDS

Record of Accounts, 1856-1880, 1888-1969; 5 reels.
Administrators' Bonds, 1868-1917; 1 reel.
Appointment of Administrators, Executors and Guardians, 1868-1905; 1 reel.
Record of Administrators and Executors, 1915-1949; 2 reels.
Record of Administrators, 1949-1969; 2 reels.
Record of Executors, 1940-1969; 1 reel.
Guardians' Bonds, 1868-1913; 1 reel.
Record of Guardians, 1911-1969; 1 reel.
Record of Indigent Children, 1946-1969; 1 reel.
Inheritance Tax Records, 1923-1969; 1 reel.
Inventories of Estates, 1851-1888; 1 reel.
Record of Settlements, 1872-1969; 6 reels.

Index to Estates, 1911-1947; 1 reel.

LAND RECORDS

Record of Deeds, 1851-1963; 52 reels.

Index to Real Estate Conveyances, Grantor, 1850-1969; 3 reels.

Index to Real Estate Conveyances, Grantee, 1850-1969; 4 reels.

Land Entries, 1852-1940; 1 reel.

Federal Tax Lien Index, 1925-1969; 1 reel.

Index to Plats, 1911-1969; 1 reel.

Record of Resale of Land by Trustees and Mortgagees, 1923-1969; 1 reel.

MARRIAGE, DIVORCE AND VITAL STATISTICS

Marriage Bonds, 1850-1868; 4 reels.

Marriage Licenses, 1867-1969; 11 reels.

Marriage Registers, 1851-1969; 1 reel.

Index to Births, 1914-1995; 2 reels.

Index to Deaths, 1914-1993; 2 reels.

MILITARY AND PENSION RECORDS

Record of Armed Forces Discharges, 1918-1994; 3 reels.

Index to Armed Forces Discharges, 1917-1969; 1 reel.

MISCELLANEOUS RECORDS

Lunacy Docket, 1944-1969; 1 reel.

Orders and Decrees, 1871-1955; 5 reels.

Cross Index to Special Proceedings, 1871-1943; 1 reel.

Index to Orders and Decrees and Special Proceedings, 1940-1969; 1 reel.

OFFICIALS, COUNTY

Minutes, Board of County Commissioners, 1868-1942; 4 reels.

TAX AND FISCAL RECORDS

Tax Register, 1851-1862; 1 reel.

Tax Scrolls, 1925, 1935, 1945, 1955, 1965; 3 reels.

Minutes, County Board of Equalization and Review, 1950-1969; 1 reel.

WILLS

Record of Wills, 1851-1969; 3 reels.

Cross Index to Wills, 1851-1957; 2 reels.

YANCEY COUNTY

Established in 1833 from Buncombe and Burke counties.
Many early court records are missing; reason unknown.

ORIGINAL RECORDS

BONDS
> Apprentice Bonds, 1874-1912; 1 volume.
> Apprentice Bonds, 1893, 1909; Bastardy Bonds, 1866-1914; Officials' Bonds, 1872-1891; 1 Fibredex box.
> Bastardy Bonds, 1875-1879; 1 volume.

COURT RECORDS
> County Court of Pleas and Quarter Sessions
>> Minutes, 1834-1868; 4 volumes.
>> Execution Dockets, 1835-1848, 1855-1859; 5 volumes.
>> State Dockets, 1834-1861; 2 volumes.
>> Trial and Appearance Dockets, 1834-1861; 3 volumes.
> Superior Court
>> Minutes, 1834-1913; 12 volumes.
>> Equity Minutes, 1845-1868; 2 volumes.
>> Equity Execution and Trial Docket, 1845-1863; 1 volume.
>> Execution Dockets, 1835-1849; 3 volumes.
>> State Docket, 1835-1855; 1 volume.
>> Trial and Appearance Docket, 1855-1868; 1 volume.
>> Civil Action Papers, 1861-1914; 7 Fibredex boxes.
>> Civil Action Papers Concerning Land, 1867-1923; 8 Fibredex boxes.
>> Criminal Action Papers, 1865-1920; 12 Fibredex boxes.

ELECTION RECORDS
> Record of Elections, 1878-1933; 3 volumes.

ESTATES RECORDS
> Record of Accounts, 1870-1917; 1 volume.
> Administrators' Bonds, 1870-1900; 1 volume.
> Appointment of Administrators, Executors, Guardians and Masters, 1870-1904; 1 volume.
> Record of Administrators, Executors and Guardians, 1901-1928; 1 volume.
> Estates Records, 1853-1915; 31 Fibredex boxes.
> Guardians' Records, 1874-1921; 2 Fibredex boxes.
> Guardians' Bonds, 1872-1902; 1 volume.

LAND RECORDS
> Deeds and Miscellaneous Land Records, 1847-1915; 1 Fibredex box.
> Attachments, Executions, Liens and Levies on Land and Personal Property, 1866-1915; 1 Fibredex box.
> Record of Probate, 1834-1871; 3 volumes.

MARRIAGE, DIVORCE AND VITAL STATISTICS
Divorce Records, 1866-1914; 8 Fibredex boxes.

MISCELLANEOUS RECORDS
Alien Registration, 1940; 1 volume.

Orders and Decrees, 1869-1909; 2 volumes.

Miscellaneous Records, 1854-1915; 2 Fibredex boxes.

Records of Assignees, Receivers and Trustees, 1887-1916; 1 Fibredex box.

ROADS AND BRIDGES
Bridge Records, 1899, 1903; Road Records, 1867-1915; 1 Fibredex box.

Railroad Records, 1877-1918; 6 Fibredex boxes.

WILLS
Record of Wills, 1857-1869; 1 volume.

Wills, 1885-1909; 1 Fibredex box.

MICROFILM RECORDS

CORPORATIONS AND PARTNERSHIPS
Record of Partnerships and Corporations, 1908-1967; 1 reel.

COURT RECORDS
County Court of Pleas and Quarter Sessions
Minutes, 1834-1868; 2 reels.

Superior Court
Minutes, 1866-1956; 10 reels.

Equity Minutes, 1866-1868; 1 reel.

ELECTION RECORDS
Record of Elections, 1878-1966; 1 reel.

ESTATES RECORDS
Record of Accounts, 1870-1967; 4 reels.

Appointment of Administrators, Executors and Guardians, 1870-1928; 1 reel.

Record of Administrators, Executors and Guardians, 1909-1961; 1 reel.

Record of Administrators and Guardians, 1922-1934; 1 reel.

Record of Administrators, 1934-1967; 1 reel.

Record of Guardians, 1956-1967; 1 reel.

Inheritance Tax Records, 1923-1967; 1 reel.

Record of Settlements, Wills, Inventories and Accounts, 1855-1869; 1 reel.

Record of Settlements, 1870-1923; 1 reel.

LAND RECORDS
Record of Deeds, 1831-1958; 55 reels.

Cross Index to Deeds, 1831-1944; 3 reels.

Index to Deeds, Leases and Options, Grantor, 1944-1967; 1 reel.

Index to Deeds, Leases and Options, Grantee, 1944-1967; 1 reel.

Land Entries, 1851-1946; 1 reel.

Record of Surveys, 1909-1933; 1 reel.

Record of Probate, 1834-1846; 1 reel.

Record of Resale of Land, 1923-1967; 1 reel.

MARRIAGE, DIVORCE AND VITAL STATISTICS
     Marriage Licenses, 1870-1967; 8 reels.
     Marriage Register, 1851-1967; 1 reel.
     Record of Marriage Certificates, 1851-1879; 1 reel.
     Maiden Names of Divorced Women, 1941-1967; 1 reel.
     Index to Births, 1913-1986; 2 reels.
     Index to Deaths, 1913-1986; 1 reel.
     Index to Delayed Births, 1873-1949; 1 reel.

MILITARY AND PENSION RECORDS
     Record of Armed Forces Discharges, 1945-1986; 6 reels.
     Index to Armed Forces Discharges, 1898-1967; 1 reel.

MISCELLANEOUS RECORDS
     Orders and Decrees, 1869-1952; 3 reels.
     Special Proceedings, 1919-1952; 3 reels.
     Cross Index to Special Proceedings, 1919-1967; 1 reel.

OFFICIALS, COUNTY
     Minutes, Board of County Commissioners, 1870-1967; 7 reels.

SCHOOL RECORDS
     Minutes, Board of Superintendents of Common Schools, 1842-1868; 1 reel.
     Minutes, County Board of Education, 1885-1953; 1 reel.

TAX AND FISCAL RECORDS
     Tax Scrolls, 1936, 1945, 1955, 1965; 2 reels.

WILLS
     Record of Wills, 1838-1967; 2 reels.